D1608044

Decolonial Feminism
in Abya Yala

GLOBAL CRITICAL CARIBBEAN THOUGHT

Series Editors:

Lewis R. Gordon, Professor of Philosophy, UCONN-Storrs, and Honorary Professor, Rhodes University, South Africa

Jane Anna Gordon, Professor of Political Science, UCONN-Storrs

Nelson Maldonado-Torres, Professor of Latino and Caribbean Studies, Rutgers, School of Arts and Sciences

This series, published in partnership with the Caribbean Philosophical Association, turns the lens on the unfolding nature and potential future shape of the globe by taking concepts and ideas that while originating out of very specific contexts share features that lend them transnational utility. Works in the series engage with figures including Frantz Fanon, CLR James, Paulo Freire, Aime Cesaire, Edouard Glissant and Walter Rodney, and concepts such as coloniality, creolization, decoloniality, double consciousness and la facultdad.

Titles in the Series

Black Existentialism: Essays on the Transformative Thought of
   Lewis R. Gordon
Edited by danielle davis
A Decolonial Philosophy of Indigenous Colombia: Time, Beauty, and Spirit
   in Kamëntšá Culture
Juan Alejandro Chindoy Chindoy
Blackening Britain: Caribbean Radicalism from Windrush to
   Decolonization
James G. Cantres
Systemic Violence of the Law: Colonialism and International Investment
Enrique Prieto-Rios

Decolonial Feminism in Abya Yala

Caribbean, Meso, and South American Contributions and Challenges

Edited by

Yuderkys Espinosa-Miñoso, María Lugones, and Nelson Maldonado-Torres

ROWMAN & LITTLEFIELD

Lanham • Boulder • New York • London

Published by Rowman & Littlefield
An imprint of The Rowman & Littlefield Publishing Group, Inc.
4501 Forbes Boulevard, Suite 200, Lanham, Maryland 20706
www.rowman.com

6 Tinworth Street, London SE11 5AL, United Kingdom

Copyright © 2021 by Yuderkys Espinosa-Miñoso, María Lugones, and Nelson
Maldonado-Torres

All rights reserved. No part of this book may be reproduced in any form or by any elec-
tronic or mechanical means, including information storage and retrieval systems, without
written permission from the publisher, except by a reviewer who may quote passages
in a review.

British Library Cataloguing in Publication Information Available

Library of Congress Cataloging-in-Publication Data

ISBN 9781538153116 (cloth) | ISBN 9781538153123 (electronic)

♾™ The paper used in this publication meets the minimum requirements of American
National Standard for Information Sciences—Permanence of Paper for Printed Library
Materials, ANSI/NISO Z39.48-1992.

Contents

Decolonial Feminism in the Caribbean, Meso, and South America

An Introduction

Yuderkys Espinosa-Miñoso, María Lugones, Nelson Maldonado-Torres

It has been more than a decade since the emergence of decolonial feminism and much has happened since then. The Latina philosopher María Lugones played a major role in the formation of the movement through her creative combination and expansion of (a) Black and U.S. Third World women of color theorizing, including her own, (b) the analysis of the impact of colonialism in precolonial societies, particularly in Africa and Abya Yala, and (c) the work of an array of scholars and activists from different parts of Abya Yala, including Lugones herself, whose work explicitly thematizes and explores multiple dimensions of coloniality and decoloniality. Also central in Lugones's formulation of decolonial feminism was a critical assessment of intersectionality as a category for analyzing the imbrication of oppressions and the possibilities of building coalitions, and the creation of and participation in international and transdisciplinary spaces in the U.S. and Latin America dedicated to flesh out the multiple dimensions of the coloniality of gender and of decolonial feminism.[1]

INITIAL ENGAGEMENTS

Lugones put together the first network dedicated to explore the idea and project of decolonial feminism in around 2006. This network included participants from Bolivia and Mexico, as well as from two universities in the United States: the Center for Philosophy, Interpretation, and Culture at Binghamton University, where Lugones led a group of doctoral students and faculty working on the topic, and the Department of Ethnic Studies at the University of California at Berkeley (UC Berkeley), where Nelson Maldonado-Torres and Laura Pérez convened and facilitated discussions with doctoral students.[2] Binghamton and UC Berkeley had already become important sites in the formulation of U.S. women of color feminism—with, for example, Lugones's presence at Binghamton and that of figures such as Laura Pérez and Norma Alarcón at UC Berkeley—, and in the elaboration of modernity/coloniality—e.g., Quijano taught regularly at Binghamton in the 1990s and visited Berkeley multiple times in the early 2000s.[3] UC Berkeley also became the scenario of various events and conversations on coloniality at that time, including the 2005 conference organized by Maldonado-Torres entitled "Mapping the Decolonial Turn," which included the participation of Lugones, Quijano, Chela Sandoval, Sylvia Wynter, Paula Moya, Walter Mignolo, Linda Martín Alcoff and others.[4]

Lugones also participated in meetings and conversations organized by the Grupo Latinoamericano de Estudios, Formación y Acción Feminista (GLEFAS), founded by Yuderkys Espinosa-Miñoso, who invited Ochy Curiel and Breny Mendoza, among others, to be part of the group. GLEFAS emerged in around 2006–2007 as a space to promote the formation of counter-hegemonic voices in Latin American feminism. Other scholars and activists who have joined the group since then include Aura Cumes (Maya), Carmen Cariño (Ñuu Sabi), Bienvenida Mendoza (Afro-Dominican), María Teresa Garzón (Colombian) and Lugones herself. After a restructuring, GLEFAS conceives itself today as a "weave" that combines and connects individual and collectives of intellectuals and activists. GLEFAS has been the principal engine for the exploration and dissemination of decolonial feminism in Latin America and the Spanish speaking Caribbean.[5] Different from the typical white and mestiza-led spaces of mainstream Latin American feminism, GLEFAS was led by racialized women and by some mestiza women who were committed with feminist forms of analysis that were not centered on gender and that explored, instead, the ways in which racialization and racism as well as the various forms of domination in our contexts play a major role in the understanding of the condition of women in lesser positions of privilege.

The historical conditions that led to the formation of GLEFAS also help to explain the context that prompted an impressive adoption of decolonial feminism among an important number of Black, Indigenous, and racialized women in Latin America and the Spanish-speaking Caribbean, including the contributors to this volume. Latin American feminism was highly invested in the opposition to dictatorships in the region during the 1970s and 1980s, and at least part of the movement had committed with popular struggles. The spread of feminism among women from these sectors led to an increasing awareness about the limits of a feminist discourse based on the unity among apparently "equal" women with a common objective. There were episodes, initially sporadic, through the 1980s when the differences in power and interests among white-mestiza women leaders and other women who came from racialized sectors that had been negatively impacted by the republican projects of the left and the right became obvious and when they were contested. Indigenous movement uprisings of the late 1980s and through the 1990s, the land-back movements among Indigenous and Afro-descendent peasants, and the increasing consolidation of an anticolonial, anti-imperialist and antiracist movement through the 1990s and the start of the new century had a strong impact in various spaces of the feminist movement. They led some feminists to look for a different genealogy and different analytical concepts to do our work. GLEFAS was founded as a space where to continue these pursuits.

AN ENTHUSIASTIC RECEPTION IN LATIN AMERICA

When Lugones's article entitled "Colonialidad y género" was published in 2008 it immediately became obvious that it offered what many of us were looking for: a new type of analytic, a new lexicon that would allow us to develop our own voice and to express a series of political intuitions, grounded on our unspeakable experiences of negation and wounds, that we were barely prepared to outline in a coherent form.[6] Since then, we called ourselves decolonial feminists and took on the task of educating new and previous generations of feminists in this framework while also recovering the voices of combative women who had been hidden and invisibilized by the hegemonic feminism. We became actively involved in the production and amplification of the analytical and theoretical bases of decolonial critique at the interior of feminism, as well as in the production of new conceptualizations grounded on an understanding of domination in terms of fusion.

Decolonial feminists in GLEFAS and a few other spaces in Latin America and the Caribbean were then for the most part a small amount of racialized and mestiza women who were committed with antiracist, anticapitalist, Indigenous, and antiforced heterosexuality struggles. At that time, like it is still the case now, they—including many of the contributors in this anthology—entered the spaces for discussion within the feminist movement to denounce hegemonic feminism and the hegemonic positions within the sexuality movement. These positions interpreted "the women problem" and represented our struggles from the position of their white and white-mestizo privilege. In spite of the different trajectories from which they came and experiences that they had, and in spite of their differences, they were moti-vated to produce other approaches to interpretation, different from those of the most widespread feminism; other approaches to interpretation that were based on their experiences and those of other women in less privileged conditions.

In Latin America, they were not more than ten at the start, but they were able to open a path that was useful for many others who came after them. From very early on, they faced an opposition to recognizing their capacity to produce knowledge and were accused of dividing the movement, of being a danger for feminism and of falling into essentialism. They, including most of the contributors in this volume, were labeled a transient trend. But their and our persistence, passion, insistence, and rage rose to the occasion, as well as their working capacity, and their faith in themselves, the forgotten and rejected. Also important was their recognition of the contributions of the few women who, coming from the unauthorized worlds of modernity, were able to enter academic spaces, produced critical thinking, and write for publications that would soon be forgotten if it were not because their desire to remember them. The value that they gave to these other women's words and their warnings was so great that they stubbornly insisted in reading them, listening to them, making them known to other women, and attempting to extend their legacy.

It was in this way that decolonial feminists convened internal spaces of debate and participated alongside other feminist groups in university halls and activist spaces even at points when their work was barely valued. They published anthologies with their own thinking and that of other women who they found on the same path. They did research and called for the need to do new studies and interpretations of the fundamental themes of feminist theorizing. They wrote, wrote, and wrote. They offered interviews and spoke at universities when they open their doors to us. They used social media as a training method, facing the common racist and imperialist positions of the known and established feminism. They committed themselves/ourselves with the ample formation of an antiracist and decolonial consciousness at the international level. They accompanied and relieved the voices of partners who were involved in a wide array of struggles in the territories. They cited each other and introduced their contributions to the training programs that they created and to those where they were invited. They sought to demon-strate the value of their wagers and of the knowledges that were rejected by dominant feminist theorizing. They produced research projects that showed the academic dependency of their southern feminisms. They committed with the propagation of the voices that had been and continue to be silenced and deauthorized by feminist knowledge.

Now more than ten years after the call to shape decolonial feminism the movement has increased exponentially. From permanent disqualification and epistemic violence, little by little we have been transitioning into a movement with more legitimacy, but, above all, into a moment where we can start to see the specific impact of the movement in new generations and in the construction of new forms of leadership among women, lesbian, and non-normative identities of gender and sexuality who are part of or descend from negatively racialized groups. Decolonial feminism today is more valued internationally and has an impact on the feminist movement inside multiple nation states and at the international level.

Today's decolonial and antiracist feminists are frequently found in university hallways and they demand training programs that are less Eurocentered. They also organize study groups outside of the official programs and denounce the epistemic violence and racism within the university and within the scholarship of gender and sexuality. Decolonial feminists plan, develop and search for resources to finance other kind of research with new themes, approaches, and methods that challenge the most known basic tenets of classic feminist research and theorizing.

There are certainly risks with the dissemination and incorporation of decolonial feminism and of decolonial thought at large in universities, even in small collectives, since universities are heavily institutionalized spaces that are driven by liberal imperatives and neoliberal interests that preserve and further solidify the modern/colonial order. Anyone who wishes to contribute to anti-racist and decolonial feminist work must constantly work with others, inside and particularly outside of the university, to avoid reproducing the elitism, arrogance, and entitlement that has often been part of academic knowledge production in universities. This is as true in the Global North as in the Global South, which points to the importance of collaborations and solidarity among decolonial feminists everywhere, crossing geographical boundaries and linguistic differences. We hope that this book contributes to these efforts and that it is read and studied with this epistemic and political goal in mind. Much more needs to be done: we hope to generate not only critics and readers, but also and most importantly co-participants.

If decolonial feminism has entered new spaces in universities in the north and south, it clearly never left its presence among communities and collectives outside the university. Antiracist feminist organizations have emerged in multiple places and they are formed by Black, Indigenous, Romani, Asian, and East Indian peoples as well as migrants and many others. These organizations have incorporated the analyses and contributions of decolonial feminism. In these and other ways, antiracist struggle has been strengthened, revitalized, and radicalized. This has also led to modifications in mainstream feminism, which has been forced to introduce changes in its public representations, its discourses, and its agenda. We are no longer a small, reduced, and unacknowledged group that remains at the entrance or the margins of the feminist field without saying anything. We have grown and we are maroon women, men, and two-spirit peoples, as well as combative subjects, collectives, and communities who are willing to reclaim our place in the production of knowledge and to challenge and debate about the meanings of the world that we want and to which we belong.

We cannot forget that decolonial feminism had been slowly coming to be before it emerged as a project. We cannot forget the antecedents that made its emergence possible, and the bases on which its basic tenets and goals are founded. As it has been mentioned, there are two important traditions of critical thinking that combined and served as a foundation to our interpretations: Black and women of color feminist theorizing, and Latinx, Latin American, and Caribbean thought, particularly in its most recent decolonial turn. For us, women of color feminism becomes decolonial when we struggle against and when we seek to end the coloniality of gender. An explanation of the coloniality of gender is then necessary to understand decoloniality.

HUMAN/NON-HUMAN, COLONIALITY OF GENDER AND THE COLONIALITY OF FEMINIST REASON

The violence of the kingdoms of Castille and Leon against the peoples they found in the sixteenth century in what they called America, and what we call, following a great number of Indigenous and increasingly also Afro-descendent organizations, Abya Yala, cemented and further transformed a criteria for the classification of people on the basis of their supposedly superior or inferior nature. The prior and subsequent incursions and aggressions of kingdoms in the Iberian Peninsula, including what we call today Spain and Portugal, in Africa also played a major role in the fabrication of race as a paradigm at the center of defining relations among world habitants at a global scale—the so-called civilization mission of Western modernity.[7] Indigenous people in Abya Yala were designated as Indians, and indigenous people of Africa, particularly those who were taken from their lands and subjected to racial slavery, were called Negroes.[8] The Christian kingdoms of what we call Europe today began to increasingly recognize themselves in their process of expansion as civilized and white subjects and communities with their own family of nations. They also considered themselves naturally superior to the rest of humankind. Thus, only Europeans could be truly human, in the account of humanity that was beginning to be drawn by philosophers like Hobbes and Descartes.

The distinction between the human and the non-human became central to the expansion of Europe to Abya Yala including the Middle Passage and later incursions and conquest in other parts of the world.[9] The non-human included what the Europeans called "nature." Nature was thought to include earth, rivers, plants, animals, all to be used for the benefit of Man. Feminist science historians have identified and commented on the use of sexist and rape metaphors in influential Western scientists such as Francis Bacon.[10] The basic idea was that the earth should be raped for the benefit of man. Quijano referred to this violence that encompassed all there was and the relations among everything as "the coloniality of power."[11] Since animals do not have gender, Lugones referred to the dehumanization of the peoples of Abya Yala, as the "coloniality of gender."

The coloniality of gender is about violence against body, mind, soul, heart, spirit. Because the coloniality of gender is the violence of poverty for the non-white women of Abya Yala, the violence of land dispossession, the violence of disruption of peoples and communities, of ignoring, de-authorizing, destroying the peoples' knowledges, including ritual knowledge, because of its complexity that weaves capitalism, racism, colonialism and hatred of non-white women, the coloniality of gender endured. The violence of the coloniality of gender is also the process of deteriorating, with an aim to destroy, peoples' selves, their relations to each other and to the habitat. Indigenous and African people's labor produced surplus labor for capital and exploited Indigenous peoples and African peoples, often to death. The reduction of people to animals, a thorough dehumanization, conceived them as highly and brutally sexualized, but their sex and their sexual difference was not socialized, it was not gender. Gender became one of the marks of the human. The Indigenous and African peoples of Abya Yala were thrown out of civil society, without recourse to the protection of government, including the law. The law negated their humanity. This helps to explain why today, in the U.S.A. Black, Indigenous and women of color do not exist in the law as such.

Intersectionality and decoloniality are two philosophical understandings of the dehumanization of the peoples of Abya Yala. It is clear that given the coloniality of gender, non-white women, women indigenous to Abya Yala and Afro-diasporic women are not women in the sense that white women are women. Yet, for dominant, white, hegemonic feminisms "woman" is a universal. At the intersection of woman and race, we understand the falsehood of that universal. It is Black, Indigenous and women of color, non-white women, and their struggle against the coloniality of gender in all its multidimensionality that is a fundamental moment of decoloniality. Several of the papers in this volume engage this aspect of decolonial feminism.

The second aspect of decolonial feminism is the struggle against the modern/colonial gender system and the coloniality of gender, none of which was part of the forms of social organization of the peoples of Abya Yala, who for the most part ancestrally lived in relations of equality and reciprocity as well as in non-heterosexualist communities. This includes contestations of and opposition to social organizations premised on the centrality of gender, most notably against the nation-state, which are different from forms of relations organized on cosmologies that understand the plurality of beings in a habitat as seeking a balance between equivalent opposites. Unless the opposites are conceived as equivalent, no balance could ever be possible. Passing on the cosmologically grounded systems of thought, the languages, communal practices of creating life, fluid understandings of sexuality, communal understandings of the self in relation are all as constitutive of decoloniality and of decolonial feminism as the struggles against the violences of coloniality, the nation-state, and capitalism. Several of the papers in this collection of decolonial feminist work exhibit this second aspect of decolonial feminism.

In addition to the combination of the borderlands experience where histories of migration and racism meet, and the Latin American and Caribbean critique of Eurocentrism and modernity/coloniality, for many of us who received the proposal of decolonial feminism in Latin America and the Caribbean, the ideas and analysis of decolonial feminism connected with long standing concrete concerns. For us, decolonial feminism amplified the epistemic bases for the understanding of the "women's problem" through the acknowledgment and legitimation of the local traditions of thinking in our lands and our willingness to engage in the dialogue of knowledges.

Decolonial feminism has thus walked between the academic space, and the experience in activism, social movements and in struggles for land that are connected to world and ways of understanding and gathering knowledge that are generally considered illegitimate. Decolonial feminists have become bridges and facilitators in the crossing of specialized critical thought and knowledge otherwise. From this crossing, from this "being in between," have emerged our most central questions and contributions.

Decolonial feminists have gone over old themes in feminist theorizing. They have provided new approaches and interpretations on the basis of historical experiences in the Global South. For example, we have reopened the debate about patriarchy and the category of gender, which are two key concepts in feminist analysis. Our critique of dominant approaches to patriarchy and gender is based on the decolonial feminist suspicion of universalist analyses that reduce the historical experiences of women and people with non-normative sexualities in the extra-European world to the history of Europe. The concept of the "Colonial/Modern Gender System" shows the connections and the inseparability of the history of the concept of gender and patriarchy with the history of race, class, and the emergence of the project of modernity.[12]

Revealing and analyzing the complicity between dominant feminism and Western modernity, as well as the commitment of the former to the latter, has been another important task. Thus, Espinosa-Miñoso's project of critically revising the feminist program has been fundamental in demonstrating the coloniality of feminist reason, and it has made it possible to unveil this complicity in the foundations of explanation and the program of liberation of the best-known feminisms. This task has led to the critical revision of the entire conceptual framework of feminist epistemology. As part of this effort, exploring the question of intersectionality and the need to overcome the fragmented understanding of the world and domination has been a singular contribution.

These critical analyses have led to the review of other important theses in feminist theory such as the old explanation of the sexual division of work and the constitution of the two spheres of life that would separate the two sexes: the private world/public world split. This split is the basis of an entire analysis about care, as well as about sexual, physical and psychological violence toward women. This analytic serves as a ground for models of action and social and institutional policies that pretend to be universal. However, recent work inspired by decolonial criticism refute the fundamental ideas that sustain this analytic, showing its limits and discussing its final goals. The contributions in this anthology are part of this work.

Sexual domination is another important theme in decolonial feminist analyses and contributions. These analyses have been demonstrating that domination on the basis of dimorphic sexual difference, that is between men and women, has not been eternal or universal. It also functions differently in the sphere of the human and the sphere of the non-human, or dehumanized. We have also emphasized the various ways in which Black women have provided historical responses to the problem of sexual domination in modernity/coloniality that have been ignored or silenced by feminism.

Another important topic in our reflections has been the question about the models for research and knowledge production, and as part of this, the relation between the academy and local knowledges. This also involves a return to a revision of feminist epistemology, which in turn is part of a critical analysis about the reproduction of the coloniality of knowledge and the construction of truth on the basis of the propagation and imposition of ideas elaborated by a small group of women with race and class privilege.

There is also the question of the control of the historical representation of the world by modern institutions and the role of feminism in perpetuating it. This theme has been at the core of various initiatives by researchers, activists, and artists interested in aesthetics and visual production.

There are naturally many more themes. This introduction and anthology aim to offer a glimpse into a rich variety of approaches, voices, questions, and contributions that are part of Latin American, Caribbean, and Latinx decolonial feminism recently, with an emphasis in the Spanish speaking parts of Abya Yala. Nine of the eleven chapters in this anthology were exclusively translated from Spanish for publication in this anthology. This volume will therefore provide access to a large array of decolonial feminist questions, concerns, sources, and projects that are not well known in English speaking contexts. We are aware that much more work is needed to foment the kind of intellectual production that we envision: more translations of work in Spanish to multiple other languages other than English, and more translations from English and other languages to each other, including Spanish. This volume shares a multiplicity of analyses and a new bibliography for many readers of this text. We also want to make more Black, Indigenous, and decolonial feminist bibliography in English accessible in Spanish and in the many other existing languages that precede Spanish in Abya Yala. This volume is not the end of any analysis, but a point of juncture as well as an invitation to continue making our critical analyses accessible across borders and linguistic differences. We invite you to respond to the gaps that you will undoubtedly find here with translations and analyses that seek to build connection among related struggles against coloniality.

This volume is divided in four parts, the first of which is entitled: "Decolonial Feminism: A Critique of Eurocentered Feminist Reason." This part focuses on major debates, key concepts, as well as on genealogical and methodological aspects that help frame the decolonial feminist field of discourse and intervention. Here we find contributions by María Lugones, Yuderkys Espinosa-Miñoso, and Ochy Curiel. In the opening chapter of the anthology, María Lugones argues that while feminisms of women of color have made major advances in the critique of the universality of the category "woman," that it is necessary to become critical of the category of gender itself and of its supposed universality.[13] Failure to do so can lead to a reassertion of Eurocentrism and colonialism even in work that could otherwise be described as anti-or decolonial. Lugones's alternative is not relativism, but a material and discursive critique of the many ways in which gender operates as a system that is intrinsically connected to capitalism, racism, and the nation-state, among other areas of modern/colonial power. Gender reproduces differences between men and women, while it serves to establish a problematic norm and aspirational goal to subjects regarded as lesser humans or non-humans. Gender remains a possibility or a temporary, inconsistent, and conditional attribute of colonized subjects in the modern world. Coloniality includes gender as a strategy of control; decolonization, in turn, cannot mean the equality of gender relations, but the overcoming of coloniality and the gender system itself. This opens up a myriad of possibilities for the unfolding of the multiple forms of resistance that can inform decolonial coalitions.

Multiple are the ways and subterfuges in which coloniality can reproduce itself and compromise the work of decolonization. Like Lugones, Yuderkys Espinosa-Miñoso is concerned about the reproduction of coloniality in the assertion of the universal meaning of "woman" and in mainstream feminism. Espinosa-Miñoso turns her attention more specifically to Latin American feminism. She employs a genealogical approach to reveal ways in which Latin American feminism has not only repeated problematic tendencies of mainstream feminism, but also reproduced lethal dimensions of the coloniality that is embedded in the very idea of Latin America. While Latin America is sometimes taken as an "other" to the West and modernity, and therefore as an alternative to the dominant West, a closer look exposes Latin America as for the most part a project of "white-mestizo elites." It is then not rare to find a systematic elision of the voices, questions, and contributions from Black and Indigenous women in the project of Latin American feminism. These voices happen to be among the most critical of the alleged universality of feminism, of its commitment with Eurocentric rationality, and of Latin Americanism.

A frequent question in explorations of decolonial thinking is the relationship between postcolonial theory and decoloniality. Ochy Curiel explores this question in the context of offering decolonial feminist methodologies. While she notes that postcolonial criticism and postcolonial feminist analysis remain for the most part caught within the poststructuralist linguistic turn, she nonetheless finds important contributions in it, such as Stuart Hall's concept of disengagement. For Curiel, disengagement includes a more critical distance of the poststructural linguistic turn than what we tend to find in postcolonial approaches, and a serious effort to recognize the epistemic viability and relevance of knowledges produced by Black and Indigenous peoples. Curiel does not primarily refer to scholars and other experts who happen to be Black and Indigenous. For her, a decolonial feminist methodology has to consider scholars and activists whose work aims to respond to challenges and questions that are central to Black, Indigenous, and Third World peoples. This does not mean that any theory that is formulated by a committed scholar or activist of color is devoid of problems or issues. Curiel warns us, for instance, about certain limits of intersectionality theory, and proposes ways to overcome these limits from the point of view of decolonial feminism. At stake is a recognition of the formative role of coloniality in the creation of structures of oppression in modernity.

The second part of the anthology, "Democracy, Citizenship, and Public Policies: A Decolonial Feminist Critique," explores the impact of coloniality and the coloniality of gender in the field of law, in democracy, and in public policies about women. Here Breny Mendoza, Iris Hernández Morales, and

Celenis Rodríguez Moreno mobilize decolonial feminist concepts, analytical frameworks, and sources to address these issues.

A central tenet in the idea of the superiority of Western civilization is that the West is the home of the one and only viable conceptualization of democracy, and that every political authority on the planet needs to adopt it and apply it. Breny Mendoza finds this issue to be one of the most dangerous dimensions of the coloniality of Western reason, and a major area of concern for decolonial feminism. Failure to critically engage Western ideals, such as democracy, can easily lead feminists to reproduce an imperial attitude in face of non-Western societies.

Like Espinoza-Miñoso, Mendoza believes that genealogy is an important conceptual exercise to unveil the coloniality of Western modernity. In this case, for Mendoza, genealogy takes the form of exposing the mythical character of the very concept of the West and of is political theories. She draws from the important work of historians such as John M. Hobson and David Cannadien, who offer a critical view of the triumphalist conception of Western history. However, Mendoza calls for more radical and complete critical examinations that consider the relationship between the West, Abya Yala, and Africa, instead of solely the East. The critique of a failure to engage in a more expansive and global critical examination of the myth of Western civilization also applies to feminist studies of Western civilization, which question the absence of a reflection on gender in major critical genealogies of the West, but that also tend to ignore the relevance of Abya Yala and Africa. Once Abya Yala and Africa are brought to the picture, then, it is impossible to refer to gender and civilization without acknowledging coloniality. Mendoza uses this argumentation as a basis to introduce an examination of coloniality and of the coloniality of gender in accounts of democracy and in social contract theory.

Along with the ideas of reason, civilization, and democracy, citizenship is yet another key concept in the conceptual arsenal of modernity/coloniality. Citizenship is a formal indication of belonging in a modern nation-state. It serves to acknowledge and protect certain rights. While citizenship is supposed to apply equally to everyone who receives it, the story of each nation-state shows how incomplete and variable the recognition of the rights that come with citizenship is. Struggles to obtain a better recognition of rights and citizenship are oftentimes taken in critical scholarship as unqualified positive contributions to the search for liberty and happiness, yet, Iris Hernández Morales warns us that struggles for citizenship can easily reproduce the colonial dimensions that serve as foundations for the nation-state. Hernández Morales takes the LGBTI movement's struggle for rights as an example of this serious problem and demonstrates how decolonial antiracist feminist practices and genealogies of power, gender, and sexuality in the modern world contribute to a conceptualization of struggles that avoid complicities with coloniality.

If social movements for citizenship and rights can reproduce coloniality, one can anticipate the multiple ways in which institutionalized feminism can also do so. Institutionalized feminism refers to offices, departments, and ministries for women's rights and other sites that focus on developing public policies on women and gender. In her contribution to the volume, Celenis Rodríguez Moreno's offers arguments and concepts to understand the various ways in which public policies on women and gender often reproduce the patterns and roles that they apparently seek to challenge. In her acute analysis of a large array of documents that seek to address women's rights in Colombia, she finds that policies of gender equality tend to work as "technologies of modern colonial gender." Problematic binaries of gender, the public/private distinction, and the divide between center and periphery are reproduced in documents that continue subordinating the most vulnerable among women and creating impediments to advance decolonial responses to injustice and right abuses in the state.

The third part of the anthology, entitled "Decolonial Interpretations of Violence toward Women," consists of two contributions—one by Norma Cacho and Sarah Daniel, and the other by Betty Ruth Lozano Lerma—that offer fresh and distinct but also related critical analyses of violence toward Black, Indigenous, and impoverished mestiza women. These chapters challenge traditional interpretations of violence toward women in feminist theorizing, exploring the linkages between coloniality, militarization, extractivism, and feminicides in the living conditions and struggles of mainly racialized and impoverished women.

The struggles for rights fail to capture the grave condition of the most vulnerable women in Latin America and the Caribbean. More than a struggle for rights, many of them struggle for survival and for land in largely militarized contexts. Militarization in Latin America and the Caribbean, as well as in the United States and other former colonies, one could argue, cannot be divorced from practices of removal and control of indigenous populations and undesirable sectors in the colonies. In their contribution, Norma Cacho and Sarah Daniel, help us to understand the phenomenon of feminicide in relation to the coloniality of military organization and violence. Viewed in this way feminicide is not a specific affront to women, but part of a way to shape the world according to logics of colonialism and capitalism. What is at stake in acts like feminicide and rapes of Black and Indigenous women is both, the very existence as well as the collective and individual dignity of these women, and the continued reproduction of a colonial order of things in Latin America and the Caribbean. Recognition of these conditions, lead Cacho and Daniel to propose a "decolonial and antiracist lesbofeminist" approach as a way of "defending the territories—body, culture, and land—" of Black and Indigenous women and peoples.

Betty Ruth Lozano Lerma also pays attention to the concrete forms of brutal violence and murders of women in the ordinary heavily militarized context of Buenaventura, Colombia. Lozano Lerma's contribution provides a lucid description of the systemic and systematic forms of violence in the Colombian Pacific region with a strong Afro-Colombian presence. So-called development projects led to the increase in the militarization of the region, leading to forced mobilizations of Afro-Colombians and severe deterritorializations. With land and life in peril, so it happened with the communal forms of living in the region. Killings, rapes, and tortures became instruments of deterritorialization. Feminism, therefore, has to take into consideration and respond to the politics of development and to the effects of militarization in the decimation of communities and the appropriation of land. Justice, reparations, and decolonization need to be a central part of any such response.

In the fourth and last part of this volume, we find works by Jessica Martínez-Cruz, Carmen Cariño, and Catherine Walsh, that explore "Indigenous Cosmologies, Struggles for Land, and Decoloniality." With these chapters, which focus on Nicaragua, Mexico, and Ecuador respectively, the critique of Eurocentered feminism that appears at the start of the volume reappears but now in the form of a sustained engagement and exploration with Indigenous cosmologies and movements. Attention to Indigenous cosmologies as well as to Afro-descendent views of community and ancestral relations with land demonstrates the existing plurality of epistemologies and forms of organization that inform decolonial feminist proposals and interventions. These chapters also highlight the indispensable work of "women" who struggle to live in and who fight for decolonized community formations.

In her contribution, Jessica Martínez-Cruz carefully considers both, the important perspectives and knowledges of Indigenous peoples, and the institutional practices that maintain them at the margins, including Eurocentered feminist analyses. She focuses on the identification and treatment of Grisi Siknis, an apparent mental condition and disorder that affects some members of the Indigenous Miskito communities in Nicaragua, particularly girls, boys, and young and adult women. Martínez-Cruz compares the Miskito approach to understand Grisi Siknis with that of the primarily Mestizo experts that were sent by the government to the region. She identifies and critically analyzes the instrumentalization of Indigenous knowledge by the Nicaraguan biomedical system and the state's naturalization of the point of view of scientists and anthropologists. Here one can observe coloniality at work, not directly through the military, but through the health institutions of the state and through the university and scholarly disciplines. Martínez-Cruz's also underscores the need of engaging Indigenous healers as producers of knowledge and leading figures in the search for solutions, and of recognizing that violence against Indigenous and Black women is inseparable from other forms of state violence, a point that is at the center of the concluding two chapters.

If violence that specifically or overwhelmingly targets Indigenous, Black, and impoverished Mestiza women cannot be separated from other forms of violence that affect entire communities or other sectors in those communities, then, it should not be surprising that these women's struggles tend to target multiple and interconnected forms of violence. In her contribution to this volume, Carmen Cariño Trujillo shares analyses that are part of a dialogue with her Indigenous and campesina sisters in Mexico. She focuses on Indigenous and campesina leadership in struggles for the defense of lands and territories. Expulsion from lands and territories is part of the violence that Indigenous, Black, and campesina face as women and as part of their communities. As a result, their struggles often involve the creation of community-based women's organizations against extractivism, dispossession, and pillage. Indigenous and campesina women have taken important leadership roles, not only in Mexico but through Abya Yala, in opposition to the destructive forces of coloniality and its nexus with state "development" policies and neoliberalism in the region. In doing so, they have tended to affirm a thought and praxis of defending life in community and with harmony with the environment.

In the twenty-first century, most states in Abya Yala have been plagued with either the legacies of dictatorships, the "adoption" of developmentalist and neoliberal models, or both, none of which can be understood without the role of the United States and other organizations such as the World Bank and the International Monetary Fund in the region. Since the 1990s, increasingly visible forms of resistance to this order emerged, including renewed calls for different forms of socialism, which led to the formation of explicitly "left" governments in states like Venezuela, Bolivia, and Ecuador. A long-time decolonial intellectual militant in the United States and Ecuador, Catherine Walsh, takes Ecuador's "progressive" state to task, showing the ways in which leftist politics can also reproduce the coloniality of state violence. Most importantly, Walsh demonstrates the continued insurgency and leadership of Indigenous and Black communities in Ecuador and other parts of Abya Yala in face of their struggle against left-and right-wing Mestizo creole elites in the region. Indigenous and Black women often lead these organizations, which tend to reflect major tenets in decolonial feminism, including, to echo Walsh, an acute awareness of systemic epistemic and military violence, and the search for robust decolonial intercultural formations that seek to affirm processes not only of resistance but also of re-existence—and therefore a re-writing of norms and roles on the basis of collective wisdom and commitment with the unfinished project of decolonization.

It becomes clear in the various contributions listed so far that decolonial feminism exceeds the interest in the critique of patriarchy and gender discrimination. They reveal that there is a danger in pursuing these forms of critique by themselves: reproducing imperial attitudes and coloniality. Instead, for the editors and authors in this volume decolonial feminism has to do with living and building community in spite of and against the violent interventions of the coloniality that is part of state institutions, including the university, systems of public health, and the military, as well as of hegemonic private enterprises and supra-state organizations. We hope that these pages contribute to the growth and continued inter-weaving of decolonial attitudes, ideas, theories, and projects in Abya Yala and the Global South, particularly the souths in the north and south.

Acknowledgments and Dedication

We cannot conclude this introduction without expressing profuse thanks to the translators and editorial assistants who made this possible. Most of the translators were—and some of them still are—doctoral students at Rutgers University, New Brunswick, when they translated six of the eight chapters in this volume that were originally written in Spanish. All of these students and former students had been part of seminars that explored different areas of decolonial thought and are doing research in this area. They are Carolina Alonso Bejarano (now at the University of Warwick), Shawn González (now at Princeton University), Amanda González Izquierdo, María Elizabeth Rodríguez, Jennifer Vilchez, and Rafael Vizcaíno (now at DePaul University). They were joined by Verónica Dávila—a doctoral student at Northwestern University—, Carlos Ulises Decena—faculty member at Rutgers University, New Brunswick, and Geo Maher—visiting faculty at Vassar College—in the translation of the other two chapters.

The translations of the chapters that were originally written in Spanish went through at least two rounds of revision. Man Kaplan, Kelly Roberts, and Alexandria Smith participated in the first round, while Amanda González Izquierdo took a lead in the second. Amanda González Izquierdo and Rafael Vizcaíno served as research and editorial assistants, a process that also involved reviewing the chapters for style and content. Maldonado-Torres actively coordinated and contributed to the translations, the comments on the translations, and the review of the notes and bibliography. He also translated Yuderkys Espinosa-Miñoso's contributions to this introduction.

Clearly, the principal note of thanks goes to each of the contributors for not only making their work available for publication in this anthology but for working with the editors in responding to their comments—particularly to María Lugones's careful and sometimes extensive comments to their chapters—and to the comments and recommendations that they received from the translators and the reviewers. All the authors and the editors feel privileged that we embarked in this project with María, our *maestra* and now *ancestra*, who we will always remember and to whom we will remain grateful. In her absence, we counted with the extraordinary assistance of two of her closest companions and interlocutors to make sure that this anthology was published: Joshua Price and Gabriela Veronelli. We thank them for their dedication and generosity.

The idea for this book originated in the context of discussions among Yuderkys Espinosa-Miñoso and Nelson Maldonado-Torres about the importance of creating connections between decolonial and anticolonial feminist work in Latin America and Africa. Espinosa-Miñoso was working on a selection and translation of works by African anticolonial and decolonial feminists in Spanish for circulation among activists and engaged scholars in Latin America, and Maldonado-Torres was contributing to debates about the decolonization of the university in the context of the 2016 Rhodes Must Fall and Fees Must Fall protests in South Africa, where questions about gender and intersectionality were prominent. They wished to help bridge the gap between anticolonial and decolonial feminist perspectives in Abya Yala and Africa, particularly among movement-based struggles, and by extension between the Spanish-speaking and English-speaking Caribbean and Americas, including the United States, where monolingualism unfortunately continues to dominate in the academy.

While Espinosa-Miñoso and Maldonado-Torres had only met each other recently, each of them had a close relationship and an ongoing dialogue with María Lugones, who first coined and sought to develop the concept of coloniality of gender and the project of decolonial feminism. They had also participated with Lugones in various spaces dedicated to explore the significance and potential of decolonial feminism in Latin America and the United States respectively.

Lugones was the ideal additional editor, an invitation that she quickly accepted. Her dedication to the curation and production of this volume was highly significant, as she carefully read and commented on the great majority of the works published here. Lugones also helped to craft the first draft of this introduction, and she was developing one of her most recently published writings for inclusion in this volume when she suddenly and unexpectedly passed away.

María's passing was and remains a profound loss for us and so many others who have learned from her through her teaching and writing through the years. María was a *maestra* and an interlocutor like no other. She was passionately invested as well as intellectually and politically committed to the consistent, rigorous, and systematic exploration of ideas and practices that challenged the coloniality of gender and that promoted decoloniality in all its forms. For this and so many other reasons, this book is dedicated to the memory and life of our dearest friend, teacher, and accomplice, María Lugones, precursor and mother of decolonial feminism and co-editor of this anthology. She did and so far has done more than anyone else to build bridges between decolonial feminists in the north and south of Abya Yala and the Global South, a goal to which this book seeks to contribute. María's prints remain in each of the pages in this publication as an infinite breadth that moves us and reminds us of her words "I don't want to talk for you, but with you." Thanks for your leadership, passionate engagement, and commitment with the cause of the rejected, the dehumanized, the colonized, the *atravesadxs* and of Black, Indigenous and women of color in struggles for liberation, *maestra*! We close this introduction with what you shared with us about it:

"This anthology is a crossing toward creating a bond, from Abya Yalan women to South African sisters involved in the fight against violence in its complexity: the violence against our bodies, against our possibilities as creators of knowledge, of art, of music, of a world in which we can know the experience of a freedom from violence, an experience that becomes an enduring one. That is why we fight.

All the work in this collection is cognizant of the struggles that Abya Yala takes on against the coloniality of gender, a pervasive violence that takes many forms. Every author is committed to a new understanding of the situation of Afro and indigenous women's, and of their own perception of the situation of unbearable harm inflicted on them. In taking up the struggle from a decolonial perspective in their analysis, the authors shift, often very explicitly, from a reality of domination that declares Afro and indigenous to be not quite human, not capable of agency, not capable of analysis and direction to the reality they inhabit as their own persons and as members of people who share a history with them. The reality of violence thus moves in two planes. On the one hand in their living in the violence that is one of the faces of domination. The other is that of understanding their world and situation of violence with the knowledges from below, from their people, a world in which they are active agents. . . . Because when seen from below, women can see a decolonial account of their situation and of their possibilities, the authors can be followed by the readers in their creative proposals. A sense of communality and traditions of active engagement are among what many of the women have even when the violence used against them seems insurmountable. The collection gives a rich sense of what is happening in Abya Yala, both the horror and the liberatory turns. A theorized understanding of decoloniality is present in each piece. There are differences in the understandings which enriches our discussions of what decoloniality can be."

NOTES

1. Early essays that demonstrate these various elements include: María Lugones, "Heterosexualism and the Colonial/Modern Gender System," *Hypatia* 22.1 (2007); María Lugones, "The Coloniality of Gender," *Worlds and Knowledges Otherwise* 2.2 (2008); María Lugones, "Toward a Decolonial Feminism," *Hypatia* 25.4 (2010). It is worth mentioning in this context that Lugones published "The Coloniality of Gender" in a special web dossier on "Gender and Decoloniality" that she curated for the open access web publication project *Worlds and Knowledges Otherwise* (Vol. 2, dossier 2, 2008). The dossier includes a preface by Walter Mignolo, a short introduction by Lugones, and three additional articles by Isabel Jimenez-Lucena, Madina Tlostanova, and Svetlana Sharikova. Notable in this web dossier is the global and international scope of the reflections, which include reflection on Abya Yala, Africa, Morocco and Southern Spain, Russia and the (post) Soviet "Orient," and Central Asia. Lugones's work was also central in the publication of a volume on gender and decoloniality that Mignolo put together and published in 2008, also with widely international contributions by Lugones, Jiménez-Lucena, and Tlostanova. It is also notable here that Lugones participated in the translation to Spanish of "Coloniality of Gender" for this edited volume and made changes in the process of translating the article, including the title. This chapter, "Colonialidad y género: hacia un feminismo descolonial" [Coloniality and gender: toward a decolonial feminism] is clearly part of the path that led from the 2008 to the 2010 publications in the journal *Hypatia*, demonstrating the multilingual context within which decolonial feminism emerged and the generative role of translation in it. This multi-lingual approach was crucial for Lugones too, who dedicated herself to learn Aymara. See María Lugones, "Colonialidad y género: hacia un feminismo descolonial," trans. Pedro DiPietro with María Lugones, *Género y descolonialidad*, ed. Walter Mignolo (Buenos Aires: Ediciones del Signo, 2008): 13–54.

2. The impact of this network dedicated to exploring decolonial feminism is evident in publications such as a special dossier in the journal *Qui Parle*, in which the editor, Marcelle Maese-Cohen, who was then one of the doctoral students who participated in the decolonial feminism group at UC Berkeley, seeks to place postcolonial studies in conversation with decoloniality. Maese-Cohen pursues a connection between decolonial feminisms as a category, and Gayatri Chakraborty Spivak's concept of planetarity. Maese-Cohen built from the international scope that was already part of the conversations about decolonial feminism, which are evinced, not only in the network that Lugones put together with participants in Bolivia, Mexico, and the U.S. but also in Lugones's engagements with the work of the African feminist Oyeronke Oyewumi and her attention to coloniality and the coloniality of gender as a global pattern of power that is constitutive of the globalized project of Western modernity. That Lugones saw decolonial feminism as a project with global relevance

was also already clear in the open access special dossier on "Gender and Decoloniality" that Lugones put together and published in 2008 for *Worlds and Knowledges Otherwise*. See, María Lugones, "Introduction," *Worlds and Knowledges Otherwise*, 2.2 (2008): https://globalstudies.trinity.duke.edu/projects/wko-gender; Marcelle Maese-Cohen, "Introduction: Toward Planetary Decolonial Feminisms," *Qui Parle: Critical Humanities and Social Sciences* 18, no. 2 (2010). The international scope of decolonial feminism and the impact of Lugones's teaching in Binghamton, including the involvement of her students in the decolonial feminist network, is also transparent in Pedro DiPietro, Jennifer McWeeny, and Shireen Roshanravan, eds. *Speaking Face to Face: The Visionary Philosophy of María Lugones* (Albany: SUNY Press, 2019). It is also important to note that Lugones was working in at least two anthologies with a clear international component when she passed away: this one, which focuses on bridging the gap between decolonial feminist scholarship in different parts of Abya Yala, including the gap between English and Spanish, and a second one on various forms of feminism in the Global South, which Lugones was preparing for the book series "On Decoloniality," co-edited by Walter Mignolo and Catherine Walsh.

3. For an account of several activities at Binghamton University and UC Berkeley that played an important role in the development of modernity/coloniality and decoloniality as a transdisciplinary theoretical framework, including the emergence of the conceptualization of the project as a "decolonial turn," see Nelson Maldonado-Torres, "El caribe, la colonialidad, y el giro decolonial," *Latin American Research Review* 55.3 (2020), and Nelson Maldonado-Torres, "The Decolonial Turn," *New Approaches to Latin American Studies: Culture and Power*, ed. Juan Poblete (London: Routledge, 2018).

4. Maldonado-Torres later served as guest editor of two special issues that included papers originally presented in the "Mapping the Decolonial Turn" conference. For an introduction to the special issues see Nelson Maldonado-Torres, "Thinking Through the Decolonial Turn: Post-Continental Interventions in Theory, Philosophy, and Critique—An Introduction," *Transmodernity* 1, no. 2 (2011), and Maldonado-Torres, "Decoloniality at Large: Towards a Trans-Americas and Global Transmodern Paradigm (Introduction to Second Special Issue of 'Thinking Through the Decolonial Turn')," *Transmodernity* 1, no. 3 (2012).

5. One of the most important anthologies on decolonial feminism in Spanish is largely the product of GLEFAS in collaboration with supporters and participants at the University of North Carolina, Chapel Hill, and the press of the Universidad del Cauca in Colombia, among others. See Yuderkys Espinosa Miñoso, Diana Gómez Correal, and Karina Ochoa Muñoz, eds. *Tejiendo de otro modo: feminismo, epistemología y apuestas decoloniales en Abya Yala* (Popayan, Colombia: Editorial Universidad del Cauca, 2014).

6. As it was pointed out earlier, "Colonialidad y género: hacia un feminismo descolonial" was not only a translation but also an expansion of the 2007 article "Coloniality of Gender" that anticipated ideas that were later going to appear in the 2010 "Toward a Decolonial Feminism." In this section the "we" refers principally to the individual women and collectives in Latin America and the Spanish speaking

Caribbean that adopted the concept of decolonial feminism to identify their work and who called themselves decolonial feminists.—Eds.

7. See, among others, Aníbal Quijano, "Coloniality and Modernity/Rationality," *Cultural Studies* 21 2–3 (2007): 168–178; Aníbal Quijano, "Coloniality of Power, Eurocentrism, and Latin America," *Nepantla: Views from South* 1.3 (2000); Sylvia Wynter, "1492: A New World View," in *Race, Discourse, and the Origin of the Americas*, ed. Vera Lawrence Hyatt and Rex Nettleford (Washington, D.C.: Smithsonian Institution Press, 1995): 5–57.

8. See Aníbal Quijano, "Coloniality of Power,"; Aníbal Quijano, "Que tal raza!" *Revista Venezolana de Economía y Ciencias Sociales* 5. 1 (2000).

9. Quijano, "Coloniality of Power"; Wynter, "1492."

10. See, for example, Sandra Harding, *The Science Question on Feminism* (Ithaca: Cornell University Press, 1986); Sandra Harding, *Whose Science? Whose Knowledge?* (Ithaca: Cornell University Press, 1991).

11. See Quijano, "Coloniality of Power."

12. See María Lugones, "Heterosexualism and the Colonial/Modern Gender System," *Hypatia* 22, no. 1 (2007).

13. Note that Lugones was in the process of revising this chapter when she passed away. We are reproducing the published version of the chapter in *Critical Philosophy of Race* with some notes indicating the paths that Maria was taking when revising it. See María Lugones, "Gender and Universality in Colonial Methodology," *Critical Philosophy of Race* 8, nos. 1–2 (2020).

PART I

Decolonial Feminism: A Critique of Eurocentered Reason

Chapter 1

Gender and Universality in Colonial Methodology

María Lugones

I understand the concept of gender as a central organizational element of the modern neoliberal nation-state that continues to be at work.[1] Anibal Quijano argued that since the sixteenth century race became constitutive of the conquest and colonization of Abya Yala. A central element of the racialization of the peoples of Abya Yala, which came to include Africans who were sold and worked as slaves, was their reduction to subhuman beings, referred to in the chronicles, for example, of Diego Encinas, Francisco López de Gómara, Jose de Acosta among others as animals, beasts, primitives. Sylvia Wynter has argued that Africans came to be later conceived as the missing link between apes and human beings.[2] I have argued elsewhere that the gender system that came to the colonies, organizing the relation between European (later white) human beings as part of what Quijano calls the modern colonial capitalist global model of power, included a veiled sinister turn: neither male nor female Indigenous people nor people kidnapped from the African continent and enslaved were considered and treated as gendered. Since animals are not gendered, gender became one of the marks of the human. The Spanish Crown itself found Indigenous people not to be human. The lack of gender was left implicit; my argument demonstrating the coloniality of gender unveils it.[3]

This piece goes further than the above summary of my views. It takes up another important aspect of the question of decolonization: What allowed for resistance by the peoples of Abya Yala against their violent conquest and colonization by the Europeans? Here I shift from naming them colonized and slaves and think of them as, and name them as, the peoples of Abya Yala, including the peoples of the Caribbean and the southern and central regions: Mapuches, Onas, Sirionós, Chimú, Aymara, Diaguita, Tehuelche, Chiquitano,

Tlaxcala, Aztecs/Mexicas, Maya Quiche, Guaraní, Toba, Chiquitano, Taino, Yanomami, Carib, Pueblos such as Taos and Santa Clara, the Anishinaabe in Canada, and the people of the British colonization of what came to be called the United States such as the Cherokee, Sioux, Piute, Muskogee, Cheyenne, Crow, Comanches, Osage, and many others who were not wanted for their labor, as were the Africans and the peoples from the South, but for their land. Under the "Indian Removal Acts" across the United States, the Sioux and many others were removed from their lands and forcibly relocated to urban sites without any place of their own. Despite these genocidal attempts, the Indigenous peoples of what came to be called the United States resisted continuous attempts at extermination by settler colonials and the ferocious destruction by the armies of the colonizing government and of the "independent Americans." Those armies included people who were killers and admired by the settlers and the rest of the white population, such as Andrew Jackson, nicknamed "Indian killer," who became the president of his country and is called by Roxanne Dunbar-Ortiz, a "genocidal sociopath."[4] African peoples were bought or abducted into a new economy away from the Mediterranean through the triangular Atlantic trade—European ports, African ports, Caribbean ports and back—were also dehumanized and bestialized in all of the aspects central to the idea of race. When Bartolomé de las Casas argued that the peoples indigenous to the colonial territories were human, he did not assert the same for the African peoples. In time, he came to believe in their humanity.

The Haitian rebellions showed at many levels how mulattoes and Africans had different interests in the plantations and different relations to the plantation masters. Marronage also showed different attitudes and possibilities to those of the Indigenous peoples.[5] The development of new religiosities and language expressed not just their intelligence, creativity, and their fundamental rejection of slavery but also their capacity to create communal relations. The brutality of their treatment by the colonizer, the clearest expression of a non-seminal economy, attempted to thoroughly dehumanize enslaved Africans. Slavery presented the captured and enslaved Africans with only one alternative: "to work to death in a plantation without respite or to struggle for their freedom and independence from a small society."[6] "The plantation system has two poles: the planter and the captive subjected to slavery. [The planters] do not distinguish between bambaras, mandingas, ibos, ashantis, or congos. The 1804 State limits the origin of the population of African origin to the color of their skin. The planter is not interested in the knowledges brought from Africa."[7] As they did struggle, the relation to whites is well captured by Casimir's reference to articles 6 and 7 of the Constitution of 1846: "All Africans or Indians and their descendants are entitled to be Haitians [. . .]. No whites, whatever their nation, will be able to acquire the condition of being

Haitian."[8] Casimir's central position is, "The Haitian nation is the result of a cultural synthesis, which is the product of the collective exercise within the same medium of those diverse features from Africa's many ethnicities."[9]

Both the Indigenous and the African peoples were constituted culturally by preconquest societies of great age. Their encounter with the Europeans placed them in systems of coloniality so that now something crucial becomes clear: By seeing coloniality, one sees the territories and the peoples in the double visions/realities: the ways of being, relating, and knowing of Indigenous and African peoples and the ways of knowing, being, and relating of Modern Europeans in relation to the inhabitants of Abya Yala whom they reduced to beings inferior by nature. By seeing coloniality, one sees both the reduction and the resistance of people instead of dependent nation-states. By seeing coloniality, one comes to see the resistance exercised by Indigenous and African peoples as a complex fabric that includes transculturation as well as the keeping of some beliefs masked through the process of taking Catholic liturgy and imbuing them with their own religious meaning.[10] This point connects to my previous work in *Pilgrimages*: the coloniality reveals more than one reality.[11] The reality of the dominators who imagine the peoples to be animals, beasts, dangerous cannibals and aggressive sexual beings; the realities of those who see and resist the coloniality within it and are as resistors constituted by the cultural, relational, cosmological shared practices, values, knowledges that animate their resistance. Though they change, the changes are not out of the creative control of their constitution as peoples of Abya Yala.

This piece offers a decolonial methodology that is frankly political in its confrontation with feminism in its universal face. Yet, I offer it as a conversation with social scientists, feminist philosophers, and theorists to think together about gender. I mean gender, the concept, not specific instances of use or unexamined common usage in which "gender" has become interchangeable with "women" in many contexts. Here, I am questioning the universality tied to the concept, not the characteristics of particular gender systems. I am not questioning that the modern/colonial capitalist gender system is an oppressive, variable, systemic organization of power, I am just arguing that it is not universal, that is, that not all peoples organize their relations in terms of and on the grounds of gender. This gender system that applies most forcefully to bourgeois white women has been resisted, but this resistance continues to retain two egregious faults: (1) it does not address the conditions of subordination and oppression of non-white women,[12] and (2) it fails to offer another humanity, another sense of being a woman, if such a being should continue to exist under that name. That is, it fails to offer a sense of being a woman who does not follow the positions and aspirations of white men, but rather is a being different, distant, and at odds with whiteness, capitalism, and neoliberalism; a sense of being a woman that arises from an understanding of and dealing with the travails, difficulties, and possibilities of the times we live in. They fail to conceive the possibility that other peoples have knowledges that constitute "woman" and the "human" with very different, appreciable meanings.

Feminist anthropologists of racialized peoples in the Americas tend not to think about the concept of gender when they use the term as a classificatory instrument, they take its meaning for granted. This, I claim, is an example of a colonial methodology. Though the claim that gender, the concept, applies universally is not explicitly stated, it is implied. In both group and conference conversations I have heard the claim that "gender is everywhere," meaning, technically, that sexual difference is socialized everywhere. The claim, implied or explicit, is that all societies organize dimorphic sexuality, reproductive sexuality, in terms of dichotomous roles that are hierarchically arranged and normatively enforced. That is, gender is the normative social conceptualization of sex, the biological fact of the matter. The claim regarding the necessity of gender in the organization of social, political, economic life is sometimes justified or explained in terms of the nature of humans, their experiences, and the nature of biological and social reproduction. No characterization of particular social, political, economic, religious, or moral life is given as necessitating gender given the assumed facts of sex or of reproduction. The claim is not about desirability of oppression but about a descriptive fact: gender is a reality of social, economic, and political organization, though the forms it takes are variable.

The position is stated briefly, for it is treated as obvious—"gender is everywhere, of course." It is the "of course" that betrays the universalism. It is not a claim that results from a critical use of gender, the concept. Indeed, to claim the necessity of gender is quite different from claiming the necessity of sex. The latter, sex, is a given, assumed to be dimorphic as a fact. The former, gender, is the socially necessary regulated version of sex, necessary because sex needs to be regulated as the case of the colonized and enslaved makes clear: without regulation sex is wild. Though variation among societies is quite possible, gender is generally understood to take a normative, dichotomous hierarchical form. The term "gender" was introduced into the vocabulary of feminism and psychology with this meaning rather than the prior grammatical one of the early 1970s. For example, in Spanish words which end in "a" are feminine while those ending "o" are masculine. Thus, ciruela and máquina (plum and machine) are feminine and cuadro and perro (frame and dogtractor and color) are masculine.[13] Before the 1970s there was no sex/gender distinction, gendered social roles as well as biological marks were thought to be natural.

New thinking about gender has accompanied the critique of the binary provoked by focusing on intersexuality, transgender, transsexuality, and the introduction of "queer" as a non-binary understanding of gender. Yet, the critique of the binary has not been accompanied by an unveiling of the relation between colonization, race, and gender, nor by an analysis of gender as a colonial introduction of control of the humanity of the colonized, nor by an understanding that gender obscures rather than uncovers the organization of life among the colonized. The critique has favored thinking of more sexes and genders than two, yet it has not abandoned the universality of gender arrangements. So, given the critique of the binary, one can think of gender as the socialization of reconceived sexual differences, remembering that not all sexual differences have been unambiguously socialized.

In giving attention to gender, the concept, the direction of this piece is to theorize the relation between the user of the concept and the one being referred to as situated in particular geographies, times, and worlds of meaning that permeate the structures and institutions of particular societies. My focus on methodology is an attempt to offer a decolonial methodology to both study colonized people who live at the colonial difference, but also to engage in decolonial coalition. To see the colonial difference is to see coloniality/modernity as the place the colonized inhabits and the situation of oppression from which the colonized creates meanings that are not assimilated; meanings that are not the "original" Indigenous meanings but new meanings that reject, resist, and decry the coloniality/modernity relation and its logics. Thinking about this direction, I need to answer the question I ask myself when I address this task: Why am I spending so much of my time and intellectual energy addressing a question that seems banal or misguided to people? Why am I not happy with letting go and telling myself, "There is gender everywhere, of course. I see it. It is obvious"?

WHY METATHINK GENDER

I can state why I am keen on scrutinizing gender in this direction briefly:

1. Indigenous and African people in the Americas were denied humanity, and thus, gender.
2. Their struggle against the denial of humanity did not lead to acceptance of the colonial culture's gender system by Indigenous women and women of African descent.[14] Even when their ways transculturated, the "hard core," as Sylvia Marcos calls it, that is, the cosmological grounding, continued to have vitality, particularly in their ritual knowledge.[15]

3. If we take seriously that the denial of humanity of the people of Abya Yala and the people of the African diaspora is still very much with us, then using gender when entering into a study of people who have been dehumanized is to deny or hide the colonial denial resulting in a double denial.

4. Understanding the group or people under study with gender on one's mind, one would indeed see gender everywhere, thus imposing an order of relations uncritically as if coloniality had been completely successful both in erasing other meanings and in people having totally assimilated. The claim that "there is gender everywhere" thus becomes a necessary, if unfounded, denial of my claims.

5. The emphasis on the human/non-human dichotomy was accompanied by the imposition in Abya Yala and other colonized territories of the structural differences of modern/colonial life. Differences understood as dichotomies in the organization of life in terms of the knowledge, economics, politics, institutions, and practices of modern/colonial thought. Paradoxically the emphasis on the human/non-human dichotomy also emphasized the logic of quantities and of the same. The logic of quantities is in the language and understanding of the production of profit/surplus value of those who produce it, where it is produced, what is its value, a non-seminal economy where seminality conceives an economy "uniformly tinted by sentiment," in which the individual accepts regulation by the community. Labor is sacred.

Through these logics, the people of the African diaspora and the colonized of Abya Yala have come to be conceived as not-quite-human. Elizabeth Spelman clearly expresses the logic of the same as she says, "[W]hite kids like [her] were taught that blacks are just like whites but that whites are not like blacks."[16] The same and yet fundamentally different.

Without further development, these five reasons will probably be dismissed as contrary to good reason and very much in need of argument, so I begin by elaborating them. It is in relation to the process of argumentation that I welcome dialogue. Understanding the forms of organization and relations that people who were and continue to be racialized had and have in their own habitat is a complex task that requires the intelligence, energy, and desire for interculturality of many people. It is a necessary task toward decolonial coalition and toward the study and learning of people with a history of colonization and racialization. In what follows I provide my reasoning and further clarification in correspondence to the points raised above. The unveiling of the relation between "gender," colonization, and race is a decolonial task, one that I pursue because I continue to be interested in questions of liberation, and possibilities for those of us who have survived in spite of the coloniality.

REASONING AND CLARIFYING POINTS 1–5

Point 1

Spanish and Portuguese colonizers perceived, conceived, and treated the peoples in the Americas as non-human. What I think of as the "modern, capitalist, colonial gender system" includes the conception of the human of early European modernity, thoroughly developed during the sixteenth, seventeenth, and eighteenth centuries. In this system, the human was separated from the non-human emphatically. "Nature" is non-human in this view and it is to be treated so as to reap the greatest benefits from it for the Man of Reason.[17] To the colonizers, the Church and the Crown, the people they encountered in what they came to call América, after the Italian Amerigo Vespucci, were animals and so they were classified as inferior by nature to European men.[18] As animals, they could not be gendered, that is, they were not men and women; they were like other animals classified as male and female only based on their sexual organs.[19] They were also property and, as property, useful bodies to be bought and sold on the block.

In the fully developed understanding of man as human under this system, it is rationality that is the central characteristic of humanity, and what enables men to govern, to know, to separate the body and the mind. Because Rousseau understood European bourgeois women as properly charged with the moral education of children,[20] and Hobbes understood them as instrumentally rational,[21] I think of bourgeois modern women as gendered and human, for moral education is seen as a human task, and, most importantly, they are seen as capable of reproducing the human, namely, the men of reason as well as capital, and during coloniality, also race. Even at a time when their reason was not considered fully functional in the respects necessary for producing knowledge and engaging in moral decision making, they were still considered able to teach right-and wrongdoing to their children. Thus, the human/non-human distinction plus the gendering of bourgeois European women made gender a mark of the human heterosexual couple. This is what I call the "coloniality of gender," the dehumanization of colonized and African-diasporic women as lacking gender, one of the marks of the human, and thus being reduced to labor and to raw sex, conceived as non-socializable sexual difference—their offspring also slaves from birth and thus not their own, as Hortense Spillers says, the female slaves were denied mother right.[22]

This denial of humanity, or of full humanity, is still alive in the Americas. People, both men and women, who are racialized with a history of colonization are criminalized and denied authority, including the authority of knowledge. They are taken to be ignorant of how to conduct themselves with respect to the duties of citizenship, of the family, of health. They are also not

considered rapeable, that is, their violation is not a crime. They were sexualized as predatory animals—as females and males—given the recent sexual
dimorphic model. Thus they were males and females, not men and women.
The gender system introduced by the colonizers only constituted European
bourgeois men and women as gendered, their sexual difference socialized as
emphatically heterosexual. The sexual difference of the colonized was not
socializable; rather, it was understood as raw, animal biology, outside civil
society. Thus, gender became a human trait that was codified and normed in
the social, political, and economic structures of European modern societies.
However, gender did not become a category of thought, an a priori without
which the human could not be human for a thinker like Kant, like the necessary relation between cause and effect.[23] Indeed, Kant did not try or think it
valuable to derive gender through transcendental argumentation, even when
the experience of being gendered could not be separated from the lives of animals except through the pairing of men and women given the a priori concept
of being human in modern European eyes, outlined above.

Point 2

When someone is oppressed, particularly in the brutal ways that the colonized
and enslaved in the Americas have been oppressed, they resist. For human
beings not to resist the dire circumstances of being dehumanized, their ways,
practices, personalities, selves, ways of relation, access to cultural and shared
social backing, and practices of ritual knowledge would have been erased.
Not resisting means the person's motivational structure must have been
undermined. It is to be expected that those who are in the process of being
disintegrated and feel it as something terrible will resist, even if in impercep-
tible ways to the oppressor. Indeed, the communal feeling of pain at the lashes
inflicted on a member of one's oppressed group is a form of resistance that
does not issue from a calculated strategy.[24]

Foucault's account of resistance coincides with my argument in thinking
that oppression calls resistance forth, but he misses what I think is crucial to
resistance.[25] He does not see that the agency of the resistor in these cases is
what I call "active subjectivity,"[26] a minimal form of agency that includes
habit, reflection, desire, the use of daily practices, languages, ritual knowledge, a thinking-feeling way of decision making, which may not be part of the
meanings of the institutional and structural meanings of the society but may
be part of the meanings in the resistant circle. Thus, the meaning of the resistance will be unintelligible to the oppressor and may be done with or without
critical reflection, but always without an understanding in common between
oppressor and oppressed. In the terrible encounter with the conqueror and the
colonizer, Indigenous and African resistors were fully formed as people in

communities and worlds of sense. So, their resistance is thoroughly informed by that constitution and by the communal circle of meaning that permits the exercise of oneself as a person.

In her description of transculturation, Mary Louise Pratt tells us that "though subjugated people cannot readily control what emanates from the dominant culture, they do determine to varying extents what they absorb into their own and what they use it for."[27] Transculturation speaks to the multifaceted process in which hegemonic cultures influence subjugated ones, in which subjugated cultures give up old and acquire new values and meanings, and in which completely new cultural forms are created.[28] The creation of new cultural forms, then, needs to be understood through accessing the process of the creation, the process of transculturation, rather than taking at face value the organization of the social. Here questioning one's locus will disallow interpreting the new as acculturation. Transculturation always brings in the shared culture, ways of life, ways of knowing, understanding of the self in relation that are not static, rather they are always changing and transforming the meanings of colonial, modern, capitalist structures of meaning.[29] That is, not passively taking those meanings *in toto* from the colonial direction.

Point 3

If something has been broken, to call it "whole" hides or denies the breakage. Paradoxically, then, if a human being has been denied and continues to be denied her humanity, that person has been made real as an animal in a version of reality that is Western, colonial, and powerful. Thus, for a person from the outside of her history of resistance to that denial of humanity to come into her community and say, "You are human," in the sense of "human" of the version of reality controlled by power, will hide something since the denial of humanity is itself being denied without the necessary move of *joining the resistance*. That is, this person is just taking up the Western, modern, capitalist understanding of "human" and thus of gender.

When Sojourner Truth asked her famous and powerful question, "Ain't I a woman?,"[30] she was uttering the question to a group of white women going for the vote for white women. It was certainly clear, then, to Sojourner Truth that "woman" is not a universal term. The used and abused body is not socializable as that of a woman. Sojourner Truth interpellates the white women powerfully, exploding the sound WOMAN with the meanings of her body: her body is just as strong as a man's, thus she is a producer of surplus value, her body and work quantified. She also reproduces, but what issues from her body is not hers, it is property, and the extremity of reaping her off is that white women's babies suckle the milk that should make her baby strong. The white woman benefits from the black slave woman's bodily productive coercion. So, is she a woman? How can the meaning of the word include her, a quantity, productive, non-human? The desire for an organic creation of a new meaning can be heard as an echo in her invasive interpellation. When Fanon, in the inescapable split between black and white, asks whether he is human, he calls for an alternative understanding of the human, since the human/non-human distinction in the modern/colonial matrix of power denies his humanity.[31] Following that alternative understanding of the human, I am also calling for a new understanding of human relations toward what Fanon called for, a new humanity and thus new men *and* new women, or not necessarily men and women but new people—*gente*—the peopled habitat.[32] Gender as a concept does not belong in this alternative vision; thus to presuppose that standing at the colonial difference the new men and new women would understand themselves in terms of a socio-economic-legal-political-Western modern/colonial form of society is to make the wrong presupposition. I want to repeat that it is within our possibilities to desire a sense of being a woman who does not follow the positions and aspirations of white men, but rather is a being different, distant, and at odds with whiteness, capitalism, normative heterosexuality, and neoliberalism, who arises from an understanding of dealing with the travails, difficulties, and possibilities of the times we live in.

Point 4

Understanding the group with gender on one's mind, one would see gender everywhere,[33] imposing an order of relations uncritically as if coloniality had been completely successful both in erasing other meanings and people had totally assimilated, or as if they had always had the socio-political-economic structure that constitutes and is constituted by what Butler calls the gender norm inscribed in the organization of their relations.[34] Thus, the claim "There is gender everywhere" is false, given my elaborations in points one to three, since for a colonized, non-Western people to have their socio-political-economic relations regulated by gender would mean that the conceptual and structural framework of their society fits the conceptual and structural framework of colonial or neocolonial and imperialist societies. The only way they could be seen to fit is when they are already looked at as attachments to those frameworks, erasing them as the people they have been, are, and are becoming in a line of continuity woven by resistance to multiple forms of coloniality and in so doing maintaining their belief system or transculturating it to some extent in resistance to colonial domination.

Point 5

The distinction between human and non-human beings is at the center of my concerns in this article. Indigenous and Afro-diasporic peoples are not human in the colonial logic yet they produce surplus value and thus they fit in the logic of the same through the quantification of labor and its products.[35] In the colonial imagination they are active but not agents, certainly not autonomous agents as are wage earners. The Argentinean philosopher of liberation Rodolfo Kusch finds in the Indigenous people a way of thinking and of producing that he calls "seminal." A seminal economy is an economy not tied to the ego, non-quantifiable, guided by an organic vision of reality "uniformly tinted by sentiment, in which the individuals are regulated by the community and labor is sacred."[36] In contrast to the urban economy, for Kusch, the urban South American acts and understands his world in terms of causes, activity, individual autonomy, quantities over qualities, the value of work and production in terms of rationality, solutions, money, science. Kusch explains: "In indigenous society the individual cannot use his ego as a weapon, but rather allows himself to be led by custom, which in turn is regulated by the community. Furthermore, his regimen will also be irrational, and thus the individual will not quantify either his labor or his production."[37] Thus, labor cannot be quantified and there cannot be a separation between the individual and the community. Labor exists in the tension—opposition—between the favorable and the unfavorable, germination on the one hand and disease, death, devastation on the other. The community in the habitat enacts germination through labor. On the other hand, the fiction that separates a person from his labor in the causal living of the urban South American informs the fiction of autonomy.[38] But the fiction is central to who the worker is, an autonomous individual. As such, his individual labor and production have a quantifiable value. The autonomous individual is split, not active, not an agent except as a seller of his own labor. This is not a communal act, it cannot be. He does not acquire worth through the value of his labor, his rationality does not lie in the market, his price is fixed, the price of his labor is his autonomy. But labor is not, as it is for the Indigenous people, sacred. "A seminal thinking humanizes the habitat in which one lives";[39] "in South America there is an indigenous cultural structure mounted on a thinking through inward directness which personalizes the world; it emphasizes its globality because it faces the original tearing between the favorable and the unfavorable."[40] The contrasts are ubiquitous, they permeate everything, and they are, as Kusch says, impermeable to each other. A seminal economy and seminal thinking constitute the person who resists the reduction to a working beast who produces surplus value, reduced to a quantity both in terms of what it produces and in terms of its being a piece of property. Food and people are quantified. "It is most of

all a reaction to a quantitative economy that places a price on bread."⁴¹ Kusch
seeks to understand the possibilities of their interaction.

The relation of opposition as tension that transcends a causal logic is for
Kusch present in many Indigenous peoples. I think that one such opposition
is between sexed beings who produce together the food for the community.
"The" sexes are opposites in this sense of tension seeking for balance and
germination. The colonizers broke this relation in production. The community was thus seriously broken, split in colonial halves and thus placed in a
situation of disintegration.

A Decolonial Methodology Toward Decolonial Coalition

I am ready, then, to suggest a decolonial methodology in the study of colonized people who live at the colonial difference with respect to the attribution
of gender, and thus with respect to an understanding of their relations to self,
to others, to their community, to their habitat, and to the cosmos in a historical
line that takes into account their resistance to the denial of their humanity and
to the complexity of what decolonial thinkers such as Walter Mignolo, Anibal
Quijano, Nelson Maldonado-Torres, Arturo Escobar, Madina Tlostanova,
Rolando Vazquez, and Catherine Walsh call the coloniality of power, knowledge, being, and gender.⁴² I am also suggesting that this methodology is
important if we want to form decolonial coalitions among colonized peoples.
As coloniality is constituted by a denial of coevalness, resistance to coloniality denies the linearity of colonial time. Methodologically, then, I will suggest
the following:

- The people, nation, community that are being approached by those who
  are not of them, outsiders to the communities, who want to learn them
  for the sake of coalition or who want to study them in an academic vein,
  need to be understood historically, not in the linear progressive understanding of the history of Western modernity, but with an understanding
  of Indigenous conceptions of time, including the sense of time arising
  from the history of encounter and of resistance to dehumanization.⁴³ It
  is the Indigenous peoples' own understanding of time, such as the balancing of opposites for example, *pachakuti* and *pachayachachic*—the
  unnameable opposites—in the Andean case that the historization needs
  to consider. The time of the outsider invades colonially.
- In this history people come to be at the colonial difference and the colonial wound, which are terrifying positionalities from which coloniality
  is vivid and is resisted non-dichotomously.⁴⁴ Dichotomous and categorical thinking are central to Western modernity and are absent in all the
  Indigenous understandings of reality with which I have become familiar.

I know the Andean and Mesoamerican cases the best. For Andean peoples the mountain and the valley are opposites, but like night and day, man and woman, they are not dichotomous opposites. None of these are bounded categories; indeed, they do not make sense except as interconnected, inseparable, fluid.

- Colonized peoples face colonial domination *as fully constituted peoples* who make life in their habitats rather than work for others for profit or surplus value. As people who hold particular understandings of knowledge, values, and relations in the extensive world that includes all there is and, in particular, in relations to understandings of self, relations to the spirit world, relations to other people in the communities, nations, tribes, groups, communities that they call their own, they do not separate the human and the non-human, or the human from nature, that Modern/colonial invention. Everything is interconnected, including the *almas*, souls, everything in the cosmos. There are no transcendent, nonconnected beings.
- Whether they are the same or different, the sameness is not reciprocal. Sameness is weighed in terms of abstract measurement of land, labor, production. It is clear that it is neither a reciprocal difference nor those non-hegemonic differences that Lorde celebrates when she thinks of differences as "a fund of necessary polarities between which our creativity can spark like a dialectic." Differences enable different women to interdependence that "allows the I to *be*, not in order to be used, but in order to be creative. This is a difference between the passive *be* and the active *being*."[45] A shift to a creative sense of being.
- Attention needs to be paid to the concepts behind any assertion of gender. Western/colonial understanding of concepts construes them as a universal. The concept can be applied differently by different people but it is the same concept, even by those who acknowledge different gender arrangements, for example what Rita Segato calls "a low intensity patriarchy" and "high intensity patriarchy" or what Julieta Paredes calls "patriarchal entronques."[46] Thus, my critique of the use of gender as it is used in the study of colonized peoples is that it is a concept to be understood and used by experts from the outside. As a "meta" conceptual category it is not used as if it needs to be clear and useful to those studied. Paradoxically, the category does not apply to the colonized because they are not human, or they are human anew, in a double denial since the colonial relation is not undone but repeated. Indeed, this exclusion as well as the lack of its use by the colonized themselves does not invalidate its use by experts in the experts' own judgment. Why not? It is their life, their communities, their realities being organized against their possibilities. This indifference regarding the usefulness of the category

to the subjects under study demonstrates that the exclusion is methodologically colonial in its imposition.[47]

- A presentist interpretation of a people without a historico-cultural
understanding is one that lacks a history of colonial domination and of
resistance to colonial domination. Neither transculturation as a creation
or oppression are unveiled by a presentist interpretation. The claim that
"history does not matter" supports and denies the "all people are the
same as human." Thus, presentism and universalism go well together.

- Gender has been understood as the socializing of the sexual difference
in terms of power.[48] I think that the sexual difference implies relational
individualism among separate people, even when we are thinking of
more than two genders. The colonized have kept a sense of self struggling against dehumanization, against assimilation, keeping resistant
senses of self, transculturated, recovered, or new. In particular, they
have struggled to keep a communal sense of self. Whether they have
become gendered is a question to investigate, not to assume.[49] That is a
legal, political, economic, social question that goes to the structure of the
society and the grounding of that structure. Whether it is the community
or the nation-state that is the point of reference is a central question
for the investigation. It is also a question that needs to take carefully
and seriously the meanings from below, of individuals and groups who
resist dehumanization and assimilation. Of course, if the group of people
have been thoroughly colonized and have completely lost their world of
meaning, they will be attached to the colonial world of meaning, but that
is a part of the investigation. The social scientist is placing or replacing
the relations among the people directly to the colonial structure, bypass-
ing their own sense of themselves which in the organizing relations may
be in cosmological terms.

I suggest this methodology or these first steps toward a decolonial methodology as necessary for those of us committed to decolonial coalition among
colonized peoples. The fact that European colonizers reduced people to animality and thus distinguished between the human and the nonhuman does
not mean that Indigenous people anywhere in Abya Yala made this human/
nonhuman distinction themselves. Gender is tied to the distinction, so for
peoples who do not make that distinction, gender cannot be part of their relational organization. So, in understanding their socio-political-economic organization, it is important to understand whether reproduction of Indigenous
peoples was given a specific conceptual understanding that does or does not
incorporate the distinction between the human and the nonhuman and thus the
distinction between human and non-human reproduction.

"Do not forget sociogeny," Fanon would tell us as he asks for an alternative understanding of the human.[50] How the people under study or with whom one seeks coalition understand themselves as people, as the people they are individually and collectively, is the beginning of a search as to whether the effects of colonization produced an unescapable split between being human—and thus like the colonizer—or non-human—and thus colonized. Looking to Fanon's work points us to a sociogenical understanding of people in their history. For the colonized and the enslaved, the split makes attempting to live a human life in the colonial matrix of power impossible. For the colonized and the enslaved to live a human life requires a new understanding of the human and a new understanding of relation; but that is an understanding outside the colonial matrix. Assimilation, loss of value and accepting the imposition of colonial values produced and produces an impasse, a crossroads, a giving up, and so requires a new understanding of "human" and "humans in relation."

We must move away from gender as a reduction through the governmental apparatuses that inscribe it everywhere in the social and reduce men and women to an understanding of relations tied to the development of capitalism in global modernity. As I am understanding the concept of gender, there is no escaping the tie between the Western modern/colonial capitalist conception of humanity and the concept of gender. The split between white human (man of reason, woman as reproducer of humans and moral educator) and non-human (animal, nonwhite) is not an escapable split without a different understanding of the human than the modern colonial capitalist one.[51] For example, *warmi*, an Aymara word that is usually translated as *mujer* (woman) is decidedly not "woman." The meaning of *warmi* is tied to the cosmology and to the organization of the *ayllu*, the Aymara and Quechua community, which is itself organized in cosmological terms. "Woman" is constituted differently. It is tied to modern Western law, the Western production of knowledge, the nation-state, individualist morality, capitalist economy, all in modern Western terms, thus it is tied to state and colonial power. The nature of the modern concept of law and the modern/colonial capitalist understanding of law is not a question that arises in Indigenous communities in Abya Yala, since the institution of the law and its nature is not part of societies for which ritual knowledge and cosmology are central to the organization of the social. The nation-state is a problematic introduction for Indigenous and Afro-diasporic people seeking a new possibility for themselves not allowed by the human/non-human split.

If we think of transculturated Indigenous ways of living, the question is whether our interpretation of the organization of relations reproduces colonial relations where the relation is to the nation-state, global capital, and the enduring conceptual framework of modernity. Is the Foucaultian understanding of power that Foucault sees in the people of modern nations also held in Afro-descendant and Indigenous communities with a history of colonization who may have transculturated?[52] In this investigation one wants to know whether and how people want to recover the ways of relation that have been destroyed and replaced with colonial ones. For example, how do we understand Indigenous people who are members of communities with a history of colonization who relate to national governments "representing" their communities and who make pacts with the government? Do they include or exclude women? Is the inclusion one that is poorly understood as exclusion? Are the women included in a manner that does not count as representation in the liberal sense? Is the exclusion transculturated? Does the exclusion change women's standing, rendering women secondary in decision-making?

Gloria Wekker interprets the meaning of "woman" among the Surinamese creole as very different from any colonial understanding.[53] Jean Casimir thinks of what Wekker is describing as a creation that also obtains in Haiti where those who were captured, sold into slavery and treated as animals created an arrangement of the social that, in Haiti, is what constitutes the Haitian people as a sovereign people. According to Casimir, this is a creation done by women.[54] In Wekker, women are central in the organization of the social world in which they live. Their principal ritual and social relations are to other women with whom they do the *matti work*.[55] Women are central in the creolization of Surinam and Haiti according to both Wekker and Casimir. Among the Aymara, *chacha* and *warmi* are opposites but they cannot be hierarchal opposites, one inferior to the other, because there could not be any searching for balance between *pachakuti* and *pachayachachic* between them as there is between all opposites in the order of the cosmos. Unless attention is paid to the changes in the understanding, grounding, and practices of sexuality in particular Indigenous societies and the deep changes constituted by coloniality regarding the body, the sensual, and the sexual such as changes in meaning and the demonization of non-heterosexual practices, including ritual practices, the reductive centering of the reproductive organs in the animal body will not be seen and the heterosexual matrix will be presupposed. For example, Sylvia Marcos finds in many Mesoamerican understandings of opposition the idea that day and night mutate, they touch each other every day, and the sexual in us does the same.[56] In her work on religiosity in Mesoamerica, she has found an understanding of sexuality as fluid and mutating, not fixed but in "homeorrheic equilibrium."[57] The same can be said about hot and cold, night and day, and other extremes in oppositional fluid change. As part of the creolization in the Caribbean context, the understanding of what it is to be a sexual person became important in the creation of spiritualities such as Voudun, Santería, and candomblé, new creations in colonial Abya Yala, where sexualities are also mutating and cosmologically grounded.

CONCLUSION

To end, the question is whether gender is a meaningful concept—understood, as I have shown, as a system of control and classification that splits up people hierarchically in fundamental ways—without the Western legal structures, the non-seminal economic system, the system of production and legitimation of knowledge, and the moral order; without the modern/colonial Western understanding of humanity that gives "human" meaning; without the Western system of thought and cosmology that give meaning to gender; without transcendent understandings of religion that make people into either fallen flesh or self-determining beings—both Western understandings. It is almost obvious that approaching the people whose lives one seeks to devote one's attention to and looking for their place and who they are in it, whether as someone to enter into coalition with or someone to be studied without generalization as a member of an Indigenous or Afro society, searching only for gendered forms of sexual difference will not do.

Yet, this colonial attitude persists and the Indigenous person and African descended person have been and continue to be reduced to animality. Suppose that with our investigation of any animal we begin there with sexual difference, recognizing the organs of reproduction and categorizing them as male and female, leaving those considered abnormal by the scientist aside, and examine their behavior: The male takes care of the eggs till the babies are independent and can be on their own. The female kills the male after impregnation. Both get the meat out of the nuts by throwing them on the road and waiting for cars to run over them, both communicate by turning their lights on. The female carries the baby close to her chest, the male sleeps all day. The female kills prey for the pack, the drones build fantastic nests with saliva and sawdust and so on. If "male" is the biological classification and taking care of the eggs is what they do, what are they socially? In assigning gender to them, one puts the reproductive traits together with tasks done by the one, with this or that trait, and one still could not assign gender because there is no clarity about the organization of the social, the economy, and the order of relations. Clearly doing this would not make the animals whose behaviors I described above "men" or "women," nor would it make them in the same situation as the inhabitants of Abya Yala or those who were from other continents who were dehumanized, bestialized by the modern/colonial capitalist gender system.

This dehumanization and bestialization occurred precisely because these people were not understood by the colonizers and enslavers as social agents, and thus their sexual difference not socializable. Thus, one does not find gender; animals do not have gender. But, I think, neither do those who ground the order of their world in cosmological terms. But not for the same reasons, that should be clear. If one recognizes the denial of humanity to Africans and Indigenous peoples in Abya Yala by the modern/colonial capitalist system, a denial that also excluded them from participating in the colonizing civil society, and centrally, if one recognizes that these denials meant a further denial that they, in their own communities, have structured civil societies—structures with a human grounding, where human is understood in modern/colonial terms—then one can recognize that they cannot have gender. Further, their lack of humanity consistently indicates that they cannot be said to have membership in the structures or institutions of colonizing civil society that order their world and thus give their gender a modern/colonial meaning in the very conceptual constitution of those structures and institutions.

The contradictions that I see as I see the coloniality keep me from forgetting that gender is irrevocably white, European, and modern and that the modern/colonial capitalist gender system necessarily denies gender to the colonized and enslaved. Rather, they are not human, non-human, not fully human. It is interesting and important that in their understanding of their own racial superiority, Anglo-, European-, white women struggle both to keep and to change gender. Their struggle for change does not address the inhumane and inhuman positions, tasks, and conceptions of the racist white imagination nor the social, political, and economic structure of racial states but rather their attempts continue to universalize the category "woman" as if the colonized and enslaved females of the planet were included among the human. While the concept of gender is deeply embedded in the structure of Western nation-states, societies, and economies, it is absent in the racist, colonial imagination and conception of the non-white, non-human. To approach Indigenous and Afro societies under the colonial nation-state as if they had gender is to deny them twice as I have argued. Why does anyone want to insist on finding gender among all the peoples of our planet? What is good about the concept that we would want to keep it at the center of our "liberation"?

NOTES

1. This text was previously published in *Critical Philosophy of Race* 8, no. 1–2 (2020) and it has been minimally amended for this publication. The published article has a bibliography and no endnotes, while the version published here has endnotes with bibliographic information along with comments or observations by Yuderkys Espinosa-Miñoso and Nelson Maldonado-Torres—identified as editors or *Eds*. Most of the comments and observations address the similarities and differences between the chapter published here and another version of it that María Lugones was preparing for

publication in this volume before she passed away. The previously published version of this chapter reprinted here, as well as the version that Lugones was preparing for publication in this volume, start with an initial heading with the word "Introduction," which has been removed from this version to follow the formatting guidelines for this anthology. The initial paragraphs in this introduction are quite different in the two versions of the article. The unpublished version had a slightly different title too, "On the Universality of Gender in Colonial Methodology." The unpublished version starts with a line that reads: "In this chapter I am beginning a conversation with feminist theorists and social scientists to think about gender, the concept, together." Lugones argues that "gender is the arrangement of social relations determining who is a man and who is a woman in the West among bourgeois men and women" and that the socialization of this sexual difference is deeply embedded in the "social/political/economic structures in formation" in the modern world. She recognizes that this is part of what she refers to as the Modern Colonial Capitalist Gender System, but she is emphatic that she wishes "to argue for something more radical." This more radical argument has to do with the recognition of the colonial difference between the presumably socializable subjects of western modernity, and the presumably non-socializable, and therefore not completely human, groups that were perceived as permanent colonial subjects or as slaves. Lugones's conclusion is that "In any of these degrees of non-humanity, the colonized and the enslaved were not agents in these social, political, and economic structures. As not human they were not gendered." The point is that "Gender, then, is quite particular, modern, colonial, capitalist but it has operated as universal in the conquering, colonial ventures, colonizing the relation among peoples." Lugones adds that "The direction of this chapter is to see the coloniality of power in terms of dehumanization and to see the assimilation of the colonized organization of human relations to modern gender: the dichotomous, hierarchical, heterosexual modern organization of human relations, the female as subordinate, sex as dimorphic, normal sexuality as heterosexual. I aim to theorize the relation between the user of the concept and the one being referred to as situated in particular geographies, times, and worlds of meaning, a relation of power through this piece. I will attempt to offer a decolonial methodology to both study colonized people who live the colonial difference, but also to engage in decolonial coalition." In comparison with the chapter that is published here, the unpublished version starts with a more extensive critique of the claim that "gender is everywhere," but the published article comes back to this theme in the final two paragraphs of the chapter.—*Eds.*

2. Sylvia Wynter, "Unsettling the Coloniality of Being/Power/Truth/Freedom: Towards the Human, After Man, Its Overrepresentation—An Argument," *The New Centennial Review* 3, no. 3 (2003): 266, 301, 304.

3. María Lugones, "Heterosexualism and the Colonial/Modern Gender System," *Hypatia* 22, no. 1 (2007); María Lugones, "Toward a Decolonial Feminism," *Hypatia* 25, no. 4 (2010); María Lugones, "Methodological Notes Towards a Decolonial Feminism," in *Decolonizing Epistemologies: Latina/o Theology and Philosophy*, eds. Ada María Isasi-Díaz and Eduardo Mendieta (New York: Fordham University Press, 2011); María Lugones, "A Decolonial Revisiting of Gender" (unpublished manuscript).

4. Roxanne Dunbar-Ortiz, *An Indigenous Peoples' History of the United States* (Boston: Beacon Press, 2014), 94.

5. For consistency, we added an initial capital letter to the word "Indigenous" in most instances.—Eds.

6. Jean Casimir, *Haití de mis amores* (Isla Negra, Chile: Ambos Editores, 2012), 32. We added a colon in this sentence.—Eds.

7. Ibid., 56. We deleted the ellipsis at the end of the quote to follow the formatting guidelines in this volume.—*Eds.*

8. Ibid., 45.

9. Ibid., 48.

10. José Carlos Mariátegui, *Seven Interpretive Essays on Peruvian Reality* (Austin: University of Texas Press, 1971); Sylvia Marcos, *Taken from the Lips: Gender and Eros in Mesoamerican Religions* (Leiden: Brill, 2006); Mary Louise Pratt, *Imperial Eyes: Travel Writing and Transculturation,* 2nd ed. (New York/London: Routledge, 2008); Fernando Ortiz, *Cuban Counterpoint: Tobacco and Sugar* (Durham: Duke University Press, 1995).

11. María Lugones, *Pilgrimages/Peregrinajes: Theorizing Coalition Against Multiple Oppressions* (New York: Rowman & Littlefield, 2003). We added this bibliographic information here.—Eds.

12. Valerie Amos and Pratibha Parmar, "Challenging Imperial Feminism," *Feminist Review* no. 17 (1984).

13. The original publication offered "tractor and color" as translations for "cuadro and perro." We have changed it to "frame and color" here.—Eds.

14. Aníbal Quijano, "Colonialidad del poder y clasificación social," *Journal of World Systems Research* 6, no. 2 (2000); Aníbal Quijano, "Colonialidad del poder, eurocentrismo y América Latina," in *La colonialidad del saber: eurocentrismo y ciencias sociales* (Buenos Aires: CLACSO-UNESCO, 2000); Aníbal Quijano, "Colonialidad del poder, globalización y democracia," *Revista de Ciencias Sociales de la Universidad Autónoma de Nuevo León* 4, no. 7–8 (2002).

15. Marcos, *Taken from the Lips.*

16. Elizabeth Spelman, *Inessential Woman: Problems of Exclusion in Feminist Thought* (Boston: Beacon Press, 1988).

17. Wynter, "Unsettling"; Michel Foucault, *The History of Sexuality, vol. 1: An Introduction* (New York: Random House, 1978).

18. Quijano, "Clasificación Social"; Quijano, "Eurocentrismo y América Latina," Quijano, "Globalización y democracia."

19. Lugones, "Heterosexualism"; Lugones, "Decolonial Feminism"; Lugones, "Methodological Notes"; Lugones, "A Decolonial Revisiting of Gender."

20. Jean Jacques Rousseau, *Èmile* (CreateSpace Independent Publisher Platform, 2017).

21. Thomas Hobbes, *Leviathan* (Indianapolis: Hackett Classics, 1994)

22. Hortense Spillers, "Mama's Baby, Papa's Maybe: An American Grammar Book," *Diacritics* 17, no. 2 (1987).

23. Immanuel Kant, *Critique of Pure Reason* (New York: Penguin Classics, 1994).

24. Alexander G. Weheliye, *Habeas Viscus: Racializing Assemblages, Biopolitics, and Black Feminist Theories of the Human* (Durham: Duke University Press, 2014); Lugones, *Pilgrimages*.

25. Foucault, "History of Sexuality."

26. Lugones, *Pilgrimages*.

27. Pratt, *Imperial Eyes*.

28. Michael Horswell, *Decolonizing the Sodomite: Queer Tropes of Sexuality in the Andean Culture* (Austin: University of Texas Press, 2005), 6.

29. Ortiz, *Cuban Counterpoint*; Pratt, *Imperial Eyes*.

30. Sojourner Truth, "Ain't I a Woman?," Women's Convention, Akron, Ohio.

31. Frantz Fanon, *The Wretched of the Earth*, trans. Richard Philcox (New York: Grove Press, 2005). The editors added "the" before "modern/colonial matrix of power" in this sentence.—Eds.

32. Ibid.

33. Oyèrónkĕ Oyĕwùmí, *The Invention of Women: Making an African Sense of Western Gender Discourses* (Minneapolis: University of Minnesota Pres, 1997).

34. Judith Butler, *Undoing Gender* (New York: Routledge, 2004).

35. Quijano, "Clasificación Social"; Quijano, "Eurocentrismo y América Latina," Quijano, "Globalización y democracia."

36. Rodolfo Kusch, *Indigenous and Popular Thinking in América* (Durham: Duke University Press, 2010)

37. Ibid., 135. The editors added a colon after "Kusch explains."—Eds.

38. The editors deleted a comma before "informs."—Eds.

39. Ibid., 141.

40. Ibid., 126. The editors deleted ellipses at the end of the quoted text for consistency in the anthology.—Eds.

41. Ibid., 140.

42. The editors added first names for Mignolo, Quijano, and Maldonado Torres here. They also added a hyphen in Maldonado-Torres's last name. Eds.

43. The editors added "be" after "need to" in this sentence.—Eds.

44. Walter Mignolo, *Local Histories/Global Designs: Coloniality, Subaltern Knowledges, and Border Thinking* (Princeton: Princeton University Press, 2012).

45. Audre Lorde, "The Master's Tools Will Never Dismantle the Master's House," in *Sister Outsider: Essays and Speeches* (Berkeley: Crossing Press, 1984), 111 (italics in original).

46. Rita Segato, *Género y colonialidad en ocho ensayos* (Buenos Aires: Prometeo, 2015); Julieta Paredes, *Hilando fino desde el feminismo comunitario* (La Paz, Bolivia: El Rebozo, Zapateándole, Lente Flotante en Cortito que's p'a largo y Alifen AC, 2010).

47. Lila Abu-Luhgod, *Writing Women's Worlds* (Berkeley: University of California Press, 1993); Oyĕwùmí, *Invention of Women*.

48. Joan Wallach Scott, *Gender and the Politics of History* (New York: Columbia University Press, 1999).

49. The editors added a comma after "investigate."—Eds.

50. Frantz Fanon, *Black Skin, White Masks*, trans. Richard Philcox (New York: Grove Press, 2008). This reference has been added by the editors. Fanon introduces the concept of sociogeny in the "Introduction." "Do not forget sociogeny" is not a literal citation, but meant to refer to Fanon's call to consider sociogeny in the examination of blackness, antiblackness, racism, and alienation.—Eds.

51. Fanon, *Wretched*; Donna Haraway, *Primate Visions: Gender, Race and Nature in the World of Modern Science* (New York: Routledge, 1998).

52. The unpublished version that Lugones was preparing for this volume reads: "Is Foucault's understanding of power that is at work in the notion of the people of modern nations, also one that applies to Afrodescendents and Indigenous people"?—Eds.

53. Gloria Wekker, *The Politics of Passion: Women's Sexual Culture in the Afro-Surinamese Diaspora* (Durham: Duke University Press, 2016).

54. Casimir, personal correspondence with author.

55. The editors added italics to "matti work," as it appears in the unpublished version.—Eds.

56. Marcos, *Taken from the Lips*.

57. Ibid., 13.

Chapter 2

Toward a Genealogy of Experience

Critiquing the Coloniality of Feminist Reason from Latin America

Yuderkys Espinosa-Miñoso
Translation by Carlos Ulises Decena and Geo Maher

This text aims to answer a key question proposed by the genealogical method and which, applied to feminism, can be translated as the following: How have we become the feminists we are? What are the conditions of possibility which have allowed feminism to believe what it believes, to say what it says, to do what it does even in a space geopolitically conditioned by its "Third Word" status, of a region marked by a colonial wound?

Starting from these questions opens up space to reconstruct some clues for thinking feminism in Latin America and its history of dependency. And here, we refer not to Latin American feminism, but to feminism in Latin America, since there is but one feminist reason with universalist pretensions which local feminism has tenaciously embraced. If it seems nobody is apparently surprised at hearing that feminism is a response to modernity, we will need to ask why we have been willing to follow it in those regions of the world where modernity cannot but reveal itself for what it is: racist, Eurocentric, capitalist, imperialist, colonial.

Maybe women as well as those subject to discrimination for their gender or sexual identities have succumbed to the idea, foundational to feminist theorization and thought, that the past has always been worse for us. Maybe feminism might say that our struggle cannot but be modern, cannot but proclaim modernity as the historical temporality that allows us to pursue our freedom. This argument would reveal (or does in fact reveal) without a doubt how the interests of feminism differ from those of antiracist, anticolonial, and decolonial struggles in the region. It exposes the hidden plot of feminist struggles and their commitment to coloniality.

In this essay, I advance a methodological proposal for a genealogy of experience to approach and develop a critique of what I call at the outset the coloniality of feminist reason. Latin America, from where I develop this project and from where I write, provides simply the case study from which I approach the question and seek to demonstrate my claims.

THE PROJECT OF A CRITIQUE OF MODERN, EUROCENTRIC FEMINIST REASON

This project starts from a question about Latin American feminism: How do we document struggles over its meaning and the construction of hegemonies and counterhegemonies stemming from those struggles? In what way do we contribute towards the construction of a countermemory that will allow us to reveal the power games and hierarchical relations that obscure and collaborate with the local production of subalternity within the "Global South," the internal fracture of the "colonial subject"? If Mohanty has warned us about the discursive colonialism of feminisms from the Global North, subaltern activism has shown us the internal colonialism, mechanisms of control, and tactics for the production and preservation of the power of a minority within feminism in Latin America.[1] The colonial wound bleeds more in some of us than in others. Hegemonic feminisms of the Global North have needed the complicity of the hegemonic feminisms of the Global South to give continuity to the history of colonization and dependency. This is why an analysis of feminisms of the South and their dependent relationship to those of the North requires a complex engagement that allows us to dismantle the myth of the supposed internal unity of the collective subject "women," and thus allows us to observe a field of live contestations of meanings in post-independence Latin America. These disputes are resolved through the imposition of symbolic and material violence on those whose bodies are marked by processes of racialization and continued exploitation—what I have called *la otra de la otra*, or: the other of the other (woman).[2]

It is from this location that an awareness emerges of the need to take up a critical genealogy of the present when it comes to the feminist politics and thought in Latin America, to show what is twice hidden by colonial and postcolonial plots, to reveal the coloniality of feminist reason. This is a project that seeks to denounce and thereby contribute to dismantling feminism's commitment to the presuppositions of modernity and its contribution to modernity's expansion. Our task, in other words, is the decolonization of feminism.

To this end, I develop a methodological proposal that leans, on the one hand, on the genealogical method articulated by an important tradition within modern philosophy itself. If the genealogical method has been useful for anti-Enlightenment proposals within Western modernity, can it be useful to the project of demonstrating feminism's committments to Eurocentric modern ontologies even in regions like Latin America? What implications would this have in terms of radical antiracist and decolonial critique? Setting out from the critical frameworks developed by Black, Indigenous, and other people of color, and anti and decolonial theories in Latin America, this project is linked to a perspective that contests Western modernity as the maximum expression of human evolution, unveiling what it has been in reality: an imperialist, racist project of domination and death.

On the other hand, I embrace developments within feminist, Black feminist, and feminist of color epistemology in the proposal for situated knowledges grounded in experience. For this purpose, I focus on revisions of what has been called standpoint theory, which seeks to overcome the pretensions of scientific knowledge to "speak from nowhere,"[3] and I review the critiques formulated by Joan Scott of the uses of experience as basis for our explanations so as to avoid falling into the same errors she documents.[4]

ON THE GENEALOGICAL METHOD
AND THE IDEA OF THE ARCHIVE

Traditionally, Latin American philosophy has approached the historiography of the region's thought through the History of Ideas, convened by several of the best known Latin American philosophers—Cerutti, Alberdi, Zea, Rodó, Bello.[5] Following this legacy, the feminist philosopher Francesca Gargallo has embraced the construction of a history of Latin American feminist ideas in her project *Latin American Feminist Ideas*.[6] Even though I have been motivated to continue that task for a while, as my engagement deepened and my questions about the trajectories of (what I then called) Latin American feminism, I began to find clear differences between what these authors were doing within philosophy and, in particular, what Francesca Gargallo was engaged in from the perspective of Latin American feminist philosophy. It was not long before I fortunately found myself reading the philosopher Santiago Castro-Gómez and his *Critique of Latin American Reason*, during the course of my engagement with thinkers committed to the decolonial turn.[7] And it was there that I found clues to what I wanted to do and what I was in fact already doing without meaning to. In Castro-Gómez's text, he recalls the proposal made by another great Colombian philosopher, Roberto Salazar Ramos, a member of the "Bogotá Group," who encouraged the development

of an archeology of what is "Latin American," seeking to discover the mechanisms through which a series of discourses have been constructed that have
granted Latin America a specificity and exteriority vis-a-vis modern, Western
reason. As Castro-Gómez himself explains, what interests him is to "critically
examine that family of discourses that made possible the creation of an entity
called 'Latin America,' endowed of an ethos and of a cultural identity that
supposedly distinguish it from modern, European rationality."[8] The question
that would definitively guide his work was no longer about what characterizes a predetermined Latin American identity, but instead what makes it possible—its conditions of possibility. How has Latin American identity been
produced as a way of being and of thinking and what has philosophy had
to do with that project? To answer this question, Castro-Gómez proposes to
observe the production of philosophical thought in Latin America not to construct a "history of ideas" as proposed by Latin Americanist philosophy, but
instead to develop a "localized genealogy of the practices" that would help to
critically reveal how philosophy in Latin America has contributed to producing the idea of "Latin Americanness."[9]

For Castro-Gómez, the genealogical task is inevitably linked to the task not
so much of finding what unifies us, but instead of showing the antagonisms,
the dilemmas, the power games, "the ruptures, the empty spaces, the fissures,
and the lines of flight . . ."[10] In his rigorous study of Michel Foucault's work,
Castro-Gómez observes how the genealogical task can be useful for scrutinizing our present to determine the historical contingencies and the power strategies that have made it possible. In this way, the Colombian philosopher shows
us a genealogy in the modality that Foucault takes up from the Niezschean
model, as a *critical ontology of the present*. He finds and helps us discover
Foucault's genealogy as an effective method that allows for a new

> way of philosophically approaching the problem of modernity, where before
> uncovering the "truth" of its inherent promises (liberty, equality, fraternity),
> what is being sought are the technologies of domination that contributed to its
> construction, as well as the diverse forms in which that truth constitutes our
> contemporary subjectivity.[11]

In this way, the author seeks to demonstrate the usefulness of the genealogical method for unveiling coloniality in Latin America. His rigorous study
allows us to see, based on the concrete experience of Colombia, how the ideals of progress and modernization sustained by white-Mestizo elites in Latin
American countries have been built on Enlightenment ontological foundations.[12] In this way, Castro-Gómez takes up the Foucaultian wager insofar as
it helps us "draw up a cartography of the forces that constitute us in what we
are" and thereby unveils coloniality.[13]

Since the genealogical method interrogates present facts in order to identify the interests and historical and cultural conditioning that have determined
those facts, and the will to power that has produced them, it can be effective
in producing critical thought that is prepared to unveil the political economy
of truth that legitimizes the web of meanings and practices of the present.
This is why it becomes necessary to interrogate practices and their effective-
ness: what do we really do when we speak or act? To turn the question about
identity into a question about what we do, to the practices to make us what
we are. The investigation of practices leads us to wonder what counts as a
practice, how does it work, what are the rules that make it work. To do genealogy allows us to distance ourselves from the present to see the conditions
of possibility that constitute us, to see these a priori and problematize and
denaturalize them. To trace the history of practices in order to denaturalize
them, to observe how, when, and why they have emerged.[14]

Inspired by these ideas and by the questions posed by the genealogical
method, I came to formulate the questions necessary for observing and analyzing feminism in Latin America correctly: How have we come to be the
feminists—"advanced" women at the "cutting edge of our time"—that we
claim to be? What is it that we do, as feminists in Latin America, when we
call a march for "the right to abortion," when we shout "mi cuerpo es mío"
(my body is mine) or "libertad en la calle y en la plaza" (freedom at home and
in the plaza), when we pressure institutions and the state to approve a law for
"gender equity," when we open spaces at the university and we ask women
to enter it en masse, when we establish a gender and sexuality studies program, when we talk about reproductive rights, when we give speeches at the
United Nations, when we formulate and develop projects for "poor women,"
or when we develop campaigns against street harrassment? What is it that we
feminists do when we say what we say and do what we do? What is it that we
feminists in Latin America do when we do and when we speak?

And it was at this point that I began to formulate the existence of a universal and Eurocentric "feminist reason." Because when I looked back from the
vantage point of these questions, what I was able to document is that there is
no history of the specificity of our feminism. Instead, there is a history of the
will to not distinguish ourselves, to not set ourselves apart from the theories,
the wagers, and the mottos of the feminism produced in the Global North.
There is an effort to adjust to theories produced in the USA and Europe, in
a way to allow into those theories women from the most dissimilar contexts,
those cross-cut by coloniality.

Attempting to explain the feminist present in Latin America—its dilemmas, contradictions, disputes, central issues, political strategies, discourses,
and practices—allowed me to notice something like a shared feminist reason, a series of principles on the basis of which feminists have all settled

irrespective of times and from the most diverse contemporary locations, in the United States, Europe and Latin America, Asia, or Africa. A series of principles that contribute to the production of one narrative: we the women, we as the ones who have always been dominated. And its flipside: we the empowered, we women who are owners of our destiny and who become somebody thanks to feminism (and, therefore, thanks to modernity).

I have thus taken up the task of reviewing the dilemmas and the limits of the theoretical-political practices produced, sustained, and nurtured by feminism and contemporary sociosexual movements viewed from the particularities of the Latin American context and its history of coloniality. My genealogical project seeks to interrogate the discourses to which we have adhered regarding sexuality, gender, the sex-gendered subject, and the ways in which we have applied those discourses to think "Latin Americanness" as a globalized space seeking integration into the (truly) human. What I propose is a critical exercise that will allow us to become aware of how we have become the feminists and/or the "free, transgressive, and advanced" sexed-gendered subject that we claim to be. The goal is to reveal the "political economy of truth" evident in the political and discursive practices around gender and sexuality (patriarchy and heterosexual regime) to which we have contributed insofar as we have subscribed to a blind faith and contributed to feminist postulates cast as universal.[15] I am interested in pausing to reflect on those postulates in order to denounce mechanisms of regulation, hierarchization, and the legitimation of some forms of understanding over others.

To be able to stage this critique of the present of our feminism, it is also necessary to appeal to archeology; to play the role of the archivist and cartographer "of our memory, revealing old testimonies as symptoms of the present"; to construct an "audio-visual archive" and slog through the widest variety of available documents, together with "muted practices, sideway behaviors, heterogenous discourses," and to be willing to "excavate and plumb the depths, to bring to light what is hidden."[16] In sum, as Foucault himself points out, the objective it to bring together a series of rules that operate for a group of people during a specific period so as to be able to determine (1) "the limits and forms of the *sayable*": what can or cannot be said; (2) "the limits and forms of *conservation*": which discourses are counted and seen as an important part of memory and which pass "without any trace"; (3) "the limits and forms of *memory* it appears in different discursive formations. Which utterances does everyone recognize as valid, or debatable, or definitely invalid?"; (4) "the limits and forms of *reactivation*": which discourses "are attempts made to reconstitute?"; (5) "The limits and forms of *appropriation*. What individuals, what groups or classes have access to a particular kind of discourse?"[17]

If it is true that genealogy must record the singularity of events outside of any monotonous finality; it must seek them in the most unpromising places, in what we tend to feel is without history—in sentiments, love, conscience, instincts; it must be sensitive to their recurrence, not in order to trace the gradual curve of their evolution, but to isolate the different scenes where they engaged in different roles.[18]

Then I had already been preparing for this task, in fact I had already been carrying out this task for a while. I began without knowing a long time ago when for some reason I started to construct, obsessively and fastidiously, an archive of the practices and the discursive practices of lived and experienced feminism. Motivated by this archivist obsession, I started writing a long time ago, and the practice of writing helped to record in my memory and in collective memory every moment of lived feminist politics, first locally, and, to the degree that I became part of a more international movement, regionally as well. It was an exercise that was shared by several of those who have walked with me. I put together a digital and physical archive where I saved original texts published here and there in virtual spaces, blogs, pamphlets, and non-specialized journals alongside photographs and images of our activities and half-finished drafts that were never published. But there is something else that escapes the physical archive: the systematic exercise of consciously holding in memory the recollection of affects, images, feelings, but also of words said and not said, analyses shared in workshops for political reflection or afternoons of (re)encounters with friends and heated discussions with my antagonists of then and of now.

I have appealed to all of this in my interrogation of the experience of feminist practice. I have resorted to the idea of experience and of active witnessing for the construction of my archive. As an activist earnestly engaged in the work and in debates about feminism in Latin America, I have asked myself if it was possible to appeal to my own historical memory, to my almost 30-year trajectory and participant observation in crucial moments of the medium-term history of regional feminism. I constructed my archive with notes from meetings I attended, activities I helped organize, discussions in which I participated, reflections that emerged from these and that have accumulated in essays, notes, published articles, and unpublished manuscripts. With the one thousand and one stories that I keep in my memory and the ones in which I have played the role of participant witness or not, but which I have learned about through different accounts by those who were there. There is also the corporeal and visual memory that accompanies the speeches, the sensations of joy, of pain, of victory or defeat, of expectation, incredulity or certainty. In sum, I have challenged myself to construct and propose the possibility of creating a genealogy of the experience of feminism in Latin America, to use my own experience as a substantial and fundamental document in my archive and to appeal for corroboration to other sources: to articles, essays, video and audio recordings, photographs produced by other activists and thinkers who have also been part of this trajectory and who have moved through feminism in Latin America during the period I have lived and that I now try to document.

To establish a foundation for this methodological choice, I have decided to review all of the critiques of the scientific method's pretention of objectivity whether produced within feminism or outside of it. And I want to take stock of the way standpoint theory can help me discover arguments to validate my use of experience as an archive from which I can carry out this critical genealogy of the feminist present and demonstrate its coloniality.

USING EXPERIENCE TO CONSTRUCT THE ARCHIVE OF A GENEALOGY OF FEMINIST REASON IN LATIN AMERICA

As we know, feminist epistemology in its totality and specifically within the tradition produced by Black and women of color feminisms, in their critique of the scientific method, have proposed and thematized the "experience" of women and of Black women and women of color as legitimate grounds for the production of knowledge.[19]

Concretely, it has been the so-called "standpoint" perspective—developed by white feminist epistemology and taken up by Black women and women of color feminists—which has been focused on developing a critique of the methods for knowledge production in modern science and has proposed in its place the use of experience as an effective mechanism for the construction of knowledge. While white feminists have focused on androcentrism and the pretension of objectivity in the scientific method, Black and women of color feminists have developed a trenchant critique of the universality of the category "women" in classical feminist theory, pointing out that what counts as feminist theory is only one "standpoint" produced by white women with access to university training thanks to their class and race privileges.[20] Some Black feminists have proposed their own theorization as a standpoint of its own based on the experience of Black women.[21] Something similar would happen in the past two decades in Latin America, when the reappearance of a strong continental anticolonial and decolonial movement called into question the history and knowledge produced by the social sciences in the hands of white-Mestizo intellectuals. Thus the production of a voice and interpretation of their own became one of the key tasks for these movements and for decolonial feminism.[22]

Black and women of color feminist critiques, and more recently decolonial feminism, ended up performing the same critique within feminism
that feminist epistemology had made toward Western scientific knowledge
production: that they conceal beneath objectivity and universality what is
in reality a partial perspective since it emerges from a particular historical
experience and concrete interests.[23] What is clear is that standpoint theory did
not in itself guarantee overcoming the obstacles posed by either the universalist essentialism of the category "women," or the racism, Eurocentrism, and
coloniality of the most influential feminist theories. As Harding points out,
recalling the critiques of thinkers such as Haraway, "standpoint epistemology,
like other kinds of socialist feminist theory is guilty of this theoretical and
political error."[24]

Despite these shortcomings, the contributions of standpoint epistemology
to the construction of a method of analysis grounded in experience as source
for knowledge are undeniable. First proposed by Nancy Hartsock and Dorothy
Smith, standpoint epistemology first argued that the point of view of women
offers far broader explanations to the social life as a totality than those that
men tend to be able to provide, given the greater visibility that women enjoy
thanks to the activities assigned to them within the sexual division of labor.[25]
While the male gaze cannot observe or take into account a large part of social
activities, since these are seen as tasks of a "natural" order—the reproduction
of life and care—women, who are responsible for these activities, can see
them, and from this perspective can also see those ("abstract") tasks carried
out by men and which enjoy social value. This is what Harding calls "bifurcated consciousness" and which feminist researchers concretize through their
research and analysis.[26] In this way, feminist standpoint theorists suggest that
more adequate research can be carried out when investigators ask themselves
about the world and activities of women, since this provides a bottom-up
view of the social that is more encompassing, complete, and less distorted.

In that way, if the social order is a power matrix where race, class, and
gender are superimposed and codetermine one another, a feminist standpoint
approach to research would render more visible how that matrix operates
by taking as point of departure the experience of those at the lowest rung of
privilege hierarchies. In this way "what is a disadvantage in terms of their
oppression *can* become an advantage in terms of science."[27]

This idea is reminiscent of and seems to me to be related to Du Bois' idea
of "double consciousness": the privileged perspective on the world that the
racialized subject enjoys insofar as they cohabitate the subaltern world, subjected to oppression, while also entering as subaltern into the world of the
dominant classes, the white world. This way of inhabiting the world produces
the possibility of a doubled perspective, an alternative gaze (second-sight)
which allows them to become conscious of their subaltern position.[28]

It is a peculiar sensation, this double consciousness, this sense of always looking at one's self through the eyes of others, of measuring one's soul by the tape of a world that looks on in amused contempt and pity. One ever feels his two-ness—and American, a Negro; two souls, two thoughts, two unreconciled strivings.[29]

If Du Bois laments the presence of that double, bifurcated consciousness, which leads to us "losing focus," from the vantage point of standpoint theory this is not merely an obstacle but also the condition of possibility for a fuller and more heterogeneous view of the world.[30] It is from this double consciousness that a more radical critique committed to social transformation can emerge, insofar as this perspective reveals what is hidden by power games and, in the case of countries in the Global South, internal colonialism as well. As we now know: explaining the world and events purely from the vantage point of those who occupy a privileged location gives us a partial and distorted understanding of the world that can be sorted out through the doubled gaze and experience of those who occupy a subaltern position.

One might arrive at the logical conclusion that the subaltern gaze is doubled, contradictory, conflicted, paradoxical, impure . . . and that precisely as a result, it offers a greater source of knowledge. But I wonder then why it is that the gaze produced by white and white-Mestizo feminism has always been incomplete, shedding light only on one aspect of how oppression operates. This incomplete gaze not only prevents us from accounting for the opressions of disadvantaged subjects, but also prevents us from seeing the complexity of the matrix of oppression in its totality, or the intrinsic relations between projects of domination.

I would therefore like to introduce a small but major distortion into the feminist standpoint. If Mohanty celebrates the epistemic privilege that emerges from the experience of women in the Global South insofar as they find themselves at the bottom of the hierarchy of privilege, and if we accept the critiques of Black women and women of color feminisms that at the base of the pyramid of power we find the racialized woman, then the subject of this privileged standpoint is not just any woman but the subaltern woman—in Latin America, the Indigenous and Afro-descendant woman, the peasant, the poor and landless.

And so the perspective that I want to produce based on my own experience of moving through feminism in Latin America is the point of view produced by being/inhabiting a body subjected to impoverishment, dispossession, and the systematic negation of her capacity to produce knowledge, critique, and a project for the future. It is from the experience of coming from a dehumanized people, of a people subjected to servitude and the negation of themselves from which I will attempt to answer some of the questions that I pose to Latin American feminism. The idea of a genealogy of experience starts from recognizing the locus of enunciation from where one writes. The question of how we have come to be the feminists we are and what it is that feminists in Latin America do when they do what they do will be answered from the perspective of the subject produced between worlds: the woman on whose body the poor, Black barrio will always be present as a birthmark; the woman who saw the world of rich white people on television, at the movies, in the face of the boss, in the group of upper-class, white-mestiza girls who made fun of her at school; the woman who, when she accesses a university education and feminism—spaces of racial and class privilege—ended up understanding that peculiar sensation of "always looking at one's self through the eyes of others."[31]

But to avoid confusion, the one who practices genealogy with the archive of her own experience will need to avoid the mistake of using it as foundation or as proof, as the foundation for her explanation. Heeding Scott's warnings about the bad uses of the archive of experience means understanding that it has to become that which must be explained: how have we become the feminists we are, the advanced women we claim to be?[32] That is the question that I ask of the experience of feminism. But there is also a hidden and personal question: how did I learn to read myself fundamentally as a woman who is part of a global community of women? How did I come to construct a history of myself from the vantage point of that category so foundational to feminism? Why could I not for so long explain all of the rest of my experience which feminism could not account for? In the case of the genealogy of feminism in Latin America and the ways it (re)produces a Eurocentric Reason, appealing to the experience of three decades of activism allows me to question it, interrogate it, critique it. How is the difference established between the "advanced feminist subject" and the subject rendered illegible as if trapped by ignorance and lack of consciousness about her own oppression? What are the truths that we have accepted and which define our practices? How do these operate? How and in what ways does feminism constitute subjects that see and act upon the world in a given way?

HOW AND FROM WHAT PERSPECTIVE I ARGUE THAT THERE EXISTS A WESTERN FEMINIST REASON AND THAT IT IS COMMITTED TO COLONIALITY

The fundamental ideas that I want to affirm and propose as conclusions to my inquiries and simultaneously as hypotheses to be confirmed or disproven in the future debate are, (1) that there exists a universal feminist reason, and (2) that this reason has been characterized by its commitment to modernity and, therefore, to the hidden face of coloniality and the racism that defines it.

By the coloniality of feminist reason I understand a series of practices, including discursive practices—in the Foucaultian sense—that have been agreed upon and developed by feminists of any tendency, and through which they have contributed to the production of a universal subject "woman/ women." This is a series of discourses that—despite debates and the acceptance or not of internal differences within this subject—sustains certain basic agreements about this subject within the social, alongside a series of prescriptions about which practices will lead to its emancipation. Feminist theorizing has produced and deployed a representation and image of "the woman"—beyond any difference, spatial or temporal—as always in a state of subjection, with less power and in a hierarchical relationship to "man" (also viewed as universal). Taking sexuality as given and contributing in paradigmatic fashion to the production of a technology of "gender" without questioning the ontological basis of either, feminists have given continuity to the modern myth and its Eurocentric reason.

Here, it is important to explain the concept of "reason" and how I am conceptualizing it. By reason, I allude to four fundamental issues that have been substantive pillars for philosophy and modernity and therefore, for coloniality as well:

One: On one hand, the pretension that one arrives at true knowledge of the world through trustworthy explanations that lead one out of a state of apprenticeship. True "reason" in this sense—mature reason—is inevitably linked to the advent of the Enlightenment. This "perspective imagined modernity and rationality as exclusively European products and experiences," as Quijano reminds us.[33]

To make use of reason in this sense means that "man" is capable, for the first time, of producing his own understanding of the world "without the guidance of another." Thus, for Kant,

> Enlightenment is man's emergence from his self-incurred immaturity. *Immaturity* is the inability to use one's own understanding without the guidance of another. This immaturity is *self-incurred* if its cause is not lack of understanding, but lack of resolution and courage to use it without the guidance of another. The motto of enlightenment is therefore: *Sapere aude!* Have courage to use your *own* understanding![34]

If, for Kant, enlightenment is a time of arrival at maturity, this "maturity" refers to the fact that "man" stands against the authority of tradition, instituting in its place a regime that subjects all belief to the "court of reason" to be judged according to universal principles, principles that—through study and the command of nature—lead to inevitable progress and an escape from ignorance.[35]

While feminist theory and research have been constructed in opposition to a positivist Cartesian method that presents itself as neutral, uncontaminated, and capable of discovering the true laws governing the natural and social order, the fact is that in order to gain a space within the production of a truth about "women," gender, and sexuality, feminism has needed to resort to certain forms of knowledge validation, accepting and being a part of the knowledge/power mechanism through which the border between legitimate and illegitimate knowledges is established.

Aside from that, the fact is that feminism and feminists have positioned themselves as possessing a series of truths that challenge common knowledge about social reality and about the subject "woman," a subject that these truths have helped to define and on the basis of which they offer a diagnosis of the world. Feminists are convinced that, as bearers of this truth about "women," they more than anyone else are able to establish a liberatory program that will allow women to escape their state of historical subjection. With this certainty, feminists have developed a global agenda for women's liberation and equality that they preach and impose by various means on the rest of the world, and particularly on women from those countries they consider less developed. This is what has been denounced by Third World women as a "savior complex" that is nothing less than imperialist.

Two: When I refer to reason I also use it in the sense that Hegel does in his *Oldest Systematic Program of German Idealism* when he speaks of the "mythology of reason" as what Castro-Gómez describes as "an organic system of beliefs firmly grounded in the ethos of the community, able to bind individuals together and give meaning to collective action."[36] Once we embraced the need to undo the organic communal bond that gave meaning to early communities, seen by modernity as the source of backwardness, we feminists called for the construction of new communities of women liberated from the burden of tradition. We feminists thus invented the "community of women" in order to give meaning to a struggle and a common life.

Three: I am also thinking about it as rationalization in the Weberian sense, i.e., and to put it in Castro-Gomez's words: "the methodic organization of life and the subjection of human conduct to a specific set of rules with the goal of obtaining some expected results.[37] In this sense, we feminists—the feminists that we claim to be—prescribe a series of practices within the communities that we develop, and we *are* a series of practices governed by a series of prescriptions about what "the liberated woman"—the subject of liberated gender and sexuality—would look like. Feminist ideas and truths do more than simply create an idea of the world and produce subjects. Just like any other discourse, feminism contains implicit prescriptions about what it means to be a woman today, or rather a woman in search of self-determination.

Four: Finally, when I speak of feminist Reason, I allude in reality to a form of critique. Feminist Reason responds to the arrogant and imperialist gesture of modern reason as that which proclaims itself to be the only true existing reason, its highest stage of evolutionary development, that which in other words develops within its own historical time and within a specific space: Europe. Authors like Dussel and Quijano have denounced this operation, arguing that what the West has named reason is in reality an effect of Eurocentrism, a program that seeks to annul and refuses to recognize any other forms of thought as valid forms of knowledge and reasoning.[38]

If Dussel sees modernity as a phenomenon that is possible for all cultures and all historical epochs, it is thanks to the colonial enterprise that Europe managed to impose itself on all other conquered peoples and civilizations, thereby defining itself "as the new and at the same time, most advanced [part] of the species."[39] According to this myth, humanity evolves along a unilinear and unidirectional path from a state of nature to a state of maximal cultural development, whose culmination is European or Western civilization. The idea of race is the cornerstone upholding the entire scaffolding that frames Europe as superior and as an example to follow.

So the success of Western Europe in imposing itself as the center of the modern world consisted in simultaneously developing Eurocentrism as a shared feature of the colonial and imperialist enterprises in conjunction with the development of race as a form of global classification (coloniality), which allowed Europeans to develop "a new temporal perspective of history and relocated the colonized population, along with their respective histories and cultures, in the past of a historical trajectory whose culmination was Europe."[40]

In this same sense, Mario Blaser proposes that we consider modernity "the state of being that obtains from the enactment of a modern myth composed of three basic threads: the great divide between nature and culture (or society), the colonial difference between moderns and nonmoderns, and unidirectional linear temporality that flows from past to future."[41] There are many examples of how feminist reason adheres to these precepts in its interpretation of the world. Demonstrating that feminist reason is a form of modern, Eurocentric reason would mean focusing our attention on how these elements are reproduced in our theoretical-discursive practices, in our political practices, and in our projects for the future.

I should say that when I speak of feminist reason as a form of modern, Eurocentric reason, I accept the revisions carried out by some authors in the direction discussed here. Feminism as a global project that universalizes an interpretation of society and the condition of women—and also of women as a universal subject—is clearly committed to coloniality and modernity. The neoliberal period that began in the late 1980s, and which I should say marked my own incursion into Latin American feminism and therefore provides the basis for my own critical genealogy of feminism in Latin America, has been fundamental for the full expansion of these ideas and ideals of feminism(s). Research currently underway will account for this.

NOTES

1. Chandra Mohanty, "Under Western Eyes: Feminist Scholarship and Colonial Discourses," *boundary 2* 12, no. 3 (1984); Chandra Mohanty, "'Under Western Eyes' Revisited: Feminist Solidarity through Anticapitalist Struggle," *Signs* 28, no. 2 (2003).

2. Yuderkys Espinosa Miñoso, "Etnocentrismo y colonialidad en los feminismos latinoamericanos: Complicidades y consolidación de las hegemonías feministas en el espacio transnacional," *Revista Venezolana de Estudios de la Mujer* 14, no. 33 (2010).

3. Sandra Harding, "A Socially Relevant Philosophy of Science? Resources from Standpoint Theory's Controversiality," *Hypatia* 19, no. 1 (2004).

4. Joan Wallach Scott, "The Evidence of Experience," *Critical Inquiry* 17, no. 4 (1991).

5. Santiago Castro-Gómez, *Crítica de la razón latinoamericana,* 2nd ed. (Bogotá: Editorial Pontificia Universidad Javeriana, 2011): 245–47.

6. Francesca Gargallo, *Ideas feministas latinoamericanas* (México, DF: Universidad Autónoma de la Ciudad de México, 2004).

7. Castro-Gómez, *Crítica.*

8. Ibid., 12.

9. Ibid., 245–47.

10. Ibid., 117.

11. Santiago Castro-Gómez, "La filosofía latinoamericana como ontología crítica del presente. Temas y motivos para una 'Crítica de la razón latinoamericana,'" accessed April 22, 2014, https://www.insumisos.com/lecturasinsumisas/LA%20FILOSOFIA %20LATINOAMERICANA%20COMO%20ONTOLOGiA%20CRiTICA%20DEL %20PRES.pdf.

12. Santiago Castro-Gómez, *La hybris del punto cero ciencia, raza e ilustración en la Nueva Granada (1750–1816)* (Bogotá: Editorial Pontificia Universidad Javeriana, 2005); Santiago Castro-Gómez, *Tejidos oníricos: movilidad, capitalismo y biopolítica en Bogotá (1910–1930)* (Bogotá: Editorial Pontificia Universidad Javeriana, 2009).

13. Castro-Gómez, *Crítica,* 256.

14. *Revista La Cicuta,* "Lanzamiento *La Cicuta Revista*: Santiago Castro-Gómez - 'Michel Foucault: El oficio del genealogista," YouTube, published October 4, 2013, https://www.youtube.com/watch?v=033YTK-t0zo.

15. Castro-Gómez, *Crítica,* 12.

16. Luis Gonçalvez, "La metodología genealógica y arqueológica de Michel Foucault en la investigación en psicología social," 1–2, accesssed April 22, 2019. http://

www.fadu.edu.uy/estetica-diseno-ii/files/2015/06/transitos-de-una-psicologia-social -genealogi%CC%81a-y-arqueologi%CC%81a.pdf.

17. Michel Foucault, "Politics and the Study of Discourse," in *The Foucault Effect: Studies in Governmentality*, eds. Graham Burchell, Colin Gordon, and Peter Miller (Chicago: University of Chicago Press, 1991), 59–60 (emphasis in original).

18. Michel Foucault, "Nietzsche, Genealogy, History," in *The Foucault Reader*, ed. Paul Rabinow (New York: Pantheon, 1984), 76.

19. Dorothy E. Smith, "Women's Standpoint: Embodied Knowledge versus Ruling Relations," in *Gender Inequality: Feminist Theory and Politics*, ed. Judith Lorber (New York: Oxford University Press, 2010); Sandra Harding, "Is There a Feminist Method?," in *Feminism and Methodology*, ed. Sandra Harding (Bloomington: Indiana University Press, 1987); Nancy Hartsock, "The Feminist Standpoint: Developing the Ground for a Specifically Feminist Historical Materialism," in *Discovering Reality: Feminist Perspectives on Epistemology, Metaphysics, Methodology and Philosophy of Science,* eds. Sandra Harding and Merrill Hintikka (Dordrecht: Reider Publishers, 1983); Patricia Hill Collins, *Black Feminist Thought: Knowledge, Consciousness, and the Politics of Empowerment* (Boston: Unwin Hyman, 1990).

20. bell hooks, "Black Women: Shaping Feminist Theory," in *Feminist Theory from Margin to Centre* (Boston: South End Press, 1984).

21. Hill Collins, *Black Feminist Thought.*

22. Sueli Carneiro, "Ennegrecer al Feminismo," presented at the seminar *La situación de la Mujer negra en América Latina, desde una perspectiva de genero*, São Paulo, Brazil, 2001; Breny Mendoza, "La epistemología del sur, la colonialidad del género y el feminismo latinoamericano," in *Aproximaciones críticas a las prácticas teórico-políticas del feminismo latinoamericano*, ed. Yuderkys Espinosa Miñoso (Buenos Aires: En la Frontera, 2010); Aura Cumes, "Multiculturalismo, género y feminismos: Mujeres diversas, luchas complejas," in *Participación y políticas de mujeres indígenas en América Latina,* ed. Andrea Pequeño (Quito: FLACSO Ecuador/ Ministerio de Cultura, 2009); Zulma Palermo, "Conocimiento 'otro' y conocimiento del otro en américa latina," *Estudios*, no. 21 (Fall 2009).

23. Yuderkys Espinosa-Miñoso, "Una crítica descolonial a la epistemología feminista crítica," *Revista El Cotidiano* 29, no. 184 (March-April 2014).

24. Sandra Harding, "Feminism, Science, and the Anti-Enlightenment Critiques," in *Women, Knowledge, and Reality: Explorations in Feminist Philosophy*, ed. Ann Garry and Marilyn Pearsall (New York/London: Routledge, 1996), 299–300.

25. Hartsock, "The Feminist Standpoint"; Dorothy Smith, "Women's perspective as a radical critique of sociology," *Sociological Inquiry* 44, no. 1 (1974); Dorothy Smith, *The Everyday World as Problematic: A Sociology for Women* (Boston: Northeastern University Press, 1987).

26. Harding, "Feminism, Science," 313.

27. Ibid., 314 (emphasis in original).

28. W.E.B Du Bois, *The Souls of Black Folk* (New York: Penguin, 1989), 2–3.

29. Ibid.

30. Doris Sommer, "A Vindication of Double Consciousness," in *A Companion to Postcolonial Studies*, ed. Henry Schwarz and Sangeeta Ray (Malden: Blackwell, 2000), 165.

31. Du Bois, *Souls.*

32. Scott, "Evidence."

33. Aníbal Quijano, "Coloniality of Power, Eurocentrism, and Latin America," *Nepantla: Views from South* 1, no. 3 (2000): 542.

34. Immanuel Kant, "An Answer to the Question: 'What is Enlightenment?,'" in *Kant: Political Writings*, ed. Hans Siegbert Reiss (Cambridge: Cambridge University Press, [1784] 1991), 54 (emphasis in original).

35. Castro-Gómez, *Hybris*, 22.

36. Castro-Gómez, *Crítica*, 132.

37. Ibid., 53.

38. Enrique Dussel, "Europe, Modernity, and Eurocentrism," *Nepantla: Views from South* 1, no. 3 (2000); Quijano, "Coloniality."

39. Quijano, "Coloniality," 542.

40. Ibid., 541.

41. Mario Blaser, *Storytelling Globalization from the Chaco and Beyond* (Durham: Duke University Press, 2010), 4.

Chapter 3

Constructing Feminist Methodologies from the Perspective of Decolonial Feminism

Ochy Curiel
Translation by María Elizabeth Rodríguez

The decolonial approach, in its several expressions, has offered critical ways to understand the historical and political specificity of our societies from non-dominant paradigms.[1] These ways of understanding show the relationship between Western modernity, colonialism, and capitalism, thus putting into question the narratives that are present in official historiographies and showing how social hierarchies have been formed.

More specifically, decolonial feminism, by reclaiming a substantial part of the propositions of both the decolonial option and of critical feminisms, offers a new analytical perspective to understand in a more complex way the relationships derived from race, sex, sexuality, class and geopolitics in an overlapping form. These proposals made mainly by Indigenous feminists and feminists of Indigenous origins, Black feminists, working class feminists, and lesbian feminists, among others, have questioned the ways in which hegemonic, white, white-Mestizo and class-privileged feminism has understood the subordination of women by having done so from their own situational experiences, which reproduce racism, classism, and heterosexism in their theories and political practices.

These critical feminisms have turned feminist theories and practices upside down. However, there is yet more excavating to do in relation to political practices, methodologies, and pedagogies, with the intention that the decolonial approach is not limited to epistemological analysis. In this article, I intend to further advance this aspect and for this I propose, first of all, to clarify and problematize what I understand as postcolonial and as decolonial feminism, since there are confusions and various interpretations with regard to them. Secondly, I will characterize decolonial feminism, its main sources and proposals; and thirdly, I will address some issues that I believe are central to problematize feminist methodology(ies) and propose what I consider to be central aspects of the construction of decolonial feminist methodologies. I will now proceed to develop every aspect I propose.

IN REGARD TO POSTCOLONIALISM

In the social sciences as well as from the perspective of activism, it is often assumed that the epistemological and political perspectives of what is called "postcolonial feminism" are the same as in "decolonial feminism." Nevertheless, there are important differences that need to be clarified.

We could say that many societies have at some point been colonized—i.e., they have experienced the colonial event. Even countries that are now imperial centers, such as the United States, have been colonized at some point. However, not all societies have been colonized in the same manner; therefore, they are not postcolonial in the same way. The type of colonization that the United States experienced is not the same as the type that India experienced, and both of these differ from the type that most of the Latin American and Caribbean countries experienced.

Postcolonialism, in its historical meaning, begins in 1947, with the independence of India from the British Empire and with the end of World War II. Postcolonialism is also linked with the emancipatory processes in Asia and Africa, with the emergence of "Third World" nationalisms, and with the massive exodus of immigrants to industrialized countries. The term has had ambiguous inscription in the areas of influence defined by the Cold War.

The postcolonial, as a category, concept, and perspective—that is to say in its epistemological meaning—arises from the "postcolonial theories" during the 1980s in England and the United States. The Palestinian scholar Edward Said's book, *Orientalism*, in some way provides the parameters of these theories and makes a link between the European humanities and imperialism through the construction of the East (the Orient) as an Other in relation to which the West (the Occident) is constituted.[2] Subsequently, other academics stand out, particularly Indian scholars such as Gayatri Chakravorty Spivak, Homi K. Bhabha, Ranajit Guha, and Chandra Talpade Mohanty, among others. The concept of the postcolonial has wide-ranging positionalities, historical uses, and even several theoretical and political ambiguities.

Ella Shohat, an Iraqi of Jewish descent, has pointed out some of these theoretical and political ambiguities. She asserts that many formulations of the postcolonial do not make clear whether this periodization is epistemological or historical, also adding that they have universalizing and depoliticizing pretensions, dissolving the politics of resistance. Due to its multiple interpretations, Shohat proposes that the "post" in postcolonial should not refer to what comes after, or what has overcome colonialism; rather, it would be more precise to refer to a theory which goes beyond, or "post," the fixed and stable binary relationships of First world/Third World, colonized/colonizer, center/periphery.[3]

Anne McClintock, from Zimbabwe, also criticizes the concept of the postcolonial for its linearity, as if colonialism and its effects have ended.[4] Arif Dirlik, from Turkey, on the other hand, points to the postcolonial as a poststructuralist and postfoundational discourse whose specific linguistic and cultural trends are used, particularly by displaced Third World intellectuals seated in prestigious universities in the United States and Britain, as if these terms were universally consistent. For Dirlik, the notion of identity that is assumed from these positions is discursive and non-structural. In other words, it is a culturalism that downplays how capitalism structures the modern world.[5]

For the Puerto Rican Ramón Grosfoguel what is understood as postcolonial studies has a theoretical and political problem, namely that it understands colonialism as an eighteenth and nineteenth century "event," from the perspective of the British colonization of India and the British and French colonization of the Middle East.[6] For Grosfoguel, as for other Latin-American decolonial thinkers, the colonial experience begins in 1492, that is to say, 300 years earlier. In this view, 1492 is a fundamental starting point, since it is from this point that the modernity/coloniality relation that constructs the epistemic and political superiority of the West over the rest of the world is concretized. According to the author, postcolonial studies conceals this phenomenon. However, I will return to this point later on.

Although the Afro-Jamaican Stuart Hall agrees with some of Shohat's, McClintock's, and Dirlik's critiques, he also emphasizes how the concept of the postcolonial can help to describe or characterize the changes in global relations that take place as part of the (necessarily unequal) transition from the epoch of the empires to the moment of post-independence or post-colonization.[7] The concept also helps to identify the new relationships and arrangements of power that are arising in the new context. For Hall, the postcolonial is a process whereby all the worlds that were marked by colonialism disengage from the entire colonial syndrome. In this sense, postcolonialism is not only about describing "this" society instead of "that one," or describing "then" versus "now," but about re-interpreting colonization as part of a transnational and transcultural global process, an interpretation which produces a decentered, diasporic, or global rewriting of the great imperial narratives, which were previously centered on the nation.[8] I adopt Hall's proposal of "disengagement" since, although it refers to the postcolonial, this approach serves to construct proposals around decolonial methodologies, a matter that I will develop further below.

There are very few works that establish clear differences between what is understood by postcolonial feminism and decolonial feminism. Nevertheless, I will risk proposing that postcolonial feminism offers a narrative from the position of "Third World" women that challenges the hegemonic, generally white, and Western feminism. This narrative introduces the importance of considering race, class, and geopolitics to the understanding of geopolitical relations.

The contributions of postcolonial feminisms include the analysis of *discursive colonization* proposed by Chandra Mohanty and the idea of *epistemic violence* proposed by Gayatri Spivak, both of Indian origin.[9] The central argument of these two concepts refers to the critique of knowledge production by intellectuals who are generally white and from the North over women from the Third World. These women are assumed to lack agency and are seen only as victims, which creates a relationship of knowledge-power from positions of privilege of sex, race, sexuality, and geopolitics.

Although the contexts in which these authors have applied these concepts have been different from Latin America and the Caribbean, they apply perfectly to our context. Theories, categories, and concepts are transported, without contextualization from Europe and North America to our region in order to analyze the realities of many women, who then become objects of study of many feminists who have institutional and academic privileges, as well as privileged race, class, and sexuality positions.

Most postcolonial feminists, both in this region and beyond, are embedded in academic spaces, which, while they are spaces of political discourses, are minimally involved with social movements. This limits the ways in which knowledge is decolonized, because (a) it does not facilitate a recognition of categories, concepts, and epistemes that arise from the political practices that many women with underprivileged race, class, sexuality, and geopolitical positions produce in their communities and collectives, and, above all (b) it does not facilitate anchoring these analyses to the material realities and the concrete struggles that are being carried out in different places. Like the postcolonial project, which has been interrogated as a whole, very often postcolonial feminist analysis remains within a poststructuralist linguistic turn, which, although it opens doors for "other" interpretations, does not stop reproducing the discursive coloniality of knowledge.

CONCERNING DECOLONIAL FEMINISM

I assume, as do many others, that the struggles of Indigenous and Black peoples against colonialism in Abya Yala generated processes of decolonization, which included the emergence of important epistemologies whose further study is very much needed. Therefore, decolonizing practices precede everything that has been conceptualized as decolonial. This is a starting point for decolonial feminism.

What is called decolonial feminism, a concept proposed by Argentinian feminist María Lugones, has two important sources.[10] One source is the set of feminist criticisms made by Black feminists, women of color, Chicanas, working class women, the Latin American feminist autonomy movement, Indigenous feminists, and French materialist feminism against hegemonic feminism in its universalization of the concept of "woman," and, therefore, its racist, classist, and heterocentric bias.[11] Another source is the proposals for what is called decolonial theory or the decolonial project that different Latin American and Caribbean thinkers have developed. I will discuss these two points further, and I will start with the latter because it offers me a more general framework of analysis and gives me the possibility to include some of the criticisms that decolonial feminists have made of some of the decolonial Latin American and Caribbean thinkers.

The decolonial project, or, as it is also called, the modernity/coloniality group or network, arises from a group of Latin American, Caribbean, and Latinx intellectuals and activists, located primarily in U.S. universities including the State University of New York (SUNY) and Duke University, as well as in Latin American universities, specifically in the doctorate program in Cultural Studies at the Universidad Andina Simón Bolívar in Quito (Ecuador), the Master's program in Cultural Studies of the Javeriana University in Bogota (Colombia), the Master's program in Research on Contemporary Social Problems of the IESCO (also in Bogota), the seminar-workshop "Factory of Ideas" in Salvador de Bahia (Brazil), and the Central University of Venezuela, among others. Some of its members are involved with the Indigenous movement in Bolivia and Ecuador and the Colombian Afro-descendent movement, while others organize activities within the framework of the World Social Forum. This group is an expression of contemporary critical theory closely related to the traditions of the social sciences and humanities of Latin America and the Caribbean.[12]

There are several important issues that decolonial feminism incorporates from the decolonial project. First is the concept of *decoloniality*. This concept can be explained departing from the idea that the end of colonialism as a geopolitical and geo-historical constitution of European Western modernity did not lead to a significant transformation of the international division of labor between centers and peripheries, as well as between the ethnic-racial hierarchy of peoples and the formation of nation-states in the periphery. On the contrary, what has happened is a transition from modern colonialism to global colonialism.

The decolonial implies a new understanding of global and local relationships. This understanding requires us to see Western Eurocentric modernity, world capitalism, and colonialism as an inseparable trilogy, as Enrique Dussel has proposed.[13] The Americas are a product of modernity in the construction of the world system. In order to establish itself as the center of the world, Europe created the Americas to serve as its periphery since 1492, when capitalism became a global phenomenon through colonialism.[14]

From that Eurocentric perspective, Western modernity is assumed as emancipation, as utopia, as the myth that defined the dominance of Europeans over others who they considered barbarians, who they categorized as immature, whom they had to help develop—even if it had to be done through war and violence—and these others were ultimately seen as guilty of their own victimization.[15] In this way, this relationship between modernity and colonialism/global capitalism creates a global pattern of power that the Peruvian Aníbal Quijano defines as the *coloniality of power*, another important concept that decolonial feminism adopts.[16]

The coloniality of power has encompassed social relations of exploitation/domination/conflict around the dispute for the control and dominance of labor and its products, nature and its resources for production; sex and its products, the reproduction of the species; subjectivity and its products, both material and intersubjective, including knowledge and authority along with its instruments of coercion. For Quijano, this global pattern was sustained around the idea of race, which imposed a racial/ethnic classification: Indians, Blacks, olives, yellows, whites, Mestizos; and a geocultural classification: America, Africa, East Asia, Middle East, West Asia or Europe.

Although Lugones welcomes Quijano's proposal on coloniality, she points out that race is not the sole determinant for the configuration of the coloniality of power. For Lugones, along with race, there is gender and thus heterosexualism.[17] Lugones also argues that Quijano assumes a notion of hyper-biological sex. She analyzes how the gender he refers to has to do with a type of human relationship reserved for the European white male who possesses rights, and for his female companion, who serves for the purpose of their reproduction as species.[18] For this decolonial feminist, the type of differentiation that applies to the colonized and enslaved peoples is *sexual dimorphism*, male and female, which for Lugones accounts for an encompassing reproductive capacity and animal sexuality. In this logic, enslaved females were not women. In other words, Lugones argues that gender is a modern and colonial category. This is linked to the notion of humanity that was imposed by Western modernity, a notion that begins by questioning if Indigenous and Black people were human.

The colonized females and males were neither women or men, nor were they considered human. On this aspect, the Puerto Rican Nelson Maldonado-Torres develops the concept of the *coloniality of being*, another important concept that decolonial feminism embraces, and defines it as the denial of humanity to certain peoples (especially Indigenous and Afro-descendants peoples) who have been considered as an obstacle for Christianization, and then for modernization.[19] This negation of *being* (Dasein) has been the justification for enslaving them, taking away their lands, waging war on them, or simply murdering them. They are, as Frantz Fanon would say, "the wretched (*damnés*) of the Earth."[20]

Western Eurocentric Modernity also generated the *coloniality of knowledge*, another important concept that decolonial feminism adopts, which is a type of techno-scientific, epistemological rationality that is assumed as the acceptable model for knowledge production.[21] This knowledge, from this point of view, must be neutral, objective, universal, and positivist. As the Colombian Santiago Castro-Gómez points out, this colonial knowledge aims to be at a point zero of observation, capable of translating and documenting with fidelity the characteristics of an exotic nature and culture. It is an imaginary that pretends to emerge from a neutral platform, a single point from where you can see the social world that cannot be observed from any other point, just as the gods would.[22] From there, a great universal narrative is generated in which Europe and the United States are, simultaneously, the geographical center and the culmination of a temporal movement for knowledge, where the knowledge of subaltern populations is undervalued, ignored, excluded, silenced, and made invisible. The subalternity here is "the other" insofar as this other is not man, heterosexual, father, Catholic, educated, with racial and class privileges. Now, there are also many women with these privileges, and so it is clear that "otherness" must be studied, investigated, exoticized, exploited, developed, and mediated.

The coloniality of power, of being, and of knowledge, therefore, is the dark side of modernity, of that Western modernity from which feminism also arises as an emancipatory proposal that is supposedly for "all" women. These interpretations have been key to decolonial feminism. Yet another source has been the ideas and forms of thinking that have emerged from collective political practices, of which many of us have been part. These practices have to do with critical and counterhegemonic feminisms.

The Afro-Dominican, lesbian, feminist, autonomous, and decolonial thinker and activist Yuderkys Espinosa-Miñoso, has started to systematize what we in Latin America and the Caribbean call decolonial feminism.[23]

For Espinosa-Miñoso, decolonial feminism "is a movement in full growth and maturation that is proclaimed to be revisionist of the theoretical and the political proposal of feminism given what it considers its western, white, and bourgeois bias."[24] Espinosa-Miñoso posits that decolonial feminism aims to revise and problematize fundamental bases of feminism and to broaden key concepts and theories of what is known as the decolonial theory proposed by many of the aforementioned Latin American thinkers. Espinosa-Miñoso identifies US Black women and women of color feminisms and their proposal to consider the imbrication of the oppression of race, class and sex as important sources. Also relevant are the contributions by Afro-Latinx and Afro-Caribbean women, who make visible the relationship between racism and sexism in contexts that are dominated by the ideology of mestizaje. As Espinosa-Miñoso makes clear, their work also denounces the invisibility of feminist and Black movements in the region.

Espinosa-Miñoso further clarifies that decolonial feminism includes a consideration of key issues in postcolonial feminism, such as epistemic violence and strategic essentialism, and she regards central ideas in the current of Latin American autonomous feminism as important. Latin American autonomous feminism started in the 1990s with the denunciation of the developmentalist policies implemented by Northern countries in "Third World" countries, which included the institutionalization of social movements, including feminism.[25] Espinosa-Miñoso also points out that some decolonial feminists incorporate proposals submitted by French materialist feminism with its early questioning of the idea of nature, its understanding of the categories of men and women as types of sex, and the analysis of heterosexuality as a political regime. The poststructural feminist challenge of the essentialism of identities in political action is also a point of reference for some decolonial feminists.

On the basis of these contributions, key feminist categories have been problematized because they take for granted and reproduce the universalization of the subordination of women. They do so by only considering gender (from a binary and heterocentric perspective) in their analysis, and by relying on generalizations that have involved concepts and categories such as patriarchy, women, and sexual division of labor, that do not consider experiences of women affected by racism, classism, heterosexuality, and geopolitics. Therefore, the *modern/colonial gender system* has affected interpretations, theorizations, research, methodologies, and many political practices, by reproducing racism and colonization.[26]

Next, I will focus on some important issues raised by feminists who call ourselves decolonial, whose work includes contributions to and problematizations of what is called "the" feminist methodology. These explorations are necessary to understand the complexity of social relations, in addition to creating other categories, concepts, and theorizations, thus achieving an epistemological and political disengagement in the ways in which we produce knowledge.

A FEMINIST METHODOLOGY? THE POINT
OF VIEW AND INTERSECTIONALITY

Many feminists like myself have recognized the contributions of Sandra Harding to thinking about an epistemology and a feminist methodology that should question the masculine logic of science. Harding's work has also offered important insights about the value of reflexivity and its role in avoiding the "objectivist" position, which aims to hide the cultural beliefs and practices of the researcher. Also important has been Harding's call for making explicit the gender, race, class, and cultural traits of the researcher and to consider this effort as part of the researcher's positionality.[27] However, Harding ultimately reproduces the universalization of gender, as well as its binary oppositions, therefore making her proposal quite essentialist: it suggests that the feminist methodology is a perspective that is grounded on women's experiences as opposed to the experiences of men. This dualist point of view assumes that "women" and "men" are all equal, decontextualized, and universal. Although Harding proposes that we consider the race, gender, and class of the researcher, her proposal is limited to understanding the feminist methodology only on the basis of gender.

Donna Haraway, known for her contributions around reflexivity and positionality, has also invited us to historicize those who do research.[28] That is to say, she has called to demonstrate a place of enunciation that definitely affects the interpretations of the research that is carried out. This is important—it is even an essential ethical starting point—but reflexivity from a decolonial point of view is not only about self-definition in the production of knowledge; it is also about assuming a position in the production of knowledge that should consider geopolitics, race, class, sexuality, and social capital, among other positionalities. This other, decolonial, view of reflexivity includes key questions such as: what is knowledge for? How do we produce knowledge(s)? Who produces knowledge and in accordance with which political project(s)? Within which institutional and political frameworks do we produce knowledge?

The African-American scholar Patricia Hill Collins has expanded on the question of positionality on the basis of the reconstruction of Black feminist thought.[29] For Collins, this viewpoint has two components:

1. *Political-economic experiences*, which provide a set of different experiences, a different perspective on the material reality that African-American women live.
2. *A Black feminist consciousness about material reality.* This means understanding how consciousness is created from the experience of a reality that is best interpreted by African American women.

For Collins, both the experience and the awareness of that experience by African American women are traversed by how they face, problematize, and act upon what Collins calls the *matrix of domination*.[30] These activities presuppose an understanding of how racism, heterosexuality, colonialism and classism interact. The matrix of domination is composed of four characteristics: *structural elements*, such as laws and institutional policies; *disciplinary aspects*, which refer to bureaucratic hierarchies and surveillance techniques; and *hegemonic elements or ideas and ideologies*, which include interpersonal aspects and quotidian discriminatory practices.

Collins's analysis invites us to consider two ideas:

1. If the Black feminist consciousness arises from experience, and if Afro-feminist women—and not only feminists of African descent, since this could also be extended to other subalternized subjects—are the ones who, from their realities, can interpret these experiences better, it is because lived experience is a source of knowledge, and therefore these women themselves should be the ones investigating it.
2. If the interpretation of that reality implies understanding how the matrix of oppression acts upon their own lives, characterized by how they are affected by oppressive forces such as racism, heterosexuality, colonialism and classism, with its structural expressions, ideologies and interpersonal aspects, then all this is not about analytical categories, but about lived realities that need a deep understanding of how they occurred.[31] Therefore, it is not a question of describing that they are Black, that they are poor and that they are women; it is about understanding why they are racialized, impoverished, and sexualized. This is what interests us as decolonial feminists because it allows us to show that these conditions have been produced by coloniality.

I am not suggesting that only those who have suffered the oppressions have the capacity to understand and investigate the realities that affect others, but I posit that there is *an epistemic privilege* that is important to consider in the production of knowledge, and that means that the subaltern goes from being object to being subject of knowledge production.[32]

To consider Collins's matrix of domination, or as Maria Lugones would put it, the mutual constitution of the oppressions, is different from assuming the intersectional as a perspective, a concept proposed by Kimberlé Crenshaw.[33] That intersectionality is the most successful concept to understand oppressions in feminist research and in feminist proposals is not coincidental, for in the end it is a liberal and modern proposal, even though it has been proposed by an African-American female scholar.

Intersectionality refers to an acknowledgement of the differences between intersected categories, in which race and gender, for example, are presented as axes of subordination that at some point have been separated, with some level of autonomy, and that are then intersected. The metaphor of the crossroads that the author uses is an indicator of the political and theoretical problem contained in this proposal. Intersectionality asks very little about the production of these differences contained in the experiences of many women, mostly racialized and impoverished ones. Therefore, it tends to incline toward a liberal multiculturalism that pretends to recognize differences, including them in a model of diversity, without questioning the reasons for the need of such inclusion. In other words, intersectionality is defined from the modern Eurocentric Western paradigm. In contrast, a decolonial feminist position implies understanding that race and gender as well as class, heterosexuality, and related categories have been constitutive of the modern colonial episteme. These are not simple axes of differences, but differentiations produced by the overlapping oppressions produced by the modern colonial system.

Based on all of the above, a feminist decolonial methodology should ask itself several questions: What is the significance in the points of view of feminist research? How much do we impose gender on investigative and epistemological processes when we study racialized, primarily Black and Indigenous, women? How much do we reproduce the coloniality of power, of knowledge, and of being when race, class, and sexuality become only analytical or descriptive categories that do not allow us to establish a relationship between these realities and a modern/colonial capitalist world order?

THE SUBJECT-OBJECT RELATION

Another issue that I want to highlight here is the subject-object relationship. In feminist methodologies, who are the subjects and who are the objects of our research? One of the characteristics of the coloniality of knowledge, as we pointed out, is to assume that those who have been defined as others—who represent the colonial difference—are generally the objects of research: women, Black, impoverished, poor, Indigenous, migrants from the Third World, as if critical feminist research is done only from assuming them as raw material. Generally, the place of privilege of those who build knowledge on these "others" seems unquestionable. What does it mean for white feminists of the Global North to study women of the Global South, or for academic feminists of the South to study the "other" local women of their own countries? Under what kinds of relationships are these investigative exercises done?

Research is an important task that should be done by social scientists and activists. What typically happens, however, is that those who have privileges of race, class, sexuality and geopolitical location engage in discursive colonization and epistemic violence.[34] They do this through interpretations of the social and cultural practices of the groups who are assumed as "others." This activity continues a path that tends to limit academic credentials to those in hegemonic positions who continue to study those who are considered "different."

THE EPISTEMOLOGICAL DISENGAGEMENT

Recalling Stuart Hall's conception of disengagement, the decolonial approach proposes a delinking from the coloniality of power, of knowledge, and of being, which justify the rhetoric of modernity, of progress, and of democratic "imperial" administration.[35] This delinking/disengagement implies several inquiries in relation to the knowledges that are produced, how they are produced, and for what they are produced.

The Recognition and Legitimation of Subalternized "Other" Knowledges

This aspect starts from the recognition of the points of view that are produced from the lived experiences that contribute to proposing other, more fair and humane worlds, outside the liberal/colonial matrix. "Other" knowledges cannot simply be used to assuage epistemological guilt, nor is the task just to cite Black, Indigenous, or impoverished feminists to give an aura of criticality to research, knowledges, and thoughts in construction.[36] It is about identifying concepts, categories, and theories that arise from subaltern experiences, which are generally produced collectively and have the possibility of generalizing without universalizing. It is about explaining different realities with the goal of breaking the conceptualization of these knowledges as local, individual, and impossible to communicate.

This assumes what Zulma Palermo has defined as a liberating ethic with its own genealogy. This ethic requires us to place ourselves outside the categories that have been created and imposed by Western epistemology, and to break with the epistemic colonial difference between the cognizant subject and the subjects to be known. This epistemic colonial difference has imposed the exclusion and invisibility of the knowledges of subaltern subjects.[37]

An example of disengagement from a particular point of view is found in what the Bolivian of Aymara origin Silvia Rivera Cusicanqui has proposed as the *ch'ixi*, which refers to another notion of mestizaje that does not have to do with politics of whitening or hierarchical structuring, which was the case with the formation of the national states in Latin America and the Caribbean, where institutional and structural racism has been established.[38] In the Aymara language, *ch'ixi* means a juxtaposed fabric, something that is and is not at the same time, a heterogeneous grey, a mixture, contrary to each other and at the same time complementary. According to Rivera Cusicanqui, this notion characterizes a large part of our peoples of Latin America and the Caribbean.

The Guatemalan Maya Kaqchikel Aura Cumes has proposed retaking the category of *winaq*, which appears in the Popol Wuj and that questions the notion of modern gender, to explain the ways in which, before colonization, the Mayas were called "people" without gender attribution.[39] Gladys Tzul Tzul, also Guatemalan Maya Kaqchikel, proposes the tension *transformation/conservation* to understand the policy of Indigenous women in Guatemala, who, while struggling to ensure the conservation of communal land to avoid expropriation by the state, allow access to use these lands. Tzul analyzes how women who participate in communal activities, principally in relation to the defense of land, employ a series of strategies that prevent the total control of capital, which seeks to dismember the land. Women participate in production through the collective decision-making for the regulation and administration of common use, particularly with respect to the control of land and reproductive work. They engage in strategies that allow for disengagement from the control of the state and the logics of capital.[40]

Another effort of epistemological disengagement, regardless of our agreement or disagreement with the content, is what communal feminists have called "patriarchal entronques" ["entronques de patriarcado"].[41] They use the concept to explain the existence of patriarchy among various Indigenous peoples before colonization, and how this patriarchy was modified in conjunction with the new forms of modern patriarchies.[42]

The epistemological disengagement implies doing what I have called *anthropology of domination*, which implies unveiling the forms, ways, strategies, and speeches that define certain social groups as "others," emerging from places of power and domination.[43] To participate in and create *anthropology of domination* means doing ethnography of the North and of the North that exists within the South. It also involves doing ethnographies of the academic practices, methodologies, and pedagogies that contain the idea of development and a transnational solidarity based on privilege, which entails making an ethnography of the logics of international cooperation, of the social intervention, of our own places of knowledge production, of the theories that we use and legitimize, and of the purposes for which these theories are made. In other words, the anthropology of domination requires an ethnography of subjects and social practices from the positions and places of production of privileges.

All these are efforts of epistemological disengagement made from the political practices of activists and thinkers with particular points of view––such as Indigenous or of Indigenous origin and people of African descent in Abya Yala—that propose new, non-Western categories or re-elaborate from Western categories new non-hegemonic concepts that open possibilities for "other" interpretations.

This disengagement also assumes "other" pedagogical processes ("procesos pedagógicos 'otros'"). For Yuderkys Espinosa-Miñoso, Diana Gomez, Karina Ochoa and María Lugones, this activity involves a "relationship between doing and thinking as well as the reverse: thinking from doing. In this way, an experience of knowledge while doing is generated, of producing knowledge that links theory and praxis."[44] The authors propose co-research and theorizing by organic intellectuals in communities and organizations, and by activists committed in processes that involve struggle, resistance, and action, all from their own communitarian processes.[45]

To Problematize the Conditions of Knowledge(s) Production

Finally, I think that it is important to contest the conditions of knowledge(s) production which imply what Rivera Cusicanqui calls *the economy of knowledge* that questions the geopolitics of knowledge.[46] This is important to keep in mind because even in many decolonial and anti-colonial proposals there is a recolonization of the imaginaries and of the minds of intellectuals. With this proposal, the author points to the need to abandon the spheres of superstructures and the material mechanisms that operate behind anti-colonial discourse, such as high salaries, luxuries, privileges, and publishing opportunities, to actually make a decolonization in the very practice.

But a feminist decolonial proposal is not limited to analyzing that economy of knowledge; rather, it seeks to do research and to make methodological and pedagogical proposals from collective processes and from organizations and communities to strengthen their own analytical frameworks that lead to better ways to search for social transformation.

NOTES

1. This text was presented to a large extent in the "Conference on Feminist Research Methodology and its Application in the Field of Human Rights, Violence, and Peace," which took place on June 19 and 20, 2014, in the city of San Sebastián-Donostia, Basque Country. It has been amended in some of its parts for this publication for the purpose of continuing to problematize what I understand by decolonial methodologies.

2. Edward Said, *Orientalism* (New York: Pantheon, 1978).

3. Ella Shohat, "Notes on the 'Post-colonial,'" *Social Text,* no. 31/32 (1992).

4. Anne McClintock, "The Angel of Progress: Pitfalls of the Term Post-colonialism," *Social Text,* no. 31/32 (1992); Stuart Hall, "When was 'The Post-colonial'? Thinking at the Limit," in *The Postcolonial Question: Common Skies, Divided Horizons,* eds. Ian Chambers and Lidia Curti (New York/London: Routledge 1995).

5. Arif Dirlik, *Postmodernity's Histories: The Past as Legacy and Project* (Lanham: Rowman & Littlefield, 2000); Sandro Mezzadra and Federico Rahola, "The Postcolonial Condition: A Few Notes on the Quality of Historical Time in the Global Present," *Postcolonial Text* 2, no. 1 (2006), http://postcolonial.org/index.php/pct/article/view/393/819.

6. Avila Pacheco and Wilson L. Peña Meléndez, *Ramón Grosfoguel. La descolonización de la economía política* (Bogotá: Universidad Libre, 2010).

7. Hall, "When was 'The Post-colonial'?"

8. Ibid.

9. Chandra Mohanty, "Under Western Eyes: Feminist Scholarship and Colonial Discourses," *boundary 2* 12, no. 3 (1984); Gayatri Spivak, "Can the Subaltern Speak?," in *Marxism and the Interpretation of Culture*, eds. Cary Nelson and Lawrence Grossberg (Urbana: University of Illinois Press, 1988).

10. María Lugones, "The Coloniality of Gender," *World & Knowledges Otherwise* 2, no. 2 (Spring 2008). https://globalstudies.trinity.duke.edu/sites/globalstudies.trinity.duke.edu/files/file-attachments/v2d2_Lugones.pdf.

11. Yuderkys Espinosa Miñoso, "Feminismos descoloniales de Abya Yala," in *Le Dictionnaire universel des Créatrices. A paraître à l'automne* (Paris: Des Femmes-Antoinette Fouque Publishing, 2013), https://www.dictionnaire-creatrices.com/fiche-feminisme-decolonial-abya-yala?q=yuderkys.

12. Santiago Castro-Gómez and Ramón Grosfoguel, "Giro decolonial, teoría crítica pensamiento heterárquico," in *El giro decolonial. Reflexiones para una diversidad epistémica más allá del capitalismo global,* eds. Santiago Castro-Gómez and Ramón Grosfoguel (Bogotá: Siglo del Hombre, 2007).

13. Enrique Dussel, "Beyond Eurocentrism: The World-System and the Limits of Modernity," in *The Cultures of Globalization*, eds. Fredric Jameson and Masao Miyoshi (Durham: Duke University Press, 1998).

14. Ibid.

15. Enrique Dussel, "Europe, Modernity, Eurocentrism," *Nepantla: Views from South* 1, no. 3 (2000).

16. Aníbal Quijano, "Coloniality of Power, Eurocentrism, and Latin America." *Nepantla: Views from South* 1, no. 3 (2000).

17. Lugones, "Coloniality of Gender."

18. Ibid.

19. Nelson Maldonado-Torres, "On the Coloniality of Being: Contributions to the Development of a Concept," *Cultural Studies* 21 no. 2–3 (2007).

20. Frantz Fanon, *The Wretched of the Earth*, trans. Richard Philcox (New York: Grove Press, 2004).

21. Edgardo Lander, "Ciencias sociales: saberes coloniales y eurocéntricos," in *La colonialidad del saber. Eurocentrismo y Ciencias Sociales. Perspectivas latinoamericanas*, ed. Edgardo Lander (Buenos Aires/Caracas: CLACSO/UNESCO, 2000).

22. Santiago Castro-Gómez, "Decolonizar la universidad: la hybris del punto cero y el diálogo de saberes," in *El giro decolonial. Reflexiones para una diversidad epistémica más allá del capitalismo global*, eds. Santiago Castro-Gómez and Ramón Grosfoguel (Bogotá: Siglo del Hombre, 2007).

23. For a discussion of Autonomous Feminism and how it relates to Decolonial Feminism see Yuderkys Espinosa Miñoso, Diana Gómez Correal, and Karina Ochoa Muñoz, "Introducción," in *Tejiendo de otro modo: Feminismo, epistemología y apuestas decoloniales en Abya Yala*, eds. Yuderkys Espinosa Miñoso, Diana Gómez Correal, and Karina Ochoa Muñoz (Colombia: Editorial Universidad del Cauca, 2014).—Trans.

24. Yuderkys Espinosa-Miñoso, "De por qué es necesario un feminismo descolonial: diferenciación, dominación co-constitutiva de la modernidad occidental y el fin de la política de identidad," *Solar* 12, no.1 (2016): 150.

25. Ibid., 151.

26. Lugones, "Coloniality of Gender."

27. Sandra Harding, *Whose Science? Whose Knowledge?: Thinking from Women's Lives* (New York: Cornell University Press, 1991).

28. Donna Haraway, *Simians, Cyborgs and Women: The Reinvention of Nature* (New York/London: Routledge, 1991).

29. Patricia Hill Collins, *Black Feminist Thought: Knowledge, Consciousness and the Politics of Empowerment* (New York/London: Routledge, 1990).

30. Ibid., 18.

31. Lugones, "Coloniality of Gender."

32. Collins, *Black Feminist Thought.*

33. For more on intersectionality, see Kimberlé Crenshaw, "Demarginalizing the Intersection of Race and Sex: A Black Feminist Critique of Antidiscrimination Doctrine, Feminist Theory, and Antiracist Politics," in *Feminist Legal Theory: Foundations,* ed. D. Kelley Weisberg (Philadelphia: Temple University Press, 1993). See also Lugones, "Coloniality of Gender," 12.

34. Mohanty, "Under Western Eyes"; Spivak, "Can the Subaltern Speak?"

35. Hall, "When was 'The Post-colonial'?"

36. Thanks to Rafael Vizcaíno for assistance with the translation of a part of this sentence. *–Trans.*

37. Zulma Palermo, "La opción decolonial," *CECIES: Pensamiento Latinoamericano y Alternativo*, accessed October 3, 2013, http://www.cecies.org/articulo.asp?id =227.

38. Silvia Rivera Cusicanqui, *Ch'ixinakax utxiwa. Una reflexión sobre prácticas y discursos descoloniales* (Buenos Aires: Tinta y Limón/Retazos, 2010).

39. Aura Cumes, "Cosmovisión maya y patriarcado: una aproximación en clave crítica," paper presented at the Centro Interdiciplinario de Estudios de Género de la Universidad de Chile, Santiago, Chile, 2014.

40. Gladys Tzul Tzul, *Sistemas de gobierno comunal indígena. Mujeres y tramas de parentesco en Chuimeq´ena´* (Guatemala: SOCEE/Maya´Wuj Editorial, 2016).

41. We are using the term for "entronques de patriarcado" that appears in María Lugones, "Gender and Universality in Colonial Methodology," *Critical Philosophy of Race*, 8, nos. 1–2 (2020).—Eds.

42. Julieta Paredes, *Una sociedad en estado y con estado despatriarcalizador* (La Paz, Bolivia: Ministerio de Justicia, 2008).

43. Ochy Curiel, *La nación heterosexual. Análisis del discurso jurídico y el régimen heterosexual desde la antropología de la dominación* (Bogotá: Brecha Lésbica and *en la frontera,* 2013), 28.

44. Yuderkys Espinosa, Diana Gómez, Karina Ochoa, and María Lugones, "Reflexiones pedagógicas en torno al feminismo descolonial. Una conversa en cuatro voces," in *Pedagogías decoloniales. Prácticas insurgentes de resistir, (re)vivir y (re)vivir*, ed. Catherine Walsh (Quito: Ediciones Abya Yala, 2013), 409.

45. Ibid., 411.

46. Rivera Cusicanqui, *Ch'ixinakax utxiwa.*

PART II

Democracy, Citizenship and Public Policies: A Decolon. Feminist Critique

Chapter 4

The Question of the Coloniality of Democracy

Breny Mendoza
Translation by Rafael Vizcaíno

"Thus, in the beginning, all the World was America."

John Locke

This essay is part of a larger project that seeks to argue that Western democracy is an artifice and a device of colonial-imperial power that the West established starting with the conquest of America in 1492. From this perspective, the kind of democracy that today we understand as Western is not primordially understood as a benign and emancipatory form of government that creates equality and justice between peoples, irrespective of their sex, race, class, caste, or religion. On the contrary, it is understood as a form of domination that was constituted historically through the usurpation of territories and the rights of the peoples of the world, colonial wars, and the violent destruction of other forms of government and social organization that were sometimes more egalitarian. Furthermore, it creates extremely oppressive and exploitative social, political, and economic forms that are still held to today through violence and the same excessive power that the West managed to obtain from its colonial expansion beginning in 1492. Western democracy, to which so many oppressed peoples of the non-West still aspire today, originates from nothing less than the historical facts of their defeat and colonization by Europe and its successors. That is, the idea of Western democracy is born of the colonial fact itself. Recognizing the colonial and imperial origins of Western democracy is increasingly urgent. This is not only because the West redoubles its efforts to completely deprive the non-West of its resources and tries to impose its model of democracy on the world through political violence and war—as evidenced in the war against terrorism in the Middle East or in the fabrication of violent *coups d'état* in Honduras, Venezuela, Ukraine, etc.—but also because many oppressed peoples of the world continue to bet on a democratic model which, in its essence, depends on their exclusion, elimination, and oppression.

It is no coincidence that the model of democracy that the West chose as its historical referent was the democratic state of ancient Athens, which was a slave state where slaves and women were excluded from citizens' rights granted to free men. The non-democratic character of the Athenian state, however, has been systematically sidelined by Eurocentric historians who have erected ancient Greece as the pillar of Western civilization and democracy. But in these historical narratives not only are the non-democratic foundations of Athenian democracy hidden; so, too, are the material conditions that actually allowed for the construction of Western democracy.

To demonstrate the roots of democracy as a project of domination that emerged from European colonial expansion into the so-called New World, one should begin by demythologizing the genealogies of the West as well as its political theories. The myths of the origins of the West as a "civilization" that develops autonomously from the rest of the world's civilizations must also be questioned.[1] These genealogies of autonomy that refer to Greece, Rome, Christianity, the Renaissance, and the Enlightenment, from which the modern ideas of political democracy, the industrial revolution, and capitalism emerge—and which culminate in the U.S. American model of democracy with its seductive ideas of the right to life, freedom, and the pursuit of happiness—must be reinterpreted as spells that erase not only the origins of democracy in the conquest of America, but also the extreme violence with which it is born and maintained. In turn, it is necessary to reveal how systems of power based on gender and racial discrimination and created in the process of conquest and colonization are central to the ascent of the West and the constitution of democracy as a system of domination.

THE RISE OF THE WEST

Within the Anglophone political sciences, historians such as John M. Hobson have contributed significantly to the destabilization of Eurocentric historiography by recuperating the importance of China, the Middle East, India, Japan, and North Africa in the development and rise of the West. Hobson criticizes what he calls the logic of immanence of traditional historical narratives, which argues that Europe triumphs over the world because it possesses innate qualities and virtues that make it superior to all other cultures and civilizations in the world. The traditional Eurocentric vision that Hobson criticizes imagines Europe as blessed by unique virtues that make it more rational, laboring, productive, selfless, frugal, liberal and democratic, honest, paternal and mature, advanced, witty, dynamic, independent, and progressive. The "East," in turn, is conceived in feminine terms as its opposite: irrational and arbitrary, lazy, unproductive, indulgent, exotic and seductive, promiscuous, despotic, corrupt, infantile, immature, retrograde, unoriginal, passive, and immutable.[2] Drawing on vast empirical evidence, Hobson tries to demonstrate not only how this Eurocentric imaginary rests on false premises, but also how the West could never have triumphed without what he calls the "resource portfolios" (Eastern ideas, technologies, and institutions) that the East provided and which the West borrowed, assimilated, and then denied and passed off as its own.[3]

Hobson undertakes a formidable historical rehabilitation of Asia, the Middle East, North Africa, and, in particular, China, recognizing its advanced economic, political, and social systems, its high technological development, and its world hegemony from the year 500 to the 1840s, when China finally succumbed to Western power. Europe appears in this historical perspective as one of the most backward, patriarchal, and obscurantist regions of the so-called Old World, which only managed to move forward because of the advances of the East. The East, and especially China, is established as a region that managed its own development, that established itself as a world economic power for more than a thousand years, and that made possible the rise of Europe. It seems, however, that Western scholars on both the left and the right erase this appropriation of and dependence on Eastern breakthroughs for European development. In its place, they construct a triumphalist teleology that ascribes to Europe a retroactive superiority that begins in ancient Greece, persists until today, and has no end.

Hobson does not entirely deny the active role that Europeans had in their own development. What Hobson considers crucial here is an imperial identity based on the supposed superiority of Christianity over Islam, which the West started to develop early on toward the end of the first millennium and which led first to the crusades and then to the wrongly-called "voyages of discovery," when Europeans managed to reach the shores of Abya Yala, aided by the technological advances of the East. Christendom, which had been defined against and imposed on Islam and Judaism (and even the European peasantry and women during the witch-hunts), was then established as a model of domination in the so-called conquest of America. The supposed superiority of Christianity served as justification for subjecting Indigenous peoples, African slaves, and later the rest of the non-Western world, as well as for defining these peoples as either barbarians, savages, subhumans, or nonhumans. From Hobson's Anglo-centric view, European imperial identity was consolidated only recently in the nineteenth century, when the idea of race gained more prominence and when the belief in the West's moral necessity to carry out civilizing missions around the world through, if necessary, violence became more forcefully rooted in the European mentality.[4]

It is important to note that while Hobson rescues the East from the dump of history, Abya Yala continues to be omitted in this review of Western history. Abya Yala is recognized as the place where Europeans extracted large quantities of gold and silver by exploiting Indigenous labor and African slaves. But Hobson only makes a brief mention of the conquest's contribution to Europe's economic development; its inclusion in the story is completely marginal and isolated from the process of appropriating/assimilating/usurping the East's "resource portfolios" he describes.

The East, and China in particular, remains central to the "triumph of the West" as well as the British Empire, which managed to replace China in world domination by 1840. In this way, Abya Yala is out of history, categorized as the only region of the world—both Old and New—that preserves a status of timeless backwardness, defined by its isolation from the rest of the world, contributing only raw materials and free labor to the triumph of the West. Since it is the British to whom the defeat of China is attributed, the Spanish Empire and the Portuguese colonizers are, of course, erased from this historical revision. There is nothing in this history that sheds light on the importance of the usurpation of the Abya Yala peoples' vast territories, their genocide, the appropriation of their knowledges, technologies, and forms of social and political organization, or their economic development, which the Iberians found or introduced to Abya Yala, for the rise of the West. There is not a word about how social relations and new forms of labor and colonial institutions such as the encomienda, the mita, slavery, and *repartimiento* contributed to the development of capitalism— a system which is to give the West a comparative advantage over the rest of the world. In short, there is nothing that establishes the conquest of America as an important factor contributing to the defeat of China, the rise of the West, the consolidation of capitalism, the creation of the modern state, or the Western democratic system.[5]

It is the modernity/coloniality group that adjudicates to Abya Yala and the Spanish and Portuguese conquest a preponderant place in the history of the rise of the West. Authors such as Enrique Dussel, Aníbal Quijano, Walter Mignolo, and Ramón Grosfoguel have demonstrated in several of their writings and lectures how colonialism constitutes the darker side of Western democratic capitalist modernity or the modern/colonial system. They make us see how the processes that led to the original accumulation of capital, the generalization of free wage labor among Westerners, and the ideas of emancipation and liberal democracy were only made possible in the West by the colonial conditions that Europeans imposed on Abya Yala and eventually the rest of the world. Quijano's concept of the coloniality of power speaks to a global pattern of power based on an idea of race that was established in 1492 and persists to this day.[6] These decolonial authors from Abya Yala agree with Hobson that Europe developed an imperial identity that will come to define not only its mentality, or what Dussel calls the *ego conquiro*, but also the construction of Eurocentric knowledge through the epistemicide of non-Western knowledges (the coloniality of knowledge) and an epistemic apartheid.[7] Furthermore, they also grant Abya Yala a much more important role in the historical developments of capitalism, modern nation-states, and democracy. More importantly, what interests us here is the way in which the imperial attitude, what Maldonado-Torres describes as the mentality that emerges from the *ego conquiro*, established a genocidal reason in what will be defined as Western civilization, to which I will turn now.[8]

THE CONCEPT OF CIVILIZATION AND THE QUESTION OF THE COLONIALITY OF GENDER

Studies on the concept of civilization have resurfaced as the language of civilization and barbarism has once again become central to Western imperial discourse, especially in its new crusade against Islam since 9/11. But here again we find that studies of civilization rarely include Abya Yala. In general, they begin with prehistory—Mesopotamia and Egypt—and then quickly focus on what is considered central to Western civilization: Greece and Rome. They discuss the Athenian State, Sparta, Roman society, then the Middle Ages, the Renaissance, the Enlightenment, and European and U.S. history of the nineteenth and twentieth centuries.[9] One of the most important articles recently published on this subject is "Civilization" by David Cannadine. In this work, Cannadine tells us a story in which the concept of civilization entered the European vocabulary in 1775, once it was admitted to the British *Ash's Dictionary*.[10] The concept of civilization is binary, as all concepts of Western political philosophy are. More specifically, it was built in relation and in opposition to barbarism. The concept of barbarism, which is said to be older, originates with the Greeks who denominated "barbarians" those foreigners who did not speak Greek and who did not enjoy the political rights of the Athenians, as the Romans would also do to the peoples who did not conform to Roman society or speak Latin.[11] Barbarians were always foreigners considered to be political and cultural enemies and naturally inferior to their opposites, the civilized. Civilization, Cannadine tells us, was defined as the highest stage to which a society could aspire and often referred to forms of collective identity and political, social, and cultural achievements located in the West. Tracing the classical canons of studies of civilization, Cannadine describes an interesting trajectory of the concept of civilization along which we can observe Europeans—only the English, French, Italian, and Germans—not only appropriate the status of civilized in contradistinction to the well-known figures—the European Christians in front of the infidels, the pagans, the Muslims, the Jews, the Chinese, the Slavs, the Turks, the Africans, the Abya Yala Indians, etc.—but also dispute among themselves the status of civilization. In this debate, the fall of the Roman Empire was central because it was supposed that the immeasurable superiority of Rome declined as a result of the invasions of Germanic hordes considered barbaric. And yet, as though a sort of hoax or semantic trick, not a moment later in this nineteenth century debate, the barbaric became the positive element: the Germanic wild hordes breathed new life into the decaying empire of Rome.[12] The barbaric became positively understood as the very element that gives new energy to decaying empires, which the Germans would then use to justify their genocidal policies and to differentiate themselves from the English, French, and Italians, with whom they identified Latin decadence and the idea of civilization. The Spaniards and Portuguese were not even mentioned, but, as we well know, these peoples were branded as barbarians nearer to the Muslim world than to Europe. Later, during the two World Wars, the Germans were once again labeled the barbarian villains and enemies of Western civilization, which the English, French, and US Americans now had to save. Interestingly enough, is that, at this historical moment, the concept of civilization did not apply to peoples outside of Europe, but rather referenced an internal dispute between the English, French, Italians, and Germans. Later, the concept underwent new changes, which enabled civilization to be comprehended in a plural sense.[13] Western civilization suddenly appeared as a civilization among others, where each civilization was essentially understood in terms of its swing from emergence to inevitable fall, as almost always developing autonomously, and as entering into contact with other civilizations only at the time of its decadence. In this conception, attention is paid to the role that "creative minorities" or elites had in preventing the fall of a civilization. The elites who failed to prevent a fall are charged with the destruction of civilization while those elites who avoided a fall are characterized as having known how to infuse new life back into their civilization, especially through spirituality, religion, high political values, and war. In this manner, the U.S. appears as that which prevented, by virtue of its supposed democratic, liberal, and progressive values, the fall of Western civilization.

Samuel Huntington, however, in *The Clash of Civilizations and the Remaking of World Order*, alerts us to the dangers that Western civilization is constantly running up against: the hostility and rise of the Muslim world, the Chinese, and others including Latin America, which Huntington does not know whether to locate within or outside the West—but, in any case, does not pay any more attention to it.[14] What is interesting in Cannadine's historical account of the concepts of civilization and barbarism is how he manages to give us a history of these concepts without making any mention of the colonial and imperialist history of the West. As did Hobson previously, Cannadine focuses exclusively on the West's relations with the East, obfuscating the conquest of America while also using a narrow concept of the West that only includes five countries: England, France, Italy, Germany, and the United States. Despite these oversights, it is clear that the Eurocentric standard of civilization stands as that feature which defined the Western world and distinguished it from the non-Western world. This reinforced a hierarchical vision of the world derivative of a series of characteristics that put the West on top and, as Huntington points out, are unequivocally linked to Western qualities like individualism, Christian religion, separation of temporal and spiritual authorities, the rule of law, and the values and practices of democracy and social pluralism.

Feminist studies of Western civilization, while questioning authors like Hobson, Cannadine, and Huntington's absolute silence on the question of gender, nonetheless focus on the relation of the West to the East. Here, their greatest contribution has been revealing how, in the debates on civilization, representations of women's status and gender were crucial to differentiating the West from Islam.[15] These feminist works often argue that gender and sexuality, not the question of democracy, were the defining features of the conflict between the West and Islam. It is from this perspective that some Western feminists begin to worry about Islam's possible influence on Western women. Adopting a clearly imperial attitude, these Western feminists assume that female empowerment is unquestionably derivative of Western values and traditions.[16] There are some authors, however, who recognize the diversity of opinions on the issue of women's rights that exists within the Islamic world, attributing the inequity that occurs between genders to the possession of oil, not Islam, without mentioning, however, the colonial history in the region.

Other feminist authors question the glorification of the West by calling attention to the high status of women in ancient Egypt and the Roman Empire, the exclusion of women in Athenian democracy, and the way in which the status of Western women deteriorated in the eighteenth and nineteenth centuries.[17] However, their narratives follow the same pattern characteristic of those studies of civilization written by Western male theorists. All of them continue to define the West by the same geographical limits and the same historical chronology. As Ann Towns points out, Western feminists have neither broken with the Eurocentric vision of civilization nor integrated the role of colonialism into their histories of Western civilization, even though some theorists have recognized that Enlightenment ideas of civilization used the status of women as a measure of the development of a society.[18] There are those who question the portrayal of savage women as extremely oppressed and that of Western women as freer, feminine, and companions to civilized European man. They point at the same time to the contradictory character of representations of Western women's femininity, which was also always described negatively as a manifestation of inertia, weakness, and emotionality and used to denigrate societies considered savage and inferior.[19] According to these feminist theorists, Enlightenment defenders further contradicted themselves in other writings where they described the supposed savages as possessing masculine attributes such as aggressiveness, physical force, and courage, which contrast with their picture of civilized men as peaceful, dialogical, genteel, sociable, refined, and of good customs.[20] The few feminist studies that analyze the intersection of gender and race mention how some Enlightenment defenders feminized the native peoples of North America because they did not find in these societies clear norms of masculinity and femininity that hierarchically separated men and women. These peoples were considered effeminate and their conquest proof of their lack of virility. Moreover, in a contradictory and arbitrary way, African slaves were described as belonging to a lewd, overly sexual, aggressive, and muscular race. Finally, it is worth mentioning that nineteenth-century Western anthropologists destabilized these racist and sexist discourses by claiming that the supposedly savage societies were matrilineal and that these women enjoyed a higher status than Western civilized women did, especially after the Industrial Revolution.[21] In spite of these important contributions by feminist scholars of civilization and some anthropologists, none of these works discredit the Western canon that self-adjudicates the status of civilization nor incorporates the conquest of America in its account. It is Maria Lugones, an Argentine decolonial feminist, who introduces elements to the analysis of the idea of civilization that not only center the conquest of America, but also complicate our understanding of gender and its relation to ideas of barbarism, savagery, and bestiality.[22]

Lugones turns to Quijano's concept of the coloniality of power and Nelson Maldonado-Torres' concept of the coloniality of being to reinterpret the standard of civilization that Westerners use to differentiate the gender status of Western women and men as well as that of women and men from the colony.[23] For this, it is important to note that the conquest of America is the moment at which, for the first time in the history of humanity, a zone of non-being, as Frantz Fanon calls it, was formed to establish not only hierarchies between barbarian or savage and civilized peoples, but also that particular place where the line separating those considered human from those considered non-human is drawn.[24] Combining elements from intersectional and decolonial analysis, Lugones establishes how the idea of race that originates in the conquest of America and carries in its lexicon a division between the human and the non-human determines not only who enjoys the status of the human, but also who can represent the standard of civilization and the status of gender.[25]

In this sense, when, during the conquest of America, the question "Do the Indians have souls?" was posed for the first time, not only was their humanity put into question, but also, for the first time in history, conquered peoples were bestialized.[26] Based on these premises and Abya Yala's colonial experience, as recounted in Lugones' work, the following conclusions can be drawn:

1. The women and men of the colony were not understood as human beings, but as beasts of burden that could be forced to work to death; genocide could be committed against them with impunity. Here, there is neither the feminization nor masculinization of the peoples of Abya Yala, but simply their bestialization.

2. As racialized and bestialized beings, the women and men of the colony did not belong to the world of the social. Their bodies could not carry the sign of gender because they only manifested the biological sex of females or males, belonging to the animal kingdom. Therefore, they could not symbolically represent figures of women or men whose membership in human society could be presupposed. It follows from here also that those who were outside the social world were also those who were outside the political world.

3. In the colonial process, European men appropriated the status of the human and civilization. They conferred on European women a conditioned human status or, rather, a subhuman status. Closer to the animal world than to the social and cultural world, Western women were thought to deviate from the human ideal represented by European man. But as biological reproducers of the white race and the Western civilization that would emerge from the debris of Abya Yala, European women were allowed to bear the mark of the human, the social, and gender in a manner consistent with their subordination to European men. Gender and race constituted them as "natural" complements to European man; they were subordinate to him, without political and labor rights, but crucial to the reproduction of the new social world born out of the first genocide in history.

4. Finally, given that it was the European who defined who is human and only the human is eligible for racial, social, and political status as well as civilization, it was the standard of civilization that ultimately afforded the embodied mark of gender. The gender mark on bodies became the hallmark of civilization that only Westerners could carry and thereby distinguished them from the world of beasts. This is what María Lugones calls the coloniality of gender.[27]

THE COLONIALITY OF WESTERN POLITICAL THEORY

The coloniality of gender allows us to historicize and conceive of gender as a criterion of civilization in relation to the processes of racialization and bestialization that proceeded from the conquest of our lands in 1492. Although it does not refer directly to the political forms that emerged from it, the coloniality of gender enables us to see its effects on the configuration of citizenship, modern states, and Western democracy. That is why we now turn our attention to Western political theories to gradually establish the intersection of civilization, bestiality, gender, and democracy. Here, Hobson also provides us with some necessary tools for glimpsing the way in which the political sciences have been imbued with the concept of civilization.[28]

In his book *The Eurocentric Conceptions of World Politics*, Hobson describes how the discipline of International Relations has been plagued, since its Anglo-centric beginnings in 1760, by Eurocentric and racist conceptions that attribute to the West not only an exclusive status of self-generated civilization, but also a racial, cultural, and social superiority that gives it the absolute right to intervene militarily, impose its political institutions and way of life, and even exterminate non-Western societies that refuse to accept their supposed destiny.[29] Despite the numerous variations of Eurocentrism and racism that, according to Hobson, have been created throughout history, both ideologies have consistently permeated right as well as left political thinking and adapted to the different conjunctures of world politics. Right and left political theories differ only in the degree to which they accept imperialist intervention, paternalism, or the intensity of racism; all, however, whether directly or subliminally, grant the West the exclusive status of civilization. All, regardless of their political color, share what he calls the Eurocentric Big Bang theory, which attributes to the West not only autogenetic superiority and civility, but also what is for some essential and for others pitiful: the moral obligation to civilize barbarians and savages and the resolute conviction that barbarian and savage peoples are obliged to succumb to the Western civilizational missions.

Depending on the intensity of their racism, political theorists prioritize civilizing missions differently. For example, some grant non-Westerners some capacity to adapt to Western rationality and civility and so presume civilizing missions to be benign in their effects on Westerners. But those who perceive non-Westerners anxiously and as a threat to the West invoke their direct or indirect extermination. Here, the civilizing mission bespeaks racial apartheid because non-white contact is thought to contaminate the Western world like a virus. For some, this can even mean rejecting the colonial and imperial wars out of fear that the best elements of the white race will perish in them, just as they supposedly did in the case of the *mestizaje* or the occupation of land in tropical climates. However, for other political theorists, the civilizing mission must become lethal since the threat of barbarian contamination is perceived as too dangerous. In this case, the total extermination of non-Western peoples is invoked.

The non-Western danger is perceived according to the degree to which different non-Western peoples are treated as protagonists and are recognized as possessing redeeming qualities. The West is portrayed as reserving for itself the ideal role of the protagonist, which is meant to guarantee its establishment of civilization and to license its civilizing mission. The East, by contrast, understood here as primarily Asia (although Russia is included), is imagined as a second-rate protagonist; sometimes, though, this protagonist is portrayed as aggressive and predatory, as in the case of China and the Middle East. Africans and Abya Yala peoples, it must be said (because they are barely mentioned), are given no redemptive qualities, presumably because they are too far from the human world and therefore do not have a historical role.

Eurocentrism and racism also infuse political theory's most central categories such as sovereignty, anarchy, and democracy. Hobson calls into question three of the principles governing political theory in particular, within the discipline of International Relations: (1) sovereignty is strictly exclusive to the State *qua* State; (2) all states are sovereign and rational; and (3) all states are politically and culturally self-determined and enjoy legal equality, that is, coexist in existential equality in an anarchic world (where there is no imperialism). It is obvious that, in a world governed by the coloniality of power, these theoretical premises not only are false, but also are themselves responsible for exerting the coloniality of power. As I point out in another place, the Treaty of Westphalia signed in 1648 in Germany did not primarily seek to create sovereign nation-states in European territories, as is commonly understood; rather it more so sought to establish an agreement between European colonial powers that would ensure mutual respect during the territorial occupation of the colonies.[30] That is, the concept of sovereignty, and the European nation-state itself, arose from the usurpation and colonial occupation of non-Western peoples' lands. The blueprint for this concept of sovereignty, as we shall see later, was first realized during the occupation of the Abya Yala peoples' territories. It would then be extended to the rest of the non-Western world, preventing the Indigenous nations of North America from being recognized, on their own lands or by the international community, as sovereign, and allowing for the perpetual usurpation and dispossession of Indigenous territories in the colonies.[31] From this perspective, notions of sovereignty and indigeneity appear as oxymoronic.

Hobson agrees. The standard of Western civilization dictates that the civilized world cannot recognize the sovereignty of barbarian and savage peoples. According to Hobson, from 1760 onward, Western political theories did not view sovereignty as an attribute of all states and so thought that civilized nation-states should be treated differently than the so-called non-civilized nation-states.[32] It is interesting how Western political theorists made distinctions between peoples they considered barbarians, savages, and nonhumans; they present us with a stratified concept of sovereignty. The West reserved for itself a hyper-sovereignty that gave it extraordinary powers to intervene in not only non-Western nation-states, but also those territories claimed by the West, but occupied by Indigenous peoples. However, the West gave barbarian states such as China, India, Japan, and Russia a limited or calibrated sovereignty based on this uneven, racial, and hierarchical concept of civilization. Within this logic, the Abya Yala peoples of the whole continent, and, we can assume, the Mestizo-Creole nation-states and Africa too, did not enjoy any degree of sovereignty because they were not even ascribed the status of barbarians. The West could therefore wage war against them, intervene militarily, and interfere in their internal affairs whenever necessary. In this system of stratified sovereignty, any attempt to recognize cultural pluralism or the cultural self-determination of barbarian, savage or non-human peoples will always be viewed as an affront to Western civilization that gives rise to the problems of the world. The West has the moral obligation to contain barbarism and savagery in order to save the civilized world.

Hobson's work is very useful not only for understanding the history of the West as a political invention, but also for seeing how Western political thought is deeply Eurocentric, racist and imperialist. However, as mentioned earlier, his work does not pay due attention to the conquest of America, and his chronology of colonialism starts with the British Empire. His interlocutors remain the Anglo-Saxon world and the subjects of the British Empire, that is, postcolonial theorists and critics of Orientalism who come from Asia and the Middle East. This leaves a very large theoretical and historical void in his conversation. However, within the Anglo-Saxon academy, there are Native American theorists who analyze the implications of Western political theory alongside the history of colonialism. Unlike Hobson, they theorize from the colonial fact that is the conquest of America; and yet, in turn, they also only focus on the founding of the settler-colonial states of the U.S. and Canada. That is, Abya Yala is equally outside the parameters of these theories. However, some of the elements of these theories remedy some of the problems of Hobson's work and are very helpful for understanding our own reality. Especially their critique of Western thinkers such as Hobbes, Locke, Rousseau, Kant, and of Rawls' social contract theory, but also their critique of anti-racist thinkers who were trained in the social contract tradition, like the Jamaican Charles Mills, provide us with important elements with which to build our own political theories.

THE SOCIAL CONTRACT'S CRITICAL THEORY

Indigenous studies authors like Robert Nichols reveal the hidden ways in which the theorization of the social contract has been, since its origins, founded on the usurpation of Indigenous territories and the extermination of Indigenous peoples.[33] Likewise, these authors show how political concepts such as sovereignty, private property, law, and rights are born of the colonial fact. As Nichols shows us, during colonial expansion, the concept of political sovereignty, for example, was closely linked to the need to claim individual ownership of Indigenous peoples' communal lands. Historically, it was in the colony where notions of natural law and communal property were distorted and denied for the first time to argue that property can never be communally owned, that it can only be individually owned and the result of a social contract between sovereign (read: civilized) individuals. This clearly facilitated the distribution of Indigenous lands among colonizers. Social contract theorists during this period followed the denial of communal land ownership with a new "productivity clause" that justified the occupation and annexation of Indigenous lands; these lands, they said, were occupied by unproductive people who did not practice agriculture and therefore could not enjoy any rights over their land. To rationalize this clause, these theorists not only constructed a link between the notion of productivity and the right to individual property, but denied the agricultural development that Indigenous peoples had achieved, defining them as nomadic peoples that depended exclusively on hunting and harvesting roots and fruits.

Under this new colonial property regime, Indigenous peoples were forced to cede their lands to the civilized because their lands were neither cultivated nor cultivable, given the technological means at their disposal. Indigenous peoples' supposed primitive and savage state, more beastly than human, caused them to automatically lose their rights to their lands. In losing communal property rights over their lands, Indigenous peoples also lost their rights to form or even participate in a political society and to exercise political sovereignty over their territories. In fact, they could not even collaborate with the settler-colonial state that imposed itself on their territories. Worse still, as communal property did not grant and the productivity clause essentially denied Indigenous peoples rights to their lands, it is concluded that they never had sovereign rights over them; thus, usurpation of Indigenous lands does not constitute an illegal act or crime. That is, Indigenous peoples could not have rights to protect or the sovereignty to claim lands over which they, presumably, never presided in the first place. This is where the idea of America as *terra nullius* comes from.

In this sense, the idea of America as *terra nullius* constitutes an imaginary, but founding element in the modern theory of social contract, which was written by authors like Hobbes and Locke precisely at the historical moment of England's colonial expansion into America. This timing reveals the colonial and expansionist nature of the social contract itself and of the nation-states that emanated from it. First, the social contract spun the fiction that the lands usurped by the colonizers never had legitimate owners. Then this fiction became reality: colonizers dispossessed the Indigenous of their lands, carried out genocide, disabled their autonomy, political sovereignty, and even status as constituting a human society, and implanted a settler-colonial state based on a logic that justified their physical and cultural elimination.[34] In this sense, social contract theory, which presumes a pre-political state of nature where anarchy reigns to be resolved through individual agreements that then form a political collective, instead of being a fiction or, as some argue, a heuristic metaphor with which to understand the origin of the modern state, is based on the real fact that is the conquest of America. Insisting then that the state of nature is but a theoretical metaphor not only conceals its foundational role in the conquest of America; it also sustains the colonial state or the *colonial contract* or *settler contract* that comes out of it. As Nichols reminds us, Locke himself, in describing the state of nature that preceded the formation of the State, claimed, "in the beginning, all the World was America."[35]

Feminist political philosophers like Carol Pateman in her famous work *The Sexual Contract* published in 1988 had already drawn attention to the patriarchal and fraternal character of the social contract and how it depended on the exclusion of women.[36] However, in her collaborative work with the political philosopher Charles Mills she reflected on how the racial discrimination against enslaved Africans also had to do with the sexual contract's conception, and even acknowledged that the usurpation of Indigenous lands and extermination of Indigenous peoples were foundational to the social contract. As we will see shortly, Pateman's collaboration with Mills opened a new chapter in the debates about the social contract that reveals a series of fissures between different colonized peoples based on their gender and race.[37]

Charles Mills introduces the dimension of race and white supremacy in his critique of social contract theory. He defines racism and white supremacy as a political system, a formal and informal power structure that determines socio-economic privileges and norms, which dictate a differentiated distribution of wealth, opportunities, obligations, benefits, and rights. Mills, like Quijano, thinks that the idea of race began 500 years ago with the conquest of America and that it perseveres as a world political system to this day by way of what he will call the racial contract. But unlike Quijano (and, for that matter, Nichols), Mills does not focus on the colonial fact. On the contrary, his analysis focuses on what he calls the epistemology of ignorance or white ignorance that is subsumed and made integral to social contract theory and, according to Mills, ultimately prevents white people from understanding the social contract's racist foundation. The problem is therefore epistemological and based on the cognitive inability of whites to understand the world they have created. From this perspective, it was not so much the colonizers' territorial occupation of Indigenous lands but the manner in which racial discrimination based on skin color excluded non-whites from the social contract between white men, and how invisible and unexplained racism remained within the theorization itself. The problem then for Mills lies not only in the racist agreements between whites, but also in social contract theory's internal argumentation, which itself rests on racist premises, and the way in which these premises become invisible to social contract theorists. For this reason, despite the racist premises of the social contract between white men, Mills still finds redemptive qualities in the concept of the social contract because he believes that it is there where the collective and political identity necessary to construct non-racist justice and peace can be erected. According to Mills, the only thing left to do is to bridge the gap between the ideal of the social contract and the reality of the racial contract by reforming the social contract in a manner that, this time, recognizes the humanity of racialized beings. That is, the racial contract can be rescued by universalizing the idea of the human such that it includes those excluded from the social contract between whites. In other words, all that is needed to rescue the contract's political goodness is to de-racialize it. This position distances him from Pateman and Nichols who do not recognize any redeeming quality, nor any decolonial or feminist utility for the social contract. Nichols, who speaks of a colonial, rather than a racial contract, calls attention to the way in which the new social contract of Mills—now reformed—ends up supporting and even strengthening the colonial contract that is based on territorial occupation and a logic of Indigenous peoples' physical and cultural elimination or extermination. Once situated within the colonial fact and not just alongside its racist internal argumentative structuring, the social contract appears as a structure of domination that not only arose from the usurpation of Indigenous lands and the gradual disappearance of Indigenous peoples, but would be utterly impossible without the occupation and elimination of the Indigenous. Nichols presents us with several examples from the histories of Canada and the United States that illustrate how policies concerned with the inclusion or integration of Indigenous peoples into white political society amount to the usurpation, occupation, and elimination of the Indigenous by the colonial state. What is for Mills favorable—inclusion in the social contract for non-whites—represents, for natives, political suicide and extermination. Mills' proposal is therefore actually hege-monic and conservative.

I want to conclude with a very brief discussion of the book *Decolonizing Democracy* written by feminist theorist Christine Keating in which she ana-lyzes what she calls the postcolonial contract that emerged in India during the process of independence from England.[38] In this study, Keating presents a variation of the colonial (settler), racial, and sexual contracts; unlike Nichols' colonial contract and Mills' racial contract that require categorical dehuman-ization and the exclusion of the colonized, the contract Keating analyzes seemingly harmonizes the interests of both the colonizers and colonized, at least during certain historical colonial conjunctures. Keating describes for us moments during the colonization of India in which the British tried to legitimize their dominion by appealing to a racial and cultural kinship with the Hindus. The British who promoted this colonial policy sought alliances with the local Bengali elites to build fraternal bonds that were based on a fictitious line of descent that the British allegedly shared with higher castes of Hindus.[39] According to this legend, Hindus, an Aryan race like Europeans, were once defeated by barbarian Muslim hordes and now had, if they were to submit to British colonial rule, the opportunity to resurge. Keating shows us how these alliances were woven through a sexual subcontract that under-mined Hindu women's property and inheritance rights and gave Hindu men rights to control women and family property that did not previously exist. She speaks in this context of a social contract that emphasized the fraternity between or connivance of colonizing and colonized men, or what she calls domination by compensation. That is, Hindu males yielded political powers in public in exchange for greater individual rights over the property of women and the family. However, this fraternal contract eventually succumbed to the paternal social contract proposed by other sectors of the British colonial administration. Keating attributes the emergence of the paternal contract not only to a rejection of this fraternal harmonization of Hindu and British interests, but also to its distortion. For British colonizers who held this view, Hindus did not have redeeming qualities enough to participate in a fraternal social contract. Rather, they affirmed that Hindu women should be rescued from the barbarity of Hindu patriarchal institutions and customs that were oppressing them.[40] Ultimately, according to this line of argumentation, Hindus did not have the capacity for self-government and had to be subjected to colonial rule to prosper. The resultant social contract thus required the sub-ordination of Hindu men to the paternal domination of the British and used the liberation of Hindu women as pretext. Here, the social contract based on the dominion of the father (the British colonizer) persevered over the fraternal contract. Keating observes how both of these colonial contracts were, in the process of independence, preserved for the postcolonial state, which would emerge after independence. In the postcolonial historical context, then, there was a paradox: Hindu women were granted political rights at the same time as their individual and property rights were limited. Within these relatively benign colonial contracts, as compared with the colonial contract that Nichols describes and Keating overlooks, Keating, like Mills, finds remedies for the social contract. In this case, the existing gap between the ideal of the social contract and its material reality can be overcome by reaching different agreements on non-domination at the interpersonal, local, and state levels. That is, for Keating it is possible in India to break with domination by compensation and to create a social contract that refounds society as that which is, this time, free of power relations that are based on hierarchies of caste, gender, race, and religion.

As we see, Keating, like the other authors discussed here, excludes the colonial experience of Latin America or Abya Yala. In this sense, the latent Anglo-centric bias has the function of reifying the colonial difference characteristic of the world of the colony established by Europeans in 1492. It is also possible to find subtext concerning the Black Legend in these historical narratives, as Iberian empires are placed outside the history of modernity and capitalism. Hence, it should come as no surprise that, with the exception of Native North American theorists, both Mills and Keating still find room for reform in the social contract. The myth of the Anglo origin of democracy operates even in those theoretical discourses that claim to question it. It must be clear, however, that the conquest of America, the usurpation of territories, and the physical and cultural elimination of Indigenous peoples constitute the precondition for the social contracts between Western men and even those that emerge in India centuries later. A reformulation of the colonial and racial contracts under the former conditions is more difficult to imagine than such a reformulation within a context where there is recognition, however conditioned or partial, of the humanity of the colonized, as appears to have been in the case in India. However, we find some of the elements of domination by compensation that Keating analyzes in our own colonial experience. Julieta Paredes, Lorena Cabnal, Rita Segato, and I have spoken in our writings of something similar in the Spanish colony. Perhaps Paredes's phrase of "patriarchal entronques" is the most eloquent we have to describe the silent pacts between the colonizers and the colonized in our territories.[41] But the figure of *mestizaje* that is born only out of the conquest of America and not other colonial experiences also introduces new elements that mystify the conglomerate of power relations that arises within colonial societies. However, it is important to recognize that the Creole-mestizo nation-states also act as settler-colonial states insofar as they operate by way of a logic of elimination and are hyper-patriarchal. In this sense, perhaps instead of a refoundation of the State through constitutional reforms, what we most need is a refoundation of society. Any state that, at the level of civil society, is based on colonial, racist, and hyper-patriarchal social pacts is incompatible with notions of justice, equality, and democracy. To the extent that the new constitutions of countries like Ecuador and Bolivia often serve to strengthen mestizo-Creole patriarchal power or generate new fraternal alliances between Indigenous and mestizo-Creole men, this incompatibility should become clearer. In any case, we must not forget that the possibility of refounding our societies in a world where we do not enjoy sovereignty or juridical equality in the international community is limited. In a world that is literally being devoured by the genocidal logic of Western civilization, our salvation depends entirely on a monumental, world-scale political cataclysm.

NOTES

1. John M. Hobson, *The Eastern Origins of the West* (Cambridge: Cambridge University Press, 2004).

2. Ibid., 7.

3. Ibid., 2.

4. John M. Hobson, *The Eurocentric Conception of World Politics* (Cambridge: Cambridge University Press, 2012), 25.

5. Charles C. Mann, *1493: Uncovering the New World Columbus Created* (New York: Vintage Books, 2011).

6. Aníbal Quijano, "Coloniality and Modernity/Rationality," in *Globalization and the Decolonial Option*, ed. Walter D. Mignolo and Arturo Escobar (New York/London: Routledge, 2010), 25.

7. Enrique Dussel, "Europe, Modernity, and Eurocentrism," *Nepantla Views from South* 1, no. 3 (2000).

8. Nelson Maldonado-Torres, 2007. "On the Coloniality of Being: Contributions to the Development of a Concept," *Cultural Studies* 21, no. 2–3 (2007).

9. Ann Towns, "Civilization," in *The Oxford Handbook of Feminist Theory*, ed. Lisa Disch and Mary Hawkesworth (New York: Oxford University Press, 2015).

10. David Cannadine, "Civilization," *The Yale Review* 101, no. 1 (2013): 1

11. Ibid., 2.

12. Ibid., 8.

13. Ibid., 16.

14. Samuel Huntington, *The Clash of Civilizations and the Remaking of World Order* (New York: Simon & Schuster, 1996) quoted in Cannadine, "Civilization," 27.

15. Towns, "Civilization."

16. Ibid., 81.

17. Ibid., 83.

18. Ibid.

19. Ibid., 89.

20. Ibid.

21. Ibid., 90.

22. María Lugones, "Towards a Decolonial Feminism," *Hypatia* 25, no. 4 (Fall 2010): 744.

23. Ibid., 745.

24. Frantz Fanon, *Black Skin, White Masks,* trans. Richard Philcox (New York: Grove, 2008), xii.

25. María Lugones, "Heterosexualism and the Colonial Modern Gender System," *Hypatia* 22, no. 1 (Winter 2007): 187.

26. Ramón Grosfoguel, "The Structure of Knowledge in Westernized Universities," *Human Architecture: Journal of the Sociology of Self-Knowledge* 11, no. 1 (2013): 82.

27. María Lugones, "The Coloniality of Gender," in *The Palgrave Handbook of Gender and Development,* ed. Wendy Hartcourt (London: Palgrave MacMillan, 2016).

28. Hobson, *Eurocentric.*

29. Ibid.

30. Breny Mendoza, "La cuestión del imperio español y la Leyenda Negra," eHumanista: Journal of Iberian Studies 50 (2022).

31. Robert Nichols, "Realizing the Social Contract: The Case of Colonialism and Indigenous Peoples," *Contemporary Political Theory* 4, no. 1 (2005): 4.

32. Hobson, *Eurocentric.*

33. Robert Nichols, "Contract and Usurpation: Enfranchisement and Racial Governance in Settler-Colonial Contexts," in *Theorizing Native Studies*, ed. Audra Simpson and Andrea Smith (Durham: Duke University Press, 2014).

34. Nichols, "Contract," 102.

35. John Locke, *Second Treatise of Government* (Indianapolis: Hacket, 1980), c.V, section 49, 29, quoted in Nichols, "Contract," 112.

36. Carole Pateman, *The Sexual Contract* (Palo Alto: Stanford University Press, 1988).

37. Carole Pateman and Charles Mills, *Contract and Domination* (Cambridge: Polity Press, 2007).

38. Christine Keating, *Decolonizing Democracy* (University Park: Pennsylvania State University Press, 2011).

39. Ibid., 21.

40. Ibid., 30.

41. Julieta Paredes, *Una sociedad en estado y con estado despatriarcalizador* (Bolivia, La Paz: Ministerio de Justicia, 2008).

Chapter 5

The Limits of Civic Political Imagination

Sexual citizenship, Coloniality, and Antiracist Decolonial Feminist Resistance

Iris Hernández Morales
Translated by Shawn Gonzalez

There is a colonial division of the world into two zones: "the visible" and "the invisible." Within "the visible," there is the binary of legal/illegal. Here, access to rights makes it possible to move from "illegal" to "legal." This binary obscures those who do not speak in these terms, supporting the foundations of modernity. These considerations problematize the notion of citizenship, which, being part of a legalistic framework, reformulates the practices of disappearance and extermination in the conquest of Abya Yala. If citizenship, in general, has been the political objective of various social movements, it can be inferred that the realization of this goal has extended until today the coercive relationship between these two zones. Here, the visible is dominant to the extent that it is consistent with hegemonic mandates. Understood in this way, the "right to have rights" mobilized by the new social movements is a global, neocolonial strategy, because, in order to exist, "the visible" actively produces "the invisible." That is to say, it produces forms that are incomprehensible for the legal/illegal binary, or rather, "extralegal."

The project of universal liberty and equality imposed by modernity produced a dominant normativity that established the boundary between "the visible" and "the invisible." "The visible" refers to modernity, which was forged through the intersection of Eurocentric thought, capitalism, and structural variables of oppression—race, class, sexuality, gender—as markers of hierarchical differences. In "the visible," the hierarchy is represented by modern reason, modern law and its legal/illegal binary, and the capitalist productivity associated with white, bourgeois, heterosexual men. "The invisible" is coloniality, or what is rejected by modernity for being what it is. This is how "the invisible" contains "extralegal" subjects who are not important to modernity, because they and their knowledges are transformed into modernity's waste.

Subjects who are not important to modernity and, therefore, are excluded from its proposal of equality and freedom, try to overcome this tension because, as María Lugones states, there is no oppression that exists without some degree of resistance.[1] However, when this resistance emphasizes the access to and exercise of rights, it demonstrates a failure to question the foundations of modernity. Everything stays in the same place, so the waste of knowledge upon which modernity is constructed remains intact. Therefore, making oneself part of "the visible" in order to enjoy the benefits of citizenship permanently reasserts structures of domination.

This reassertion of structures of domination is linked to the supremacy that hegemony grants to certain social demands. In order to preserve its power, hegemony encourages dominance in alignment with its founding order: the matrix of colonial power. In this way, I demonstrate the need to be alert to the dominance of some social movements, given that, as bears repeating, they sustain themselves within the aforementioned matrix. In this sense, I am particularly interested in the oppressive practices that these movements reproduce internally and externally and their connection to the reaffirmation of the limits that define "the visible" and "the invisible" through the model of citizenship they promote.

From here, I focus on the notion of citizenship in the LGBTI movement. Since its appearance in Abya Yala toward the end of the 70s, the movement has progressively become part of the world of "the visible." It suffices to say that in less than fifty years, it has achieved political demands that greatly surpass the gains made by Indigenous communities in more than five hundred years of struggle. In this sense, the centrality of the LGBTI struggle exists in direct relation to the marginality of other struggles. In other words, the centrality of the struggles of the LGBTI movement is interwoven with the coloniality of other social movements, which demonstrates its lack of liberatory political imagination.

This analysis leads into the primary objective of this essay, which is to describe how the colonial imaginary is reactivated in our times and how resistance, or other struggles, work to speak in their own terms and not in those imposed by modernity. To accomplish this objective, this text is organized in three parts. The first centers on the way in which the notion of citizenship produces coloniality, emphasizing how it maintains the "visible"/"invisible" division, denying a common territorial space of coexistence. Here, the return to coloniality, the construction of sites of dominance through categorical thinking, and the production of the extralegal subject will be critical.

Secondly, I will connect the previous point to the LGBTI movement and its notion of citizenship centered on the access to and exercise of rights. The idea is to discuss how it has become a global, neocolonial axis of the survival of Western racism. Finally, I will highlight the contributions of decolonial antiracist feminism, emphasizing its efforts to create symmetrical encounters across differences as an exercise in weakening the borders between "the visible" and "the invisible." Without focusing on citizenship, decolonial antiracist feminism has emphasized a reflection on coexistence within the great Latin American house of differences, promoting a political imagination that does not restrict itself to the terms imposed by modernity.

In what way is the notion of citizenship an instrument of modernity/coloniality? How does the LGBTI movement's struggle for rights reactivate the colony in our times, fundamentally affecting racialized subjects? How does the decolonial antiracist feminist genealogy contribute to the creation of a power that responds to neocolonialism? I attempt to respond to these questions in order to undo the colonial anchors that maintain racism in contemporary societies. This does not only affect the movements in question, but every social movement. Herein lies its importance.

THE PRODUCTION OF COLONIALITY
IN THE NOTION OF CITIZENSHIP

I approach the study of modernity/coloniality as a theoretical lineage of the criticism of modernity that is committed to the radical transformation of imperialist logics. This radicality connects to the exercise of thinking about the causes of oppression, instead of its consequences, in order to keep visible alternative possibilities of transformation. From here, to expose how the notion of citizenship produces coloniality, it is necessary to consider the causes that created its organization and current manifestation. This is vital and requires a return to the colonial period in Latin America, the moment in which Abya Yala was reinvented by the colonizer.

The conquest imposed Western culture as the only legitimate axis of civilization and progress, which required erasing the existing diversity of Abya Yala. In this way, the establishment of a single system of meaning and interpretation of reality became a defining vector of modernity. I focus on modernity's capacity to create and recreate a constricted present, determined by what it, and only it, has to offer. I emphasize this point because it informs the selective exercise of modernity, which cartographically divides a single territory into that which is consistent with modernity and that which is not, and therefore cannot be part of it. This model universalized its ideologies, suppressing the diversity of Abya Yala and preventing Abya Yala from expressing itself in its own terms.

That which cannot be part of modernity is violently inscribed in a dark and invisible side: coloniality. In this way, a single territory contains the boundaries that form "the visible," or, "modernity," and "the invisible," or, "coloniality," through the coercive relationship between them, making visible only one side of reality and covering and obscuring the other. Following Santos's definition of the characteristics of abyssal thinking, I argue that the part of reality that is inscribed in "the visible" determines that the other zone does not exist "in any relevant or comprehensible way of being."[2] That is to say, "what is worth being lived" is an imposition of modernity. "What is not worth being lived" encapsulates the set of experiences created by coloniality.

This production of irrelevance negates the co-presence of both zones, which removes all possibility—following Audre Lorde—of creating community in Abya Yala's great house of differences.[3] The negation of this possibility occurs through the construction of conditions that, by universalizing the modern experience of "what is worth being," transform into the "should be" of those who inhabit the zone of "the invisible." Coloniality represents a violent normativity that recovers and updates colonial relationships. In other words, it activates the colonial matrix of power. In this sense, I note that the co-constitutive modernity/coloniality relationship is the cause of the asymmetrical organization of power in our time. From here, analyzing this asymmetry makes it possible to intervene in its causes and not only its consequences, the latter of which leaves everything in the same place, since they do not transform the foundations that produce them.

On this point, Aníbal Quijano proposes that coloniality constitutes the global pattern of capitalist power imposed by European rationality. This pattern—which originates and globalizes through America—imposes a racial/ethnic classification at the global level, operating in each of the dimensions—material and subjective—of social existence.[4] I present, therefore, the importance of race in shaping the zones I have identified and the hierarchical relationships between people and cultures that they imply. An exercise will further illustrate this point, allowing me to enter into the territory of this text: the coloniality produced by the notion of citizenship.

Imagine a citizen.

What is he or she like? What do they do?

. . . .

Did you think about it? Respond now about the citizen you imagined.

Was he or she a poor person? An Indigenous person? A Black person?[5]

In general, responses to these questions provide images that the culture imposes as dominant. The images that emerge from the responses—in agreement with Quijano—are those of white subjects. Therefore, I demonstrate that race continues to operate as a limit between "the visible" and "the invisible," which is to say, that more than 500 years after the conquest of Abya Yala, Western rationality continues to define the forms of learning, being, and relating among ourselves, with other people, and other living beings. This pattern of colonial power is globally hegemonic today.[6] Therefore, and I stress this, if the majority of people do not include images of Black, Indigenous, and poor people, then neither does the concept of citizenship and its rights. On the contrary, it serves the white dominance that extends far beyond the borders of Abya Yala.

The central role of race in Quíjano's theory indicates the influence of race in the development of the notion of citizenship, which relates to one of the limits in the coloniality of power: it ignores the fact that the centrality of race naturalizes the irrelevance of other variables of oppression. Lugones illuminates this covering-up, denouncing the coloniality that pervades gender.[7] Following her remarks, there are hidden processes related to the ignorance—produced by Eurocentric thinking—of the multiplicity of subjects, which obscures the fact that "categories and categorical thinking are tools of oppression."[8] Failing to consider this is "presupposing the categories of oppression to be separable."[9]

Lugones states that the erasure of diversity in Abya Yala naturalized male control, an issue that explains Quijano's omission of the relationship between gender and race. This omission occurs because he could not see that women were reinvented "according to the discriminatory codes and principles of Western gender."[10] This takes place, without a doubt, within the formal contents of citizenship because the existence of gendered pact associated with the racialization of salaried labor "had political implications for the establishment of citizenship and not only economic ones in the construction of classes."[11] I emphasize, then, that the matrix of colonial power supports citizenship's substance and that it should not be restricted to a single oppressive variable. It is sufficient to consider that the Indigenous man was not only subalternized for the color of his skin, but also for characteristics that made him similar to a woman: he had no beard, he wore his hair long, and he was smaller.[12]

Mendoza adds that although salaried labor was associated with capitalist exploitation, it establishes the foundation of a masculine citizenship that excluded women and slaves. Therefore, she argues that without the colony, citizenship would not exist, because Western race and gender are the basis of capitalism, liberal democracy, and the limits that define who is or is not important for this notion. Racial differences were produced to establish these limits through the consolidation of a "should be" that at its peak regards the white, male, hetero, bourgeois citizen as the comprehensible subject of modernity. In this way, the author visualizes the intersection of the heterosexual system and the modern, colonial gender system with capitalism and liberal democracy.

What Mendoza demonstrates is significant because the social pact she refers to prevents poor white men from falling into slavery, liberating them from domestic work. This establishes the basis of modern citizenship: free, with rights, and therefore legal, with time to participate in public life (which is to say, everything that was off limits to racialized subjects and "women"). In this way, I argue for an understanding of oppression based on the intersection of class, race, sexuality, and gender, established by the profitization that modern categorical thinking makes of these intersections. By this, I refer to the fact that power encourages the disaggregation of the analysis of reality, but strategically utilizes these intersections, strengthening citizen demands centered on one variable of oppression, but utilizing the multiplicity it detects to its advantage. In other words, it liberates on one side and represses on the other, leaving everything as it was before.

This dynamic is synthesized in Lugones' search for the cause of the indifference of Black men toward the violence that affects women of color. As Mendoza describes "the subordination of gender was the price that colonized men paid to maintain a certain level of control over their societies."[13] This negotiation produced male collusion with violence toward women. Or, rather, the complicity between colonizing and colonized men permitted the latter a certain level of control at the cost of the subordination of women, which never removed them from their place of subordination but did limit solidarity between men and women. In this way, dominant categories arose among the subordinated—colonized men above colonized women—which safeguarded the white foundations of citizenship.

Therefore, citizenship protects the privilege of the political subject who is valued by modernity. This does not refer only to the production of this subject, but rather, and most importantly, to the operation of the logic of citizenship. This logic consolidates an ideology of exclusive equality because its object is the territorial division between "the visible"/ "the invisible." The aforementioned centrality of race is crucial in this respect because it warns that racial equality is not neutral, because it operates only between white men and racialized men. This illuminates what exists beyond affirmations like "what is not seen, does not exist; what does not exist, does not have rights" because what citizenship allows to be seen always benefits the dominant order since the subjects it makes seen only exist in the zone of "the visible." Citizenship does not exist in the zone of "the invisible." I explain this more clearly below, since modernity articulates a false "invisible."

For Santos, two pillars sustain reality.[14] The pillar of regulation/ emancipation operates in the zone of "the visible"; the pillar of violence/appropriation in "the invisible." The point is that it is not a question of incorporating "the invisible" in "the visible" as if it were about taking a step forward. It is a question of understanding that "the invisible" is beyond what citizenship makes comprehensible. Citizenship only exists as a product of the pillar of regulation/emancipation, which in modern law expresses the limits that define "the legal" and "the illegal." In this way, I assume "the illegal" as a false "invisible," since this position obscures the radicality of the inexistence of those who do not even exist under this form. The legal/illegal binary is the product of regulations and emancipations that allow the second component to move toward the first component of the binary; what does not possess a legal or illegal form is suppressed.

"The invisible" is beyond citizenship, which is to say, it has been subjugated by the pillar of appropriation/violence. It is the nonexistent, what is not officially recognized, "the extralegal." Therefore, in modernity/the visible, the debate is between the legal/the illegal; in coloniality, "the extralegal" exists, which is worse than being illegal, because in lawless territory, the strongest always prevails. This foreshadows the coloniality of the notion of citizenship, because the legal/illegal is presented as the only intelligible possibility, obstructing the emergence of other alternatives, distinct from its perspectives and the ways in which they are constructed. This constrains the political imagination of social movements because they are subjected to the order of hegemonic power and collaborate with the imprisonment of the extralegal subject in "the invisible" and with the terms this establishes.

I demonstrate in this way that the desire for liberation based exclusively on the access to and exercise of citizenship is pervaded by an intense desire for hegemonic norms. For this reason, entering "the visible" is merely symbolic, since the movement between the illegal and the legal does not harm the production of extralegality. On the contrary, it often exacerbates the invisibility of those who do not comply with hegemonic norms, since these norms not only define what is legal and illegal in "the visible," but also possess the capacity to transform what is illegal into legal in the invisible zone. From here, it is important to recognize the ways in which some movements extend, preserve, and/or return to colonial domination and its waste of knowledges.

The recuperation of wasted knowledges is fundamental because they can transform the organization of the colonial matrix of power. The various elements obscured by the boundary between "the visible"/"the invisible" expose, on the one hand, the possibility of radical transformation—because if these knowledges were incorporated into reality they would modify the terms of conversation used up to this point. On the other hand, they demonstrate that colonial power never ended, a point that affects every relationship we engage in. I continue to develop this final aspect by analyzing the power exercised by the LGBTI movement.

THE LGBTI MOVEMENT'S PRODUCTION OF COLONIALITY

Before anything else, I emphasize that the LGBTI movement produces coloniality. It is not the only social movement that does this, but it is an ideal one for understanding how its demands strengthen monocultural power. Its transformative potential remains trapped in "the visible," so its liberation remains consistent with the pillar of regulation/emancipation and it has emphasized demands that subscribe to the universal legalistic character of citizenship, subordinating the forces from "the invisible" that seek to contaminate the limits of modernity.

According to Santos, two movements have emerged since the 1970s and 1980s, originating in struggles from "the invisible" that have contaminated "the visible."[15] He calls the first *the return of the colonial* and *the return of the colonizer*; the second, *subaltern cosmopolitanism*. I will linger on the first movement, which alludes to those who rebelled against having their life experiences relegated to "the invisible." Their struggles produced a radical response from "the visible" that continued to submerge them in the extra-legal zone, because their interventions undermined the metropolitan order. The state discourses and practices that criminalize indigenous struggles and that represent them as terrorism are an example of this. This response, among others, naturalizes the fact that while the LGBTI movement constructs rights, others are inscribed in a political void that creates states of exception. For example, in Chile, this results in Indigenous people being imprisoned long-term without proceedings to protect them and in evidentiary processes that allow statements from faceless witnesses, among other things, exposing a normativity that undermines the right to due process. That is to say: what is illegal in "the visible" is legal in "the invisible."

Interwoven with this, *the return of the colonizer* recuperates the forms of colonial management and subordination, enabling the construction of reality to remain at the mercy of those who hold power. Here, what Santos calls *societal fascism* takes place, which reproduces the life experience of the extralegal subject, allowing, it bears repeating, "the stronger party has a veto power over the life and livelihood of the weaker party."[16] Every type of existing societal fascism constructs reality by wasting knowledges and confining them to "the invisible" zone. For example, territorial fascism naturalizes the fact that dominant power operates freely in geographical zones that were generally subjected to European colonialism without considering the participation of their inhabitants. Therefore, these two movements delineate the coloniality of the LGBTI movement.

I maintain that the democratic recuperation(s) occurring in Abya Yala since the 1980s operate under colonial logic. On the one hand, they open liberatory spaces; on the other hand, they repress anything inconsistent with social hegemony, reigniting the paradox of modernity: liberty is founded on the repression of those who do not fit within the universal truths of a democratic reconstruction based on the access to and exercise of rights. In this context, the pillar of regulation/emancipation operates, as previously stated, according to the legal/illegal binary. The legal regulates and the illegal emancipates, advocating for "*the right to have rights*" as an axis on which post-dictatorial citizenship is established.

This review of the coloniality of citizenship allows for the critique of certain aspects of this process. To begin, the struggles against oppression primarily focused on liberating themselves from the yokes of dictatorship (clearly, a necessity) but without questioning the causes that produced these states, which, therefore, perpetuated the paradox of modernity. The recuperation of democracy kept the colonial past in the same place, just as the earlier project of democratization did not eradicate the practices of disappearance and extermination of the Indigenous communities of Abya Yala. Although elements existed that destabilized the "Iberian heritage" that understood the continent as a tributary of the conquistador's model, the truth is that categorical thinking, the centralities it produces, and the failure to question capitalism defined the political limits of the New Social Movements (NSMs).[17] These movements, attached to the legal character of the demands for rights and the universality of these demands, demonstrate the acritical posture of the hegemonic terms that govern the citizenship debate, which is linked to the neoliberal establishment and reinforces the state as the administrator of diversity, despite its homogenizing focus.[18]

Although a citizenship mobilized "from below" breaks with citizenship's classic liberal character, it still relies on the censure of differences. This is paradoxical because the struggles of the NSMs are based on cultural recognition. Nevertheless, it is not difficult to understand that by centering itself on separately overcoming oppression based on gender, class, race, and sexuality, these movements would reinvent power, anchored in the production of centers and peripheries. This is the result of various factors promoted by the "new" perspectives that administer power and continue to reinforce the boundary between "the visible" and "the invisible."

The factors I refer to form the foundation of post-dictatorial homogeneity. From this, I highlight two facts: the first is that the new paradigm of cultural recognition promoted by the NSMs is superimposed on the paradigm of economic distribution, encouraging a valorization of identity that fails to reduce inequality and social inequity, because it improved people's coexistence with capitalism. That is to say, it didn't question capitalism and, therefore, did not correct it as a cause of asymmetries in the exercise of power. This often occurs in the form of trying to provide for people's basic needs without this meaning a shift toward the equitable redistribution of resources. This is a conducive environment for societal fascism's processes of exclusion.

The failure to correct social inequalities promotes a state that, within a multicultural environment, fosters "certain cultural identities and consequently disadvantages others."[19] This tendency acquires a macabre character in the hands of the post-dictatorial Latin American state and its two primary features: participatory citizenship and the neoliberal establishment.[20] For Dagnino, this fact outlines the *perverse confluence* between the state, citizen participation, and neoliberalism because it affirms that neoliberalism was only possible with the participation of civil society, which, it is worth stating, refers to the group of people who construct the instituting/instituted tension or the legal/illegal binary within the regulation/emancipation paradigm, always in accordance with the official state and with international law.

Accordingly, the notion of citizenship synthesizes this pillar's operation because it defines the limitations within "the visible" of the legal/illegal by announcing this tension, since its perspectives do not question the operative terms. In this way, citizenship status is consistent with the censure of difference, because its knowledge is colonized by the monocultural meaning of the modern world. From here, the spaces of affirmation that the nation-state opens for what it considers illegal is related to the subjectivity of its power. The perverse confluence of participation and citizenship is an example of this, because it reproduces one of the primary critiques of liberal citizenship: rights that equalize through the status of citizenship do not modify the capitalist foundations of modern societies.[21]

This reinforces the position of extralegal subjects in the space of "the invisible," because their life experiences will not be part of civil society's demands. It suffices to consider the fact that citizenship emerges under the auspices of an idea of the subject that does not represent the Latin American subject, nor the diverse components associated with slavery, reciprocity, and small-scale production, nor with the notions of mestizo, Indian, or Black as a colonial structural foundation. Therefore, it is no coincidence that Indigenous struggles represent an extraordinary counter-hegemonic strategy that remains located in the extralegal, because they represent a radical struggle against capitalism, through systems of belief that, in connection with the land, distance themselves from the exploitative logics of this model. Utilizing their knowledges, which are wasted by the West, could paradigmatically transform the relationships between individuals, cultures, and nature.

This waste of knowledges is connected to the fact that the lesbian, gay, bisexual, trans, and intersex (LGBTI) movement is, ultimately, gay. This underrepresentation of lesbians and trans people—following a logic of the interrelation of power—means that the demands of the former are expressed publicly, erasing the lived experiences of the latter. It does not matter how many lesbian or trans activists there are; the gay male subject, who holds the majority within the LGBTI movement, takes over representation, producing a schism within these spaces. Outside, they form organizations that fall under new systems of under-representation, because there are more LGBTI organizations than lesbian or trans ones, which keeps everything in the same place. Therefore, equitable power relationships do not exist within LGBTI identities nor between LGBTI organizations and lesbian or trans ones, because gay centrality co-opts all representative spaces.

This co-optation reproduces the coloniality of power because the coloniality that restrictive "LGBTI diversity" imposes on lesbian and trans knowledges and experiences only permits sexual diversity to speak in gay terms. They are blind to the totalizing character of their sexuality that makes invisible not only the gender of lesbians and trans people, but also race and class. In this way, what the gay movement does, according to Lugones, is to establish itself through a categorical analysis that naturalizes its masculine privilege, recuperating the masculine/feminine tension. In this way, the non-neutrality of its sex determines—just like racial equality—that sexual equality is only accomplished between straight men and white gay men. The story of Simón Knkoli in South Africa demonstrates this.

Simon Knkoli denounced the limitations of the gay movement. When he was detained in a march against apartheid, he experienced the fragmentation of struggles due to his homosexuality. GASA, an international organization of gays and lesbians to which he belonged, kept silent about his imprisonment, which he understood "as a continuation of the organization's racism and its unwillingness to recognize that homosexual liberation was also related to anti-apartheid struggles."[22] GASA, informed by the whiteness of gay activists, subordinated race to the struggles of homosexual liberation, illuminating the totalizing character of their sexuality, failing to understand that racism also affected them and thus indicating complicity with white, heterosexual, male power.

This incident describes the depoliticized arrangement of the LGBTI move-ment grounded in national discourses. This arrangement strengthens a project of citizenship that reproduces the parameters that the nation-state imposes on their lives, turning the pluralism of its discourses into mere decoration. Gay centrality and the development of its political agendas based on sexual equal-ity support a dominant idea that is clarified by Eric Fassin's thinking. Fassin argues that sexuality defines a state's modernity or lack thereof, an issue that refigures Western supremacy, allowing for the survival of the hegemony that characterizes nationalist discourses and imaginaries.[23] The centrality of sexu-ality rearticulates colonial hierarchies and order because its agenda for rights only constructs equality between sexes and sexualities, excluding race from this project: "Therefore, I think that where the West determines that sexism exists, it allows for the naturalization of racism."[24] If nationalist democratic discourses emphasize a democracy based on sexuality, it is not illogical to think that those who join 'the visible' reproduce the racist colonial history of Latin American states, given their coherence with these states.

Concretely, the limits of democracy are extended through the centrality of the sexual rights agenda. Revising the group of juridical norms with the intention of creating equal rights between men and women and between heterosexuality and homosexuality demonstrates that these groups acquire rights at the same time that the return of the colony and the colonizer becomes consolidated, since "the new wave of antiterrorism and immigration laws follows the regulatory logic of the appropriation/violence paradigm."[25] This pillar allows the colonizer to divide, imposing his contractual terms despoti-cally, militarizing territories to ensure their exploitation. This exposes the fact that citizenship is dispensable because it obscures the operation of a societal fascism occupied with ensuring that "the invisible" does not transgress met-ropolitan boundaries. This cover-up contributes to the way that citizenship and its calls for equality and liberty naturalize its relationship to capitalism without connecting it to the violence this entails for Indigenous communities and/or with the inhuman cases of exploitation of racialized migrants, among other things. This again articulates the fragmentary LGBTI logic which is evident in the central role that equal marriage occupies in its agenda of rights.

Marriage rights discourses imply an understanding of oppression based on a single variable of oppression. Translated into Quijano's terms, sexuality replaces race in a framework based on a Eurocentric perspective of relation-ships between couples. The transformation of marriage into a right exposes the universalizing logic that characterizes this perspective. If I add to this its relationship with capitalism, what results is the reproduction of the coloniality of power. I would like to note that marriage reaffirms a social classification based on sexuality which revives Quijano's boundary, naturalizing the irrelevance of other variables in the oppressive phenomenon, which vitalizes the coloniality of gender, race, and class. In other words, this demand conceals the foundations that support the causes of this difference, reactivating the colony in our times.

In addition, stable, matrimonial identity strengthens a notion of social respect based on the capacity for consumption. This respect connects love with the economic capacity of a couple to support needs related to the state's economic model. That is to say, it is not that gay love only strengthens the structure of marriage; gay love also strengthens the stability of capitalism through apolitical behavior that places the struggles against its oppression in favor of capital, or, from another angle, against anti-capitalist struggles. In this way, the limit observed by Knkoli is reactivated because the LGBTI movement exists on a racist continuum which obscures the fact that its liberation is related to these other struggles. An example of this is that the legalization of gay marriage is often followed by demands for retail stores to include gay couples in their wedding lists, which evinces once again a trivial political imaginary that is committed with the idealized effects of consumerism.

The demand for marriage rights produces trivialization, it needs to be stressed, since once it is accomplished, they demand that retail stores include them in their sales, which again exposes complicity with the idealization of consumerism.[26] In this way, the market is exposed as an axis of integration that extends the perverse confluence of participation and neoliberalism, with the latter being a crucial component of the return to the colony and the colonizer.

The preceding example demonstrates the importance that the family and the couple possess for homonormative gay politics; that is, a model of homosexuality that mirrors the heterosexual model. I stress that while the LGBTI movement and even certain radical lesbian feminist groups strive to criticize the heterosexual normativity of the nation, they ignore the fact that this analysis of sexuality subordinates other variables of oppression, which, as I said, collude with classism and racism. Gay marriage validates this organization because it is reasonable to consent to it and through this ascend in the hierarchical system of sexuality, at whose peak are white, married, heterosexual couples.

Marriage is a normativized space of "dissidence" that connects with the cartography that differentiates between wilderness and civilized space. Here, "gay friendly" promotes the capitalism of homosexuality, which submits gay couples' aspirations to a socioeconomic circuit of class. This obscures the precarity of other subjects and other affective configurations, reinforcing the hegemony of Western thought through one variable of oppression that establishes itself as dominant. I stress: gay sexuality, being non-dominant with respect to heterosexuality, is dominant with respect to lesbian gender, which shows that relationships of domination/subordination are reproduced inside subaltern groups. The story of Knkoli, in fact, demonstrates that gay sexuality is dominant and subordinates race, which exposes its commitment to the white, heterosexual, racist imaginary as the naturalized boundary of its liberation. In this way, the ideals of the nation-state are preserved, strengthening hegemonic codes at the global level because it is undeniable that a hierarchical relationship of states exists in the transnational arena.

Jasbir K. Puar expands this last point. She coined the term "homonationalism" to explain the acceptance and tolerance of gay and lesbian issues after the attack on the twin towers.[27] Puar claims that Western powers have used LGBTI rights to condemn certain Eastern cultures for "barbaric" homophobic practices, while justifying Western oppression of the East. That is to say, the violence towards "women" and homosexuals in these territories justifies imperial neocolonialism. For example, through Pinkwashing, Israel transforms its international image, uniting gay love to the war against Palestine.[28] For this reason, photographs of gay soldiers have spread virally, exposing Israel's support of LGBTI demands, which has been applauded by this group, despite international condemnation of the state for violating the human rights of the Palestinian people. In this way, gay sexuality appears in an intelligible framework that inscribes within "the invisible" those who are associated with barbaric backwardness, reinforcing military operations whose goal is ethnic cleansing.[29] In other words, Islamic terrorism facilitates a colonial return that revives the colonizer through a territorial fascism that bans life within the "axis of evil."

The LGBTI movement does not question the form of its inclusion, facilitating repressive politics in the Middle East, as well as in militarized Indigenous territories throughout Abya Yala. Here, I again warn that the visibility acquired has been utilized in the service of power. Its centrality is determined by its consistency with the system of dominant beliefs that excludes "the feminine" and racialized subjects, among others. This is the product of an understanding of oppression limited by sexuality and the legalist logic of citizenship and inextricably linked with the Eurocentric, racist, neoliberal enclaves that make up the pillar of regulation/emancipation. Here, speech only occurs in the terms of power, preventing the enunciation of the knowledges it wastes, which is a focus of the decolonial, antiracist feminism I turn to now.

LINES OF FLIGHT: THE CONTRIBUTIONS OF THE DECOLONIAL ANTIRACIST FEMINIST GENEALOGY

Here I discuss the tension that in the 1990s divided feminism into two branches: institutional and autonomous. The former formed part of the perverse confluence driven by the state, which is criticized by the latter, causing the latter to remain confined to the periphery. In this way, the technocratic notion of gender obscures the differences between poor, lesbian, Indigenous, and Black women that shape the developing political repertoire of autonomous feminists.[30] Nevertheless, the coloniality of autonomy is a practice that is reactivated within the movement which mobilized another displacement. Yuderkys Espinosa-Miñoso detects an organization of power inside the movement based on first-and second-generation voices.[31] The first defined their principles; the second had to assume the mandates of the first, which omitted their experiences. The first generation's power was connected with class, whiteness, and academic rank, which contributed to a reluctance to dialogue with the social movement.[32] All of this fostered an autonomous feminist political subject unaware of the struggles of women of African and/ or Indigenous descent.

This demonstrates a sedimentary, colonial, racist practice that universalizes the notion of "woman." This issue allows me to demonstrate a turning point in the perspective that the decolonial antiracist genealogy puts at our disposal, since it is through lived experiences—particularly of racialized women—that the limits of the comprehensive feminist narrative of oppression can be transcended. An intense debate that is still in progress has allowed decolonial antiracist feminism to understand that the experience of modernity is much larger than what is known and that, therefore, it is necessary to develop responses that overcome the Western limitations that restrict the political imagination trapped in its margins. Hence the importance of dialogue and encounter with the social movement.

The expansion of the present that this implies has been consistently developed by voices such as Yuderkys Espinosa-Miñoso and Ochy Curiel, whose work has produced a political-philosophical development that criticizes Eurocentric epistemology, recovering a group of feminist perspectives to analyze oppression in a broader narrative than the one enabled by gender and sexuality. Their relational analyses challenge a view of the variables of oppression as disconnected, and offer the possibility of approaching social movement as problem and solution, depending on how its privileges create disadvantageous positions within and beyond the movement.[33]

To synthesize: decolonial antiracist feminism creates an intersectional perspective on oppression and the ways in which it is produced by capitalism, racism, liberalism, and Eurocentrism. It recognizes that social movements' political practices have collaborated with the reproduction of modernity, excluding subjects and knowledges. It is enough to return to the coloniality that pervades feminist autonomy and the second generation's autonomy, which excludes lived experiences associated with race. This last consideration allows for the discernment of this variable in feminist thinking, trying to re-envision the forms of relation between people, cultures, and nature, which overcomes the limitations created by struggles exclusively linked with citizenship, not only for feminist political imagination, but also for the entire social movement.

This last point leads to the inscription of decolonial, antiracist feminism in the second movement outlined by Santos: subaltern cosmopolitanism.[34] I assume that one of its intentions is to overcome the limits that separate "the visible" from "the invisible," exposing the ways in which the return of the colony and the colonizer imposes colonial terminology. In this vein, exposing what is hidden is paramount for expanding modernity's systems of representation and meaning. Efforts to overcome monocultural representations are based in a constant struggle, as I understand it, to incorporate wasted knowledges.

On this topic, I return to some previously established points. If variables like sex/gender/sexuality have contributed to a global neocolonialism tied to sexual rights agendas and to specific political movements, then the participation of those who are overlooked by these projects creates the possibility of radical articulation. This articulation responds to structural violence with terms that are unknown by "the visible" and are required to transform the restrictive codes of modern co-presence and coexistence. This is how I define subaltern cosmopolitanism as an effort to engage with wasted knowledges through a critique of dominant thought that integrates the analysis of oppression in a broad system of domination that, as is revealed by examination, is marked by the racism and classism of modern society. Decolonial, antiracist feminism strives to configure this articulation. It does not interpret all of the realities through a common perspective, because this reconstructs colonial foundations. It understands that illuminating what has been silenced makes available knowledges obscured by modernity/coloniality, and that this transforms reality.

I highlight now Lugones's decolonial feminist contributions, who outlines two steps that support the unmasking of coloniality: intersectionality and fusion.[35] The first is a comprehensive state, the second a state of action. Intersectionality makes visible categories that are obscured by discourses that select the dominant, as seen, for example, in my exercise that asks you to imagine a citizen. In this way, it initiates a process that destabilizes the ornamental status of social struggles inscribed in central and, therefore, dominant, cultural features, which are produced by the universalization of a single and always dangerous viewpoint. Fusion positions the experiences of oppression/ resistance relationally and, therefore, forms the foundation of resistant coalition. It is not theory, but a lived possibility that connects resistances, opening up space for common concerns and the diverse forms in which they have been addressed.

A graphic example illustrates the possible dangers of not applying these two steps. In 2007, the Mapuche activist Patricia Troncoso, after a long hunger strike, was on the brink of death. The nascent idea of an antiracist, lesbian feminist support network circulated among metropolitan Chilean activist networks, but was rejected on the grounds that Indigenous oppression was not their struggle and that even if they supported her, they would not get involved with this community because of the violence that Mapuche men inflicted on Mapuche women.[36] The reference to violence towards women prevents intersectionality, which is to say, that there was a failure to understand the relational character of oppression, in favor of the continuity of racist state violence toward this community. In this way, the accusation of sexism colludes with Chilean racism because its centrality subordinates racism, obscuring it.

I proceed with caution on the previous point. It is not that violence toward women is not relevant. No. What I am trying to emphasize is that there is a Western interpretation of violence that coincides with the agenda of sexual rights, whose contribution to neocolonial processes has already been established. I am not trying to propose that this is a struggle that should be abandoned; what I suggest is that when struggles are linked to prominent variables of oppression, they run the risk of naturalizing and universalizing a viewpoint that subjugates the differences of other struggles and their extension in different geographical locations. This—I stress—prevents the transformation of strategies for approaching violence because it assumes knowledges that reproduce what occurred with the Indigenous in the colony. The Indigenous were constructed as non-human through the association of their color with practices forbidden by Western culture. In this case, race is marked as a bestial sign of "violence against women," preventing the coalition between lesbian feminism and Mapuche communities.

I do not want to be trivial; I aim to warn about complex practices that for more than 500 years have produced the extralegality of racialized people. Not listening to them allows social struggles to be strategically used in the service of power as occurs with LGBTI sexuality. Therefore, I propose that it is not sufficient to understand intersectionally: a crossing point between resistances is necessary to promote counterhegemonic coalitions. I insist: I do not justify violence toward women; I emphasize that resistance to it cannot inscribe itself in perspectives that omit non-Western points of view because this limits relational analyses and the radical intervention of violence. Based on this case, the question emerges: In what way are struggles antiracist if they do not encounter the diversity of oppressions that define racialized experience? For me, the response is that this does not strengthen the counterhegemonic coalition and, therefore, it is difficult to imagine changing modern hegemony because the understanding of oppression derives from non-relational imaginaries of identity that compete among themselves, generating a spiral of relations of domination/subordination that particularly obscure race.

Lugones allows for envisioning a path of action that will not be possible without creating the conditions for symmetrical encounters between differences. This requires overcoming the ways in which our own terms stabilize the existence of "the invisible." "This is an exercise in abandoning certainty, of enunciation of the resolution of conflicts that aims to transform ourselves through the incorporation of Other knowledges."[37] In this sense, lesbian feminist encounters have put into play some of the conditions of encounter that I connect with the contributions of Santos in this respect.

Santos describes five conditions—each connected to one another—that contribute to the realization of the conditions of encounter to which I refer.[38] The first condition transitions from *cultural completeness* to *cultural incompleteness*, which understands that our knowledges require other forms of thinking, apart from Western ones, in order to create radical transformation. If struggles do not transform reality, it is because they require distinct knowledges in order to do so. The second condition moves from *narrow cultural accounts* to *broad cultural accounts*, putting into play common preoccupations and distinct ways of approaching them. The third transitions from *unilateral times* to *shared times*. This involves eradicating the idea that power's time is the only correct time. "If the time to deal with a topic belongs to dominant subjects, it is likely that their hegemonic character will be reproduced in their demands. If it respects non-dominant desires, it supports strategies that destabilize monoculturality and, therefore, allow for adherence to counter-hegemonic, collective proposals. . . . If time belongs to dominant subjects—whether hegemonic (white, middle class, heterosexual, men) or non-hegemonic (white, middle class, gays, others)—hegemony is reproduced. It is necessary to approach topics based on the abandonment of colonizing practices that determine the what, the how, the when, and the why."[39] The fourth condition requires that *unilaterally imposed topics and partnerships* are replaced by *mutually chosen topics and partnerships*. The fifth brings us from *similarity or difference* to *similarity and difference* in order to break down hierarchical relationships and mobilize partners in dialogues to have the right to be similar when difference makes them inferior and to be different when similarity would put their identity in danger.[40] This only works when the voices rejected by modernity are heard.

Given the aforementioned, I argue that decolonial, antiracist feminism represents an expansion of the present because it puts oppression in a broader framework of understanding due to its permanent efforts at dialogue with the social movement. The autonomy/institutionality tension, the fractures within Latin American autonomous feminism, the persistent effort to create autonomous enunciation in lesbian feminist encounters—where second-generation racialized voices, among others, are relevant—will be fundamental in interweaving the analysis of reality and strengthening subaltern cosmopolitanism. This idea assumes a concrete position in the VII Encuentro Feminista de América Latina y el Caribe (EFLAC) in Chile, from which an explicit commitment to antiracist and anticapitalist struggles emerged, an issue which, as I already stated, has not been simple.[41] In fact, the events related to Patricia Troncoso took place that same year.

Without a doubt, this commitment complicated the interpretation of reality, which in 2009—when Espinosa-Miñoso and Curiel began to dialogue with the decolonial turn—put into circulation "Una Declaración Feminista Autónoma. El desafío de hacer comunidad en la Casa de las Diferencias" [An Autonomous Feminist Declaration: The Challenge of Creating Community in the House of Differences] synthesizing the foundations of this approach. The declaration outlines, among other things, the connection with the community, continuous questioning of the state, and the importance of the coexistence of counter-hegemonic differences, all of which refocus attention to the axes of the struggle against oppression, overcoming the limits of citizenship and classic lesbian feminist themes. An intense process of construction led to thinking of the conditions for encounter with wasted knowledges, which was exposed clearly in the Encuentro Lésbico Feminista de Abya Yala (ELFAY) [Lesbian Feminist Encounter of Abya Yala – ELFAY, 2014—]. The important influence of Yuderkys Espinosa-Miñoso, Ochy Curiel, and Celenis Rodríguez inflected the encounter with the Other to expose common preoccupations that emphasized the participation of racialized lesbian feminist voices, allowing for a displacement of the classic topics of white lesbian feminism that excluded or only nominally assumed the topics proposed by lesbians of color.

This rests on the assumption of the incompleteness of the lesbian knowledges that expanded cultural accounts of the themes and approaches of oppression. This is not a simple question because it implies a displacement that is not well received by the hegemony, which is perceived as an oppressive imposition and, as such, provoked responses at ELFAY. Among these were those of some Chilean lesbian feminists who argued that decolonial feminism "resulted more in a proletarian and anti-racist revindication than in a systemic and thought-out critique." They added, "to consider Marxism or racism as political solutions is a waste of time and energy."[42] To consider this as a waste of time supports hegemonic time because it suppresses other knowledges, strengthening the power that sustains extralegality. Beyond this, I argue that constructing counter-hegemonic spaces of enunciation enables antagonisms that try to erase the Other, above all if it is someone who mobilizes displacement, making concrete the objective of citizenship: the continuation of the boundaries between "the visible" and "the invisible."[43]

This raises various challenges that highlight how and around whom common preoccupations are translated. Nevertheless, I emphasize that this benefits the resistant coalition. In this sense, I highlight the importance of balancing the decision of which topics to approach, emphasizing the importance that invisible voices possess for our struggles. Creating the conditions to do this requires a process that connects with the causes that originally produced oppression, which deepens processes of enunciation that are symmetrical and continually more human in order to overcome the restrictions of citizenship, which, without making use of these terms, only recreate the colony in our times.

CONCLUSION

This reconsideration exposed how citizenship reinforces hegemonic power, given its colonial baggage, and how the LGBTI movement was transformed into its tool through the use of demands that incorporate variables of oppression in its favor. This reinforces the limits between "the visible" and "the invisible," aiding the return of the colony and the colonizer, which fundamentally affects racialized subjects. In this context, the decolonial antiracist feminist genealogy is resistant, responding through an intersectional understanding that advances to fusion. Their action fosters symmetrical enunciations that destabilize the colonial matrix of power, which also operates within oppressed groups, through the construction of conditions that incorporate the knowledges erased by modernity. Without focusing on citizenship, they emphasize a challenging reflection on the coexistence of differences, fostering a political imagination not restricted by the limits of modernity and its terms.

NOTES

1. María Lugones, "Radical Multiculturalism and Women of Color Feminisms." *Journal for Cultural and Religious Theory* 13, no. 1 (2014).
2. Boaventura de Sousa Santos, "Beyond Abyssal Thinking: From Global Lines to Ecologies of Knowledges," *Review* 30.1 (2007): 45.
3. Audre Lorde, "Poetry Is Not a Luxury," accessed November 19, 2020, https://makinglearning.files.wordpress.com/2014/01/poetry-is-not-a-luxury-audre-lorde.pdf.
4. Aníbal Quijano, "Coloniality of Power, Eurocentrism, and Latin America," *Nepantla: Views from South* 1, no. 3 (2000): 545.
5. This is an exercise that I have repeated with modifications in various presentations, texts, and workshops. It can be found in texts in which I began to try to integrate

the oppressions. See: Iris Hernández Morales, "Arroz con leche ¿Me quiero casar?" *Revista Sociedad & Equidad*, no. 3 (2012).

6. Quijano, "Coloniality of Power," 533.

7. María Lugones, "The Coloniality of Gender," *Worlds & Knowledges Otherwise* 2, no. 2 (Spring 2008).

8. Lugones, "Radical Multiculturalism," 75.

9. Ibid.

10. Breny Mendoza, "La epistemología del sur; la colonialidad del género y el feminismo latinoamericano," in *Tejiendo de otro modo: Feminismo, epistemología y apuestas decoloniales en Abya Yala*, eds. Yuderkys Espinosa Miñoso, Diana Gómez Correal, and Karina Ochoa (Colombia: Editorial Universidad del Cauca, 2014), 94.

11. Ibid., 96.

12. Fernando Zarco, *Masculinidad y homoerotismo desde el pensamiento decolonial* (Barcelona: Universidad Autónoma de Barcelona, 2009).

13. Mendoza, "La epistemología del sur," 94.

14. Santos, "Beyond Abyssal Thinking."

15. Ibid.

16. Ibid., 59.

17. Amparo Menéndez, "El lugar de la ciudadanía en los entornos de hoy. Una mirada desde América Latina," *Revista Ecuador Debate,* no. 58 (2003).

18. The work for which I received my doctorate in Latin American Studies carried out the first part of a revision of citizenship that was focused on a diagnosis of liberal, communitarian, and multicultural citizenship and the development of this idea in Abya Yala. This allowed me to develop a group of critiques centered on the responses that each current means for liberal citizenship and the fact that they are based on a failure to question capitalism, their universal legalist character, their established participation in hierarchical relationships, and the homogenizing character of the state. It is important to note that this diagnostic recuperated the debate about "the visible" and a methodology that uses this diagnostic to propose potential solutions to the problems outlined, based on decolonial contributions and LGBTI and decolonial antiracist lesbian feminist movements' proximity to or distance from these proposals. See: Iris Hernández Morales, "Aportes, problemáticas y desafíos que la noción de ciudadanía movilizada por el Movimiento de Diversidad Sexual y sus fragmentos LTGBI y lesbofeminista antirracista decolonial significan a la radicalización del pluralismo" (PhD diss., Universidad de Chile, 2016).

19. Will Kymlicka, "Las políticas del Multiculturalismo," *Ciudadanía Multicultural: Una teoría liberal de los derechos de las minorías* (Barcelona: Paídos, 1996), 156.

20. Evelina Dagnino, "Sociedad Civil, Participación y Ciudadanía en Brasil," presented at UNICAMP, São Paulo, Brazil, 2005.

21. T.H. Marshall is considered the father of modern, classic citizenship. He tried to overcome social inequalities through citizen status. However, this did not question the class differences produced by capitalism.

22. José Fernando Serrano Amaya, "La doble salida del clóset de Simon Knkoli: heterosexismo y luchas anti-apartheid," *Ciudad Paz-Ando* 7, no. 1 (2014): 97.

23. Éric Fassin, "La democracia sexual y el choque de civilizaciones," *Mora (B. Aires)* 18, no. 1 (July 2012), accessed September 17, 2015, http://www.scielo.org.ar /scielo.php?script=sci_arttext&pid=S1853-001X2012000100001&lng=es&nrm=iso.

24. Iris Hernández Morales, "Colonialidad, Diversidad Sexual y Puntos de Fuga a la Opresión: Apuntes Generales," *Nuevas Voces Descoloniales de Abya Yala* (Madrid: Editorial Akal-GLEFAS, 2017), 12.

25. Santos, "Beyond Abyssal Thinking," 55–56.

26. In Chile, for example, the declaration of civil unions mobilized petitions of large stores to include people who signed this agreement in their sales. See "Piden a grandes tiendas que ofertas y formularios para novios incluyan al Acuerdo de Unión Civil," *Movilh*, published July 27, 2015, http://www.movilh.cl/piden-a-grandes -tiendas-que-ofertas-para-matrimonios-se-apliquen-expresamente-a-convivientes -civiles/.

27. Jasbir Puar, "Homonationalism As Assemblage: Viral Travels, Affective Sexualities," *Jindal Global Law Review* 4, no. 2 (2013): 24.

28. Israel Defense Force published a photo of two soldiers holding hands, stating: "It's Pride Month. Did you know that IDF treats all of its soldiers equally? Let's see how many times you can share this photo." The photo went viral with the applause of LGBTI groups. It can be seen on Israel Hayom (12/06/2012). Army shows its prides post illustrative gay photo on Facebook. See "Foto de soldados gays israelíes causa controversia," *BBC News* https://www.bbc.com/mundo/noticias/2012/06/120612 _soldados_gay_israel_facebook_jgc.

29. For an analysis of ethnic cleansing, see Ilan Pappé, *The Ethnic Cleansing of Palestine* (Oxford: Oneworld Publications, 2006).

30. For reasons of length, I do not differentiate between feminism, decolonial antiracist feminism, and decolonial antiracist lesbian feminism. I will use them without distinction, but without omitting the issue I signal now—the lesbian intervention in their development.

31. Yuderkys Espinosa-Miñoso, "La política sexual radical autónoma, sus debates internos y su crítica a la ideología de la diversidad sexual," in *Pensando los feminismos en Bolivia*, ed. Patricia Montes (La Paz: Conexión Fondo de Emancipación, 2012).

32. Hernández Morales, "Aportes, problemáticas y desafíos."

33. The feminist synthesis includes diverse voices embracing "The writings of Yan María Castro, Norma Mogrovejo, Yuderkys Espinosa-Miñoso, Margarita Pisano, Valeria Flores, Ochy Curiel, Toli Hernández, Marían Pessah, Chuy Tinoco, the groups Mujeres Creando, Las unas y las Otras, among others. . . . Their analyses have considered the geopolitical specificities of the region; contributing not only to feminism as theory and political practice, but also to sexual-political movements like the LGBT movement." This also recognizes all the forms of Indigenous and Afro-descendent activism, the contributions of diverse North-centric feminist thinking, and the legacy of autonomous feminists. This is contained in what is considered a founding document of this tradition, although it was not recognized as such at that time. See: "Encuentro Lésbico Feminista de Abya Yala," *Memoria X,* published August 2016, https://glefas.org/download/biblioteca/lesbianismo-feminista/memoria-x-elfay

-colombia-2014-v.pdf. See also: "Una Declaración Feminisa Autónoma. El Desafío de Hacer Comunidad en la Casa de las Diferencias," *Rumbo al Encuentro Feminista Autónomo*, published May 2009, http://feministasautonomasenlucha.blogspot.com/.

34. See Santos, "Beyond Abyssal Thinking," 63.

35. María Lugones, "Radical Multiculturalism."

36. This is described by Victoria Aldunate—Chilean, antiracist, lesbian, feminist activist—and is also noted by the author of this text. Their affirmations were shared in the Workshops of Lesbian Feminist Intersections, facilitated by Lastres Abisales in 2016.

37. Iris Hernández Morales, Unpublished manuscript, presented at Encuentro Feminista Nacional de Arica, 2016.

38. Boaventura de Sousa Santos, *Descolonizar el saber, reinventar el poder* (Santiago de Chile: LOM Ediciones, 2013). See also Boaventura de Sousa Santos, "Toward a Multicultural Conception of Human Rights," in *Moral Imperialism: A Critical Anthology*, ed. Berta Hernández-Truyol (New York: New York University Press, 2002).

39. Hernández Morales, Unpublished manuscript.

40. Santos, *Descolonizar el saber,* 84–87.

41. For information on EFLAC (in English, Latin American and Caribbean Feminist Encounters), see Encuentro Feminista de América Latina y el Caribe, *Viva Historia,* accessed November 21, 2020, https://en.vivahistoria.org/eflac.

42. Marisol Torres, "Sobre la sospecha, la crítica y la feminidad. Reflexiones tras el ELFAY," *Menjunje Lesbiano,* published December 2014, https://marisoultorresjimenez.wordpress.com/2014/12/10/sobre-la-sospecha-la-critica-y-la-feminidad-reflexiones-tras-elflay-bogota-2014/.

43. Another example is found in the correspondence debate between Francesca Gargallo y Ochy Curiel that, more than extending a bridge between common preoccupations, revealed antagonisms that as such proceed to devalue a complex process of encounters across differences and that cannot be personalized in the voices that try to construct this enunciation. See: Francesa Gallargo, "Cartas van, cartas vienen. Para una crítica de las exclusiones en el feminiso y los usos de la decolonialidad,"*Francesca Gargallo,* published November 2014, https://francescagargallo.wordpress.com/2014/11/06/cartas-van-cartas-vienen-para-una-critica-de-las-exclusiones-en-el-feminismo-y-los-usos-de-la-decolonialidad/.

Chapter 6

Public Policies on Gender Equality

*Technologies of Modern
Colonial Gender*

Celenis Rodríguez Moreno
Translation by Verónica Dávila

For the institutionalized feminism that operates inside the state in departments, offices or ministries for women's rights, as well as for some sectors of the feminist and women social movements, public policies on gender equality—also known as public policies on women and gender—are the most effective strategy for transforming the unequal gender relations between men and women. Nevertheless, despite the apparently progressive ideal that supports them, they end up reproducing the sex-gender order, operating as technologies of gender.[1]

In order to comprehend this assertion, we must first clarify how we understand these public policies on women and gender and what we mean by technology of gender. In this chapter, I approach public policies with a cognitive focus and so define them as world builders, producers of world-views. Policies, as Pierre Muller maintains, carry a specific and distinctive idea of a problem, of a social group's representation, and of a "theory of social change."[2] "Thus, public policies contribute, on the one hand, to the configuration of a 'space of meaning' (public, of course) that provides a world-vision; and, on the other hand, they act, ultimately, like a 'system of beliefs' that guides public behavior."[3] Accordingly, any public policy on gender equality produces a vision of what it means to be a woman, an idea of the world that is organized around sexual differences, and a representation of a woman's place in that world, her interests, and desires, while also setting out the "woman problem" for which the state will prescribe a number of measures.

Moreover, Italian feminist Teresa de Lauretis' concept of "the technology of gender" is based on the idea that "gender 'is the set of effects produced in bodies, behaviors, and social relations,' in Foucault's words, by the deployment of 'a complex political technology.' But it must be said . . . that to think of gender as the product and the process of a number of social technologies, of techno-social or bio-medical apparati, is to have already gone beyond Foucault."[4] To think, therefore, of a public policy on gender equality as technology of gender is to affirm that that space of sense it would create— its structure of signification—would gender the behaviors and the social relations of certain bodies with vaginas. In summary, these policies would produce women.

In order to understand how this production occurs, it is important to keep in mind that for authors like Judith Butler, "'sex' is a regulatory ideal whose materialization is compelled and this materialization takes place (or fails to take place) through certain highly regulated practices. In other words, 'sex' is an ideal construct which is forcibly materialized through time. It is not a simple fact or static condition of a body, but a process whereby regulatory norms materialize 'sex' and achieve this materialization through a forcible reiteration of those norms."[5] In this way, the fulfillment of the sex/gender ideal is a highly regulated process that is constantly intervened by social arti- facts, which indicate men and women's roles, spaces, behaviors, and ways of relating to each other. This series of practices and issues is precisely the one articulated by public policies on gender equality. In so doing, public policies emit themselves as technologies of gender.

Following Pierre Muller's idea of the structure of signification, we can understand the ways in which public policies operate as technologies.[6] According to the French political scientist, the structure of signification is composed of values, images, algorithms, and norms. Through norms and images, modes of existence—situations—are produced which put women in contact with a concrete experience of the world. This experience, in turn, contains representations charged with positive or negative meanings about how a woman should act and how a woman should be. Finally, algorithms provide constructed logics for interpreting those images that justify and make desirable the adoption of certain norms (or solutions); not only are these pre- scriptions immediate, but they also regulate the limits of a women's embodi- ment. The structure of signification concerning "woman" posits a problem as well as that which would arguably be its "logical," most desirable solution, one which "any woman would choose" given the same circumstances. It is that element of persuasion that proves to be key for understanding women's exercise of self-regulation in accordance with the proposed way of acting, even in the absence of practices of submission. What public policy ultimately achieves, then, is the creation of a mirage of coincidence between the very aspirations, wishes, hopes, decisions, needs, and lifestyles of women, on the one hand, and predetermined governmental goals, on the other, thereby making normative conduct appear good, honorable, and above all, intentional, as though a product of one's own volition.[7]

Here, it's necessary to keep in mind that the structure of signification created by public policies on gender and equality corresponds to the logic of an identity politics; because of this, it constructs a narrative of oppression shared by members of the social collective ("women"), as well as an archetypal subject with specific features, characteristics, and experiences that are closely linked to that narrative. Therefore, such policies produce particular representations of what a woman should be and what her experiences should be like that reinforce an organization of a social life based on sexual difference, reaffirming the existence of a society divided into men and women, a gendered division of labor, the separation of public and private, the idea of compulsory heterosexuality, and gender stereotypes. Thus, public policies on gender equality, insofar as they are technologies of gender, deploy and articulate discursive and non-discursive practices that re-inscribe gender ideals until they materialize.

Hence, these policies do not break gender norms; instead they reproduce them even when they try to transgress them. In regard to this, de Lauretis states: "Paradoxically, therefore, the construction of gender is also effected by its deconstruction; that is to say by any discourse, feminist or otherwise, that would discard it as ideological misrepresentation. For gender, like the real, is not only the effect of representation but also its excess, what remains outside discourse."[8]

Thus far we have tried to establish that public policies on gender equality function as technologies of gender. But in the context of Third World countries, and in the case of Black, Indigenous, and poor "women," it would be more appropriate to talk about these policies as technologies of modern colonial gender, given that they presuppose and subject these "women" to an idea of gender that is based on a racial order.

This affirmation is supported by two arguments. The first is the decolonial theoretical argument, which indicates that gender is inextricable from race, as María Lugones affirms; the socio-sexual experience that constitutes the category "woman" has only been feasible for white women, who have historically participated in the institutionalization of spaces, roles, and imaginaries that are based on this rubric of sexual difference.[9] This has not been the experience of impoverished, Indigenous, Black, or impoverished Mestizas; they have performed, since colonial times, arduous labors in the fields and in the streets, an indicator that the female sex is not fragile, intended for a specific role assignment, or, much less, destined for the private sphere.[10] This difference in experience occurs because, since the period of colonial administration, non-white peoples have not been considered humans but beasts, and in order to have a lifestyle consistent with sex/gender norms, they would need to be considered humans. This founding difference of the colonial order has persisted in those nation-states that emerged after the wars of independence, which adopted the republican principles of equality and liberty but did not break with the hierarchies and privileges imposed by the colonial government.

The second argument is functional and shows how public policies were inserted into colonial devices, to use Foucault's language, like that of development. The public policies on women and gender that were designed and put into action in Colombia—including the following publications by the Departamento Nacional de Planeación [National Department of Planning]: from *La política nacional para la mujer campesina* [The National Policy for the Countryside Woman] to the *Política pública nacional de equidad de género para las mujeres* [The National Public Policy on Gender Equality for Women], and all those in between *Política integral para la mujer* [Integral Policy for Women]; *Política de participación y equidad de las mujeres* [The Policy for Women's Participation and Equality]; and the document *Avance y ajustes de la política de participación y equidad para las mujeres* [Advancement and Adjustments to the Policy for Participation and Equality of Women]—that this paper analyzes, were first introduced to the country as part of the apparatus of development and, more specifically, through its policies.[11] This explains why policies on gender equality adopted development policies' methodologies—including their set of indicators, categories of analysis, textual and narrative structure, and methods for follow up and evaluation—and why the policies on gender equality were designed in institutions like the National Office of Planning and with the technical support of international cooperation agencies involved in development.[12]

At first glance, these public policies on women and gender were dedicated exclusively to the task of balancing the unequal relations between men and women. However, their connection with the development apparatus once again suggests that their objectives were always connected with the regulation of race and gender. In this sense, it is important to recall that technologies, like Foucault states, are not permanent; instead their use is provisional and strategic, and their ends possibly multiple, but always dependent on the device through which they are articulated.[13] We can therefore deduce, using the arguments detailed here, that public policies on gender equality are technologies of modern colonial gender, whether due to the conceptual base from which they depart or the neocolonial devices, like that of development, which organize life in the countries of the Global South around race and gender hierarchies, through which these policies are produced, and toward which these policies are geared.

Development is a knowledge/power device created in Global North countries that has, in turn, been imposed on Third World countries. Its line of action involves, first, the application of a number of scientific instruments in order to know and evaluate the economies, populations, territories, and environment that make up the Global South, and second, the prescription of formulas or recipes that, in the form of plans and policies, allow the Global South countries to overcome their main problem: poverty.[14] However, the emergence of development as this matrix of a geopolitical regulation coincided with the last wave of decolonizing processes in the African continent during the 1950s. Because of this, authors like Arturo Escobar consider development to be nothing more than a device for re-colonization, and for the rearrangement of populations and of resource centers. In this regard, he states: "Although some of the terms of this definition might be more applicable to the colonial context strictly speaking, the development discourse is governed by the same principles; it has created an extremely efficient apparatus for producing knowledge about, and the exercise of power over, the Third World. This apparatus came into existence roughly in the period 1945 to 1955 [sic] and has not since ceased to produce new arrangements of knowledge and power, new practices, theories, strategies, and so on. In sum, it has successfully deployed a regime of government over the Third World, a space for 'subject peoples' that ensures certain control over it."[15]

In that vein, the development device produced a specific type of knowledge about women, the related discourse about them and their development. This knowledge then constructed and universalized a certain Western feminist viewpoint about women of the Third World and, along with it, the customary institutional image of the poor woman as victim, both of which are based on racist ideas about certain cultures and societies:

> Women in development texts do not, as they claim, describe the situation of Third World women, but rather the situation that they themselves produce. The depiction of "Third World Women" which results is one of poor women, living in hovels, having too many children, illiterate, and either dependent on a man for economic survival or impoverished because they have none. The important issue here is not whether this is a more or less accurate description of women, but who has the power to create it and make claims that it is, if not accurate, then the best available approximation. . . . The Women in Development discursive regime is not an account of the interests, needs, concerns, dreams of poor women, but a set of strategies for managing the problem which women represent to the functioning of development agencies in the Third World.[16]

Precisely, the Women in Development discourse implicitly suggests that the "woman problem" can be managed by creating public policies on women and gender, which, in turn, will elaborate a system of social classification for the development device, just as they did in Colombia. That is to say, the discourse also produces and administers representations, roles, spaces, and imaginaries about what it means to be a woman based on gender, race, class, and sexual hierarchies. Besides formulating the ideal of the emancipated woman as implicitly white and in line with Western values, this discourse also constructs the problem of woman as the laggard, the one delayed on the path to emancipation like someone who is attached to customs, the mother of more than three children, illiterate, submerged in poverty, and, of course, non-white.[17]

Thus, the development device and, therefore, the public policies that act as technologies of modern colonial gender harness already existent homogenizing and differentiating devices, which condense the tensions within post-independence societies governed by states that proclaim equality for all but fail to detach themselves from colonial hierarchies.[18] A number of discursive and non-discursive practices are interlinked through homogenizing devices that subjectivize/gender Indian, Black, and Mestiza as women. This process is then juxtaposed with the discourses and actions of racists/classist laws, customs, and institutions that form together a differentiating device. Public policies on women and gender then gather the tensions between these two kinds of devices; its corpus is like a hinge at which many experiences are homogenized under the category woman and, at the same time, difference is rewritten, new terms are created, and hierarchies of difference are reconstructed. Public policies on women and gender take as their point of departure and evaluation the social experience and emancipatory process of white women. This reduces a multiplicity of experiences to the binary logic of Woman/"woman."

TWO "WOMEN" AND A SINGLE PUBLIC POLICY

Public policies on gender equality produce two woman subjects, which we call Woman and "woman." In this paper, I follow Lugones' proposal of placing in quotes the subject considered a version or a copy.[19] The former subject is the original, the one usually named in the singular and without adjectives, the subject that fully condenses the feminine experience; it is the one that best embodies the "must be" of the gender norm. The latter one, which is almost always accompanied by adjectives like poor, Black, Indigenous, or countryside, is the former's failed version, the unsuccessful copy. This game of dual representation tends to go unnoticed. Although for some feminists like Elsa Dorlin, it generates some questions: "We could ask if dominant discursive techniques 'would not organize,' to certain extent their own failure. The performative dimension of sexual identities, but also of social or racial identities,

would be much more effective if they did not 'make' or 'fabricate' only dominant subjects. It is as if certain performances were proposed from the start as
original, authentic and real, while others paradoxical and inauthentic. Power
relations thus orchestrate the ontologization of certain performances through
a game of imitating and more or less copying the real Subject."[20]

This way of constructing reality is characteristic of colonial discourse and
the modern colonial discourse on gender. Colonial discourse and its devices
not only imposed a regime of knowledge/power and economic exploitation
on colonized people; they also imposed an organizing system of social life
based on sexual dimorphism, which, in the beginning, during the colonial
government, only normalized the lives of white men and women but subsequently, in post-independence republics, was applied to all inhabitants of the
former colonies. Therefore, non-white bodies were gendered. Nevertheless,
since this gendering intersected with a racial hierarchy, gender norms became
more complex, corresponding, at the levels of roles, spaces, and imaginaries,
with different criteria than those contemplated for white people.[21] "Within the
apparatus of colonial power, the discourses of sexuality and race relate in a
process of *functional overdetermination*, 'because each effect . . . enters into
resonance or contradiction with the others and thereby calls for a readjust-
ment or a reworking of the heterogeneous elements that surface at various
points.'"[22]

For example, the imaginaries that were related to women's sexual passivity or physical weakness with respect to heavy labor were incompatible with
those created for Black or Indigenous women, as they were seen as sexually
lascivious or usable as cattle.[23] "They were understood as animals in the
deep sense of 'without gender,' sexually marked as female, but without the
characteristics of femininity. Women racialized as inferior were turned from
animals into various modified versions of 'women' as it fit the processes of
Eurocentered global capitalism."[24]

Despite the differences, the two subjects were and sill are both called
women, because to name the experiences and affective relations of Black and
Indigenous people as the same as that of white women is part of a strategy
for normalizing difference; it is a way of imposing, controlling, and organizing processes of subjectification, social and affective relations, as well as the
distribution of labor and spaces. This way everything is contained within a
matrix coherent with the modern colonial system of gender.[25]

An additional aspect of the public policies on gender equality that allows
for the production of the original women subjects and its copies pertains to
their complicity with identity politics, which involves the construction of
a subject meant for vindication, a subject category (as mentioned above).
Problematically, the woman subject that emerges in public policy, like feminism's woman subject, is based solely and exclusively on white women's

experiences and expressions of oppression; "White feminist struggle became one against the positions, roles, stereotypes, traits, desires imposed on white bourgeois women's subordination. No one else's gender oppression was countenanced. They understood women as inhabiting white bodies but did not bring that racial qualification to articulation or clear awareness."[26]

Following Lugones, I affirm that the categorical logic of public policies erases the differences within the woman social group while also homogenizing experiences, with the result of hiding processes of the hierarchization wherein the dominant woman sector is made to represent the whole group.[27] If the sector giving meaning to the entire woman group is white, middle-class, and heterosexual, then the rest—Indigenous, Black, poor, lesbian, or heterosexual—are only eligible for a partial or incomplete representation.

This categorical logic is part of the binary operations typical of modern colonial thinking; the subaltern is thought of as the other when compared and measured against the parameters of the normative dominant subject which becomes the universal referent. This other, viewed as ontologically incomplete, should therefore be converted, reduced to the universal subject's terms; "According to the modern and binary colonial pattern, any element, in order to reach ontological fullness, fullness of being, should be equalized, that is, made commensurable by a foundational grid of reference or universal equivalent. This produces an effect: any manifestation of otherness will constitute a problem and will only stop being one once it is sifted by the equalizing grid, neutralizer of particularities, of idiosyncrasies."[28]

In practical terms, we can observe two types of accounts in public policies: one coded as occidental and emancipatory/feminist, and with a description of the situation of woman, her problems, and her goals tied to the categorical logic; and one narrated only in the form of a problem or exception. It is precisely this latter type that is coupled with an explanation of difference, in terms of culture and customs or region, which in Colombia's case, is a subtle way of marking racial difference. Notably, the narrative of exception becomes the question of poverty in the public policies of women and gender that are part of the development device. Poverty makes reference to dark women who are limited by their oppressed cultures. As Arturo Escobar points out with regards to Chandra Mohanty's critique of dominant approaches to Third World women: "Mohanty's critique applies . . . to mainstream development literature, in which there exists a veritable underdeveloped subjectivity endowed with features such as powerlessness, passivity, poverty, and ignorance, usually dark and lacking in historical agency."[29]

For example, an appeal to liberation and "advancement," in keeping with the style of the normative account, can be found in "The Policy on Women's Equality and Participation" from 1994. Note that the noun women is not accompanied by any adjectives: "Women's situation has improved significantly during the last 40 years. Its contribution to national development has been especially effective in three fields: education, demographic transition, and the labor market."[30] However, further down in the policy is the account of the laggard, which affixes the noun woman accompanied to the adjective "poor": "The decrease in fertility has not happened homogenously. Poor women with less education continue having more children: in 1985, when the national fertility rate was of 3.2 children per women in fertile age, those of non-poor women was 2.0, poor women's 3.7, and those in conditions of misery 4.5"[31]

The contrast between these accounts conveys the concept of mimesis, which, as Bhabha explains, is central to colonial discourse.[32] As we can see, public policies on women and gender construct two subjects that are positioned against each other in a confrontation of copies/versions versus originals. One subject is the original and embodies the point of reference, while the other is but a failed subject, a lacking subject, driven to resemble the original as much as possible, by the promise of, in this case, wellbeing, a better quality of life, a life free from violence, emancipation, and liberty. Therefore, these narrations perpetuate the westernization of this failed subject.

TWO WOMEN, A SINGLE TIMELINE

Interestingly, public policies on gender equality also maintain the original/copy binary in their descriptions of a given subject's temporal and spatial location. In their accounts, "woman" is presented as living in a past time, amongst archaic and traditional practices that have to be, given her perceived motionlessness and lack of agency, transformed from the outside. By contrast, Woman is described as a contemporary, transformed subject who, being completely emancipated from her oppressive past, casts herself towards the future. In this case, the image is one of a true subject with agency and the capacity for change. To paraphrase Fanon, these narrations aim to convert the "woman" as the white woman's past; the latter becomes the former's future, its fate.[33]

Let us take an illustrative example from the "Integral Policy for Women" ratified in 1992. The paragraph reproduced below shows how certain societies—in this case, those inhabiting Colombian regions characterized by a large Black and Indigenous presence and ways of living, in this case, those of poorer social groups—are located arbitrarily in the past. It establishes a correlation between past/discrimination/local culture necessary for validating the tale of future/emancipation/westernization as the moral response: "In certain strata and regions, the most rooted forms of discrimination against women based on past cultural patterns still linger. Nevertheless, said patterns keep prevailing in the most impoverished sectors of our population."[34]

The way in which public policies on gender equality construct a timeline or a trajectory for the emancipatory process of women is based on the modern idea of temporal non-simultaneity.[35] This idea implies that two societies that coexist in the same space need not coexist in the same time because their modes of economic and cognitive production apparently differ in evolutionary development. As Castro-Gómez has pointed out, "Modern Europe's mode of production of riches (capitalism) and knowledge (new science) is viewed as the criteria according to which it is possible to measure the temporal development of all other societies. Knowledge should then pass 'through various degrees' measured by a lineal scale—from primitive mentality to abstract thought; the same can be said of the mode of production of riches, which progresses from an economy of subsistence to a capitalist market economy."[36] This operation of the senses converts other worlds and societies into strongholds of the European past, a known and outgrown experience, negating its present and, of course, its existence.

Developmental feminism also engages a similar exercise, as the Indian feminist Chandra Mohanty has shown. Mohanty criticizes white Western feminism for representing its own version of the woman subject as the norm that Third World women should follow, and, at the same time, for presenting other women—Third World women—as poor, illiterate, and politically immature; "This average third world woman leads an essentially truncated life based on her feminine gender (read: sexually constrained) and being 'Third World' (read: ignorant, poor, uneducated, tradition-bound, domestic, family-oriented, victimized, etc.). This, I suggest, is in contrast to the (implicit) self-representation of Western women as educated, modern, as having control over their own bodies and sexualities, and the freedom to make their own decisions."[37]

The situating of "woman" in the past by recurring to a stereotype based on shortages, while white woman is cast in the present and promissory future in matters like education, professions, sexual liberty, and decision power in all aspects of social life, evidences a reordering of the time of colonial discourses, since it arbitrarily locates Black and Indigenous women as well as Mestizas in the past of the white woman, hiding coetaneous historical processes and going over geographical spaces and cultural contexts.[38] In this historical account, white Woman is located at the finishing line and becomes the universal referent. Placed somewhere on that line that allegedly follows the idea of progress, non-white and poor women's best option is to "advance," to follow the stages of white women's emancipation, to become white themselves. The denial of coevalness that undergirds developmental feminism is the negation of the other, the subaltern, in the present time, as only Woman can exist.

GEOGRAPHICAL METAPHORS

These public policies on gender equality not only position "woman" according to the unique, linear history of Woman; they also engage in spatial resettlement, an arbitrary rearrangement of frontiers that creates a stage of meaning for the subjects it produces.[39] While Woman is situated in central urban contexts, "woman" is located in peripheral, marginal or regional fields that evoke poverty and migration and insinuate certain racial groups and cultural traditions, especially when the field refers to a region. This manner of situating subjects reinforces hierarchies and differences, just as the apparatus of development's First, Second, and Third World classification or North/ South division does.

Indeed, "The development discourse inevitably contained a geopolitical imagination that has shaped the meaning of development for more than four decades. For some, this will to spatial power is one of the most essential features of development. . . . It is implicit in expressions such as First and Third World, North and South, center and periphery. The social production of space implicit in these terms is bound with the production of differences, subjectivities, and social orders."[40]

This hierarchization also manifests itself in the organization of national and local spaces, a phenomenon that can be explained by Pablo Gonzalez Casanova's concept of internal colonialism. According to González Casanova, national elites reproduce colonial practices and structures that recreate the same center-periphery geography of power within the interior of the nation-state, which in turn sanction the organization, control, and exploitation of particular territories and populations.[41] It should be noted that this spatial organization is based on racial differences. In using this spatial operation, public policies on gender equality maintain the binary machinery of colonial thought, since the center/periphery relation puts back at the center colonial dichotomies: savage/civilized, white/non-white, developed/underdeveloped, western/non-western, poverty/wealth. Thus, by extension, Woman corresponds to the center, civilization, whiteness, wealth, development, and the West, while "woman" corresponds to savagery, non-whiteness, underdevelopment, the non-west, the periphery, and poverty.

In the following two fragments from the "Integral Policy for Women" of 1992, we can observe the construction of said center-periphery geography of power centers, which recreates an internal Third World: (1) "In rural areas, 17% of households are female headed, with more acute poverty problems than in urban areas"; (2) "Actions and resources are concentrated specifically in the attention of poor women in rural and urban marginal areas."[42]

MAKING PUBLIC POLICIES WITH STEREOTYPES

Up to this point we have seen how public policies on woman and gender produce two women subjects, and how each one of them is located in a differentiated dimension of time and space following either the emancipatory or problematic/exceptional logic of its respective account. In the first account, a type of woman subject is created. To do so, certain features that are considered essential and apparently persist across time are underscored or placed at the forefront—"a type is any simple, vivid, memorable, easily grasped and widely recognized characterization in which a few traits are foregrounded and change or 'development' is kept at a minimum."[43]

The second account fixes and limits its subjects to one way of doing and being, constructing a narration based on stereotypes; "*stereotypes* get hold of the few 'simple, vivid, memorable, easily grasped, and widely recognized' characteristics about a person, *reduce* everything about the person to those traits, *exaggerate* and *simplify* them, and *fix* them without change or development to eternity. This is the process we described earlier. So, the first point is ster*eotyping reduces, essentializes, naturalizes and fixes 'difference.'"[44]

Constructing subjects as stereotypes implies flat outlines and a stabile description; this means that these subjects will always be described in the same way, through a process that privileges certain hypervisible characteristics and conceal others.[45] Furthermore, stereotyping also controls and normalizes individual difference by means of racial and gender labeling; what is odd is thus sublimated into a known category—a manageable category—in which demeanor and attitude always have the same explanation, even if they are contradictory: if you work a lot, you work like a Black person; if you work too little, you are lazy like a Black person. Lastly, there is the stereotype's predictability: all of its possible answers and actions in particular situations can be anticipated. In short, under the premise of a "profound knowledge" of the other, all uncertainty is removed.[46] This transforms the subject into a being that is objectified, limited, fixed to an idea about who s/he is. Any other circulating interpretation that makes possible other ways of seeing, listening, and imagining the subject is collapsed into the stereotype and permanently interrupted. As Frantz Fanon explains, "*wherever he goes, a black man remains a black man.*"[47]

Stuart Hall indicates the principal differences between a type and a stereotype: the type determines normalcy while the stereotype sets difference. That is to say, while the type points to those who fit in, who are on the inside, the stereotype denotes those who are excluded. Stereotypes tend to be more defined, setting well-drawn limits and remaining stable across time: "Stereotyping, in other words, is part of the maintenance of the social and symbolic order. It sets up a symbolic frontier between the 'normal' and the 'deviant,' the 'normal' and the 'pathological,' the 'acceptable' and the 'unacceptable,' what 'belongs' and what does not or is 'Other,' between 'insiders' and 'outsiders,' Us and Them."[48] Finally, stereotyping tends to occur where huge power inequalities exist, where one group has enough power to impose a regime of truth, its world vision of how people and society should be, and its values: hence their prevalence in colonial discourse.

In addition, the imposition of a stereotype on an "other" implies the negation of their humanity, insofar as their status as an agential subject with capacity to reason and make decisions goes unrecognized; neither their past nor their memory are acknowledged. This sets up, once again, colonial modernity's central dichotomy between the human and the non-human, where humanity is a condition only had by white people and a prerequisite for being considered men or woman.[49] The persistence of discursive practices that strip certain social groups of—like in the case of these public policies, impoverished, Indigenous, Afro, and Mestiza women—their humanity reaffirms the long duration of the modern colonial discourse on gender and exposes who the real woman subject is for the state, who it is that can embody the ideal type Woman, and who it is that can only aspire to be the stereotype "woman."

The reduction of one subject to a stereotype and the establishment of another subject as a type is the discursive recourse that enables these public policies on women and gender to present two accounts and yet maintain the internal coherence; it is what makes their accounts impervious, eternally parallel, and capable of representing disparate subjects despite them being grouped under the same designation.

CONCLUSION

National public policies for women and gender that were designed and instituted during the 1990s strategically showcase discursive and non-discursive practices that classify them as technologies of modern colonial gender. That is to say, these practices brought gendering processes that are intertwined with hierarchies of race, class, and sexuality, which is made evident in the way in which these policies constructed representations of the woman subject as well as integrated these representations into programs and projects formulated to solve "the women problem."

To be sure, though, in order to understand the importance of technologies of modern colonial gender, it is fundamental to remember that the colonial subjectification processes are not yet finished; they continue even today through these same public policies which constantly interpellate the subject. After all, it is only through their repetition that the norms are materialized. In this case, subjectivities are fractured by the "must be" of the white gender norm and the normative limits imposed by the racial hierarchy, which are also those of the class pyramid. Nowadays, along with school texts, the law, and constitutions, public policies, operating as technologies of modern colonial gender, fulfill the role that the "encomienda," the Indian right, and urbanity manuals once did.[50] All these technologies interconnect following a comprehension field that organizes the homogenizing and differentiating devices, which orders social life and state actions through the imposition of common categories and hierarchization.

It is worth saying that the fractured subject is always desiring, trying to embody the other subject of policy: the white/Woman, the fully realized gender norm in which body, roles, spaces, and imaginaries all cohere. This desire to Westernize is also "woman's" promise of emancipation; thus it is also constructed in the mirroring accounts that run parallel to public policy texts and materialize through the programs and projects that are prescribed as solutions to their problems.

Evidently, the modern colonial gender norm is dynamic and transforms itself according to geopolitical changes in the North/South relationship; or, one might even say, they are actualized. In this regard, technologies of modern colonial gender always undergo processes that re-code what it means to be a "woman"; this, at times, implies the exaltation of certain roles or the proscription of others, the revalorization of certain spaces, a change in attitude before certain tasks, or the popularization of some imaginary. Lugones already warned us that the modern colonial system produces as many versions of woman as it deems necessary to ensure the functioning of global capitalism.[51] This is possible because the tensions between gender, race, and class that cluster under the imposition of the woman category on colonized bodies blurs the lines of coherence that do exist in the white/women subject, the ontologized subject. Thus, the number of ways of administering the differences that gendering and racializing processes as well as social class produce is presented as infinite. Whether they are schizophrenic, contradictory, or painful, the important thing is to produce the "women" that the process of colonial capitalist exploitation needs.

NOTES

1. "Technologies of gender, therefore, would be tied to sociocultural practices, discourses, and institutions capable of creating 'effects of meaning' in the production

of male subjects and female subjects. In general, gender and sexual differences would be the result of representations and discursive practices." See Hortensia Moreno, "La noción de 'tecnologías de género' como herramienta conceptual en el estudio del deporte," *Revista Punto Género*, no. 1 (2011): 49.

2. Pierre Muller, *Las políticas públicas,* 2nd ed. (Bogotá: Universidad Externado de Colombia, 2006).

3. José Francisco Puello Socarrás, "La dimensión cognitiva en las políticas públicas, interpelación politológica," *Ciencia Política* 3 (2007): 85.

4. Teresa de Lauretis, *Technologies of Gender: Essays on Theory, Film, and Fiction,* 1st ed. (Bloomington: Indiana University Press, 1987), 3.

5.Judith Butler, *Bodies That Matter,* 1st ed. (New York/London: Routledge, 1993), 1–2.

6. The structure of signification of public policies articulates four levels of perception. "Values are the most fundamental representations about what is good and what is bad, desirable or disposable . . . ; norms define the differences between real perception and real desire. They define principles of action more than values do . . . ; algorithms are causal relations that express a theory of the action. They can be expressed in the form of 'if . . . then' . . . ; [and] images ('the young, dynamic, and modern farmer' . . .) are the implicit vectors of values, of norms, or even of algorithms. They are cognitive shortcuts that *make sense* immediately." See Muller, *Las políticas públicas*, 100 (emphasis in original).

7. Santiago Castro-Gómez, *Historia de la gubernamentabilidad I: Razón de Estado, liberalismo y Neo-liberalismo en Michel Foucault* (Bogotá: Siglo del Hombre Editores, 2010).

8. de Lauretis, *Technologies,* 3.

9. María Lugones, "The Coloniality of Gender," *Words & Knowledges Otherwise* 2, no. 2 (2008), https://globalstudies.trinity.duke.edu/sites/globalstudies.trinity.duke .edu/files/file-attachments/v2d2_Lugones.pdf.

10. Note that, in this chapter, references to impoverished Mestiza women and Mestiza do not refer to the formation of creole Mestizo elites or to the process of whitening among the *criollo* population, but to the "impure mixtures," by which I mean the offspring of the various ethno-racial groups that were dominated by the colonizers.

11. *Política nacional para la mujer campesina* (CONPES 2109) (Bogotá: Departamento Nacional de Planeación, 1984); *Política pública nacional de equidad de género para las mujeres* (CONPES 161) (Bogotá: Departamento Nacional de Planeación, 2013); *Política integral para la mujer* (CONPES 2626) (Bogotá: Departamento Nacional de Planeación, 1992); *Política de participación y equidad para las mujeres* (CONPES 2726) (Bogotá: Departamento Nacional de Planeación, 1994); *Avance y ajustes de la política de participación y equidad para las mujeres* (CONPES 2941) (Bogotá: Departamento Nacional de Planeación, 1997). Other public policies on gender equality that have been produced in Colombia include: *Política de salud para las mujeres "Salud para las Mujeres, Mujeres para la Salud"* (Resolución 1531) (Bogotá: Ministerio de Protección Social, 1992) and *Política para el desarrollo de la mujer rural* (Bogotá: Ministerio de Agricultura y Desarrollo Rural, 1994). The policies *Mujeres constructoras de paz y desarrollo* (Bogotá: Consejería Presidencial para

la Equidad de la Mujer, 2003) and *La política pública nacional de equidad de género para las mujeres* (CONPES 161) (Bogotá: Departamento Nacional de Planeación, 2013) appeared in the twenty-first century.

12. "The development discourse defined a perceptual field structured by grids of observation, modes of inquiry and registration of problems, and forms of intervention; in short, it brought into existence a space defined not so much by the ensemble of objects with which it dealt but by a set of relations and a discursive practice that systematically produced interrelated objects, concepts, theories, strategies, and the like." See: Arturo Escobar, *Encountering Development: The Making and Unmaking of the Third World,* 1st ed. (Princeton: Princeton University Press, 1995), 42. Since the 1980s, national governments have made various attempts to fulfill the compromises they signed at different summits and international forums. They include: The Colombian Counsel for the Integration of Women into Development that was held in 1980; the National Department of Planning's institution of a position responsible for "the Women issue" between 1984 and 1989; and the Convention on the Elimination of All Forms of Discrimination against Women's Coordination and Control Committee, which was created in 1990 and included representatives from the Ministries of Labor, Education, and Health, the DNP (National Department of Planning), the ICBF (Colombian Family Welfare Institute), and two of the most important organizations on women's interests. See: Marta Cecilia Londoño López, "Políticas públicas para las mujeres en Colombia. Interlocución movimiento social de mujeres-estado-movimiento social de mujeres. El caso de Cali" (Master's Thesis, Universidad Nacional de Colombia Bogotá, 1999), 67. During President César Gaviria Trujillo's administration, the Presidential Counsel for Youth, Women and Family was created. It pushed the formulation and implementation of the *Política integral para la mujer* with the technical and financial support of the IBD and Unicef. It is worth noting that this policy was designed by known experts in the field of development: Cecilia López, Elsy Bonilla, Gabriel Misas, Absalón Machado, and Hernán Jaramillo. Importantly, the publication, in 1992, 1994, and 1997, of those public policies on women and gender that constructed the predominant pathway forward for women's emancipation coincided with the implementation of the first development policies.

13. "Devices are capable of consolidating together a multiplicity of techniques, abstracting them from the particular objectives they had when they were invented and putting them to work according to completely different objectives. . . . Foucault states that power techniques are 'transferable' (*Übertragbar*), given that their 'use' is not linked substantially to any objective in particular, and nor does it depend on any institution or cultural context. That is to say, any technique can be isolated from the objectives it had in a particular historical moment and put to function in strategic fields that operate with different objectives." See: Castro-Gómez, *Historia de la gubernamentabilidad I*, 36.

14. In order to understand how poverty is constructed as a world problem, this quote is key: "The perception of poverty on a global scale was nothing more than the result of a comparative statistical operation, the first of which was carried out only in 1940." See: Wolfgang Sachs, "The Archaeology of the Development Idea," *Interculture* 23, no. 4 (1990): 9. Almost by fiat, two-thirds of the world's peoples

were transformed into poor subjects in 1948, when the World Bank defined as poor those countries with an annual per capita income below $100. And if the problem was one of insufficient income, the solution was clearly economic growth. Thus, poverty became an organizing concept and the object of a new problematization. As in the case of any problematization, that of poverty brought into existence new discourses and practices that shaped the reality to which they referred. See: Michel Foucault, *The History of Sexuality, vol 2: The Use of Pleasure*, trans. Robert Hurley (New York: Vintage Books, 1985). That the essential trait of the Third World was its poverty and that the solution was economic growth and development became self-evident, necessary, and universal truths." See: Escobar, *Encountering Development*, 23–24.

15. Escobar, *Encountering Development*, 9.

16. Adele Mueller, "Power and Naming in the Development Institution: The 'Discovery' of Women in Peru," presented in the 14th Annual Third World Conference, Chicago, 1987, 4, translated by Verónica Dávila. Cited in Spanish by the author.

17. We should bring to the discussion the following quote: "In the colonies the economic infrastructure is also a superstructure. The cause is effect: You are rich because you are white, you are white because you are rich." See: Frantz Fanon, *The Wretched of the Earth,* trans. Richard Philcox (New York: Grove Press, 2004).

18. Daniel Díaz explains how race, education, and development functioned strategically to "normalize" the population. This normalization consisted in producing binaries: "To normalize life meant to binarize it (normal/abnormal), and each biopolitical strategy had its own normalization or binarization: the racial strategy operated on the useful/useless distinction, the educational strategy worked on the cultured/uncultured dichotomy, and lastly, the great development strategy invented a new cursed couple: development/underdevelopment . . . all the singularity of otherness was reduced under a new inverted image of a despotic Self ." These strategies did not work in a separate or orderly manner; instead they were superimposed on one another like layers, making it very difficult to know where one starts and the other ends. See: Daniel Díaz, "Raza, pueblo y pobres: las tres estrategias biopolíticas del siglo XX en Colombia (1873–1962)," in *Genealogías de la Colombianidad: Formaciones discursivas y las tecnologías de gobierno en los siglos XIX y XX,* eds. Santiago Castro-Gómez and Eduardo Restrepo (Bogotá: Editorial Pontificia Universidad Javeriana, 2008), 66.

19. Lugones, "Coloniality of Gender."

20. Elsa Dorlin, *Sexo, género y sexualidades*, 1st ed. (Buenos Aires: Ediciones Nueva Visión, 2009), 102.

21. "The construction of the colonial subject in discourse, and the exercise of colonial power through discourse, demands an articulation of forms of difference—racial and sexual. Such an articulation becomes crucial if it is held that the body is always simultaneously (if conflictually) inscribed in both the economy of pleasure and desire and the economy of discourse, domination and power." See: Hommi Bhabha, *The Location of Culture,* 1st ed. (New York/London: Routledge, 1994), 67.

22. Ibid., 74 (emphasis in original).

23. Lugones explains the fundamentals of the modern colonial system of gender: "I understand the dichotomous hierarchy between the human and the non-human as the central dichotomy of colonial modernity. Beginning with the colonization of

the Americans and the Caribbean, a hierarchical, dichotomous distinction between human and non-human was imposed on the colonized in the service of Western man. It was accompanied by other dichotomous hierarchical distinctions, among them that between men and women. This distinction became a mark of the human and a mark of civilization. Only the civilized are men or women. Indigenous peoples of the Americas and enslaved Africans were classified as not humans in species—as animals, uncontrollably sexual and wild. The European, bourgeois, colonial, modern man became a subject/agent, fit for rule, for public life and ruling, a being of civilization, heterosexual, Christian, a being of mind and reason. The European, bourgeois woman was not understood as his complement, but as someone who reproduced race and capital through her sexual purity, passivity, and being homebound in service of the white, European, bourgeois man." See: María Lugones, "Toward a Decolonial Feminism," *Hypatia* 25, no. 4 (2010): 743.

24. Lugones, "Coloniality of Gender," 13.

25. Regarding the effects of nomination or categorization Edward Said states: "Something patently foreign and distant acquires, for one reason or another, a status more rather than less familiar. One tends to stop judging things either as completely novel or as completely well-known; a new median category emerges, a category that allows one to see new things, things seen for the first time, as versions of a previously known thing. In essence such a category is not so much a way of receiving new information as it is a method of controlling what seems to be a threat to some established view of things . . . The threat is muted, familiar values impose themselves, and in the end the mind reduces the pressure upon it by accommodating things to itself as either 'original' or 'repetitious.'" See: Edward Said, *Orientalism* (New York: Pantheon, 1978); quoted in Bhabha, *Location*, 100).

26. Lugones, "Coloniality of Gender," 15.

27. In the construction of categories, the dominant sectors, in terms of social power, are assumed to exhaust the entire category, covering intracategorical power relations. Those subordinated sectors inside the category lack the capacity to give the category any meaning (ibid.).

28. Rita Laura Segato, "Colonialidad y patriarcado moderno: expansión del frente estatal, modernización y la vida de las mujeres," in *Tejiendo de otro modo: Feminismo, epistemología y apuestas decoloniales en Abya Yala*, eds. Yuderkys Espinosa Miñoso, Diana Gómez, and Karina Ochoa (Colombia: Editorial Universidad del Cauca, 2014), 82–83.

29. Escobar, *Encountering Development,* 8.

30. Política de participación y equidad para las mujeres.

31. Ibid.

32. As colonial mimicry seeks to transform the other to a recognizable other, it names the other as women, male, Black, Indigenous, employing the categories that the colonial discourse organizes. However, this other always overflows the category imposed or fails to fulfill it. This failure, lacking, or excess is the difference that makes the colonized subject recognizable as such, since it is always compared with the original subject. Socially pressured to reach the full resemblance, the colonized subject is always condemned to fail. See: Bhabha, *Location*.

33. "Fanon writes from that temporal caesura, the time-lag of cultural difference, in a space between the symbolization of the social and the 'sign' of its representation of subjects and agencies. Fanon destroys two time schemes in which the historicity of the human is thought. He rejects the 'belatedness' of the black man because it is only the opposite of the framing of the white man as universal, normative—the white sky all around me: the black man refuses to occupy the past of which the white man is the future." Ibid., 236–37.

34. *Política integral para la mujer.*

35. Johannes Fabian, *Time and the Other: How Anthropology Makes its Object* (New York: Columbia University Press, 1983). Sinclair Thomson's affirmation regarding the understanding of time in the work of Silvia Rivera Cusicanqui is interesting: "In the temporal plane, it posits the simultaneous coexistence of a multiplicity of historical layers, 'horizons,' or 'cycles.' This offers the conceptual framework for her work: 'a coupling of diachronic contradictions of diverse depths that emerge on the surface of contemporaneity, and therefore, cross through the coetaneous spheres of the modes of production, the state policy systems, and the ideologies anchored in cultural hegemony.'" See Sinclair Thomson, "Claroscuro andino: Nubarrones y destellos en la obra de Silvia Rivera Cusicanqui," in *Violencias (re) encubiertas en Bolivia* (Bolivia, La Paz: La Mirada Salvaje, 2010), 11.

36. Santiago Castro-Gómez, *La hybris del punto cero ciencia, raza e ilustración en la Nueva Granada (1750–1816),* 2nd ed. (Bogotá: Editorial Pontificia Universidad Javeriana, 2010), 36.

37. Chandra Mohanty, "Under Western Eyes," *boundary 2* 12, no 3 (1984): 337.

38. On stereotypes: For Bhabha, the stereotype is the primary point of subjectification in the colonial discourse: it's a fixed and detained way of representation and by being ambivalent the actions of the colonized subject will always be reduced to the same explanation. There is no possibility for change. See Bhabha, *Location;* On time: "The modern concept of time constructed a worldwide alterity based on a temporal scale that located populations and territories in relation to the new and the modern. This understanding allowed for the construction of a world order through civilizatory processes during different periods and in different ways, but always based on the same logocentric pattern of mediation A/not A, Civilized/Barbaric, Developed/Underdeveloped, White/non-White. Here is where time as world organizer gains sense, and it is here where the illusion of a universal history based on differentiated processes makes sense, but only according to the same evolutionary line." See: Andrés Arévalo, "La configuración temporal del orden mundial: una mirada moderno/colonial," *Trabajos y ensayos,* no. 9, (2009): 4.

39. In order to understand the social, political, and cultural production of spaces and frontiers, Edward Said's concept of imaginative geographies is very useful: "It is perfectly possible to argue that some distinctive objects are made by the mind, and that these objects, while appearing to exist objectively, have only a fictional reality. A group of people living in a few acres of land will set up boundaries between their land and its immediate surroundings and the territory beyond, which they call 'the land of the barbarians.' In other words, this universal practice of designating in one's mind a familiar space which is 'ours' and an unfamiliar space beyond 'ours' which is 'theirs'

is a way of making geographical distinctions that can be entirely arbitrary. I use the word 'arbitrary' here because imaginative geography of the 'our land-barbarian land' variety does not require that the barbarians acknowledge the distinction. It is enough for 'us' to set up these boundaries in our own minds; 'they' become 'they' accordingly, and both their territory and their mentality are designated as di□erent from 'ours' . . . The geographic boundaries accompany the social, ethnic, and cultural ones in expected ways." See: Said, Orientalism, 54.

40. David Slater, "The Geopolitical Imagination and the Enframing of Development Theory," *Transactions of the Institute of British Geographers* 18, no. 4 (1993), quoted in Escobar, *Encountering Development,* 9.

41. Pablo González Casanova, "Colonialismo interno (una redefinición) in *Conceptos y fenómenos fundamentales de nuestro tiempo* (Mexico City: Instituto de Investigaciones Sociales, Universidad Nacional Autónoma de México, 2003), http://conceptos.sociales.unam.mx/conceptos_final/412trabajo.pdf.

42. *Política integral para la mujer.*

43. Richard Dyer, *Gays and Film* (London: British Film Institute, 1977), 28.

44. Stuart Hall, "The Spectacle of the 'Other,'" in *Representation: Cultural Representations and Signifying Practices*, ed. Stuart Hall (London: London Sage Publications and Open University, 1997), 258 (emphasis in original).

45. "[T]he primary point of subjectification in colonial discourse . . . The stereotype is not a simplification because it is a false representation of a given reality. It is a simplification because it is an arrested, fixated form of representation that, in denying the play of difference (that the negation through the Other permits), constitutes a problem for the *representation* of the subject" See: Bhabha, *Location,* 75 (emphasis in original).

46. "The subjects of the discourse are constructed within an apparatus of power which *contains*, in both senses of the word, an 'other' knowledge—a knowledge that is arrested and fetishistic and circulates through colonial discourse as that limited form of otherness that I have called stereotype." See: Bhabha, *Location,* 77–78 (emphasis in original).

47. Frantz Fanon, *Black Skin, White Masks,* trans. Richard Philcox (London, Grove Press, 2008), 150 (emphasis in original). It is important to note that the production of subjects as stereotypes has also been criticized by postcolonial feminists like Chandra Mohanty, who, in a feminist literary review of the so-called "Third World Women," questions the arbitrary attribution of characteristics and problematics based on the universalist style of Eurocentric presuppositions: "Third World women as a group or category are automatically and necessarily defined as: religious (read 'not progressive'), family-oriented (read 'traditional'), legal minors (read 'they-are-still-not-conscious-of-their rights'), illiterate (read 'ignorant'), domestic (read 'backward') and sometimes revolutionary (read 'their-country-is-in-a-state-of-war-they-must-fight!')." See: Mohanty, "Under Western Eyes," 352.

48. Hall, "Spectacle," 258.

49. Lugones, "Decolonial Feminism."

50. "The long process of subjectification of the colonized toward adoption/internalization of the men/women dichotomy as a normative construction of the social—a

mark of civilization, citizenship, and membership in civil society—was and is constantly renewed." See: ibid., 748.

51. María Lugones, "Heterosexualism and the Colonial/Modern Gender System," *Hypatia* 22, no. 1 (2007): 203.

PART III

Decolonial Interpretations of Violence toward Women

Chapter 7

Notes on the Coloniality of Militarization and Feminicidal Violence in Abya Yala

Sarah Daniel and Norma Cacho
Translation by Jennifer Vilchez

For us, racism is the theory and structure of power that justifies colonialist ideology and colonization.[1] Five hundred years ago, our continent was invaded, the Indigenous people were subjugated or eliminated, and the transatlantic slave trade unfolded with the purpose of expanding the capitalist markets of European empires. Human exploitation was justified by a racist system organized to dominate and oppress non-European populations. Centuries of colonization have shaped the structures of Abya Yala societies, their socio-political structures, ideologies, and subjectivities.

If the historical period of colonization has ended, colonialism as a system of power—coloniality—has not; it continues in our way of perceiving reality and building social relationships, in our bodily aesthetics, in the racialization of the gendered division of labor, in the control of territories and populations, and especially in the multiple forms of violence experienced by racialized groups, particularly women.

Coloniality established colonialism; its process, according to Quijano, originates in the colonial, but also continues to be a fundamental and permanent element of the system of power that is linked to racist power relations. Coloniality produces new patterns of social domination and is based on a concept of race that goes beyond ethnocentrism and the racial domination of non-Europeans by Europeans and establishes a difference between who is considered human and who is considered not human (non-Europeans are thought of as non-human or semi-human), justifying capitalist exploitation.[2]

For María Lugones, coloniality is a system of classification that sorts people in relation to both the coloniality of power and the coloniality of gender, as well as a process of dehumanizing the colonized population.[3] Coloniality is an axis in the system of power that permeates all control over sex, collective authority, labor, subjectivity/intersubjectivity, production of knowledge, and work.

Today, colonialism and coloniality underpin new forms of neoliberal capitalism, the globalization of one model of thought, social constructs, and ways of living. In this neo-colonialism, racism is the basis for the new economic world order, neoliberal policies, and the expansion of military industry, all of which impose an idea of "development" that destroys peoples' autonomy and self-determination, further impoverishes historically marginalized populations, and yields global violence and devastation. We consider it important to contribute to the feminist movement an anti-racist and decolonial analysis, so as not to forget where we come from and where we want to go: toward an Abya Yala free from violence and classist, colonial, and heteropatriarchal domination. Thus, from a decolonial feminist perspective, we propose to address feminicidal violence in Abya Yala, particularly in Mexico and Brazil, to broaden the analysis beyond the traditional focus on gender and patriarchy and understand feminicidal violence as an instrument of control within a system of domination where patriarchy, racism, capitalism, and colonialism are co-constructed and sustained. We seek to understand how controlling Black and Indigenous women's bodies and territories is part of a military strategy rooted in colonialism. Like the coloniality of gender, which is a process of dehumanizing racialized women, control over Black and Indigenous women's bodies and territories conspires with militarization to promote feminicidal violence as a military strategy for colonizing and neo-colonizing Abya Yala.

A SHORT DEFINITION OF FEMINICIDE

Jane Caputi and Diana E. H. Russell define femicide as

> the extreme end of a continuum of antifemale terror that includes a wide variety of verbal and physical abuse, such as rape, torture, sexual slavery (particularly in prostitution), incestuous and extrafamilial child abuse, physical and emotional battery, sexual harassment (on the phone, in the streets, at the office, and in the classroom), genital mutilation (clitoridectomies, excision, infibulations), unnecessary gynecological operations (gratuitous hysterectomies), forced heterosexuality, forced sterilization, forced motherhood (by criminalizing contraception and abortion), psychosurgery, denial of food to women in some cultures,

cosmetic surgery, and other mutilations in the name of beautification. Whenever these forms of terrorism result in death, they become femicides.[4]

These authors' definition of femicide as a continuum of violence caused by patriarchy has become a reference point.[5] To speak of feminicide in Mexico is to refer to the violent deaths of women that were most prevalent in Ciudad Juárez, Chihuahua, a place that became a symbol of feminicidal violence in the 1990s. The extreme violence, brutality, cruelty, and torture inflicted on the bodies of the murdered women spoke of an unprecedented situation, forcing individuals to speak not of the "dead women of Juarez," but of "feminicide."

Feminist anthropologist Marcela Lagarde, translating "femicide" as *feminicidio* (feminicide), defines it as "the set of crimes against humanity that contains the violations, kidnappings and disappearances of girls and women within a framework of institutional collapse. It is a fractured rule of law that favors impunity. Feminicide is a state crime."[6] Lagarde states that "feminicide is the gravest visible portion of the violence against girls and women; it occurs as a culmination of a situation characterized by the repeated and systematic violation of women's human rights."[7] This assertion claims that feminicide is, first, a hate crime against women based on their gender, and, second, the culmination of a series of violent acts, which women experience continuously over the course of their lives.

Lagarde's definition of feminicide seeks to understand a phenomenon that is proliferating throughout Mexico. For several years, the number of feminicides in Mexico has grown at an alarming rate. Though the statistics vary by source, an estimated 34,176 women were violently murdered over the last 25 years and approximately 7,000 of these deaths occurred between 2005 and 2009, demonstrating the exponential growth in the number of cases. According to official figures, 1,728 women were murdered between January of 2009 and June of 2010; only 40 of these cases have been brought to trial and still, especially since the "war on drug trafficking" was launched by former President Felipe Calderón (2006–2012), the number of feminicides continues to increase.[8]

However, Lagarde does not include in her treatment of feminicide any analysis of its relationship to racism, like Jill Radford and Diana Russell do. For them, there are differences in the conditions of violence that Black women and white women face, that is, differences in the causes, effects, and consequences of feminicide: "femicide has many different forms: for example, racist femicide (when Black women are killed by white men); homophobic femicide, or lesbicide, (when lesbians are killed by heterosexual men). . . ."[9]

In addition to accounting for race and sexuality, Radford and Russell outline the contradictions and racist practices of white hegemonic feminism, which treats sexual violence as though it were a homogenous experience:

> Black women have had to insist that attention be paid to the complex interactions between racism and sexism. White feminists have had to be told how racism compounds and shapes black women's experiences of sexual violence—how, for example, racism and misogyny are often inseparable dimensions of the violence.[10]

Lagarde's "omission" of feminicide's racial differentiation can be attributed to national differences in the level of institutionalized racism. For example, the South African policies of racial segregation and apartheid made racism visible, whereas the politics of miscegenation in Mexico camouflages racism and makes it more difficult to discern.

Nevertheless, this comparison also illustrates the approach to feminicide and feminicidal violence that is most commonly used: what we could call the traditional approach. Several feminists of Abya Yala have been trained in this traditional school of thought, presuming a shared experience of gender oppression effected by patriarchy. The classical approach to violence and feminicide, which focuses its analyses solely on a matrix of patriarchal power, implies a hierarchy of violence characteristic of the modern western gender matrix. This is an example of what Kimberlé Crenshaw calls over-inclusion: "the occasion in which a problem or condition that is particularly or disproportionately visited on a subset of women is simply claimed as a women's problem."[11] That is, problems that may reflect an intersection of various oppressions are considered only in relation to gender oppression, without taking into account the role of racism, as in the case of hegemonic feminist analyses of feminicide.

The classist and racist dimension of traditional feminist theory was exposed by Black feminists in the United States including bell hooks and the Combahee River Collective, who critiqued the homogenization of women under a shared experience of subjugation and sexism that emphasizes patriarchy as the only system of oppression at work. This traditional position makes Black women, women of color, and impoverished women's experiences of racism and classism invisible, re-inscribing that hegemonic tendency to hierarchize the needs of women according to a dominant white, bourgeois, and heterosexual matrix of power. bell hooks questions feminism's subject "woman": predominately representing middle-to-upper class white feminist women, it departs from other women's realities and needs, homogenizes the feminist subject, and thus excludes other impoverished and racialized women's realities.[12] Bourgeois white feminists strategically maintain the supremacy of the "woman" subject, avoiding having to question their own class and racial privileges while simultaneously invisibilizing the consequences of racism and poverty in the construction of all other women subjects. For bell hooks, the subject "woman" must be re-constructed from the intersection of gender, race, and class oppressions if it is ever to represent an actor of counter-hegemonic social and political change.

Thus, the traditional approach to feminicides, with its hegemonic and whitened category of "woman," has as its limit the invisibility of experiences of racialized and impoverished women in Abya Yala and the complexity of the violence to which they may be subjected. This approach also prevents us from understanding the multiple causes of the feminicide phenomenon and, above all, from recognizing the bodies that are most at risk: dark, racialized, impoverished, and, in the eyes of the system, disposable bodies. Indeed, as the events in Abya Yala show us, feminicides happen primarily against Indigenous and Black women during territorial disputes.

REPRESENTATIONS OF FEMINICIDAL
VIOLENCE IN BRAZIL AND MEXICO

In Brazil, according to a 2015 mapping of violence, 4,762 women were violently murdered in 2013 alone.[13] This number translates to 13 feminicides per day and more than 60,000 women who suffered feminicidal violence such as physical, psychological, and sexual violence or torture.

In general, feminicidal violence increases every year and primarily targets afro-Brazilian women. In Brazil, the feminicide rate in 2013 was 4.8 feminicides per 100,000 women, the fifth highest in the world according to the World Health Organization.[14] Feminicidal violence is most prevalent in impoverished regions such as the Brazilian northeast, but large cities such as Rio de Janeiro and Sao Paulo also suffer from it. However, it is in the northernmost state of Roraima, which borders Venezuela, where the highest rate of feminicide exists. In addition, from 2003 to 2013, the number of Black women murdered there increased by 54.2%, from 1,864 to 2,875.[15] Therefore, in Brazil, feminicides not only manifest the extreme violence inherent to its patriarchal system; they also express the deadly rage of racism and colonialism faced by impoverished Black women.

Although the preponderance of feminicide in the north of Mexico has been addressed, the number of cases elsewhere in the Mexican Republic continues to rise, with both Chiapas and the State of Mexico recording gradual increases. According to the National Citizens Observatory on Feminicide, 1,485 women were murdered in Chiapas between 2000 and 2004.[16] The Attorney General of the State of Chiapas registered 612 cases in the period from 1994 to 2004, contrasting with the Chamber of Deputies' Special Commission on Feminicide's numbers, which count 1,456 women who were murdered between 2002 and 2004 only.[17] Based on the figures reported by the Special Commission, we can deduce that during that two-year period alone, an average of 2 women were murdered per day in Chiapas.

Between 2013 and 2015, around 7,296 women were murdered, which represented an important increase in incidences of feminicide compared to previous years.[18] It should be noted that the highest numbers of reported feminicides come from regions with high economic and social marginalization, such as the State of Guerrero, Chihuahua, and Mexico, as well as from zones wrought with territorial disputes and political conflict, particularly the State of Chiapas, which is also extremely impoverished.[19]

Following Mercedes Olivera, who defines "feminicide and the feminicidal violence that it produces as a part and direct expression of the structural violence of the neoliberal social system," we consider feminicidal violence to be intrinsically linked to the racist, capitalist, neoliberal system, which causes extreme poverty, destroys social networks, causes migratory and/or forced displacements, and exacerbates violence through class and colonial relations.[20] In this sense, we understand feminicides as situations of systemic violence occurring within an environment that not only allows for, legitimizes, and minimizes the significance of this violence, but also reproduces and normalizes its own structural conditions so that it manifests as an all-encompassing reality. We think it is necessary to explain the dynamics of feminicidal violence within a framework that attends to the numerous, concurrent, and intersecting uses of violence that impact the lives of women who, insofar as they are linked to colonial, patriarchal, and capitalist power structures, are part of a continuous process of violence that reaches its climax in the murder of women.

If we are to understand the mechanisms that make Indigenous and Black women more vulnerable to feminicidal violence, then it is not enough to refer only to the classical markers of patriarchal domination; we must also understand these markers and their functions alongside racism, capitalism, colonialism, as well as what María Lugones has called the coloniality of gender.[21] For Lugones, the logic undergirding the modern gender system and its categories is a colonial logic. This categorical logic fragments social reality into monolithic, impervious categories, which are distinct from one another. Categories are then constituted by those in power, bringing about the homogenization and intra-categorical simplification of "women." As an effect of categorical logic, "woman," for example, signifies "white-bourgeois-heterosexual woman." Subsequently, any analysis that embraces "woman" as the subject of a coalition fighting against feminicide is hegemonic because the category's signified reality does not correspond to those of racialized and impoverished women such as Indigenous, Black, and migrant women.[22]

Aníbal Quijano defines the coloniality of power as a set of material, symbolic, and economic dominations that originated in the colonization of Abya Yala. According to Quijano, this colonial matrix is central to social relations of power, particularly those of race and gender. For this reason, the colonial matrix violates Indigenous and Black women, positioning them at the margins of modernity.[23]

For the decolonial feminists, Yuderkys Espinosa-Miñoso and Lugones, it is important to analyze the modern, colonial, gender system and rethink violence against racialized women.[24] In doing so, they reveal the coloniality of gender as upholding the concept of "woman" while on a search to construct a new subject of feminism outside the modern colonial system of gender. Lugones analyzes the colonial construction of gender based on a human/non-human dichotomy in which "women" means white, heterosexual, and bourgeois women.[25] When Black and Indigenous women are not considered human, but rather the female counterparts to the males of their race, they are not "women." Lugones refers to this logic that dehumanizes racialized women as the coloniality of gender.[26]

In traditional analyses of feminicide, "woman" is considered a homogeneous category; its universal and hegemonic application, therefore, reinforces the western modern episteme's expansion. To reassert Ochy Curiel, "feminists of African descent and in particular black feminists critique the category 'woman' for its homogenization, decontextualization and the way in which it invisibilizes its relation with race. 'Woman' does not exist, she is a Eurocentric myth."[27]

Defining feminicide as, in the most colloquial sense, the murder of women, reveals a generic etymological construction that does not take into account the racialization and coloniality of gender. If "woman" in the dominant perspective refers to white woman, then feminicide denotes the murder of white woman. Consequently, in order for us to have a more complex analysis of the feminicidal violence against Black and Indigenous women, we must analyze feminicide within its colonial matrix.

If we consider feminicidal violence in the cumulative sense, such that structural violence against women reaches its climax in their murder, we can consider it to be direct expressions of the violent, heteropatriarchal, colonial, and neoliberal capitalist system that, through misogynistic and racist practices, feeds wars, poverty, militarization, and the accumulation of territory—namely, the bodies of racialized women and land—by dispossession.

This set of oppressions constitutes a racist, heteropatriarchal, colonial, capitalist system of power in its neoliberal phase. Within this system of power, these oppressions interact: they nourish and influence each other, and they exert force over one another. Each of their various expressions of violence is a weapon that maintains and reproduces this system of power and its domination. This system of power was and continues to be built on continuous colonialism: it took root during colonization and colonial capitalism, and now continues to develop with the neo-liberal phase of colonialism and coloniality. Historically, feminicidal violence has been executed against Black and Indigenous women as a means to control the colonial power system; currently, it also has characteristics specific to contemporary neoliberal globalization.

Consequently, from a decolonial feminist standpoint, in order to understand the complexity of feminicidal violence, and particularly that which is exercised toward Indigenous and Black women, we have to reflect on the colonial construction of gender.

THE COLONIALITY OF GENDER IN BRAZIL AT A GLANCE

Brazil, an extremely racist country, and its racial democracy, have been plagued by institutional racism since the beginning of colonization in 1500. Afro-Brazilian authors like Abadías do Nascimento and Lélia Gonzales criticize widely the concept of racial democracy.[28] Brazilian colonial racism is rooted in luso-tropicalism, an ideology developed by Gilberto Freyre based on two assumptions: that, as history allegedly testifies, human beings in the tropics are ultimately unable to build civilizations—the "savages" of Africa and the Indigenous people of Brazil are, in this view, living proof of that reality—and that the Portuguese, on the contrary, would have positive results; they would be able to create not only an advanced civilization, but also a true racial paradise on colonized lands.[29] This glorified portrait of the tropical Portuguese civilization depends in large part on a theory of *misgenação*, the biological miscegenation of Blacks, Indigenous peoples, and whites, which aimed to establish the "morenidade," a play on words between *moreno* (dark skin) and *modernidad* (modernity).[30] In doing so, *misgenação* actually hides the structural racism of Brazil, invisiblizing African descent through a whitening process of Brazilians' skin color and African culture.

The myth of racial democracy, which defines the Brazilian subject as the product of a fusion of African, Indigenous, and European peoples, constitutes a foundation in the construction of Brazilian identity. But in racial democracy, given the colonial matrix, its relations of power, and its racial domination, mestizaje and *miseginação* stand for whitening and anti-Blackness. That the Atlantic slave trade dispossessed African people of their humanity cannot be erased from history. That is to say, the importation of slaves for economic exploitation was justified by the dehumanization of Black people whose only role in colonial society was to exist as labor power.

Within this colonial matrix, Black women were not considered women; due to the human/non-human dichotomy, they were considered subhuman. With their bodies and lives, Black women paid for the construction of Brazil during the time of colonization and continue to pay for it now; exploitation and sexual violence are but tools of colonial and heteropatriarchal domination. On July 2, 1975, Black women denounced this process of colonization in a manifesto:

> Black women received a cruel inheritance: become an object of pleasure for the colonizers, the fruit of this violent mixture of bloods that, today, is proclaimed as the only national product that deserves to be exported: the Brazilian mulatto woman. The treatment received by this premium product is strangely degrading and disrespectful.[31]

The *misgenação* of Brazil has been made possible because of the bodies of Black and Indigenous women, because of their appropriation, violation, and now commercialization. The process of *mulattization* that is founded upon sexual exploitation also bespeaks genocidal violence; the expansion of the mestizo population is but a pretense for making the Black population disappear. With the arrival of the authoritarian regime of Getulio Vargas in 1937 and the philosophy of the Estado Novo regime, Brazil's whitening practices affected immigration politics: migrant populations of European descent were desired and welcomed in Brazil, while others were banned from entering the country. Doing so enabled the white population to increase more rapidly.

Over the course of Brazil's colonial history, Black women have been exposed to serious violations and their bodies have been reduced to territories for Brazilian conquest, suffering sexual violence, forced sterilization, and assassination.

From the beginnings of miscegenation on our continent—which were born out of the rape of Black and Indigenous women—to now, the history of the colonization of racialized women, and certainly their bodies, remains hidden. Racialized and impoverished women are still the ones who provide cheap and exploited labor in the fields, in the maquilas, in homes, and in services of care, all of which are indispensable for the global heteropatriarchal capitalist system's reproduction. These women also face ongoing structural violence in increasingly drastic ways, placing them at risk of feminicide.

When we look through the lens of anti-racist and decolonial feminism, we can understand that the logic of domination and killing of racialized women is an instrument of the system of power. Feminicidal violence against

Indigenous women, such as forced sterilization, rape, or displacement, and its use demonstrate a strategy for controlling and subjugating entire populations.

To understand the full complexity of this phenomenon, we resort to the theoretical proposal of decolonial feminists: understand oppression as imbricated or co-constitutive. Doing so allows us to analyze feminicide from a comprehensive perspective that considers this phenomenon as a technique of control used by the racist heteropatriarchal colonial modern system of power in its neoliberal capitalist phase.

But we also have to take into account the increase in feminicidal violence occurring in the context of conflict throughout many countries in Abya Yala, particularly Mexico and Brazil. The magnitude of feminicidal violence is rooted simultaneously in geopolitical and territorial conflicts, in socioeconomic disparities, and in the inequalities produced by the heteropatriarchal system and the colonial and racist matrix, as well as the trend of militarization across our continent; militarism also has a colonial and fundamentally patriarchal dimension.

MILITARIZATION AND COLONIALITY

It is interesting to recover the colonial origin of the military strategy of counterinsurgency or low-intensity conflict (LIC) used by many countries of Abya Yala. LIC is a military doctrine that was developed primarily during the Algerian War of Independence. After its defeat in Vietnam, the French army intensified the development and technical improvement of military tactics for repression and population control like torture, enforced disappearances, and attacks against civilians in order to weaken insurgents, isolate them from their civil bases, and spread terror.[32] This war strategy's enemy was a racialized and colonized internal enemy: "the native," "the savage."[33]

In his work at the Blida Psychiatric Hospital in Algeria, Frantz Fanon analyzed how psychological warfare was used to control and take away the conscience and humanity of the colonized and the oppressed.[34] In this repressive panoply, torture and rape were used against Indigenous women as weapons of war and territorial control.[35] The U.S. Army School of the Americas, located in Panama at the time, consulted with the French general Paul Aussaresse, an important military strategist of the Algerian war, to import to and spread throughout Latin America low-intensity conflict, or counterinsurgency, along with its imperial and colonial origins.

Established primarily by members of the Special Forces Airmobile Group (GAFES), the School of the Americas formed distinguished military officials following the unresolved armed conflict in Selva Lacandona, Chiapas, incited in 1994. GAFES is an elite unit of Mexican armed forces created in 1995 to suppress the insurrection of the Zapatista Army of National Liberation (EZLN).[36] In the Chiapas context, the Mexican Secretariat of National Defense (SEDENA) planned a counterinsurgency named "el Plan de Campaña Chiapas 94," increased the State's militarization, and endorsed the emergence of numerous paramilitary groups that were acting as strike teams, repression, and the demobilization of insurrections. The conflict led to the involuntary displacement of at least 12,000 people as well as to torture, enforced disappearances, and assassinations. The majority of the victims were Indigenous and, primarily, women.[37] With the rise of various paramilitary groups and as part of a systematic strategy to repress people in the resistance, a series of intimidating practices including persecution, threats, armed aggressions, enforced disappearances, and the sexual violation of women, among others, were implemented. Paramilitary groups play a critical role in contexts of war and political conflict, in geostrategic territorial regions, and as agents of community devastation.

Despite the fact that the neoliberal policy of militarism, national security, and low-intensity warfare had been a strategy of the State of Mexico for at least 3 *sexenios* (six-year terms), in 2006, during the presidential term of Felipe Calderón, military actions and strategies were intensified. The fight against organized crime, particularly drug trafficking, the State reasoned, warranted the armed forces' increased participation in matters of public security and national security policy.

Felipe Calderón defined this confrontation as a "war." Since the armed forces are used intensively in times of war, the designation granted them unlimited powers and unquestioned access to information and its circulation as a fundamental component of the State's strategy. "Enemy" losses were counted and disseminated regularly by the media, while civilian disappearances, murders, and humiliations were considered "collateral damages," made invisible, and, in the best-case scenario, justified as part of the war strategy. While war tactics like torture, rape, and persecution were carried out with impunity, military and intelligence techniques also targeted the civilian population and social movements, including Indigenous peoples and organized communities. This situation placed Mexico in a relentless spiral of violence that has not yet diminished.

Today, the outcome of the 2006 Mexican military policy on the fight against organized crime is summed up in numbers: 80,000 people were killed, more than 25,000 people were subject to forced disappearance, and at least 250,000 more people were displaced."[38] To these results, we also add the unquantifiable number of orphaned, widowed, mutilated, and exiled persons, mostly Indigenous and racialized women and minors, who were displaced from their territories by a strategy of "war" to which they did not agree and for which they nonetheless paid the most serious consequences.

The consequences of this scenario included deteriorated living conditions, exacerbated structural violence, territorial displacement and forced disappearances, a diversion of resources from basic needs to arms and espionage, an increase in human rights violations, the loss of freedom of movement, and a series of devasting mechanisms that increased violence against women like rape and sexual torture, which has led to an increase in feminicide rates throughout our country.

This wave of state violence also entailed patriarchal and colonial rhetoric, which compounded the message that Indigenous, Black, and poor women and their bodies are under the system's control and disposable. Militarization, then, "translates into a situation of extreme violence toward women, manifested in confinements, rapes, forced pregnancies, feminicides and trafficking. The complicity of governments and repressive forces exacerbates the values of patriarchy, configuring the bodies of women as territories for the horrors of war."[39] Militarism not only reflects the values of patriarchy; when articulated alongside colonial, racist, and classist conditions, it also, we affirm, materializes on the bodies of racialized, Indigenous, peasant, and impoverished women in the most aggressive and dehumanizing expression of neocolonial military war.

Military domination implies, in addition to a "security" policy, the criminalization of protesting, organizing, social movements, and also poverty. Thus, the new national security policies promote the tightening of the State and state control over a broad spectrum of populations. The expansion of the armed forces militarizes Indigenous, Black, and peasant regions where there is organized resistance against neoliberal policies for the geostrategic control of natural resources, for example. Structural reforms, which are also part of this neoliberal strategy, deepen inequalities, violence, exclusions, and poverty in the countryside and cities. These disparities push those affected to meet their needs immediately in order to ensure their survival, generating, in the hegemonically-constructed economic and cultural imaginary, an identification of impoverished areas, be they rural and peasant areas inhabited by Black and Indigenous people or destitute urban areas made up of those territories' migrant population, with crime zones. For that reason, a military intent on controlling and disciplining must intervene in those crime zones to ensure order and maintenance, thereby reinforcing these social exclusions; militarism is part of the system that produces poverty. Classist stereotypes are created that then intersect with racialized phenotypes, automatically making impoverished, racialized peoples the "enemy" of order and criminalizing poverty and precarity.

This repressive logic, advanced by the legitimizing discourse of national security, justifies different mechanisms of heteropatriarchal capitalist control and order, from militarization, military personnel, and the deployment of military apparatuses to the criminalization of dissidence and poverty. As a result, the racialized and colonized internal "enemy" continues to be Black and Indigenous people, as well as, gradually, impoverished urban migrant populations and their descendants. We can recognize low-intensity conflict's colonial heritage in the methods it prescribes to control racialized populations and in the violence it enacts against the Indigenous and Black women who resist and protect their lands whenever their bodies are violated, tortured, or killed in the name of geostrategic occupation.

In Brazil as well, the militarization process has to be understood through the colonial matrix, which exerts severe violence on racialized, Black, and Indigenous women.

Like other countries in Abya Yala, Brazil has been run by an authoritarian government since 1964, initially under the government of General Castelo Branco and later a military *junta* until 1985. Like other dictatorships elsewhere on the continent, the Brazilian government enlisted the military training of the United States to refine its techniques for repressing its people; the 1967 National Security Doctrine, for example, established Brazil's main enemy as an internal enemy to be found in the heart of the population. This doctrine also incorporated military contributions from the French school, such as the counterinsurgency executed during the colonial war in Algeria. Thus, the internal enemy of the Brazilian authoritarian state became poor, Black, Indigenous, and communist.

In effect, the Jungle Warfare Training Center (CIGS)—a center for Brazilian land armed forces officers located in Manaus in the Amazon and specializing in military training—became an important hub for the counter-insurgency led in March of 1964 by Castelo Branco, the head of the ensuing military junta. In 1973, in the middle of the dictatorship, French general Paul Aussaresses gave courses on the Battle of Algeria to several Brazilian, Chilean, Argentine, and Venezuelan soldiers. The strategy of counterinsurgency he taught is not neutral: it is a strategy of colonial war that also targets civilians and uses physical and psychological torture and rape. The civilian Indigenous, peasant, and Black populations, especially those who inhabited the areas where guerrillas advanced, such as the rural areas of the northeast and the Amazon, suffered at the hands of this repressive dictatorial regime,

The tenth chapter of the National Truth Commission's final report compiles the accounts of rape against women and torture by repressive political forces.[40] These violations are considered part of "national security."[41] The bodies of racialized women are again dominated by a military strategy for population control. Today, however, this authoritarian regime, which officially ended in 1985, is marked as a special configuration and called "a military-civil regime"—that is, a congress instituted by a military junta. This designation dilutes and obscures the borders between democracy and dictatorship, posing serious implications for the current process of militarism that circulates military doctrine and is gradually militarizing Brazil. For example, the Brazilian government has created military police forces to combat organized crime, such as the BOPE in Rio de Janeiro and the Rota in São Paulo, as well as the Police Pacification Units, which are "neighborhood" posts in several favelas of Rio de Janeiro. The presence of armed soldiers—of the military amidst the civilian population—has increased feelings of insecurity among women, as it constitutes a threat to Black and Indigenous women's wellbeing.

The racist heteropatriarchal capitalist system in its neoliberal phase strives to exploit racialized bodies and to dispossess them of their territories, demonstrating the colonial legacy of appropriating the "other." One of Brazil's most elaborate aspects is its militarization, which is understood, not only as the institution of military equipment and troops in the streets, but also as a doctrine of militarism capable of organizing a hegemonic worldview and social, interpersonal, and territorial relations that are based on control, discipline, exclusion, accusation, denunciation, and expulsion.

> For some, the term has to do with the potentialization of the armed forces; for others, it refers to the use of armed forces in non-traditional tasks, such as development. Others define militarization as the use of armed forces to combat internal threats of a non-military nature or to carry out missions that are the responsibility of the police, such as the fight against organized crime. Lastly, militarization could refer to the existence of a de facto, although not de jure, military government. It should be noted that militarization should not be confused with militarism. Militarism is the imposition of values, perspectives and military ideals on civil society, which, without doubt, is even more dangerous than militarization.[42]

Accordingly, we can also understand militarism as an ideology where military force, imposed through violence and domination, constitutes the core of national security. It is an ideology based on and reinforced through machismo, xenophobia, sexism, racism, and heterosexism. Additionally, it is an ideology that seeps into the foundations of peoples' cultural and social practices, such as their ways of resolving conflicts, organizing the economy, or relating interpersonally, among others. Understood in this way, militarism is the naturalization and implementation of military values into the social and cultural imaginaries that organize our lives. At the moment, militarism underpins a good portion of our political practices, from strictly military programs—that is to say, security programs—to the economic policies of production, "development," and cooperation. It causes both direct violence (assassinations, disappearances, feminicides, displacements) and structural violence, as it is a means to control populations for the benefit of neoliberal economic policies, the establishment of mega-investment projects, and the increasing presence of transnational corporations.

In this scenario, racialized women carry on their bodies the scars of violence produced by militarism, an imperialist strategy that does not end with the implementation of warmongering plans, but rather with the neocolonial development projects that seek to appropriate cultures, forms of community reproduction, and natural resources like water, land, seeds, and the ancestral knowledge of native people.

It is necessary to analyze further the relationship between feminicidal violence, military presence, and geostrategic resources in Abya Yala in order to understand the full complexity of this wave of racist militarism that strips people of their lands and subjects racialized women to serious acts of violence.

COLONIZATION/NEO-COLONIZATION OF TERRITORIES

Feminicidal violence is used as a tool of militarized racism to strip the Indigenous and Black populations of their territories. Sexual violations are carried out in the midst of geopolitical conflicts that destabilize organizations resisting neoliberal megaprojects and strip populations of their territories and displace them.

Since the colonization of Abya Yala, the domination of Black and Indigenous women's bodies has been used as a military strategy to control territories—that is to say, land, natural resources like water, gold, and sugar, as well as human resources like the bestialized Indigenous and Black workforce. But today, the conquest for territories continues to develop under a new violent framework; today, we have neocolonization in the context of neoliberal globalization. Throughout contemporary global conflicts for the control over territories and geostrategic natural resources—in which countries of the Global South, particularly those in Abya Yala, have a dominant role due to the richness of their soils, water, and biosphere, but also their supply of supposedly exploitable human beings—racialized and impoverished women are at the forefront. Not only are their bodies most susceptible to violence and neocolonial feminicidal risk, but they also stand at the frontlines, resisting and defending against the usurpation of their territories.

The heteropatriarchal, colonial, and capitalist system has hitherto been sustained through the extermination of Indigenous and Afro-descendant people; like the feminicide of racialized women, militarism has also been part of this logic of extermination. The militarization of Indigenous territories is justified in many ways: among them are appeals to the war against drug trafficking, social violence, and political-territorial conflicts, to name just a few. However, in Latin American contexts, militarism also coincides with strong political conflicts such that the militaristic logic develops another critical mechanism: counterinsurgency. Thus, in our region, the global model for the war against terrorism turns into, with appropriate adjustments, the fight against organized crime, which, nevertheless, has the explicit subtext of counterinsurgent war.

By this we mean to say that the military strategies for national security and territorial control are also used as catalysts for violence and targeted attacks on Indigenous and peasant peoples, their communities, struggle, resistance, and organizing. These strategies can range from purely technical components to social initiatives led by the armed forces to obtain information and identify social movement focal points. Thus, although counterinsurgency, in its most common sense, struggles for social acceptance and the support of insurgent and guerrilla groups (as part of a state policy to combat and defeat them), it also camouflages itself in areas of social conflict with other promoted interventions like the government welfare and development programs, thereby insinuating military structures into local, cultural and community contexts.

In situations of war and territorial conflict, military presence is a central part of the States' security strategy; it is used to combat not only insurgencies, but also all social and political protests staged on geostrategic territories against transnational companies. Under the pretext of fighting organized crime, armed forces are deployed in these territories to further territorial control strategies by establishing military interventions that can facilitate the exploitation of Abya Yala's natural resources.[43]

For example, in Brazil, a militaristic and racist doctrine is spreading, which, given the context of geostrategic and neocolonial conflict, is understandable. That is, parallel to the construction of an internal enemy (poor Black women and men) is the justification of "national security" measures like increasing armed forces, military training, and the profusion of weapons. Taking a decolonial perspective, we propose to look at this situation from another side, from the "light" side, of modernity: that is, light as water, like gold, like the air of the Amazon jungle, and like fresh blood.[44] Where there is an attempt by a military occupation, specifically by the United States, to have access to the natural resources and territories of Brazil and the rest of Abya Yala to build a North American military base in the tripartite border of Brazil, Argentina, and Paraguay, right next to one of the largest aquifers in the world, the Guarani Aquifer, we look from the light side of modernity. Or, at the reopening of the Alcántara base, situated at the mouth of the Amazon River, where most of the riches of Brazil are extracted, we look from the light side of modernity. But also, with the presence of North American armed forces in the Amazon, particularly in Roraima, a state rich in coltan and where the highest number of feminicides has also been recorded, and the reinforced presence of the Brazilian armed forces on the borders between northern Brazil and the Amazon, along with steady increases in violence against Black and Indigenous women, we look from the light side of modernity.

Bodies and territories are then occupied by the policies of colonial order founded on control, discipline, and violence. The bodies of racialized women have historically and systematically been used as spoils of war, as places to demonstrate power over the "enemy," as sites of domestication, and as warnings for other bodies, mainly those of their partners. Racialized bodies are territories in dispute, where sexual violence operates as a control mechanism. The racialized bodies are then privileged spaces for the neocolonial occupation of the territories.

It is important, therefore, to develop an analysis that gives voice to the memories of racialized bodies, which we understand as historical domains where racism and colonialism are embodied.

WOMEN'S BODIES-TERRITORIAL APPROPRIATION

Indigenous women, like Lorena Cabnal in Guatemala, have theorized from their daily reality and corporality the territorial concept earth-body ["cuerpo tierra"].[45] In taking up the idea that the history and survival of Indigenous peoples is connected to that of the land, Indigenous women have denounced the destruction of Indigenous territories as a simultaneous attack on both their lands and their bodies.

This territorial concept addresses the colonial history of slavery in which African women were taken from their lands and brought by force to Abya Yala. The immaterial dimension of territory, culture, and spirituality was historically linked to the corporality of the slaves, since it constituted the only thing they had left to defend and feel human. There were attempts to destroy this strength, such as obligating slaves to walk around the Tree of Forgetfulness (7 laps for women and 9 for men) in a mandatory ritual whose mission was to make the slaves forget their culture and country of origin, and then pass through the Door of No-Return in Ouidah, where enslaved women and men would leave behind their lives and become animals/commodities. Nevertheless, Black people resisted and preserved their memories through their respective African cultures and spiritualties, gradually building a relationship with these new lands of Abya Yala. To this day, Black cultures and spiritualties are criminalized and demonized in many parts of our continent.

Feminicidal violence is perpetuated as a military strategy for occupying territories through the forced occupation and sexual abuse of racialized women's bodies. According to the terms of Aura Cumes, we can say that

Indigenous and Black women's territories are violently penetrated by neocolonization and supported by the militarization of the continent.[46]

With that said, sexual violence in all of its manifestations has as its object
of war the bodies of women. Women are read as bodies with a sexual and
reproductive function, which can be attacked to disturb an entire group.
Their bodies then become preferred places to transmit messages of control,
power, and humiliation, to intimidate, control, divide, and punish people
and communities, not to mention to advance a strategy for controlling territory as well. Furthermore, wartime rape also becomes a tactic for terrorizing
populations and forcing displacement.[47] Sexual violence therefore is not only
a personal dispossession, but also a territorial one; as territories are subdued
and control and power are demonstrated, the bodies of women and girls are
made into resources suspetible to appropriation.

In addition to being one of the most widely used weapons of war in the
contexts of territorial disputes and armed conflict, rape is also an instrument
of colonization and genocide. The sexual violence and murder of racialized women corresponds to the logic of domination and extermination,
which belongs to the racist patriarchal capitalist system. Insofar as it attacks
women's reproductive capacity, rape has two aims: on the one hand, to create
pregnancies that sow the aggressor's "seed" in a given territory and children
who represent the aggressors' control over their group; and, on the other hand,
to transmit infectious sexual diseases to the community. This situation not
only leads to the rejection of women, but also stereotypes women as agents of
disease who will infect the community and/or society. Another, no less serious effect of rape is ethnic cleansing, as it violates potential mothers of the
group and their potential children.[48] In this way, sexual violations can be read
not only as violent attacks on female bodies, but also on the community and
land, according to the social and ideological implications of forced pregnancies. In each situation, enemy groups exert power over the bodies of women,
of allegedly undesirable and disposable women, to limit their reproduction
and thereby ensure another specific group and/or ethnic population's survival.

For this reason, in Brazil, as in Mexico, feminicidal violence is a tool for
controlling earth-body territories. To recognize this fact, it is necessary to
understand feminicidal violence through a decolonial lens, that is, to take
into account the colonial matrix through which heteropatriarchal, racist, and
classist systems are co-constructed and according to which violence against
racialized women constitutes a military strategy for territorial control.

The colonial matrix subjects Black and Indigenous women to violence by
appropriating and violating their bodies, by exploiting and dispossessing them
of their lands, and by discriminating against and criminalizing their cultures.

WEAVING RESISTANCES

Colonial racist domination is not just a past memory, nor does it just happen at certain historical moments; rather, it underlies the project of western modernity imposed on the world through neoliberal policies and development plans. Racism is the basis for its economic and colonial world order, and it is more present than ever before.

Today, in this hybrid world and in our contexts of violence, we have to confront the new face of racism. Technological advances of military arsenals, control, and security attempt to exterminate Indigenous and Afro-descendant people, and efforts to exploit their territories continue to be justified. Racism is recycled in a way that is reminiscent of neo-Nazi movements: institutional rights are denied while a nationalist identity that criminalizes migration is solidified through discourse. This new racism has become so normalized that walls are built and civilians are shot when crossing the border.

Given this Latin American context that is geopolitically organized around dispossession, depredation, militarism, repression, disputes over resources, and feminicidal violence, feminist movements must reposition themselves, denounce, and expose these practices as direct expressions of the structural violence inherent to the patriarchal, colonial, and capitalist system; they must show the failure of the neoliberal system as a paradigm for development and democracy.

If hegemonic feminism does not understand the role that the coloniality of gender has played in reproducing inequalities by recognizing the role that privileged women play in propagating systems of oppression, it will remain debilitated in its transformative potential. In that sense, Breny Mendoza warns that "ignoring the historicity and coloniality of gender also blinds white women of the West, who have also struggled to recognize the intersectionality of race and gender and their own complicity in the processes of colonization and capitalist domination."[49]

In Mexico, Brazil, and throughout Abya Yala, global campaigns have been organized to resist femicidal violence, the colonial matrix, and the systems of domination that compose it. For example, in Brazil, Black women have resisted colonization, slavery, and neo-colonization for hundreds of years by preserving their culture and African-based religions. The Ilaode (Mothers of Saints) are the embodiment of these Black women's strength; they preserve ancestral knowledge, but also play a political, spiritual, and social role in their communities.[50] In November of 2015, the first Black Women's March in Brazil was held, bringing together more than 50,000 women. Many of them are now very active in the movements against the parliamentary-judicial coup d'etat that took place on August 31, 2016 and the return of white, heteropatriarchal, evangelist, and militarist political force.

Throughout Abya Yala, Indigenous women, Black women, and lesbians continue to resist the colonial matrix of violence. Feminism and decolonial lesbofeminism are expressions of epistemological principles that confront expressions of intellectual and cultural hegemony, as well as political practices and forms of resistence that are rooted in Black and Indigenous cosmologies. In all corners of our continent and beyond, there are initiatives to oppose coloniality and violence led by racialized women who organize themselves into groups and networks, build political solidarities, love each other, use creativity and healing, and make themselves present in politicians' spaces, in academics' spaces, and on the streets.

Our aim is to recognize our powers, to create and act, to open up gaps in the colonial matrix. We conceive of this decolonial anti-racist lesbian-feminist proposal as a lens through which we can perceive our realities in manner that allows us to create and propose alternatives; it is anti-systemic activism against the racist, heteropatriarchal, colonialist, and capitalist system.

We have begun to weave our anti-racist lesbian feminist proposal to respond to two needs: our need to identify the traces of gender, race, sexuality, and class oppressions within us, including the ways in which, through the course of our lives, we have reproduced them, and our need to build tools with which to analyze and transform our particular realities and circumstances. It is a proposal to deconstruct the heteropatriarchal, colonial, and racist capitalist regime through multiple strategies, including daily resistances, participation in social and feminist movements, theoretical production and artistic creation, and spirituality, as well as to vindicate decolonial lesbian practices as dissenting political practices. It is also a call to think and deconstruct our own racist, classist, and patriarchal practices, for such work is fundamental to the broader transformation of our own spaces and movements.

NOTES

1. Our decolonial and anti-racist lesbofeminist proposal is dedicated to all the fighters who fell defending the earth-bodies, culture, and land of the Black and Indigenous peoples, to all those women who fell into the hands of the racist, heteropatriarchal, colonialist, and capitalist system. This proposal is one of the seeds sown by Bety Cariño and Berta Cáceres.

2. Aníbal Quijano, "Coloniality of Power, Eurocentrism, and Latin America," *Nepantla: Views from South* 1, no. 3 (2000).

3. María Lugones, "The Coloniality of Gender," *World & Knowledges Otherwise* 2, no. 2 (Spring 2008); María Lugones, "Toward a Decolonial Feminism," *Hypatia*

25, no. 4 (Fall 2010); María Lugones, "Radical Multiculturalism and Women of Color Feminisms," *Journal for Cultural and Religious Theory* 13, no. 1 (2014).

4. Jane Caputi and Diana E. H. Russell, "Femicide: Sexist Terrorism against Women," in *Femicide: The Politics of Woman Killing,* eds. Jill Radford and Diana E. H. Russell (New York: Twayne, 1992), 15.

5. Attributed to Marcela Lagarde y de los Ríos, feminicide is a political term that encompasses more than femicide—the killing of females by males because they are female—because this term not only holds the male perpetrators responsible, but also the state and judicial structures that uphold misogyny. Feminicide and femicide are often used interchangebley in spite of this distinction. In English, the use of femicide is more common. Whenever possible and appropriate, the authors' use of feminicide is maintained unless original citations specify otherwise.—Trans.

6. Marcela Lagarde y de los Ríos, "Introducción," in *Feminicidio: Una perspectiva global*, eds. Diana E.H. Russel and Roberta A. Harmes (Mexico, D.F: Universidad Nacional Autónoma de México, Centro de Investigaciones Interdisciplinarias en Ciencias y Humanidades, 2006), 20.

7. Ibid., 21.

8. "Una Mirada al Feminicidio en México 2009–2010," *Observatoria Ciudadano Nacional del Feminicidio*, accessed November 23, 2020, https://observatoriofeminicidio.files.wordpress.com/2011/09/informe-ocnf-2009-2010.pdf. Observatoria Ciudadano Nacional del Feminicidio (National Citizens Observatory on Feminicide) is an alliance made up of 49 human rights and women's organizations in 21 states of Mexico. Its main objective is to monitor and demand accountability from the institutions in charge of preventing and punishing violence against women and feminicides.

9. Jill Radford, "Introduction" in *Femicide: The Politics of Woman Killing,* eds. Jill Radford and Diana E. H. Russell (New York: Twayne, 1992), 7.

10. Ibid., 8.

11. Kimberlé Crenshaw, "Gender-Related Aspects of Race Discrimination," Background paper for Expert Meeting on Gender and Racial Discrimination, Zagreb, Croatia (EM/GRD/2000/WP.1, November 21–24, 2000), 5.

12. bell hooks, "Black Women: Shaping Feminist Theory," in *Feminist Theory: From Margin to Centre* (Cambridge: South End Press, 1984).

13. Julio Jacobo Waiselfisz, *Mapa da Violência 2015: Homicídio de Mulheres no Brasil* (Brasilia: Faculdade Latino-Americana de Ciências Sociais, 2015). http://www.onumulheres.org.br/wp-content/uploads/2016/04/MapaViolencia_2015_mulheres.pdf.

14. Ibid., 72.

15. Ibid., 30.

16. "El feminicidio más allá de Ciudad Juárez," *Observatoria Ciudadano Nacional del Feminicidio*, published 2008, http://observatoriofeminicidio.blogspot.mx/.

17. "El Feminicidio en México y Guatemala," *Federación Internacional de los Derechos Humanos*, no. 446/3 (2016): 12.

18. Carlos J. Echarri Cánovas, *La violencia feminicida en México: aproximaciones y tendencias 1985–2016* (Mexico: SEGOB, Secretaría de Gobernación INMUJERES,

Instituto Nacional de las Mujeres ONU Mujeres, Entidad de las Naciones Unidas para la Igualdad de Género y el Empoderamiento de las Mujeres, 2017): 18. Between 2007 and 2012 there was an increase of 138% in documented cases of feminicides, reaching new records. The numbers started to decrease since 2012, however, they remain much higher than the indices before 2007.

19. Ibid., 25–26.

20. Mercedes Olivera, *Violencia feminicida en Chiapas: razones visibles y ocultas de nuestras luchas, resistencias y rebeldías* (Chiapas: Colección Selva Negra and Universidad de Ciencias y Artes de Chiapas, 2008), 31.

21. María Lugones, "The Coloniality of Gender."

22. Ibid.

23. Quijano, "Coloniality of Power."

24. Yuderkys Espinosa-Miñoso, "Ethnocentrism and Coloniality in Latin American Feminisms: The Complicity and Consolidation of Hegemonic Feminists in Transnational Spaces," trans. Ana-Maurine Lara, *Venezuelan Journal of Women Studies* 14, no. 33 (2009); Yuderkys Espinosa-Miñoso, "Las feministas antirracistas teorizando la trama compleja de la opresión," Paper presented at "Género y Etnicidad: Reflexiones desde el Sur del Mundo," Centro Interdisciplinario de Estudios de Género, Universidad de Chile, Santiago, 2014; Lugones, "Coloniality of Gender."

25. Lugones, "Coloniality of Gender."

26. Ibid.

27. Ochy Curiel, "Los Aportes de las Afrodescendientes a la Teoría y la Práctica Feminista. Desuniversalizando el Sujeto 'Mujeres,'" in *Perfiles del feminismo iberoamericano,* vol. 3, ed. María Luisa Femenías (Buenos Aires: Catálogos, 2007).

28. Abdias do Nascimento, *O genocídio do negro brasileiro: Processo de um racismo mascarado* (Rio de Janeiro: Paz e Terra, 1978); Lélia Gonzales, "A Categoria Político-Cultural de Amefricanidade," *Tempo Brasileiro*, no. 92/93 (1988).

29. See: Gilberto Freyre, *The Masters and the Slaves: A Study in the Development of Brazilian Civilization,* trans. Samuel Putnam (Berkeley: University of California Press, 1986), and Gilberto Freyre, *O mundo que o português criou* (São Paulo: É Realizações, 2010).

30. Munanga Kabengele, *Rediscutindo a mestiçagem no Brasil: Identidade nacional versus identidade negra* (Petrópolis: Vozes, 1999).

31. do Nascimento, *O genocídio do negro brasileiro,* 61–62.

32. Marie-Monique Robin, *Death Squadrons: The French School* (New York: First Run/Icarus Films, 2003).

33. Mathieu Rigouste, *L'ennemi intérieur: La généalogie coloniale et militaire de l'ordre sécuritaire dans la France contemporaine* (Paris: Découverte, 2009).

34. Frantz Fanon, *The Wretched of the Earth*, trans. Richard Philcox (New York: Grove Press, 2004).

35. Raphaëlle Branche, "Sexual Violence in the Algerian War," in *Brutality and Desire: Genders and Sexualities in History,* ed. Dagmar Herzog (London: Palgrave Macmillan, 2009).

36. Jose Francisco Gallardo, *Always Near, Always Far: The Armed Forces in Mexico* (San Francisco: Global Exchange, 2001).

37. *La política genocida en el conflicto armado en Chiapas: reconstrucción de hechos, pruebas, delitos y testimonios* (San Cristóbal de Las Casas, Chiapas: Centro de Derechos Humanos Fray Bartolomé de Las Casas, 2005), https://frayba.org.mx /historico/archivo/informes/050201_la_politica_genocida_en_el_conflicto_armado _en_chiapas.pdf.

38. *Ejecuciones extrajudiciales en el contexto de la militarización de la seguridad pública* (Mexico: Comisión Mexicana de Defensa y Promoción de los Derechos Humanos, A.C, 2013), 3, http://cmdpdh.org/publicaciones-pdf/cmdpdh-ejecuciones -extrajudiciales-en-el-contexto-de-la-militarizacion-de-la-seguridad-publica.pdf.

39. "Militarización y violencia patriarcal en Haití o cómo se asocian dos viejos amigos ante el desastre," Grupo Antimilitarista Tortuga, published January 2011, http: //www.grupotortuga.com/Militarizacion-y-violencia.

40. "Violência sexual, violência de gênero e violência contra crianças e adolescen-tes," *Relatório da Comissão Nacional da Verdade,* Vol I (Brasilia: Comissão Nacional da Verdade, 2014), http://cnv.memoriasreveladas.gov.br/images/pdf/relatorio/volume _1_digital.pdf.

41. Ibid., 427.

42. Craig A. Deare, "La militarización en América Latina y el papel de los Estados Unidos," *Foreign Affairs Latinoamérica* 3, no. 3 (2008): 23–24.

43. Examples of such interventions include military plans that combat insurgencies like the "Plan Colombia" and "Plan de Campaña Chiapas 94." The former interven-tion was directed by the United States and its financing and implementation were fully documented. Both plans succeeded in displacing Indigenous populations, as they favored the entry of large megaprojects and foreign investors that seized and exploited ancestral territories for minerals and hydrocarbons.

44. Lugones considers heterosexual patriarchy as part of the "'light' side of the colonial/modern organization of gender" ("Coloniality of Gender," 2). Also relevant here is that Walter Mignolo refers to coloniality as the "darker side of modernity," which is in conversation with his account of the "darker side of the Renaissance." See: Walter Mignolo, *The Darker Side of the Renaissance*, 2nd ed., Ann Arbor: Michigan University Press, 2003; and Walter Mignolo, *The Darker Side of Western Modernity* (Durham: Duke University Press, 2011).

45. Lorena Cabnal, "De las opresiones a las emancipaciones: mujeres indíge-nas en defensa del territorio cuerpo-tierra," Pueblos–Revista de Información y Debate, published February 2015, http://www.revistapueblos.org/blog/2015/02/06/ de-las-opresiones-a-las-emancipaciones-mujeres-indigenas-en-defensa-del-territorio -cuerpo-tierra/.

46. Aura Cumes, "El Feminismo Debe Luchar contra las Múltiples Opresiones que Enfrentamos las Mujeres Indígenas y Afrodescendientes," presented at II Encuentro de Estudios de Género y Feminismos, Guatemala, 2011.

47. In the context of the Guatemalan war, cases of sexual violence against Indig-enous women have been documented both in contexts of armed conflict and ter-ritorial displacements that are advanced by transnational and national companies in the extractive industry. In both cases, the sexual abuses were often linked to forced displacements and their stories are deeply related to the continuous dispossession

experienced by the indigenous people of the area. See: Luz Méndez Gutiérrez and Amanda Carrera Guerra, *Mujeres indígenas: clamor por la justicia. violencia sexual, conflicto armado y despojo violento de tierras* (Guatemala: Equipo de Estudios Comunitarios y Acción Psicosocial, 2014).

48. Sexual violence against women in the context of war also implies two practices aimed at preventing the reproduction of racialized populations: forced sterilization and the rape and murder of pregnant women. In Mexico, particularly in the state of Chiapas, which has been experiencing a low-intensity war since 1994 as part of the unresolved armed conflict, both strategies have been used. In the Acteal massacre that occurred in December of 1997, more than half of the people killed were Indigenous women, many of whom were pregnant. According to reports, the atrocities against their bodies were such that some women's wombs were attacked and pierced and even some fetuses were extracted and stabbed. See: Martha Patricia Lopez Astrain, *La guerra de baja intensidad en Mexico* (Mexico, D.F.: Universidad Iberoamericana and Plaza y Valdes Editores, 1996).

49. Breny Mendoza, "La epistemología del sur, la colonialidad del género y el feminismo latinoamericano," in *Aproximaciones críticas a las prácticas teórico-políticas del feminisimo latinoamericano*, ed. Yuderkys Espinoa Miñoso (Buenos Aires: En la frontera, 2010), 23.

50. Jurema Werneck, "Of Ialodes and Feminists: Reflections on Black Women's Political Action in Latin America and the Caribbean," *Cultural Dynamics* 19, no. 1 (2007).

Chapter 8

The Killing of Women and Global Accumulation

The Case of Bello Puerto Del Mar Mi Buenaventura

Betty Ruth Lozano Lerma
Translation by Carolina Alonso Bejarano

In this essay I adopt a critical analytical perspective that allows me to recognize myself as a historically and socially situated being. I think from my reality as a Black woman about the conditions of oppression that I share with other Black people in Colombia. My point of departure is an epistemology of the borderlands—one that includes political necessities and ethical conceptions and operates at the limits of knowledges subordinated by the coloniality of power and Western knowledges translated into the Black/Afro-Colombian perspective. It must be recognized that our place of enunciation determines the way in which we live and understand power relations. That is why it is necessary to situate ourselves historically, socially and geographically. Our place of enunciation should be clearly stated; we must acknowledge where we stand in relation to racism, patriarchy, heterosexism, class and geopolitics.

With regard to geopolitics, I speak from Buenaventura, a seaport city located in the Colombian Pacific region separated from the rest of the country by the Western Andes. Of its nearly 400,000 people, 90% are Black Afro-Colombian, 3% are Indigenous, and a growing 7% are Mestizo or white "paisas" and come from the country's interior.[1] Buenaventura is the most important port on the Colombian Pacific coast: 53% percent of the entire country's legal imports and exports move through it.[2] The city also has many illegal ports where cocaine is exported and arms are imported, and where a variety of the legal and illegal armed groups that operate in Colombia can be found.

This situation has a history which I explore in this article that affects the population that has inhabited the area since ancestral times in a way that has particular and differential implications for Black women, something I account for in the article as well. Here, I present different aspects of the cultural and historical backdrop against which violence against women unfolds in the Colombian Pacific region. This violence finds its most cruel expression in femicide, but it manifests in multiple other ways as well.

I am especially interested in establishing that the violence experienced today in Buenaventura and the Pacific region has external roots that have nothing to do with the culture of the region, contrary to what the government wants us to believe. For example, on March 22, 2014, the Colombian Minister of Defense said in an interview that the sexual abuse of girls and women as well as the dismemberment of human bodies "has to do with a cultural practice that is unacceptable and incomprehensible" on the part of the Black people of the region.[3] Local functionaries in Buenaventura who come from other parts of the country also hold this idea. What is really happening today, and what has really happened for more than 35 years already in Colombia's Pacific region, is the processal conquest and colonization of the ancestral Indigenous and Black inhabitants' territory, bodies—especially women's—and imaginaries.

THE PACIFIC TERRITORY/REGION: AN OTHER WORLD

Black Afro-Colombian societies are worlds-other, or other worlds, built out of the necessity to create modes of life using, among other elements, those originating in the worlds from which those who were kidnapped from Africa and their descendents were taken. Foisted into America, these Afro-descendants used multiple resistance and insurgence tactics in order to give their existence a purpose and establish new relationships with their natural surroundings and with others, be they slaves or slave owners. Africans and their descendants found ways, in the midst of the most adverse circumstances imaginable, to build worlds within which they could live their lives, and in this way they created themselves anew.

The Colombian Pacific region, which includes the municipality of Buenaventura, is considered to be one of the most biodiverse places on the planet, thanks to its biological, genetic and sociocultural variety, its maritime and terrestrial ecosystems, and its ecologic and biogeographic characteristics. In spite of, or precisely because of, its isolation from the rest of society, the inhabiting population created a different world when slavery ended. As was the case in most of the country, formerly enslaved people in the Pacific region had already freed themselves by the time abolition, which took place through multiple means, became law in 1851. The new society functioned by means of peaceful conflict resolution, the authority of elders, extended families, collective childrearing, a means of production that respects nature, and cultural practices that celebrate life and death and stop people from killing each other over party differences.[4] Those who knew the Pacific region 20 years ago can testify to the diverse forms of mutual aid and collective work present there: life strategies of that "new world" in the Pacific, which Black women and men created for themselves and where harming others in irreversible ways was unimaginable.[5]

Figure 7.1 Colombia (natural regions), Carlos Eugenio Thompson Pinzón (Chlewey) (CC BY-SA 3.0)

Figure 7.2 Pacifica regions map, Peter Fitzgerald, OpenStreetMap (CC BY-SA 2.0)

AND DEVELOPMENT CAME

If the relation between the center of the country and the Pacific region was always one of extraction, where the ruling administration gave mining concessions to foreign businesses that extracted resources from supposedly vacant territory, then the violence that laid the groundwork for what is happening in the region today began with the push for development in the 1980s.

This is sufficiently documented in Escobar's and Pedrosa's work on the region.[6] Violence was imposed, not only through economic strategies, but also through subjectivizing ones: there was an attempt to change the way of thinking of Black women and men in the Pacific region so that they would produce goods for commercial exchange and not for survival. This was another "encounter" between two worlds: the peoples of the Pacific region went through a new conquest, a new colonization that sought to render them modern subjects and save them from "barbarism." Today, the Colombian government and those who support it pose to the Pacific region the same question that European conquistadors posed to Abya Yala: civilization or barbarism?[7]

This mid-1980s cultural collision came with development-oriented policies and programs consistent with the logic of a document published by the United Nations that was highly influential after World War II, which stated that "ancient philosophies"—what it called the cosmogonies of the ethnic peoples ["pueblos étnicos"] of the Americas—were an obstacle for development.[8] These policies resulted in the initial displacements that took place in the Pacific region, impoverishing entire communities that, consequently,

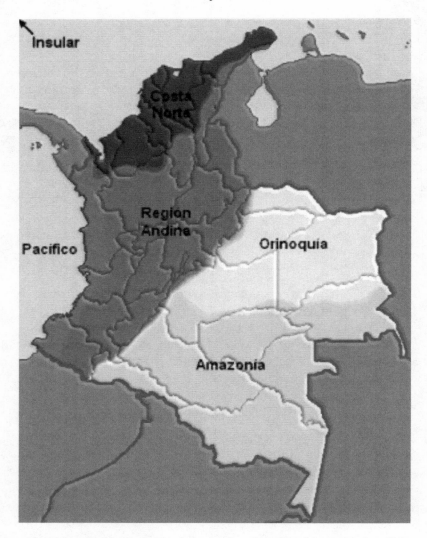

were forced to "emigrate" (a subtle way to describe this uprooting ["desar-raigo"]) in order to survive.

The Pacific region is a laboratory where the global coloniality of power expresses itself. Aníbal Quijano argues that in the 1970s—with the crisis of industrial capital, when financial capital was imposed as the new force behind modern/colonial global capitalism—the world entered a new historic era.[9] This created what he calls "structural unemployment." It is not a coincidence that Buenaventura is the city with the highest unemployment rate in the country, measuring in at 26% according to the city's Chamber of Commerce.[10]

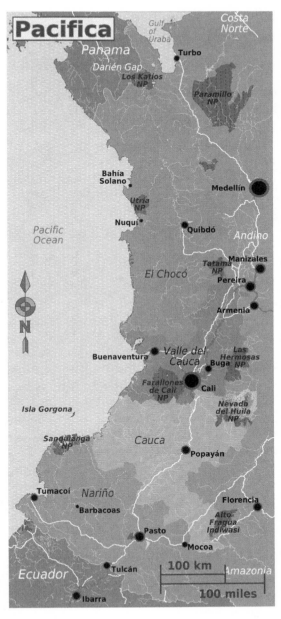

The Pacific region has been a privileged location for the strategic interests of national and transnational capital. It has been a producer of raw material since the earlier wave of colonization in the 1960s and 1980s. In the 1990s, once its biodiversity was recognized, Colombia and Northern countries created international treaties that designated the Indigenous and Black communities of the area the guardians of the land's biological resources. Since then, this biodiversity has been used more and more frequently as a platform with which to enter international markets. The Buenaventura port was privatized in 1993 as a result of neoliberal policies that rapidly impoverished the town, separating the city's social and communal dynamics from the economic dynamics of the port.

Today, the region is a field for the formulation and execution of numerous megaprojects, while the native "negredumbre" has become dispensable, an obstacle to be removed from the path toward consolidating national and international capital in the region.[11] This is how the Pacific has become a violent region, or a scene of different violences. Marginal, dependent, and absolutely poor, it is the perfect place for conflicts between paramilitary forces (euphemistically called "Bacrim," an abbreviation for "criminal mobs" ["bandas criminales"]) and the spectrum of violences that currently exist in the region.

PARAMILITARY PRESENCE IN THE REGION

In order to continue the aforementioned development policies, paramilitary forces strategically arrived in the region toward the end of the 1990s and the beginning of the 2000s. They brought with them violence that manifested itself in innumerable massacres throughout the rural areas and urban municipality of Buenaventura. Starting with their first massacre in Sabaletas, a town 45 minutes away from Buenaventura, these groups instigated an era of unprecedented terror in the region. According to paramilitary member, Ever Veloza's (a.k.a. H.H.) confession, the Calima Block (a paramilitary organization) murdered more than a thousand people between 2000 and 2001 with the sole purpose of terrorizing communities.[12] This period of time is known in the area as "the year of the thousand deaths." Carlos Castaño, paramilitary boss and top leader of the United Self Defense Forces of Colombia, told the media that paramilitaries first came to Buenaventura at the invitation of merchants and businessmen who wanted protection against the guerrillas' supposed *boleteo*.[13] Their presence led to massive displacements and, little by little, the paramilitary groups—now renamed in different ways—took hold of the city and imposed their law. The violence waged against the Buenaventura community included the particularly horrific forced uprooting and murder/disappearance of women.

Since 1999 Buenaventura has suffered crimes that remain in impunity, like the Katanga, Cisneros, Naya and Triana massacres carried out by the Pacific, Calima and Fallarones Blocs of the AUC's Valle del Cauca chapter. They were heavily denounced by the victims' families and human rights organizations in spite of the climate of terror that dominated that time, and contain a broad range of times, places, methods and responsible parties, circumstances which since 2010 have seemed almost impossible to establish due to the shifting nature and names of the groups involved. The war unleashed by groups today known as Los Urabeños, La Empresa and Los Rastrojos have covered up deaths and disappearances, causing a permanent confusion.[14]

Violence in the Pacific region has been so pernicious in recent years that it has curtailed anthropological research, which had been very prolific toward the end of the 1980s and during the 1990s. We can see how after 32 years of implementing development policies—which came with multimillion-dollar investments—the region, according to all measurements, has come today to exhibit the most dramatically low levels of wellbeing in the country. The region is even poorer and more marginal than it was before. It is not hard to deduce that the policies, plans and projects for development failed to improve the quality of life for the region's population. These policies are directly related to the increasing impoverishment of the region's people, resulting in what we can call *systematic impoverishment processes*, or *historically created poverty*. The policies also exist in direct relation to the violence that affects the region, and especially the violence inflicted on the bodies of women: dismemberments, chopping houses ["casas de pique"], *acuafosas*, public humiliation and disappearances.[15]

The communitarian values of the Pacific region, expressed in the multiple practices of mutual aid that go beyond vertical notions of Christian charity establishing horizontal relations with the other, are being transformed by the developmental logic of individual profit that imposes conflict and modern ways of organizing work which force people to be *on their own* ["estar del propio lado"].[16] Even greeting one's neighbor can be jeopardizing. The benefits of communal living are vanishing in the Pacific region, especially for women. Life becomes untenable when fear of death is linked not only to the possibility of losing one's vitality, but also to the possibility of being sexually abused, kidnapped, or disappeared (knowing that someone might be taken into the neighboring house to be chopped, which is to say cut into pieces that will later be thrown into some swamp). All of this makes communitarian life less and less viable. I call this lack of viability *deterritorialization*.[17]

The government has responded with an assistance-based approach that further fragments the community and contributes to its loss of dignity, with militarization that does not prevent violence against the community but fosters it, and with more development—for example, the 2050 Buenaventura Master Plan, which continues the mission of emptying the territory of its native population to make way for various megaprojects.[18] The plan only refers to investments for the port and infrastructure that benefits megaprojects. For example, the cost of water in Buenaventura is among the highest in the country. Water is privatized; it is not for drinking and the population still depends on rainwater. The armed conflict between groups fighting for the urban and rural territory also produces great population displacements, even from one neighborhood to another. The mining industry is knocking down the forest, considered among the most biodiverse on the planet, leaving behind a trail of poverty and death. *Mazamorreo* has turned into one of the most dangerous métiers in the region.[19] Despite the fact that the collective land titles in the region are protected by Law 70 of 1993 (known as the Black communities law), people are losing their land rights to drug traffickers and the palm industry.[20]

There are also food cartels: the plantain cartel, the rice cartel, etc. Everything that a peasant produces must go through these cartels, which belong to the armed groups. They conscript the work force into a sort of neo-slavery as a strategy to control the territory.[21] In the urban areas, new settlements are built to house people from the country's interior (paisas) who live in excellent conditions. In these spaces, access to the native Black population is stopped or restricted, which creates new segregationist neocolonial formations that intensify racial discrimination. Everyday, the killings become more brutal and there is a particularly morbid ruthlessness in the unspeakable torture and abuse with which women are murdered.

DIVERSE EXPLANATIONS REGARDING FEMICIDE

There are two explanations for the murders of women: some, taking a feminist perspective, consider them to be a consequence of patriarchy; others, defending family and traditional values, place them strictly within the frame of inter-family and domestic violence. It is common to hear the second explanation from women who are public officials or leaders in evangelical organizations, who insist on situating femicide exclusively within the framework of domestic violence.[22] This keeps the problem of violence against women in the private sphere of the home, which is considered to be a privileged place for intervention by the fundamentalist Evangelical church. This is also the model that prevails in the media. They do not understand that this is "abuse disguised as love," which takes place in the context of a war where the armed actors force women to live with them and then, "when the time comes and they are no longer needed, they are disappeared or killed and the justification is that these are crimes of passion, when in reality those young men belong to [criminal] groups."[23] Numerous testimonies refer to these types of situations, as is the case with the following observation from a woman leader interviewed by the Colombian Defensoría Delegada:

> Rapes were very frequent, especially in the neighborhoods where paramilitary and guerrilla groups had their operation centers. Both groups raped women, especially younger ones. If the headman of such and such group liked a particular girl, the only way that she could refuse him was to leave town. Otherwise sooner or later she would have to be his woman or have sexual relations with him.[24]

Local state officials interpret any analysis that goes beyond the private sphere as a threat to their administration and as a means to discredit the local government. According to the national government, as was argued in 2014 by the then-Minister of Defense in the media, these crimes are an expression of Black communities' violent cultural practices.[25]

Affirming that this violence is the cultural tradition of the region's population and confining the problem to the framework of domestic violence conceals the relationship between violence and the political and economic dynamics that function at national and global levels. Any explanation that goes beyond these assumptions is more than a simple theoretical discussion or interpretation of a phenomenon. It is an unveiling, in the broader horizon of the modernity/coloniality of power, of the complex network of relations of domination that act upon Black women and the Black population in general—which is why patriarchy is also unsatisfactory as totalizing explanation. This is about questioning the plans for development, modernity and evangelization that are presented as solutions for the impoverishment and violence experienced in the Pacific region and exposing these proposals for what they really represent: the deterritorialization of the native population, the destruction of nature, the exacerbation of individualism, the transformation of subjectivities. All of these are veiled expressions of a war over the control of territory and resources, driven by the interests of national and transnational capital. Violence against women is its most infamous expression; femicide is global capital's strategy for the deterritorialization of the Black population, granting access to its territories for business-funded megaprojects. In order to analyze what is happening to women in Buenaventura today, we must take into consideration the geostrategic and territorial importance of the Pacific region for the mega-investment of transnational capital, especially as it relates to the expansion of the port, which requires territories that have been historically occupied by Black communities and their ancestors.

MODUS OPERANDI AGAINST WOMEN

Legal and illegal armed groups use violence in a rational way in order to gain control over territory. These groups evaluate the kind of force that needs to be applied and the different ways of applying it best suited to breaking the resistance of the enemy: the communities that own the territories that these groups want to control. The abuse and torture are not irrational acts on the part of psychopaths; they are strategies carefully calculated by those who own the war and live in the country's interior.

Women in Buenaventura suffer all the forms of violence mentioned in the Rome Statute, which guides the International Criminal Court:

> rape; sexual harassment; sexual humiliation; forced marriage or cohabitation; the forced marriage of minors; forced prostitution and the commercialization of women; sexual slavery; forced nakedness; forced abortion; forced pregnancy; forced sterilization; the denial of the right to use contraceptives or, oppositely, the imposition of contraceptive methods; threats of sexual violence; sexual blackmail; acts of violence which affect the sexual integrity of women, such as female genital mutilation and examinations to prove virginity.[26]

Other forms of violence can be added to that list, including the exchange of women between the armed groups or the training of girls for *campaneo* (to be informants). Different groups, including the army and the police, recruit these girls as informants and then disappear or kill them for being *sapas*.[27] Other forms of violence include the transportation of arms, the killing of women leaders as a means to *clean* the territory, the recruitment for sexual purposes of girls and young women who are considered to be *buenas* and atrocities such as those detailed here:[28]

> They put poles up their vaginas and anuses; it's like saying, "let's destroy her because she is our worst enemy." For me those crimes are about that "let's destroy the woman" . . . "let's destroy her vagina in the most cruel and violent way possible." Maybe our power lies there and they are afraid so they want to destroy it. In so many cases when women are killed they are also horribly raped. I have always read this as a message from them; for me it's a message of fear, impotent fear, because deep down these barbarian warriors are very afraid of women and the power we have . . . They know how far we will go to defend our lives and the lives of our children.[29]

According to flyers distributed by these groups, they are *cleaning* the area by killing or disappearing women who are *sluts* and *whores*. The ways in which women are murdered—shoving poles up women's vaginas before killing them, cutting off their buttocks and playing soccer with them, cutting off their tongues for being *sapas* when they were forced into being informants by the same groups—send a message to the community about the conflict waged against the population and its collapsing moral limits.

In August of 2007, two high school 16-year olds were approached by paramilitaries on their way out of school. The paramilitaries took the girls to another neighborhood, beat them up and demanded to know the names of the women visited by the guerrillas. They then let one of the girls go, and they strolled around the neighborhood with the other girl naked. Ernestina Rivas had worse luck. Only 17, she was tied to a pole for two days, and she was tortured and raped, her breasts and buttocks cut off, after which she was buried up to her neck at the beach where the high tide eventually drowned her. Her body was found in a mangrove.[30]

Testimonies collected for a report of the Colombian Defensoría Delegada [Ombudsman's Office] mention that girls between 13 and 14 years old are forced into prostitution and end up pregnant. The racist national imagination reads these testimonies as proof that Black women are "arrechas" and have been since they were little.[31] Girls are forced into relationships and, when they refuse to have sexual relations, are publicly tortured. Many young women have to flee their communities for this reason, a reason that constitutes a form of forced displacement that is not yet formally registered.

Many mothers have left the area with their daughters after being subjected to vulgar phrases like, "that woman will be mine." So, out of fear, seeing that their daughters have been targeted, many have had to leave town . . . entire families have been displaced.[32]

Women are subjected to public nudity and other abuses as punishment for not falling in line. They are used as informants and they are murdered when they know too much.[33] Boys and girls go missing on weekends, taken to these groups' bacchanals. Some of them never return. Many women are reported missing, but many more are never reported at all because the identity of the offender is known and people are afraid for the family and children of the victim.

Disappearing the bodies of victims is a way to lower crime indicators and uphold the government and police's projected image of security. This is an old paramilitary strategy. Additionally, women's romantic partners involve them against their will by sharing information about their activities. It is for all these reasons that we women are asserting that the violence we endure does not constitute what the government calls crimes of passion that stay "between the sheets." This is not domestic violence, as state institutions and the church want us to believe.

INSISTING ON A DIFFERENT UNDERSTANDING
OF CRIMES AGAINST WOMEN

These crimes against women constitute femicide and are executed by war actors who violently defend the interests of national and transnational capital. They are not the expression of a violent culture and they do not correspond to the traditional patriarchal ways of Black men. Those are racist ideas. There are two purposes for this violence: it empties the land of its ancestral inhabitants and it blames the victims, which increases racism. When we state that violence against women is part of the culture of Black communities, we blame the victims for the deterritorializing violence that affects them. I argue that violence against women who belong to ethnic minorities is a terrorizing strategy used to deterritorialize.

In a shortsighted conception of politics, some activists, both men and women, tend to minimize the political impact of the killings of women who are not political or community organizers. This trivialization contributes to the efficacy of the death strategy used against ethnic communities, which works through the elimination of women's bodies. These killings are also belittled and depoliticized because the supposed perpetrators are delinquent groups and mafias.

It is also not recognized that these armed actors operate and commit violence according to the same logic as mafias do; all of these groups have the same orientation and (regardless of whether or not each actor is conscious of it) the same end goal: to maintain the social order—an order that obeys the principles of the neoliberal state, the economy of the free market, and the mafias by any means necessary.

Violence against women, even when their partners inflict it, damages the person, the family and the community. The purpose of this violence is to divide the community and erode the traditions of solidarity and mutual aid. That is why it can be argued that violence against women is political violence, since its end goal is the destruction of communal power. When the perpetrators of this violence are members of the community, the result is a sort of cultural hara-kiri.[34]

This violence is part of a war that hides its political character, pitting neighbors and families against each other, and individuals against everyone and everyone against each individual. The war's width, length and depth multiply as each violent act destroys the community's material base and, worse, its cultural and spiritual base, turning the traditional culture of solidarity into one of destruction and mutual hatred. It is also through the conflict's violence that hegemonic masculinity and patriarchal culture are reinforced.

We must oppose the normalization of war, especially in the Pacific region, where violence had always been an extraordinary event. Violence and death have now been turned into everyday occurrences. The daily, constant threats against youth and, increasingly, women provoke the dehumanization of everyone. We can see evidence of this in the quotidian and public expressions against women: "Don't say anything or I will chop you," "Don't act funny or you will be chopped," "Women behave because women are being chopped."[35] That is why it is impossible to stay silent. We must first scream in horror if we are to overcome the war and violence that are part of our daily lives. We must go back to seeing war as exceptional and we must demand justice and reparations.[36]

Violence against women, and particularly femicide, is symptomatic of structural and systemic problems that cannot be solved unless the underlying cause—the literal imposition through blood and fire ["a sangre y fuego"] of a hegemonic development model—is addressed. The State is incapable of solving these problems because it has been bought by corporate global capital.

Corruption invades all state institutions, exacerbating the violence against the community. The government and its justice apparatus, which act with impunity and comply with paramilitary aggressors, subject surviving victims and their families to permanent and intense insecurity, as though they do not care to dispense justice.

There is an undeclared war against women in the world, which is experienced acutely in the Colombian South Pacific region. This war is fueled by the legal and illegal actors that push a development model forward and by the global colonial matrix of power that institutes itself through megaprojects. These megaprojects endanger all life: not only human life, but also nature, which represents the possibility of human life since it offers the conditions for human existence.

DIFFERENTIAL ETHNIC AND ORGANIZATIONAL AFFECTATIONS

These crimes against Black and, in some cases, Indigenous women have differential implications for the women themselves, their families and their communities. The victims belong to both an ethnic minority and their extended families, so the effects are wide sweeping. The repercussions of femicide go beyond the personal, the family and the community: they also affect the traditional organizational forms that support the sociocultural network of life in the territory.

The death threats facing women, which are present throughout the whole country (and many other places in the world), take on particular dimensions in ethnic territories ["territorios étnicos"] such as Buenaventura.

> Women who belong to ethnic minorities encounter more obstacles accessing the justice system, both because of state officials' racism and because of the lack of differential frameworks in the institutional processes' delivery of justice. The impunity and indifference with which those who, in the name of state institutions, act are proof that women's lives and integrities are seen as disposable. Evidence tells us that crimes against women are not isolated events or crimes of passion, yet both the State and society legitimize these crimes by treating them with impunity. The death of a woman is not just the death of one woman; it is the destruction of an entire family and also a whole community if we take into consideration the extended family in black communities. The killing of women constitutes ethnocide in the context of ethnic minorities.[37]

Furthermore, women who are societal and community leaders, and women who advocate for human and land rights are all at high risk of becoming victims of femicide.

> No one wants to come forward as a leader. They are afraid someone will hurt or target them . . . At this point the organization and all of us women are very afraid. The neighborhood action boards are afraid of doing any activity, small as it might be. We are afraid to walk the land; we no longer do the normal activities we once did.[38]

The violence against women is inflicted as a means to keep other women and their organizations in line and as a threat to the general community.

> The flyer with the threat says that we who represent the organizations for the displaced population are also under threat for publishing the government's public policies. We are not asking anything of them; we are making demands of the government . . . Maybe it's the government that's threatening me . . . I'm telling the government to give me what I'm entitled to as a displaced person because it failed to guarantee the protection of the area. So I don't understand why the Black Eagles [a paramilitary group] is threatening the organizations of displaced people. That's my question: I don't know why they are threatening us.[39]

Women are direct victims of the armed conflict, as both mothers and family members of the young women and men who have already disappeared or been murdered. Traditionally, ethnic minorities regarded death as a natural event and developed cultural practices around it that allowed for the strengthening of communal life and collective mourning. Today, death is a tragedy insofar as homicides and femicides are carried out as warning signs for those who dare oppose the developmental logic of capital and the armed conflict. Disappearances and dismemberments force the community to partake regularly in the ritual of saying goodbye to the dead and thereby prevent the community from strengthening its communal ties.

In conclusion, this paper offers a general view that privileges the viewpoint and experiences of Afro-Colombian women who are subjected to multiple oppressions, resist them nonetheless, persist, and imagine insurgent processes in order to create and recreate their worlds. I hope to have corrected some of the most common erroneous characterizations which stigmatize and/or render banal the violence to which they are subjected. This violence is part of a strategy of deterritorialization, which targets the Colombian Pacific region's Black population in favor of advancing the global accumulation of capital.

NOTES

1. *Censo general de población* (Colombia: Departamento Administrativo de Estadísticas, 2005), https://www.dane.gov.co/index.php/estadisticas-por-tema/demografia-y-poblacion/censo-general-2005-1. The "paisa" region consists of the Colombian departments of Antioquia, Risaralda, Caldas, and parts of Quindío and Norte del Valle.

2. "Ventajas Competitivas," Cámara de Comercio de Buenaventura, accessed 2014, https://www.ccbun.org/articulos/ventajas-competitivas.

3.Albert Traver, "El Gobierno colombiano militariza a Buenaventura, la ciudad más violenta de ese país," *La información*, March 22, 2014, accessed June 8, 2021, https://www.lainformacion.com/espana/el-gobierno-colombiano-militariza-la-ciudad-mas-violenta-del-pais_4e33aBQli2PFJLsiGQLjA1/.

4. One of the most gruesome periods in Colombian history, known as "La Violencia" [The Violence], started with the killing of populist leader Jorge Eliécer Gaitán on April 9, 1948. This was a bipartisan and brutal conflict between liberals and conservatives, which left more than 300,000 people dead over a period of 10 years. The Colombian Pacific region did not experience this magnitude of violence.

5. See Henry Granada, "Intervention of Community Social Psychology: The Case of Colombia," *Applied Psychology* 40.2 (1991): 165–179. See also: Stella Rodríguez, "Fronteras fijas, valor de cambio y cultivos ilícitos en el Pacífico caucano de Colombia," *Revista Colombiana de Antropología* 44, no.1 (January-June, 2008).

6. Arturo Escobar and Álvaro Pedrosa, eds., *Pacífico ¿Desarrollo o diversidad* (Bogotá: CEREC, ECOFONDO, 1996).

7. Translator's note: In the Kuna Tule language spoken in Northern Colombia and Southern Panama, Abya Yala means "land in its full maturity" and is the name given to what is known today as the Americas. Bolivian Aymara leader Takir Mamani suggested that Indigenous peoples and Indigenous organizations use the term to refer to the Americas, and many organizations and intellectuals have embraced this idea.

8. Arturo Escobar, *Encountering Development: The Making and Unmaking of the Third World*. 2nd ed. (Princeton: Princeton University Press, 2012), 4.

9. Aníbal Quijano, "¿Bien vivir?: Entre el 'desarrollo' y la des/colonialidad del poder," in *Cuestiones y horizontes: de la dependencia histórico-estructural a la colonialidad/descolonialidad del poder* (Buenos Aires: CLACSO, 2014), http://biblioteca.clacso.edu.ar/clacso/se/20140424014720/Cuestionesyhorizontes.pdf.

10. Redacción Noticiero 90 Minutos, "Desempleo en Buenaventura: un panorama crítico, especialmente para los jóvenes," February 11, 2021, accessed June 8, 2021, https://90minutos.co/desempleo-buenaventura-panorama-critico-jovenes-11-02-2021/.

11. Among the projects about to be executed or currently in the process of execution: Water Industrial Project, Cement Dock, Arquímedes Project (Buenaventura-Tumaco Waterway), Delta of the Dagua River, Deep Waters Port in Bahía Málaga, Port Expansion and Pier Project in urban Buenaventura. The category "Negredumbre," coined by anthropologist Rogerio Velásquez from Chocó, refers to the "masses of Blacks that are the object of his investigation, in a semantic audacity that relates Blacks ['negros'] with crowds ['muchedumbre']. It is not just any crowd, but the one that consists of Afro-descendants put in a situation of exclusion and marginality, 'those at the bottom,' 'the cursed race,' 'the enslaved,' 'the miserable.' . . . They inhabit a specific territory: that of the rivers, the jungle and the rural world." See: Claudia Leal, "Recordando a Saturio. Memorias del racismo en el Chocó," *Revista de Estudios Sociales*, no. 27 (Summer 2007), quoted in Germán Patiño, "Prologue," in *Ensayos escogidos: Rogerio Velásquez,* ed. Germán Patiño (Bogotá: Ministerio de Cultura de Colombia, 2010), 12. They also inhabit the belts of poverty that surround the big cities. The *negredumbre* are all those who belong to the Black mass of impoverished people that inhabit this nation; it is the social block of those who are oppressed for reasons of race, ethnicity and class. This *negredumbre* is the mass, a sociological category, like Patiño proposes, more than a subjectivity. It is the people at the base of the social pyramid who are stigmatized because of the color of their skin. See: Patiño, "Prologue."

12. Javier Arboleda, "HH contó cómo fue la entrada al Valle y el Cauca," *VerdadAbierta.com*, January 22, 2009, accessed June 8, 2021, https://verdadabierta.com/hh-o-carepollo/

13. Ibid. The word *boleteo* designates a guerrilla group's war tax (extortion) levied on businesses and merchants in exchange for leaving them alone and not kidnapping them, and as a means to finance the guerrilla's subversive activities. Paramilitary groups also charge this tax and offer protection against criminals and guerrilla groups in exchange. Today, paramilitary groups levy this tax in Buenaventura, particularly on small street vendors, threatening to kill whomever does not pay.

14. Misión Permanente por la Vida en Buenaventura, "S.O.S. from Colombia's Largest Port," *Solidarity Collective,* published January 21, 2014, accessed June 8, 2021, https://www.solidaritycollective.org/post/s-o-s-from-colombia-s-largest-port---s-o-s-del-puerto-principal-de-colombia.

15. Translator's note: "Casas de pique" are houses used by criminal bands to dismember and disappear bodies. Acuafosas are clandestine cemeteries in the swamps.

16. The idea of vertical notions of Christian charity was suggested to the author by Jeannette Rojas Silva in conversation. Translator's note: By "estar del propio lado," the author refers to "a situation in which many people and communities find themselves in the context of the armed conflict in Colombia. People are afraid that those who have been their neighbors for decades and generations are secretly members of an armed group, and that just by saying hello to these neighbors one can become a target of the opposing group and be killed. This fear breaks the ancestral communal bonds that existed between people, it individualizes each person to the point that most feel that 'everyone should mind their own business'" (email to the translator, March 12, 2018). See: Betty Ruth Lozano, "Estar del propio lado," *Boletín Territorio Pacífico,* no. 1 (2007).

17. By *deterritorialization* I refer not only to forced displacement, but also to the violent processes that break communal ties and facilitate rootlessness. Deterritorialization is taking the population out of the territory and taking the territory out of the community's collective and personal imagination.

18. "Master Plan Buenaventura 2050," Grupo Gonval, published July 2014, https://www.grupogonval.com/2014/10/master-plan-buenaventura-2050.html.

19. *Mazamorreo* is a traditional way of looking for gold in rivers with a flat wooden pan used to wash the sand from the riverbed.

20. Norman Lazano Jackson and Peter Jackson, trans, *Law 70 of Colombia (1993): In Recognition of the Right of Black Colombians to Collectively Own and Occupy their Ancestral Lands*, accessed November 22, 2020, https://www.wola.org/sites/default/files/downloadable/Andes/Colombia/past/law%2070.pdf.

21. cf. Odile Hoffman, *Comunidades negras en el Pacífico colombiano* (Quito: Ediciones Abya-Yala, 2007).

22. This viewpoint has been shared at various meetings with women organizations and institutions in Buenaventura.

23. Laura Marcela Hincapié, "Violencia sexual, delito invisible detrás del conflicto armado," *El País*, published August 2011, http://www.elpais.com.co/judicial/violencia-sexual-delito-invisible-detras-del-conflicto-armado.html; *Violencia contra las mujeres en el Distrito de Buenaventura: Informe Temático*, Defensoría delegada para la evaluación del riesgo de la población civil como consecuencia del conflicto armado Sistema de Alertas Tempranas (SAT) (Bogotá: Defensoría del Pueblo, 2011), 66, https://www.sdgfund.org/sites/default/files/Colombia_VBG%20Buenaventura.pdf. All quotes from this document that appear in this chapter have been translated by Carolina Alonso Bejarano.

24. Ibid., 77.

25. Traver, "El Gobierno colombiano militariza."

26. Gonzalo Sánchez and Martha Nubia Bello, *¡Basta Ya! Colombia: Memories of War and Dignity*, trans. Jimmy Weiskopf and Joaquín Franco (Bogotá: National Center for Historical Memory, 2016), 82, http://www.centrodememoriahistorica.gov.co/descargas/informes2016/basta-ya-ingles/BASTA-YA-ingles.pdf.

27. *Sapo/sapa* ("toad" in Spanish) is a popular name given to an informant who infiltrates a group to obtain information.

28. *Buena* (literally, "good" in Spanish) is a popular vernacular to refer to attractive women.

29. "Violencia contra las Mujeres," 56, 72.

30. Jeannette Rojas, Danelly Estupiñán and Teresa Casiani, *Derrotar la invisibilidad. Un reto para las mujeres afrodescendientes en Colombia: El panorama de la violencia y la violación de los derechos humanos contra las mujeres afrodescendientes en Colombia, en el marco de los derechos colectivos* (Colombia: Proyecto Mujeres Afrodescendientes Defensoras de Derechos Humanos, 2012), 18, 24.

31. *Arrechas*: Popular Colombian expression that refers to a sexually aroused person, someone prone to sexual acts.

32. "Violencia contra las Mujeres," 64.

33. Alexandra Riveros Rueda, "¿Por qué nos duele Buenaventura? Feminicidio, racismo, etnocidio e impunidad," *Feminismo afrodiaspórico*, published November 16, 2013, accessed June 8, 2021, https://feministasafrodiasporicas.blogspot.com /2013/11/deja-de-normalizar-el-asesinato-las.html. See also: "La impunidad reina en el caso de los feminicidios en Buenaventura," *Asociación de Cabildos Indígenas del Cauca*, published October 2013, http://anterior.nasaacin.org/index.php/2013/10/12 /buenaventurala-impunidad-reina-en-el-caso-de-los-feminicidios-en-buenaventura/. "La impunidad reina en el caso de los feminicidios en Buenaventura" was originally produced by various organizations, including the Colectivo Akina Zaji Sauda, en el que participaba la autora.

34. Betty Ruth Lozano, "El feminismo no puede ser uno porque las mujeres somos diversas. Aportes a un feminismo negro decolonial desde la experiencia de las mujeres negras del Pacífico," *La manzana de la discordia* 5, no. 2 (2010).

35. Kuagro Ri Ma Changaina Ri PCN (Women's Collective of the Black Communities Process), "Shadow Report to the Committee for the Elimination of Discrimination Against Women," United Nations CEDAW Convention to Eliminate All Forms of Discrimination Against Women (2013), http://www.afrocolombians.com/pdfs/ AfroColombianWomen-AbstractCEDAWReport2013.pdf.

36. Franz Hinkelammert, *Yo soy, si tú eres. El sujeto de los derechos humanos* (Mexico City: Centro de Estudios Ecuménicos, 2010).

37. "La impunidad reina."

38. "Violencia contra las Mujeres," 57.

39. Ibid.

PART IV

Indigenous Cosmologies, Struggles for Land, and Decoloniality

Chapter 9

This Knowledge Counts!
Harmony and Spirituality in
Miskitu Critical Thought

Jessica Martínez-Cruz

The relationship between Indigenous medicine and Western biomedicine has long been fraught with difficulty.[1] In Nicaragua, long-standing institutional efforts are attempting to advance therapeutic cooperation between Indigenous and biomedical health systems in the framework of interculturality.[2] Mostly, these efforts see Indigenous knowledge as what Kyle Whyte calls "supplemental value," where Indigenous knowledge is only considered relevant when it can be put at the service of scientific knowledge by means of being translatable or translated into a Western value system.[3] At the core of the so-called cooperation, a major challenge is the undermining of traditional health systems by the Westernized hegemonic view of health that leaves aside broader narratives of wellbeing from Indigenous people.[4]

I will discuss here the slow, late and contradictory response to a crisis in the Miskitu community of Raiti by the central level of Nicaragua's Ministry of Health to reflect on the complex hierarchy of knowledge embedded in the narratives of public institutions, constitutive of the "coloniality of power" in Latin America, where other ways of knowing become "minor," "other," or not even considered knowledge, thus subalternized and colonized.[5] I refer to the term coined and developed by Aníbal Quijano and other Latin American and Caribbean thinkers to explain the Eurocentrification of modern/colonial capitalism that emerges in the colonization process of what is known today as the Americas, hand in hand with modernity.

Coloniality as power structure came with its specific cognitive model: "Eurocentrism" as a specific rationaliy or way to produce knowledge.

The latter is understood in the dominant modern/colonial worldview as the new perspective of knowledge that since its conception systematically classified non-Europe as the past and therefore inferior, non-modern or primitive and even non-human. Eurocentrism was actively formed before the mid-seventeenth century and became hegemonic with the dominion of the European bourgeois class, the secularization of its thought and the experiences and needs "of the modern colonial global capitalist model."[6]

What is of most relevance for this article is the current prevalence of Westernized views in the institutions of countries with colonialist experiences. Similar to the discussion of Indigenous environmental knowledge and governance-value in Whyte's work, the negation in Nicaragua of Indigenous knowledge by the biomedical system not only poses a serious ethical problem, but also shows the efficacy of the nation-state to produce continuous threats against Indigenous autonomy and self-determination in different ways, for instance through its politics of knowledge.[7]

I am a mestizo feminist scholar-activist from Nicaragua. While briefly working at the country's Ministry of Health from 2003 to 2004, I participated in a public health response to an outbreak of *Grisi Siknis* or *Krisi Siknis* suffered by the Miskitu population of Raiti, a community on the bank of the Wangki River in the municipality of Bocay. Raiti is part of the Indigenous territory of Kipla Sait Tasbaika (KST), between the department of Jinotega, mostly populated by mestizos, and the North Caribbean Coast Autonomous Region (RACCN). In this Afro-Indigenous region, the Miskitu people comprise the largest Indigenous population. KST is one of six Indigenous territories that make up the heart of the Bosawas Biosphere Reserve.

Unlike the Caribbean part of Nicaragua colonized by the British Empire, the Pacific region was colonized by Spaniards and their decendants forged their own version of Eurocentric rationality, what I call the Pacific Eurocentered authority, which is hegemonic in the public institutions.

As an outsider, a mestizo social researcher working on a public health response in a different and problematic place in the colonial axis of power, I remained silent for ten years about what I witnessed in Raiti: Miskitu people's experiences with *Grisi Siknis*. Silvia Rivera Cusicanqui has pointed out with great accuracy "the epistemological dilemma of ethnography: the key linguistic and cultural untranslatability, characteristic of the asymmetrical relationship between individuals and cultures whose cognitive horizon is diametrically opposite."[8] This does not mean that a critical understanding of these experiences cannot be reached by social analysis, but that the critical understanding here is in another place. It is not in social scientific narratives, but in Miskitu oral histories and in the renunciation of the notion that we, the researchers, can explain better how the world functions for others—those others who have been portrayed by the hegemonic history as perpetually in need of Western rationality, scientific knowledge, categorizations, and translations.

I kept working in these Indigenous territories in other moments of my activist and professional life. In 2014, with a mate from *Aula Propia,* my feminist collective, and the Institute of Traditional Medicine and Community Development (IMTRADEC) of the University of the Autonomous Regions of the Nicaraguan Caribbean Coast (URACCAN), an institution working with traditional healers, I regained contact with Porcela Sandino Hemsly, the Indigenous doctor who healed Raiti of *Grisi Siknis* in 2003. With her permission and because of my relationship with IMTRADEC, I put my journal notes together and did a retrospective reflexive account of what I have witnessed and have been told in Raiti over the years. Building on scholarly contributions from critical thinking in Latin America, mostly decolonial thought, appeals and practices, Miskitu intellectual production and healers' narratives, as well as my own 'ethnographic experience,' this article looks at the ways in which Western knowledge embedded in an institutional health system has worked to subordinate and negate Indigenous knowledge, in particular knowledge about health and illness processes in the *Grisi Siknis* experience of Miskitu peoples from Nicaragua.

COLLABORATION OF KNOWLEDGE? NICARAGUAN INTER-CULTURAL HEALTH MODEL

After the 1979 revolution, the Nicaraguan health model of attention changed radically. In the following decade, the country was awarded the Alma-Ata prize for Primary Health Care for their efforts to guarantee universal access.[9] Since that date on, one of the strengths of the Nicaraguan health system is its nationwide community-based health network with home-based community clinics, maternal homes (casas maternas), and extended networks of health promoters (brigadistas) and midwives (parteras).[10]

A major transformation in the 1980s was the constitution of the regional and departmental health systems. In 1985, the Ministry of Health created a program to "revitalize popular and traditional medicine."[11] From 1987 with the new Autonomy Statue—the proclaimed Law 28 for the two regions North and South of the Caribbean Coast—the relationship between the Nicaraguan state and the ethnic groups from those regions was formally acknowledged as based on historical rights.[12] By that time, the concept of *interculturalidad* (interculturality) became an important part of the conception of a new health model where cultural differences were claimed to be respected, the inter-connectedness between cultures was represented, and the inequalities based on ethnic relations constituted historically in society were acknowledged.[13] Hence, this is the place where the Indigenous knowledge acquires formal value in the Nicaraguan health system.

There are more state moves at the policy level to add as milestones in the official narratives. According to the account of Carrie, Mackey, and Laird, 1996 saw the incorporation in the National Health Plan of an aim that refers to the integration of the "cosmovision" of the communities into the health system practices.[14] In 2005, the General Health Law that followed the designed new National Health Plan 2005–2015 became consistent with the international framework for Indigenous rights. By the year 2011, with a different government elected in 2007, the health policy moved again toward the interest of universal care access, and this time a new law—No. 759, Law of Traditional Ancestral Medicine—granted space to "incorporate intercultural concepts into the health care models."[15]

Decentralization policy has been changing since the 1980s, sometimes with quite opposite strategies such as the neoliberal policy used in the 1990s, together with the current supracentralization of the state's decision-making processes, particularly in regards to the autonomous project of the Caribbean Coast.[16] What is happening in reality with cultural diversity and autonomy in a multicultural and multiethnic space, according with the National Constitution, is not easy to describe. The following poem is a glimpse of how challenging it is in practice to exercise this "constitutional right" in the country for Afro-descendant and Indigenous populations.

> This ya resitation a true reality
> So mi want unu listen to me A wa only talk the thru about we
> municipality
> And how polititian go on, about changing wi destiny.
>
> All day ne come de talk bout true democracy
> So come de tell we se we have autonomy But remember autonomy
> da self governing by
> an by me
> Then how ina the world a stranger da maniger over we[17]

Looking at experiences in the Region Autonomous of the Caribbean Coast North (RACCN), Carrie, Mackey, and Laird argue that health care accessibility and the delivery of integrated health services appears to be very deficient in Miskitu communities.[18] There are also some particularities on how it happens, when it happens, the acceptance of traditional ancestral medicine or cultural differences in the institutional Inter-cultural Health Model. Based in an anthropological fieldwork in the same region, Wedel reveals how Miskitu healing knowledge is used as last resort to face the failures of biomedical approaches and calls attention to the necessity of a better understanding from health authorities and biomedical personnel to local explanatory models of health engaging in ontological negotiations that could lead to more equal forms of therapeutic cooperation.[19] Both studies point out how medical practices in health services position biomedical providers as the medical authorities acting as gatekeepers to the traditional healers.[20]

In addition to this complexity, the majority of biomedical doctors came mostly from the Pacific dominated by Mestizo culture and the health personnel are mostly trained in the Pacific; they are the ones directly in charge of implementing an unclear "intercultural" institutional model when an Indigenous, an Afro-Caribbean, a rural woman, or the usual "other" requires health care.[21]

After almost 30 years of autonomy, there are many critics of a health model that has been ideal on paper but not quite in reality. For some, *interculturalidad* has been absent in the implementation of health policies in the autonomous regions. Even when health authorities at the different levels (central, regional, and local) acknowledge interculturality as a guiding element of the regional health system, how this is interpreted by the actors involved is very different. For national health officials, this concept "is simply recognition that culture is an important variable in health and that indigenous medicine should be accepted. [For the regional authorities] *interculturalidad* is a political concept that also refers to the transfer of decision making and power to the region."[22]

From the narrative of Miskitu people with whom I have talked about *Grisi Siknis* over the years, whether they are traditional healers, intellectuals, or health practitioners within the biomedical systems, if interculturality is ever to be a reality in the country, beyond social and political recognition of cultural differences and historical rights, it must involve the acknowledgement of a different "cosmovision" and thus of an own Miskitu epistem.[23] As Catherine Walsh has argued, this epistemic recognition has become a visible component in the struggles of both Indigenous and Afro-descendant people in Latin America in recent years, where these "struggles that . . . are not just social and political but also epistemic in nature."[24]

Locating *Grisi Siknis* in Mainstream Narratives: Health and Anthropological Texts

In biomedical language, *Grisi Siknis* is situated within the scope of mental health narratives. It is part of dissociative cultural mental disorders, together with other "culture bound syndromes," as uniquely characteristic of some Indigenous people, such as the *pibloktoq* or Arctic hysteria of the Inuit's living within the Arctic Circle, Navajo "frenzy" witchcraft, *chakore* of ngawbere of the northern Panama, and some forms of *amok* in Indonesia and Malaysia.[25] According to these sources, because of its features of a trance-like state, high levels of activity, exhaustion, and posterior amnesia of the episodes, it is also commonly known as "running" or "fleeing" syndrome.

According to the psychiatrists and biomedical doctors participating in evaluating or reporting the 2003 episode of Raiti, it was certainly a mental disorder culturally determined, very likely to be defined as massive or collective hysteria that is contagious. Some of the psychiatrists and bio-medical doctors gave relevance to the conditions under which this episode has happened (i.e., isolation and adverse economic conditions such as extreme poverty). Plenty of others within the health sector continue to think of *Grisi Siknis* as a matter of "those crazy-acting Miskitu people."[26]

The treatment has been through the use of Indigenous traditional medicine, and in the words of professionals in the health system and anthropology, this is recognized as the only possible treatment. Among the explanations that anthropologists have given to this phenomena is Phillip Dennis's, which attributes it to stress-related issues in life situations.[27] The "disease" has also been thought of as an expression of liberation of tensions in situations that need the search for solutions to a shared crisis, or the pressures on young women during their transition to womanhood, almost a ritual of such transition.[28] Others see the illness from wider perspectives, pointing at the necessity to understand the social, personal and environmental context and the role of culture in relation to illness and suffering.[29] The latter writing called attention to see *Grisi Siknis* from a cross-cultural perspective, beyond the "culture-bound condition" classification occurring only in Miskitu culture, toward an understanding of it as a Miskitu version of involuntary mass spirit possession. Some of these anthropological records also report the spreading character of the "disease."

In the first records, *Grisi Siknis* was understood as commonly experienced by female teenagers from Miskitu communities; however, there are some episodes such as the one in Awastara in 1978–1979 where five men were affected. According to Dennis and Jamieson, those men were considered "feminine" by the community.[30] In contemporary episodes, the gender feature has changed, like the event in war camps in Honduras in the late 1980s, or the event of Karata Lagoon affecting only men, or the outbreak in Raiti where 68 young and adolescent men were affected.[31]

In 2010, in a journey to Amak, the capital of the Mayangna Sauni Bu (MSB), a neighbouring territory of Raiti where Mayangna Indigenous people live, I heard for the first time from the voice of a communitarian leader that two episodes of *Grisi Siknis* occurred in 2004 and 2008 in this community to

Mayangna women; one of those women was his wife. In my experience in Raiti in 2003, when asking Mayangna people passing through the community about *Grisi Siknis*, they usually answered, "that is a Miskitu issue."

YAMNI IWAIA: MISKITU NARRATIVES OF WELLBEING FROM THE WANKI RIVER

In the narratives of Miskitu people from the community of San Andrés de Bocay, in the Indigenous Territory of Miskitu Indian Tasbaika Kum, a neighboring place of Raiti, located also in the bank of the Wangki River, *Yamni iwaia* means living according to a way of conceiving life influenced by religion, Miskitu spirituality and politics—a way of living that goes in agreement with guiding principles of individual and collective life. An important part of this is *Pain iwaia,* which means living well according to material conditions, to have a good home, to be successful in social and productive activities within the community, to have health, to dress well, to eat well, and to live without problems with other members of the community.[32]

Pain Iwaia was the most frequent term to refer to the meanings and experiences of wellbeing; according to the participatory research mentioned above, crucial principles to achieve *Pain Iwaia* were *laman laka* (harmony) and *asla iwaia* (living in unity) amongst others, and the exercise of territorial sovereignty was an indispensable condition. *Asla iwaia* is a guiding principle of collective efforts; it was also identified as the central element for the community to be able to sustain any effort in support of its wellbeing.

Miskitu wellbeing is closely related with their spiritual world. Accounts from Miskitu intellectuals and researchers highlight how in Miskitu cosmology, different spiritual beings that dwell in the environment could cause serious imbalances into the life of Miskitu people.[33] A *curandero* (spiritual/herbal healer) told me that *laman laka* is not only about relations between human beings, it is also about relations with the environment, because there must be a balance in the different realms of power. Later in a group conversation in which adults and elderly men were doing an in depth reflection about the changes in their own productive practices (i.e. fishing, hunting, and farming) they explained to us (the researchers):

M1: The kingdom is a power; it means that there is human power, the power of plants and the power of animals.

I: Do plants also have spirit? And the animals, too?

M2: That's right, it's always the same, so when you transmit all that, people respect a tree, and they don't use the machete.

M3: Because it's bleeding just as human.[34]

Fagoth argues that traditional Miskitu language does not have a word for sickness; even though in current times they use the word *siknis*, what they use to identify an ill being are imbalances with the environment.[35] Those imbalances have been translated for Western people as illnesses. Spiritual imbalance means more than physical ailments; the state of equilibrium or the lack of it is at the centre of this Miskitu cosmovision. This precept gives forms to the ways that they see their wellbeing and how they deal in practice with the world in which they live. To experience health and being well with nature and other human beings are inseparable parts in this vision.

Looking at *Grisi Siknis* can provide us with a glimpse into the Miskitu way to see and experience the world. According to the most recent Miskitu scholarly production about *Grisi Siknis*, based in a case study in the community of *Krin Krin*, black magic or occultism is the cause of the problem.[36] Through this practice, some people manipulate spirits, who later take possession of the people in the community, producing imbalances in their health and consequences in their families, as well as in the whole community. As stated by the authors, to cure this spiritual ailment Miskitu people need not only to resort to their ancestral knowledge but also to the plants and supplies that nature gives them to prepare their treatments in specific territories.[37] Thus, they need to ensure some essential rights that national and international frameworks are obliged to meet: rights intertwined with territoriality and self-determination. As pointed out by Bernal and Robertson, "cultural integrity, territorial rights and autonomy . . . form part of the 'ingredients' for healing."[38]

The ethno-history of *Grisi Siknis* has been recorded in travelers' written texts and anthropologists' accounts for more than a century. Now it is almost unquestionable that *Grisi Siknis* has a long history amongst Miskitu populations in Honduras and Nicaragua where they live; Dennis and Jamieson have identified features of "Miskitu hysteria" closely related to *Grisi Siknis* in Bell and Conzemius.[39] There are later accounts, such as Dennis's reference to the Awastara epidemic with a duration of 20 years and more than 60 people affected, and Jamieson's analysis about sporadic episodes in the 1990s in Kakabila and outbreaks in Raitipura in 1992 and 1993, which bring *Grisi Siknis* to contemporary times.[40]

Since 2000—considered a moment of the increase of registered episodes––there is also a close follow up from the IMTRADEC, the sole organization in the country working systematically to approach *Grisi Siknis*.[41] The long presence of these events, the ways that the Nicaraguan Ministry of Health has been repetitively managing the illness through the use of traditional ancestral medicine, and how *Grisi Siknis* has been dramatically affecting the lives and health of Miskitu communities, particularly women and teenagers, highlight the relevance to discuss this issue with a more critical view.[42]

NARRATIVES OF (DIS)HARMONY: THE EPISODE IN RAITI, WANGKI RIVER

In December 2003, I was part of the team of psychiatrists, doctors, traditional healers, nurses and social scientists sent by national and regional health authorities to Raiti to participate in the research and treatment of the outbreak of *Grisi Siknis,* which began almost three months before. I traveled with the Director of the National Programme of Mental Health and another psychiatrist from the central level of the Ministry of Health. At the time, *Grisi Siknis* was medically known as a "cultural-bounded syndrome." The other doctor had known about this "Miskitu aliment" since the late 1980s, when he was an authority at the National Psychiatric Hospital where some Miskitu people with mental health challenges were treated. The central level of the Ministry sent us with specific roles; while the Director would deal with Miskitu authorities and the national press, the other doctor and I were to conduct social research and accompany the healers.

We were all Mestizos, coming from Managua (the capital of Nicaragua) to Wiwilí, a municipality in the department of Jinotega, in the northern part of the country, where representatives from the Organization of American States (OAS) and a nurse joined us. They had a development project for postconflict communities in Raiti. We used their means of transport because they were better equipped for travel. We then traveled by boat through the Wangki River for almost twelve hours before reaching the community.

A well-known healer from the region, Porcela Sandino, a *prapit* (prophet)––one of the wisest in the organization of the Miskitu healer system and cosmovision—plus her assistant (and husband), two nurses, and a professor were sent by the health authorities of the RACCN and the IMTRADEC. All of them were Miskitu and arrived from the opposite direction of the river. They did a shorter but riskier traverse, coming from Bilwi, the capital of RACCN, to Waspam, the neighboring municipality, and then by river; their voyage passed through the rapids of the Wanki, a dangerous place especially in December because of the rainy season, but a very frequent passage for Miskitu people from the Wanki River.

The only doctor of the health centre of Raiti (at the same time its director) and the Miskitu authorities were expecting us. The situation was very serious. After two failed attempts in the last months to treat the epidemic with traditional healers, the illness was still spreading and affected at least 139 people, roughly ten percent of Raiti's population. The majority of them were teenagers; mostly girls and boys, but also young and adult women were suffering the illness. They constituted also a substantive part of the productive force for hunting, fishing, farming and harvesting, vital activities for Raiti's sustainability.

In the main meeting between the health authorities, the local traditional authorities, and the elderly council in Raiti, there were four demands addressed to very different actors. The first request was to the healer: they wanted to know the kind of witchcraft used, the responsible person, and a guarantee of the full recovery of all those affected. Two other demands were to the central government: They asked for better and quicker responses in emergencies such as a *Grisi Siknis* outbreak, for support to face the post-epidemic situation and the possible food shortage in the coming months, given the quantity of affected people who were not working on their harvest. Their last demand was from a very different kind and was directly addressed to the mass media: Miskitu people did not want their home and territory to be portrayed in the national newspapers and television programs as an exotic and dark place in the jungle where *Grisi Siknis* occurs.

In the national and international press, the messages from the main institutional health authorities were clear: this is an illness that can only be treated by traditional Indigenous medicine. The most renowned British newspaper, *The Guardian*, reported at the time that the Nicaraguan health minister, José Antonio Alvarado, explained why they sent Miskitu healers: "If [the affected] are given anti-convulsive drugs or anti-depressants there is no improvement, but if they are given remedies by the healer they feel better."[43] This answer was similar to the first description about *Grisi Siknis* that I heard by the psychiatrist who treated some Miskitu people in the 1980s.

The Director of the Regional Health System of the North Caribbean Region, Dr. Florence Levy, confirmed that the Miskitu healers were leading the team to face the outbreak: "There's not much our doctors can do; we are giving support to the healers as they know the problem better than us. . . . The population doesn't make use of [the Nicaraguan health services] because the illness is more spiritual than physical, so they turn to the healer for the spiritual part."[44] The anthropologists were also consulted. *The Guardian* read:

Western health care people have often been skeptical of these attacks, labelling them 'mass hysteria,' or simply 'those crazy-acting Miskitu people,'" said Professor Phil Dennis, an anthropologist at Texas Tech University who spent two years studying the phenomenon in the late 1970s. He says the attacks are very serious to those experiencing them and their families, and often to entire Miskitu communities. He witnessed four attacks during his research and said the patients were "clearly in another state of reality." . . . *Grisi siknis* is a very serious health problem for Miskitu people.[45]

The director of the health centre, a Mestizo and the only biomedical doctor in the community, showed at every moment a sensitive attitude about the suffering of the people in Raiti, without any comment about his own judgments. In the case of the Miskitu nurses accompanying the healer, their attitude to the ailment and therapy was also very respectful but less clear to me. I could not identify whether they believed in the spiritual ailment as such; or maybe their ambiguity was only an attitude in front of me, a Mestizo professional sent by the central level of the Ministry to research the situation. One of them told me that she did not know anything about "magic" because she was Christian and the Church forbids these beliefs. However, she has been with people suffering *Grisi Siknis* since the epidemic in 2000 at the Luxemburgo School in Bilwi, the capital of the Autonomous Caribbean Region of the North. Her final remarks were: "They are my people and they suffered a lot."

At the national level, in newspapers and television, the discourses of health authorities were severely criticized by religious authorities of the Pacific because they were using *sukias* (shamans in Miskitu language) to cure people instead of Western medicine. Besides that, the journalists were pointing out the lack of capacity in the Ministry of Health to deal with this situation because of the obvious length of the illness in Raiti, the quantity of people affected, and the failed previous attempts to cure them. The national controversy added more pressure to the role of the Ministry of Health; however, it was mostly because of an unresolved issue, rather than questioning the lack of understanding of the Indigenous vision of health and illness in the Ministry.

The detailed account of the journey to Raiti reveals how the response by the authorities was mediated even geographically by power relations. The Mestizo team coming from Managua, accompanied by the media, was in charge of research and public relations with the media and authorities, while the Miskitu team coming from RACCN was in charge of accompanying the healers and delivering the appropriate "therapy." This is not necessarily a negative distribution of tasks, but it does illustrate the instrumental use of the healers in contrast with the negation of their voices. It must be noted that even the strongest critics within the Ministry of Health said that the traditional healers were part of the Ministry actions.

Conversational Moments

The apparent leader of the affected people was Cornelio, who was 17 years old and with whom I had many conversations during my journey. He was a hard-working and very responsible young man: the son of a mother who raised him alone and the main support of his family. I also talked with others affected by the malady (most of them girls of about 15 years of age) and their families, as well as with some traditional leaders respected by the community, which were not present in the "formal" meetings between the Ministry of Health and Miskitu traditional authorities. They gave me important insights not expressed in the public meetings or interviews with the doctors and journalists in which I participated.

One of the issues raised by the people with whom I had these informal conversations was the abusive role played by the Mestizo guardian of the building of OAS in the community. This problematic role was expressed in two intrinsically linked ways. First, he held a lot of power: as a worker of OAS in charge of key logistic aspects—the access to the building, the keys to use some places, and so forth—his proceeding was more like gatekeeper of the material power of OAS over the community without their professional team's awareness. Second, his behavior directly toward Miskitu girls: being a foreign man in his 50s, the "seduction" of at least five of the affected girls was not only a felony under Nicaraguan Law, but also an abuse of power by all means with unknown consequences for the life of the girls. At the end of our stay in Raiti, the health authorities and the OAS team negotiated the suspension of the guardian and his immediate leave. Later, in Managua, the Prosecutor of Children's rights responsible of following up this kind of situations was informed.

When the attacks occurred, the symptoms were repeatedly the same: headaches, feelings of anxiety and fear, blurred vision, and loss of immediate (short term) memory. The manifestations were also almost the same: long periods of trance-like unconsciousness interrupted by sudden bouts of frenzied behavior, attempts to flee their communities with extraordinary strength, and sometimes seizing weapons like knifes, axes, or sticks to defend themselves against something invisible to others. Through my eyes (and understanding), the most striking feature of these collective attacks was the performance of these actions with extreme ferocity against the doors or walls of the main institutional buildings: the Moravian church, the school, the *Wihta* house (Miskitu judge house), the elderly council house, and the health centre.

For some persons with whom I talked, the girls that suffered from *Grisi Siknis* were not always safe and something had to be done. The unexpected attacks in the middle of the night led some families to tie down their affected relatives because they could flee to the jungle, river or to places away from the protection of their families. A well-respected leader told me that he had seen how some men were taking advantage of this situation, touching a girl who was in trance, and he had to intervene until her family came.

Cleaning the River, the Cemetery, and the Ceiba Tree.

My account of the successful treatment in Raiti goes far beyond the therapies described in others accounts. Perhaps this is because of the experience of the healer Porcela Sandino, who besides the preparations of some medicinal substance, individual treatment with herbs—baths and smoke—and collective ritual with the affected people, did a therapeutic journey in the community. As I remember, the spiritual therapy consisted of three main moments with the people—individual and collective—and the environment. The collective ritual was in a central place called the *auditorio*, a big *Tambo* house of a traditional construction made with wood high above the ground, high enough to avoid flooding during the rainy season. Neither I nor the director of the Health Center participated in this ritual. Porcela warned me that it could be very dangerous because of the previous attacks against health authorities, and because this time it would not be a small group of people, as the days before; in the *auditorio,* larger groups of affected people would be entering gradually.

Then came the cleaning journey through the community. I followed Porcela in this ritual. There were three spiritual and, at the same time, physical places to clean: the cemetery, the jungle through the ceiba tree, and the water of the Wangki River. Here, it must be highlighted again that in Miskitu cosmology, the spiritual beings dwell in their landscape and cosmos, such as *lasa* (spirits) that are the owners of and control nature. For Porcela, *Grisi Siknis* was caused by spirits invoked by *sukias* or *curanderos* that in order to produce damage and gain money provoke the illness. During this ritual, our longest conversation took place. According to Porcela, the severe attack in Raiti, considered the longest and the most massive in the last years, was caused by the absolute absence of harmony in the community, evidenced by the neglect of a sacred place such as the cemetery, the misuse of the water from the river, and the practice of black magic by young healers in the Miskitu communities (not necessarily from Raiti).[46] Porcela was very surprised about the abandonment of the place where their ancestors rest (cemetery) as well as angry for the use of black magic, which she considered to have begun during Nicaragua's war time (1980s), when many young Miskitu people were either displaced or combatants in Honduras. They learned in the war camps from Miskitu people that used the black book, a kind of magical knowledge, which was not taught by Miskitu healers in Nicaragua.[47]

The third and last moment of the ritual was for me the embodiment of interculturality. In a long queue, girls, boys and young women, sometimes held by their relatives, one by one stared at Porcela, who was doing their last in-depth medical review. Besides her was the assistant to help her in case she needed support, and the director of the Health Center with a notebook. The health authorities and the journalists were beside her as silenced observers also taking note. The review of the results of the therapeutic process was not only concerned with the state of the last spiritual ailment; it was also about the biomedical condition of the people. One by one, Porcela said: anemia, problems in her ovaries, and so forth, while examining the people's hands and eyes. The doctor listened carefully and registered every word Porcela said about each person examined in order to follow up his or her health situation. There were some individual minor episodes of *Grisi Siknis* during this process, but the aggressive and collective episodes that all of us had witnessed days before disappeared.

From that day, Porcela kept providing medicine to the communities until she considered the *Grisi Siknis* was over in Raiti. She returned home, received national and international media attention, and became a renowned healer beyond regional borders.

THE NATIONAL FORUM OF *GRISI SIKNIS*

In February 2004, a national forum of *Grisi Siknis* took place in Managua, the first of its kind. The institutional goal was to promote a scientific and mass media discussion around the issue and a better understanding of the illness. According to Ruíz, who, like me, participated in the forum, the objectives of the event were two: one strategic and the other instrumental.[48] The former sought to transform the negative image of the North Caribbean Coast at the national level, seen in contrast to the Pacific of Nicaragua as an exotic place of sorcery and paganism, a long standing racialized stereotype about the people from the Caribbean Coast. It also sought to make visible the role that the Regional Health System and the Regional University—through the work of IMTRADEC—have played in the health of Nicaragua. The latter sought to discuss and inform about ways to prevent and treat *Grisi Siknis* to wider audience.

The people from the Health Ministry sent to Raiti the preceding December––the traditional healer Porcela Sandino, doctors, researchers and nurses—also participated. Porcela and IMTRADEC participated as presenters in the forum, wich also counted with presentations by journalists from the national media and by the Director of the National Mental Health Program. As speakers were the anthropologists Phillip Dennis and Jorge Grumberg, who have been writing about the topic.

Ruíz makes an interesting analysis of the event, arguing that the regional health authorities were trying to validate Miskitu culture and *Grisi Siknis* as part of their world, and, in a broader context, were trying to negotiate with the national authorities a real decentralization process and inclusion of cultural diversity in the health system.[49] I add to his point that the national health authorities were trying to validate their response to the illness in front of national public opinion.

Whether the voices were from journalists, psychiatrists, or anthropologists, the leading strategy in the forum was to find ways to translate the illness into "scientific" language and through cross-cultural comparison locating *Grisi Siknis* within a broader context, leaving almost silenced the perspective of the traditional healers embodied in Porcela Sandino. Sandino's is a voice that defines *Grisi Siknis* within the domain of the spiritual world, which involves dark magic and witchcraft, thus bringing traditional ancestors' knowledge to the center of the process.

At the end, as Ruíz pointed out, the forum reinforced an institutional way to see the illness, disregarding the voices of Miskitu healers: "their approach was restricted by wider racialized perceptions in society and the academic conventions of Western knowledge."[50]

UNPACKING THE RELATIONSHIP BETWEEN WESTERN KNOWLEDGE AND 'OTHER' KNOWLEDGE

This section draws attention to the ways in which the predominance of biomedical and even anthropological views that offer explanations about this Miskitu ailment undermine the broader narratives of Miskitu people, their processes of health and illness, and thus their ways of seeing, living and enjoying their wellbeing.[51]

Critical View of the "Critical" Call: From "Local Knowledge" to Plural Thoughts

Instead of discussing the "uneasy" relation between development and anthropology widely found in the literature, I will focus on some of the arguments that anthropologists have raised within this discussion, highlighting how development promoted by international aid agencies and nation states has systematically privileged global, technological, Euro-US contemporary center knowledge over local, autonomous, traditional and non-hegemonic western knowledge.[52] Some have argued that the disregard for "other" people's worldviews reflects and promotes a view of them only as exotic beings permeated by traditional beliefs, in contrast with sophisticated, modern and formal knowledge.[53]

Sillitoe accurately calls the hegemony of Western science a "global phenomenon involving many scientists from non-Western backgrounds."[54] He also comments on the contested nature of such dominance, citing some examples, such as postmodern sociology, which raises issues as the existence of the subjective and value-laden side in the quest for truth in sciences. In a similar line, Sillitoe highlights the inquires by historians into the human side of scientific endeavors, and the work of others like Latour, who spot the impact of social interaction and values in scientific outcomes and technology.[55]

The interest of critical anthropology in validating local knowledge and experiences is an attractive but yet insufficient task. As Sillitoe argues, any attempt to incorporate "local" sciences alongside techno-scientific knowledge in development work must challenge the hegemony of "global" sciences;[56] however, it is such challenge what remains a critical endeavor of anthropology. He is trying to contribute to the connection between what they term "local" and "global" sciences, leaving out the critical understanding of the power relation between knowledges.

Put in other words, in the omission of a structural and historical analysis of the "Eurocentrism" implicit in the constitution of Western science's dominance and its effect as a universal categorizing pattern in the production of knowledge, he ignores an essential aspect of the relation of power between Western science and the other sciences.[57] For instance, in the text the lack of discussion on how the mere use of the categories "local" and "global" is naturalized in development debates.

The narratives involved in the public health response to the *Grisi Siknis* experience of the community of Raiti show some key mechanisms of coloniality. While mainstream biomedical narratives are backed by science and modern rationality, the narratives of Miskitu people are permeated by cultural beliefs in "need" of scientific rationality.[58] When acknowledged as a mental disorder, a "cultural-bound syndrome," *Grisi siknis* falls in the specialized field of psychiatry or psychology, fragmenting the Miskitu holistic and spiritual way of seeing it. By using systematically traditional ancestral doctors to cure *Grisi Siknis* and placing them in a subordinate position to the gatekeepers of scientific knowledge, the biomedical system instrumentalizes and minimizes Indigenous knowledge, traditional healers, Miskitu communities, and their relations with their territories and environment.

The biomedical mental approach and the cultural anthropological perspective are hegemonic narratives about *Grisi Siknis* in Nicaragua that act as privileged binary explanatory views which leave narrow space for Miskitu interpretations of their own reality. Beyond Nicaraguan borders, these two-fold domains—the mental and the cultural—are constituted within the same meta-narrative of Western knowledge, quite opposite to the spiritual domain in which Miskitu narratives circumscribe their health and wellbeing. The latter domain is where the healers' knowledge and experience take relevance.[59]

Of course, the problem is not with the existence of such frames but rather with the ways they have historically worked to subordinate and negate "other" frames, "other" knowledge, and "other" subjects and thinkers. That is to say, the problem is in the ways that critical thought in Latin America tends to reproduce the meta-narratives of the West while discounting or overlooking the critical thinking produced by indigenous, Afro, and mestizos whose thinking finds its roots in other logic, concerns, and realities that depart not from modernity alone but also from the long horizon of coloniality.[60]

As the discussion over *Grisi Siknis* and Miskitu thought shows, beyond the validation of "local" knowledge to address communitarian health issues, what seems to be needed is the acknowledgement of different sites of knowledge, where Indigenous views of health and illness are part of critical knowledge: "a collective mode of thinking produced and thought from difference . . . knowledges lived and constructed within and marked by the context of colonialism and its processes of subalternization and racialization; that is by the common connector of coloniality."[61]

APPROACHING DECOLONIZATION
AS A FINAL REMARK

The location of some voices in a hierarchical position over the voices of "others" in the mainstream narratives of development is a main feature of the hegemony of Westernized knowledge over "other" knowledges. This hegemony is shown in the prominence of legitimized "scientific" voices to validate *Grisi Siknis* as a relevant (public) health matter of the Miskitu populations in Nicaragua, rather than the voices of Miskitu people themselves, whether they are traditional healers, community base organizations, communitarian leaders and/or those who, at the same time, are the ones experiencing this illness directly.

How am I going to control them [Indigenous healers]? They speak for themselves. And they are the ones who know about this illness better than any of the other presenters. I can't control them, especially when I agree with them. How can we have *interculturalidad* this way? We were given very little time to present but Porcela [healer and prophet that works with *Grisi Siknis*] is presenting, she has to present.[62]

The naturalization of biomedical and anthropologists' voices as the authorized to talk about the health of Indigenous people and its consequent silencing of Miskitu voices in the public narratives and of those who know about *Grisi Siknis*, the traditional ancestral healers, give a clear message of what is allowed by the Pacific Eurocentered authority. Miskitu people can talk but just within the framework and control of biomedical knowledge, translated and brokered by anthropology, where *Grisi Siknis* is understood as "cultural sickness" and happening only in Miskitu culture because of its beliefs.[63] In this manner, the radically different onto-epistemic place from where the Miskitu people speak is erased in the public narrative. Thus, the possibility of a comprehensive intercultural process is also challenged, one in which social and political mechanisms go accompanied by epistemic dialogue. The public authority misses the opportunity to discuss Indigenous knowledge with their main holders (healers) and interconnections (community and so forth), a matter of health relevant to all, non-Westerners and Westerners.

I think that even though this disease has been horrible for those communities, it will probably help to promote the model, maybe finally they will pay more attention to the *curanderos* [healers].[64]

Healers in particular did not subscribe to an interpretation of *grisi siknis* as caused by economic conditions. As a healer argued, "We have always been poor, if it were poverty [that causes *Grisi Siknis*], almost everyone here [in the RACCN] would be affected."[65]

The instrumentalization of the labor of traditional ancestral healers, together with the negation of their voices as reflected in the discussion of the *Grisi Siknis* forum, call attention to another issue of the hierarchical positioning and negation of "other" knowledges. The healing work done by traditional ancestral healers is reduced to a simplistic task of herbal cure done by *curanderos* losing all the epistemic relevance that this healing process has in Miskitu culture. Rivera Cusicanqui's critical analysis of interculturality in Bolivia describes how crucial activities carried out by Indigenous societies, which are the axis of a worldview that represent other forms of sociability different and alternative to that of the West, are represented as minor tasks, dividing and positioning the intellectual work over the manual in a similar manner as it has been done historically with the work of women.[66]

The conflictive relations between biomedical and traditional knowledge can be traced at least to the 1920s—under US occupation. Ligia Peña points out that between 1915 and 1928, a broader project of modernization in the public health in the country, emulating the North American model of health, imposed legal and penal mechanisms in the practices of healers, leaving them in disadvantage in front of "professional" doctors and feeding negative perception and stigmatized visions questioning the validity of their knowledge.[67]

Going back to the early written descriptions about Miskitu people by Bell and Conzemius, the role of *sukias* (shamans) and spirits in curing maladies particularly called my attention.[68] Bell writes: "I have seen a young girl, who was shrieking hysterically in a dreadful manner, carried in a canoe a long distance to consult a celebrated sookia."[69] He also notes the presence of *sukias* to cure sickness and protect from spirits in every village that he has visited in the 19th century.[70] In Conzemius, the quote is even clearer:

> Presumed cause of diseases.—The cure of the sick is practically always left to the sukva; the latter is generally a clever herbalist, and the treatment applied by him is often excellent, but the remedy in itself is considered of no avail unless certain rites are observed by the healer as well as by the patient. According to these primitive people, indigenous diseases and accidents are always due to the agency of some evil spirit (M.: lasa; T., P.: walasa; U.: nawal) under whose power the sick person is supposed to be.[71]

The relevance of the healers in Miskitu worldview and in the communities is far beyond the discussion of this article; oral history in many Afro-descendant and Indigenous communities give account of powerful healers who were not only "herbalists," but also leaders of their people and of complex healing systems. Knowing this, how can we read Raiti's experience?

In a moment when historical communitarian figures have been disappeared from institutional narratives, in a community where all the institutions appear to be failing, in a context where the state intervention has impacted so negatively the community fabric, it was striking the way that the community understood and followed the healer and how Porcela Sandino moved without translation from one health system to another, from the spiritual imbalance to the biomedical condition of people with the full support of the Director of the Health Centre. What can we learn as researchers, anthropologists, and so forth, from this experience? Could we understand Porcela and her actions as embodiments of interculturality?

As a mestizo social researcher looking at the experiences of Miskitu people with *Grisi Siknis,* the answer will be probably "no," I will not be able to understand it in such a way with a Westernized critical lens. To do so, I would have to give up what academia has taught me about critical thinking, and attempt to decolonize my thoughts and practices, trying to craft a decolonizing practice of dialogue with and within subaltern groups. Rivera Cusicanqui posits how oral histories become the place of emergence for collective memories of struggle and resistance in the colonial experience; myth and history recover their hermeneutic relation beyond the Cartesian distinction, identifying the cyclical character of Indigenous resistance and retaking their character as subjects of history. Oral history is a practice that links a structural analysis with the colonial axis as the foremost articulator of the positioning and hierarchization of our socities.[72]

Oral history in this context is therefore much more than a "participatory" or "action" methodology (where the researcher is the one who decides the orientation of the action and the modalities of participation): it is *a collective act of desalienation*, both for the researcher as for their interlocutors. If this process involves the combination of conscious interaction efforts among different sectors, and if the basis of the exercise is mutual recognition as well as honesty with respect to the place occupied in the "colonial chain," the results will be so much richer in this sense.[73]

CONCLUSION

Throughout 2017, more than five outbreaks of *Grisi Siknis* were reported. The communities affected were located in the Northeastern part of the country, the last one in Walakitan.[74] In all cases, there is a striking resemblance in the way that public institutions perform their response in the public narrative, presenting it as an adequate institutional response, and once again using traditional doctors without recognition of Indigenous knowledge.

For Miskitu cosmovision, dreams, spirits and harmonious relations (in the community and with the non-human world) are key elements that constitute medicine, or, in a broader perspective, healing processes and wellbeing. Porcela Sandino opened a portal to another way of knowing. In discussing the institutional narratives about *Grisi Siknis* in Nicaragua, I am trying to highlight that Westernized hegemonic views on illness continue to displace traditional ancestral knowledge by using the knowledge and skills of Indigenous healers and their success in their treatments without recognizing of their knowledge, which is a way of knowing that cannot be replicated by Westernized science.

Mainstream health discourses and practices about processes of illness in Indigenous communities are mainly framed by the knowledge of the authorized voices, whether they are biomedical doctors or anthropologists, and not by the voices of Indigenous people or of their healers. The biomedical narratives become the gatekeepers of the appropriate knowledge about the health of the communities, and the anthropological narratives act as the authorative translations of Miskitu life experiences. These perspectives guide and inform decision-making processes concerning emergency health situations, which are realized in a top-down logic without considering, or even disregarding, the knowledge of the very Indigenous people who are supposed to receive the health services in question.

In a broader analysis, this tendency in the construction and hierarchies of knowledge is not unique to the Nicaraguan experience; instead, it is part of the coloniality of power in Latin America, where a *criolla* version of

Eurocentric knowledge continues to be hegemonic, reinforcing the colonial difference. Although such unequal power relations challenge the possibilities of interculturality, Miskitu healers' counter-narratives and practices open alternatives for collective and spiritual ways to approach knowledge and wellbeing when faced with individualistic Eurocentric views that fragment and separate reality.

My invitation here is to go beyond the recognition of the validity of "local" knowledge to the full acknowledgement of other epistemes and other ways of understanding the world and of experiencing life and wellbeing.

NOTES

1. This article is in memory of Porcela Sandino Hemsly, beloved Miskitu traditional healer who passed away on March 19, 2018. It is an expanded version of Jessica Martínez-Cruz, "Whose Knowledge Counts? Harmony and Spirituality in Miskitu Counter-Narratives," in *Latin American Perspectives on Global Development*, eds. Mahmoud Masaeli, Germán Bula, and Samuel Ernest Harrington (Newcastle Upon Tyne: Cambridge Scholars Press, 2018), 309–29. There are contributions from Serafina Espinoza (Institute of Traditional Medicine and Community Development (IMTRADEC) - University of the Autonomous Regions of the Nicaraguan Caribbean Coast (URACCAN), Marissa Olivares and Fernanda Soto (Central America University, UCA) and Goya Wilson (University of Bristol).

2. Johan Wedel, "Involuntary mass spirit possession among the Miskitu," *Anthropology & Medicine* 19, no. 3 (2012), 303–14; Heather Carrie, Tim K. Mackey, and Sloane Laird, "Integrating Traditional Indigenous Medicine and Western Biomedicine into Health Systems: a Review of Nicaraguan Health Policies and Miskitu Health Services," *International Journal for Equity in Health* 14, no. 129 (2015).

3. Kyle Whyte, "What Do Indigenous Knowledges Do for Indigenous Peoples?," in *Traditional Ecological Knowledge: Learning from Indigenous Practices for Environmental Sustainability. New Directions in Sustainability and Society*, ed. M. Nelson & D. Shilling, (Cambridge: Cambridge University Press, 2018): 62.

4. I am using the term "Westernized" to refer not exclusively to a geographic region. Instead, I use the concept in the sense of decolonial thought to speak of a hegemonic thought embedded in the institutions of non-Western geographies. I use the concept of "wellbeing" through this chapter to refer to a field that at the time of writing this article in 2017 had been problematized in Nicaragua in two ways that I am interested in highlighting: (a) as a counternarrative to the emphasis on development in the public policies in Nicaragua—this includes each government since 1988 whether named neoliberal or socialist, in both cases extractivists governments; the criticism came mainly, but not only, from the visions of Indigenous and Afro-descendent peoples in the country—, and, (b) as a counterweight to poverty studies that continue to make scientific measurements without taking into account people considered as "poor"—particularly I refer to the efforts of feminist women from the north of the

country, aiming to raise attention to the different notions of happiness and collective well-being of campesino and Indigenous women. In both forms, there are clear epistemological contributions that strain the official narratives of the nation state.

5. See Aníbal Quijano, "Coloniality of Power, Eurocentrism, and Latin America," *Nepantla: Views from South* 1, no. 3 (2000): 533. See also: Arturo Escobar, "Worlds and Knowledges Otherwise: The Latin American Modernity/Coloniality Research Program," *Cultural Studies* 21, no. 2–3 (2007); Catherine Walsh, "Shifting the Geopolitics of Critical Knowledge: Decolonial Thought and Cultural Studies 'Others' in the Andes," *Cultural Studies* 21, no. 2–3 (2007).

6. Quijano, "Coloniality," 549.

7. Whyte, " Indigenous Knowledges."

8. Silvia Rivera Cusicanqui, "El potencial epistemológico y teórico de la historia oral: de la lógica instrumental a la descolonización de la historia," *Voces Recobradas, Revista de Historia Oral* 21 (2006): 13.

9. Carlos Rodriguez and Jeannette Hamersma, *Las contrapartes en salud de América Central y el Caribe. 25 años después de Alma Ata: Experiencia en cuatro países* (Guatemala: CORDAID, 2006).

10. Magda Sequeira, et al., *The Nicaraguan Health System: An Overview of Critical Challenges and Opportunities* (Seattle: PATH, 2011), https://path.azureedge.net/media/documents/TS-nicaragua-health-system-rpt.pdf.

11. "Regulatory Situation of Herbal Medicines: A Worldwide Review," *World Health Organization*, published 1998, 8–9, https://apps.who.int/iris/bitstream/handle/10665/63801/WHO_TRM_98.1.pdf?sequence=1&isAllowed=y.

12. "The Autonomy Statue (Law No. 28)," *Centro de Asistencia Legal a Pueblos Indígenas*, published 2010, https://www.calpi-nicaragua.com/the-autonomy-statute-law-28/.

13. Edgardo Ruíz, "Cultural Politics and Health: The Development of Intercultural Health Policies in The Atlantic Coast of Nicaragua" (PhD diss., University of Pittsburg, 2006).

14. Carrie, Mackey, and Laird, "Integrating."

15. Ibid., 4.

16. Anne-Emanuelle Birn, Sarah Zimmerman, and Richard Garfield, "To Decentralize or Not to Decentralize, It That the Question? Nicaraguan Health Policy under Structural Adjustment in the 1990s," *International Journal of Health Services* 30, no. 1 (2000); Miguel Gónzalez, "La Costa del comandante Campbell," Confidencial, published August 2015, https://confidencial.com.ni/archivos/articulo/22630/la-costa-del-comandante-campbell.

17. Tishany Morales Allum, untitled poem, quoted in Diana Castillo, et al., *Mujeres Jóvenes Multiétnicas Costa Caribe Sur, Participación Ciudadana y Violencia de Género* (Maryland: Global Communities, 2017), 34. Tishany, an Afro-Indigenous poet from Pearl Lagoon in the South Caribbean of Nicaragua, performed her poetry as her answer in a group interview of a research process between 2016 and 2017, in which I participated as co-researcher. Her refusal to speak only about violence in gender terms, illustrate how for these girls violence against Afro-Indigenous women and girls cannot be separated from other forms of violence, state politics and, primarily,

from their claims about real autonomy. The above is only a piece of a longer poem handwritten in its creole language.

18. Carrie, Mackey, and Laird, "Integrating."

19. Wedel, "Involuntary."

20. Carrie, Mackey, and Laird, "Integrating," 5.

21. Pan-American Health Organization, *Health Systems Profile in Nicaragua: Monitoring and Analyzing Health Systems Change/Reform*, 3rd ed. (Washington, D. C.: PAHO, 2009), https://www.paho.org/hq/dmdocuments/2010/Health_System _Profile-Nicaragua_2008.pdf; Sequeira, et al., *Health System.*

22. Ruíz, "Cultural Politics," vi.

23. Avelino Cox, *Cosmovisión de los pueblos de Tulu Walpa: Según los relatos de los sabios ancianos miskitus* (Managua: URACCAN, 1998); Avelino Cox, *Sukias y Curanderos, Isigni en la Espiritualidad* (Managua, Nicaragua: URACCAN and BID, 2003); Ana R. Fagoth, Fulvio Gioanetto, and Adan Silva, *Wan Kaina Kulkaia: Armonizando con Nuestro Entorno* (Managua, Nicaragua: Imprimátur Artes Graficas, 1998).

24. Walsh, "Shifting," 230.

25. *Guía Latinoamericana de Diagnóstico Psiquiátrica*, Asociación Psiquiátrica de América Latina, Sección de Diagnóstico y Clasificación, 2003, http://www.sld.cu /galerias/pdf/sitios/desastres/guia_latinoamerticana_diagn_psiq_gladp.pdf; American Psychiatric Association, *Diagnostic and Statistical Manual of Mental Disorders*, 4th ed. (DSM-IV) (Ann Arbor: University of Michigan Press, 2000); *The ICD-10 Classification of Mental and Behavioral Disorders: Diagnostic Criteria for Research*, World Health Organization, published 1993, https://www.who.int/classifications/icd /en/GRNBOOK.pdf.

26. Philip A. Dennis, "Part Three: Grisi Siknis Among the Miskitu," *Medical Anthropology* 5, no. 4 (1981).

27. Ibid.

28. Jorge Grumberg, presentation at a forum on *Grisi Siknis*, February 2004, Managua, Nicaragua, quoted in Ruíz, "Cultural Politics," 188; Mark Jamieson, "Masks and Madness: Ritual Expressions of the Transition to Adulthood among Miskitu Adolescents," *Social Anthropology* 9, no. 3 (2001).

29. Wedel, "Involuntary."

30. Philip A. Dennis, "Grisi siknis una enfermedad entre los Miskitu," *Revista Wani*, no. 24 (December 1999); Jamieson, "Masks and Madness."

31. Loyda Stamp, *Prácticas de atención y tratamiento del Grisi siknis utilizadas por los médicos tradicionales en los municipios Puerto Cabezas y Waspam* (Managua: IMTRADEC-URACCAN, 2008).

32. Salvador García and Jessica Martínez-Cruz, *Significados y trayectorias sobre el bienestar y la felicidad: Una aproximación relacional y participativa Comunidades del Alto Wangki y Bocay* (Managua: Mimeo, 2014).

33. See: Cox, *Sukias y Curanderos*; Fagoth, Gioanetto, and Silva, *Wan Kaina Kulkaia*; Cipriano Henríquez Levas, Norberto Chacón Mendoza, and Serafina Espinoza Blanco, "Percepción y prácticas de atención del Grisi siknis de la comunidad de krin krin, Waspam, Río Coco," *Revista Caribe URACCAN* 16, no. 1 (2016);

Rigoberto Guido, Catalina Yunkiath, and Serafina Espinoza Blanco, "Percepción sobre Isigni de la comunidad de Sawa, Waspam, Río Coco," *Revista Caribe URAC-CAN* 16, no. 1 (2016). See also: Charles Napier Bell, "Remarks on the Mosquito Territory, its Climate, People, Productions," *Journal of the Royal Geographical Society* 32 (1862); Charles Napier Bell, *Tangweera: Life and Adventures Among Gentle Savages* (London: Edward Arnold, 1899); Eduard Conzemius, "Ethnographical Survey of the Miskitu and Sumu Indians of Honduras and Nicaragua," *Bureau of American Ethnology Bulletin* 106 (1932).

34. M1, M2, and M3 are used to distinguish the men, while I is used to distinguish the interviewer; See: García and Martínez-Cruz, *Significados y trayectorias*, 26.

35. Fagoth, Gioanetto, and Silva, *Wan Kaina Kulkaia*.

36. Henríquez Levas, Chacón Mendoza, and Espinoza Blanco, "Percepción y prácticas."

37. Ibid.

38. Ibid., 16.

39. Dennis, "Enfermedad"; Jamieson, "Masks and Madness"; Bell, "Remarks"; Conzemius, "Ethnographical Survey."

40. Dennis, "Enfermedad," 10; Jamieson, "Masks and Madness."

41. "Las epidemias de grisi siknis en la Costa Atlántica," IMTRADEC/URACCAN (n.d); Stamp, *Prácticas de Atención*; Henríquez Levas, Chacón Mendoza, and Espinoza Blanco, "Percepción y prácticas."

42. Bernadine Dixon and María Olimpia Torres, "Diagnóstico de género en las Regiones Autónomas de la Costa Caribe," *Cuaderno 3, Serie Cuadernos de Género para Nicaragua, Banco Mundial* (2008).

43. Rupert Widdicombe, "Nicaragua Village in Grip of Madness: Doctors and Traditional Healers Reach Remote Jungle Community where 60 people are Suffering from Mysterious Collective Mania," *The Guardian*, published December 2003, http://www.guardian.co.uk/world/2003/dec/17/1.

44. Ibid.

45. Ibid.

46. See numbers in Stamp, *Prácticas de Atención*.

47. For a resemblance of this thought, see Sandra Davis Rodríguez, Sasha Marley, and Gerhild Trübswasser, *Algo anda mal. El Bla o Wakni en el río Coco* (RACCN: URACCAN, 2006). In the text, adults sometimes accuse young people of lacking the will to work and of being practitioners of black magic, particularly those who were displaced and settled in Honduras in the early 1980s.

48. Ruíz, "Cultural Politics."

49. Ibid.

50. Ibid., 196.

51. There is a very strong influential religious view coming from pastors of the Moravian Church, historically the major religion adscription amongst the Miskitu people, but this is not included in this analysis.

52. I have changed the original "Euro-American" term used in Sillitoe to echo Quijano's views. "America" has been a changing term through time deeply impacted first by colonization and then by the imperialist vision of the United States of America.

See Quijano, "Coloniality," 574. By recalling an "American" vision in order to name a country, and in this case a point of view, it is easy to deny the historical and cultural realities of diverse places and geopolitics. For more on "Euro-American," see Paul Sillitoe, "Local Science vs. Global Science," in *Local Science vs. Global Science: Approaches to Indigenous Knowledge in International Development*, ed. Paul Sillitoe (New York: Bergahn Books, 2007).

53. Emma Crewe, "The Silent Traditions of Developing Cooks," in *Discourses of Development: Anthropological Perspectives*, ed. R.D Grillo and R.L Stirrat (Oxford: Berg, 1997).

54. Sillitoe, "Local Science," 6.

55. Ibid.

56. Ibid.

57. Quijano, "Coloniality."

58. This implies also that sciences are not influenced by culture (see, for instance, Karin Knorr-Cetina, Epistemic Cultures (Cambridge: Harvard University Press, 1999), quoted in Sillitoe, "Local Science," 6. A critique that many authors have pointed out about development practices and health systems too.

59. Note here that not all the healers in the communities know and can treat successfully *Grisi Siknis*.

60. Walsh, "Shifting," 224.

61. Ibid., 231.

62. Director of IMTRADEC, forum on *Grisi Siknis*, February 2004, Managua, Nicaragua, quoted in Ruíz, "Cultural Politics," 182.

63. My idea is to highlight the ways that a Eurocentered production of knowledge worked here to subordinate Miskitu cosmovision. It is not to blame anthropology; the same logic applies to other social science disciplines when scientists intend to represent realities disregarding the knowledge of racialized communities.

64. Ruíz, "Cultural Politics," 178–79.

65. Ibid., 182.

66. Silvia Rivera Cusicanqui, *Violencia (re)encubiertas en Bolivia* (Bolivia, La Paz: La Mirada Salvaje, 2010).

67. Ligia Peña Torres, "Entre curanderos y médicos: disputas por las prácticas médicas curativas en el contexto de la modernización de la salud pública (1915–1928)," presented at VI Congreso Centroamericano de Estudios Culturales, Managua, Nicaragua, July 11–13, 2017.

68. Bell, "Remarks"; Bell, *Tangweera*; Conzemius, "Ethnographical Survey."

69. Bell, *Tangweera*, 97.

70. Bell, "Remarks," 253.

71. Conzemius, "Ethnographical Survey," 123. The Eurocentric visions of Bell and Conzemius and their interpretation of the Miskitu world vision give space for other discussions. Here, what I want to note is the relevance of both the spiritual world and sukias in the records regarding to experiences of Miskitu people in the last centuries, those that could not be overlooked, even for the eyes of these Western authors.

72. Rivera Cusicanqui, "Potencial epistemológico."

73. Ibid., 20–21.

74. EFE, "Detectan nuevos casos de 'locura colectiva' en el norte de Nicaragua," *El Nuevo Diario*, published December 2017, https://www.elnuevodiario.com.ni/nacionales/450267-detectan-nuevos-casos-locura-colectiva-norte-nicar/.

Chapter 10

Fighting for Life with Our Feet on the Ground

Anticolonial and Decolonial Wagers from Indigenous and Campesina Women in Mexico

Carmen Cariño Trujillo
Translated by Amanda González Izquierdo

We have had to overcome much resistance to get here: from those who hold power, who want to keep us divided and silent; from the rich in Mexico, who want to have us as animals to exploit; from foreigners, who take our best lands and want us as their slaves; from the military, who cage our communities, rape us, threaten our children, bring in drugs, alcohol, prostitution, and violence; from those who wish to think and act on our behalf, who hate when we Indigenes speak up and who fear our rebellion. . . . We have also come this far by overcoming the resistance of members of our own communities who do not understand the importance of women participating just like men.

—Comandanta Ramona during the First Indigenous Women's Summit, Oaxaca, 1997.

In this text I reflect on what I consider to be decolonial wagers that emerge from the struggles of Indigenous and campesina women in Mexico.[1] These women, alongside their communities, build, sustain, defend, and create political strategies for the defense of their lands and territories in the face of dispossession supported by the government as well as national and international enterprises. Their struggles and forms of resistance have generated processes of decolonization that seek to shatter the models of "development" and extractivism that threaten their territories and the lives they nurture.

The reflections I share here form part of a dialogue with my Indigenous and campesina sisters who launch the struggles against various megaprojects and who oppose the dispossession of their lands and territories. They are women from the San Francisco Xochicuautla and the San Salvador Atenco communities in the State of Mexico and Triqui women displaced from the autonomous municipality San Juan Copala in Oaxaca. As sisters in the struggle, we have been reflecting on these topics in kitchens, on walks through the forests and the lands that the government and big businesses want to take from them, in marches, in the fields and campsites that they have cultivated and continue to sustain materially, emotionally, spiritually, and politically. From these spaces and with these women I look on, share, and reflect on what I consider are decolonial wagers for the defense of life and the communal.

Even though only 32 percent of Indigenous and campesina women in Mexico own land, they have been instrumental to the defense of lands and territories.[2] Not owning the land does not nullify the land-women relation. Non-propriety has led them to establish other forms of connections to the lands that go beyond "owning" them. Because of this, even though many of them do not hold land titles, they nevertheless maintain ties to their lands by developing territorialities based on celebrations, rituals, tenant farming, and committees to manage the waters, the roads, *tequio*, etc.[3] Rural Indigenous and campesina women play a fundamental role in the defense of their territories when these are threatened.

The modern/colonial capitalist system has seen Indigenous women, their communities, and their lands as objects to exploit since the beginning of colonization. Consequently, it has also persecuted these women's ways of living and relating with their territories because it is this very relation to the land that enables living in community. In this way, their modes of existing are abnegated and their lands and territories are seen as commodities for national and international enterprises in pursuit of territories rich in water, minerals, forests, etc. These territories are sacred and integral to the reproduction of the social, cultural, and material lives of their communities, not mere sites for exploitation.

In the face of threats of extractivism waged against their territories, Indigenous and campesina women have played an increasingly visible role in the defense of shared resources, so much so that they have generated and continue to generate theoretical and political proposals against dispossession, making their participation continuously more forceful. Taking up the space to raise their voices, reflect, propose, and analyze is met with challenges both within and without their communities and movement. Women confront spaces that often invalidate their ideas, which upset the patriarchal structures within and without their communities. They are also invalidated for questioning the capitalist and racist system that continues to subordinate and deny their existence, demands, and modes of being. This is the same system that sees them as enemies and as obstacles to the concretization of political projects of dispossession, culminating in their murders, incarcerations, persecutions, and the criminalization of their political participation.

Women put their bodies and souls into their participation, proposals, and actions for the defense of land-territory. This puts them in the frontlines of the struggle against the government and private enterprises scouting their lands, making them targets of aggressions that have led to their persecution, incarceration, or murder. Women are defending their territories because dispossession entails the rupture of their modes of being, the fragmentation of their social and communal fabric, the threat to their ways of working and organizing, the depravation of the fields that feed their families and constitute their legacies, the dissolution of their families and communities, the distortion of their social environment, the destruction of sacred sites, and the interruption of the continuity of communal life. Dispossession expels them from their territories either through forced displacement or other, more subtle but no less violent forms of displacement that prevent them from walking peacefully along roads, hills, and rivers, and little by little strips them of their livelihoods and their historical relation with their territories.

I therefore propose that these women's struggles for the defense of their lands question the capitalist, neoliberal, patriarchal, racist, and colonial system and that they go beyond the traditional demands of hegemonic feminism, which focuses on gender oppression without problematizing or even seeing other forms of violence against women in diverse contexts and conditions. Thus, community-based women's struggles confront questions that go beyond the scope of feminist demands to fight for their existence not just as women, but as collectives. These women launch struggles based on epistemologies and ontologies radically opposed to the logic of capitalist and racist modernity/coloniality that for more than 500 years has sought to destroy everything and everyone unaligned to the needs of those who self-attribute the right, knowledge, and power—and therefore the superiority—to call them "others."

COMMUNITY-BASED WOMEN'S STRUGGLES: ANTI-AND DECOLONIAL WAGERS

Coloniality as a constitutive element of modernity has as its origin the conquest and colonization of Abya Yala in 1492, which marks the beginning of a new global order whose impact is still felt today, as per Yuderkys Espinosa-Miñoso, Diana Gómez, and Karina Ochoa Muñoz:

> Modernity came to be in 1492 as a new world-order, built upon a European subjectivity that awarded itself a position of superiority-civility over the colonized "others": the Amerindians. The imposition of this presumption of European "superiority" was translated into a will to power that held Western civilization as the only replicable model at a global level, disavowing (overlaying) all other cultures, assumed "barbarous," "immature," and/or "underdeveloped." In this way, coloniality, as subjectivity and epistemology, played a fundamental role in the intellectual criticism of Our America, because it was understood as a founding and constitutive element of modernity.[4]

Modernity/coloniality in turn established the claim of North-Eurocentric superiority, which considers Europe as the beginning and end of History. This superiority is sustained upon the negation of the humanity of the "others," as well as of their ways of knowing, thinking, creating, and living. Thus, colonized peoples were considered "barbarous," "savages," "non-human." This *colonial model of power* ("patrón colonial de poder") persists in spite of the struggles for independence in our countries and constantly reaffirm themselves through the construction of dichotomies and hierarchies that it has imposed on all scopes of life. Ramón Grosfoguel has noted at least 14 overlapping global hierarchies that uphold what he calls the "European/Euro-American," "modern-colonial capitalist patriarchal world-system."[5]

Coloniality also manifests as discourse and practice that simultaneously proclaims the inherent inferiority of certain subjectivities and the colonization of nature, reifying some subjects as dispensable and seeing nature as a mere site of raw materials for the production of goods for the international market.[6] Coloniality as a process of dehumanization persists and acquires new characteristics. As Quijano notes, "in the past 500 years coloniality has proved to be far more extensive and enduring than colonialism. Nevertheless, colonialism was without a doubt engendered within coloniality; what's more, without it, it could not have been imposed on the intersubjectivity of the world in such entrenched and prolonged ways."[7]

Since coloniality is a current issue, decoloniality remains a pending issue. Colonization has been for a long time the *modus operandi* of globalization. Therefore, colonization reaffirms itself now, at the peak of neoliberal globalization, as "the continued impoverishment of racialized peoples, the invasion of their territories by a new imperialism that seeks to make of them key pieces in the triumph of the expansion of the logic of capital throughout the world."[8]

As Frantz Fanon noted, "the colonized world is a world divided in two," and this dichotomous and hierarchical division of the world into the fortunate and the condemned (*damnés*) has a colonial basis.[9] In this context, gender relations are also modified by colonialism. Thus, including the topic of gender in the decolonial debate is not a minor task; gender is a central category that, as Rita Segato has posited, is "capable of illuminating all other aspects of the transformation imposed on the lives of communities once they are captured by the new modern/colonial order."[10] In this respect, María Lugones proposes that from the beginning of the colonial period, the colonized deemed nonhuman could not be considered men and women and therefore only the colonizers would be considered fully human.[11] Accordingly, whenever it was of colonial interest to exploit women as if they were men, they were treated as if genderless, and when it was convenient, their female bodies were exploited as the progenitors of the enslaved workforce.

Breny Mendoza has also argued that today "colonized societies continue to be genderless societies in a perverse way, not because they lack a gender-based hierarchy like in the past, but because men and women have been dispossessed of their humanities by the *coloniality of power* and the *coloniality of gender*."[12] This is what María Lugones calls the dark side of the modern/gender system that transforms the colonized being, and the colonized woman in particular, into a being that can be mistreated, raped, exploited to death, and eliminated with impunity, physically and culturally, from the face of the earth.[13]

Today, more than 500 years after the start of colonialism, its voracity increases and its eyes are set on lands-territories that have been guarded and cared for by Indigenous peoples. Women of these communities have been essential in the care and upkeep of these lands-territories, which is why their protagonism in the struggle is increasingly visible. In the twenty-first century we are facing a reiteration of the colonial reality, as Raúl Zibechi has remarked, and thus the dichotomous and hierarchical structures are strengthened, as is the case for the human/nature binary.[14] Carefully reflecting about this binary is essential to understand the complexity of the struggles for the defense of the land and territories being led by Indigenous peoples.

The continuity of this hierarchical and dichotomous construct has as its fundamental axis not only dehumanization, but also the capacity to objectify, to make into exploitable and disposable objects people and nature, animals, waters, mountains, etc. In the logic of modernity/coloniality, nature is an exploitable object, but for Indigenous peoples, nature is not an object and thus, it is not negotiable, and it is not on sale. These opposing worldviews manifest in conflict on a global scale that increases when Indigenous peoples oppose projects of death that seek to dispossess them of their lands and territories.

In this context, it is necessary, following Sylvia Marcos, to devise new conceptual tools that account for the specificities of gender oppression in Indigenous and campesino/a contexts. In this regard, Indigenous and campesina women propose a theory "rooted in their bodies and in matter, matter which forms an unstable and fluid whole with nature and all the beings that comprise it. It is not 'theory' of ideas and abstract concepts, of symbolic and semiotic language. It is theory spoken, lived, felt, danced, smelled, touched."[15]

THE STRUGGLE FOR NATURE-TERRITORY, THE FIGHT FOR LIFE

The fight we have started does not end with the recuperation of the lands and waters. Each day and each instant is the moment to fight for life and for everything life gives us, the moment to fight for our children and for future generations. A long task awaits us in our society, and as women we know that we have the right to act and to participate.[16]

—María Antonia Ramírez, *Frente de Pueblos en Defensa de la Madre Tierra-Xochicuautla,* 2015.

The struggle for land is not recent. When the conquistadors invaded the continent, each of the Indigenous peoples had their own land propriety systems, based on a communal and sacred understanding, so they did not think of themselves as owners of the land, but as its guardians; land was not an object that could be sold or owned. For this reason, the dispossession of land denoted, from the beginning of European colonization, an attack on life and on the existence of native populations.

In post-independence Mexico, communal lands were harshly attacked; the criollos who ascended to power considered the collective ownership of land an obstacle to the nation's progress. The so-called *Leyes de Reforma* and *Ley de Colonización y Titulación de Terrenos Baldíos* (Laws of Reform and Law of Colonization and Titulation of Vacant Lands, more commonly just "Land Tenure Laws") had as their objective the privatization of land and the dissolution of Indigenous territories.[17] The collective discontent at the dispossession led the people to organize a Revolution, buttressed by men and women, Indigenous and campesinxs, whose principal demand was the restitution of their lands. The most important accomplishment was the creation of *ejidos* (communal lands), proclaimed in Article 27 of the Mexican Constitution, leading to the creation of 28,965 *ejidal* lands with an area of 85,148,116 hectares.[18] Nevertheless, in spite of this achievement of great relevance that resulted in 54.1% of the Mexican territory being socially owned, the titles for existing lands and waters—what constitutes their territorial space—remained in the jurisdiction of the state. Stemming from this control that the state exerts over lands and waters is its authority to accord them to individuals and it is the form in which the land is bestowed that determines whether it is private or social (*ejidal*, or, communal) property.[19] Thus, the last word on land ownership was constitutionally granted to the nation and not to Indigenous peoples.

In 1992, the Mexican state promotes the reform of Article 27 of its Constitution. Modifications are made to regulate *ejidal* lands under the pretext of providing legal certainty and avoiding conflicts. Thus begins another stage of threats to communal ownership that paves the way for private capital by reinvigorating the land market.

For Indigenous peoples, the land is a territorialized space. It is not simply a geographical place or a commodity; rather, the land-territory is material, social, historical, cultural, symbolic, and sacred and it grants meaning to the lives of the people and the communities that have inhabited it generation after generation. It is through the land-territory that men and women collectively build and project their conception of the world and establish their modes of living founded upon the relationship with this territory inherited from their ancestors. Therefore, without the territories, the peoples (los pueblos) do not exist.

In Mexico and in many corners of the continent, women lead the struggles for the defense of land-territory, as members of a people, always as a collective. The struggles in recent years have been against wind farms, airports, highways, dams, oil companies, hydroelectric plants, etc. All these extractivist projects appear to the peoples living in the lands-territories as neocolonial projects that continue to see Indigenous lands as sites to colonize. Through these struggles for land-territories, women confront the modern-colonial-capitalist-neoliberal logic that continues to see them, their peoples, their territories, and the Pachamama as objects to be exploited; for this reason, they posit that their struggle is for life and against the logic of coloniality.

The women who belong to Indigenous and campesina communities in many parts of the continent define their struggles on the basis of the defense of the land, waters, forests, mountains—in other words, on the basis of the defense of life. For these women, their individual rights are interwoven with the collective's rights, with the rights of Mother Earth, and it is not possible to think them separately. It is from this notion of interlinkage that they defy and challenge the canons of knowledge production and theorize, analyze their realities, and establish new anticolonial and decolonial practices and discourses. The struggles against dispossession and the destruction of Mother Earth are struggles against a way of understanding and creating the world that sees only economic gains, money, and individual benefit, as opposed to other ways of seeing and creating worlds in which relationality and caring for multiple forms of life are of the utmost importance. Forging these anticolonial and decolonial struggles entails recognizing that these sites of women's struggles are also sites of knowledge production.

For Trinidad Ramírez, from the San Salvador Atenco community, "us women are willing to defend the earth because it is Life, to put our bodies and hearts on the line to defend it. We will not allow a capitalist system to impose itself upon and make decisions about our territories, lives, bodies, and communities."[20] The struggles and contributions of these women—who in the vast majority of cases do not self-identify as feminists—pose important challenges to hegemonic feminism because they question the universal notion of *woman* along with the presumed demands that are particular to women. I believe that the actions, words, ideas, and proposals of community-based Indigenous and campesina women contribute key elements to the radical critique of hegemonic feminism that began decades ago with other racialized, Black, Indigenous, and campesina women.

There is no epistemic and theoretical decolonization without material decolonization, nor is there a single form of decolonization. This is why my thought is in plural and ongoing, with the struggles of women with their feet firmly on the ground born out of specific and politically committed contexts for the defense of life and the communal. The struggles of Indigenous and campesina women who grow up in the mountains, deserts, and valleys are built on quotidian sites of resistance: in community work, assemblies, celebrations, manifestations, etc. It is from there that they theorize, think, and fashion new strategies of resistance, as well as new ways of defending life.

In the face of deadly projects that currently threaten their lands and territories, women have risen up, defending their forms and modes of living, their sons and daughters' birthright, and Mother Nature. They are housewives, farm workers, artisans, they prepare food, cultivate crops, and live the daily struggle alongside their communities' men, children, and elderly. In most cases, they are the first to go out to protest, organize, and convene men and women to organize, to not give in, to defend what is theirs. Women have defended the land, as have men, laying down their bodies, fighting the police that guard machinery that arrives to their communities to destroy forests, lagoons, rivers, valleys, mountains, jungles. Women have not rested because they know what these projects presage, and they and their peoples will find it increasingly difficult to meet their needs because many of these projects will in the short or long term involve forced displacement, water and air pollution, the rise of unknown diseases, as well as the loss of plants and animals that also inhabit those territories. For these reasons they fight and muster up the strength to oppose dispossession.

The contributions of Indigenous and campesina women are, from my perspective, fundamental to critically rethink enlightened, hegemonic, racist, and classist feminism. Beginning with the defense of the land and their territories, these women rework women's demands and generate an other political practice that reveals interlocking oppressions. Departing from these struggles, they question the capitalist system that sees commodities in their bodies-territories and challenge the racist logic that sees them and the men of their communities as exploitable, disposable, and deserving of dispossession. From there they problematize the patriarchal system that oppresses them as women.

The struggles of Indigenous and campesina women take place in different spaces: against national and international capital and the neoliberal governments that intend to dispossess them and inside their own communities, where they question the patriarchal, racist, and sexist order that, though imposed from the outside, is reproduced within their families and communities and keeps them in positions that make their participation even more difficult. It is a simple reality that inside their own communities, there is no equity in the relationships between men and women. In that sense, the violence that women face is also reproduced inside their own families and communities. Their struggle must therefore take place on multiple fronts.

Women refuse to be mere "companions" to their male counterparts in their struggles and they play the leading role in the production of proposals, analyses, and pathways to the strengthening of their resistance. In this way they propose creative ways to launch movements, convoke and actively participate in community assemblies, prepare food, develop resources to sustain their struggles, make public denouncements, and make appearances in university campuses or spaces they had never been before to make their voices heard and demand their rights as Indigenous women and as members of native populations with ancestral rights.

These women's struggles call into question the notion that "women" are primarily concerned with gender-based violence and discrimination. Indigenous women know that this is a major problem in their daily lives, but it is not the only one and they face other forms of violence that neoliberal capitalism and coloniality reproduce on their bodies and lives at an individual level but also at a collective level inside their communities. They are distinctly aware of the importance of fighting from within to transform the systems of oppression that have relegated them to the least privileged positions, but at the same time they recognize their own capacity to enact change. They also fight from without, against the system that seeks to deprive them of their right to a harmonious life in their territories as members of an ancestral peoples. Therefore, their struggles are aimed at the defense of their land-territories, which is the defense of life as a whole. As women who are members of collectivities with their own modes of existing, they have, since the beginning of colonization, been considered an obstacle for plans of "development," first for the colonizers, and then for the nation-state.

These women's struggles are not isolated from the struggles of their people but are interwoven with the demands of their communities: the concerns of the collective are the concerns of the individual and to think of them separately is simply not possible. In that sense, these women's demands issue from the weight of interlocking oppressions on their bodies and on their lives as people who are part of a community. This is why I think that the wagers these women make go beyond gender-based demands and in this sense these wagers are more radical because they entail the defense of life in the multiplicity of its expressions and they question the structures of oppression within and without their communities.

It is important to note that these wagers are not new and that it has been Black and Indigenous feminists who, for several decades now, have denounced overlapping oppressions based on their concrete realities. These contributions have insisted on the existence of a global capitalist system (neoliberalism) in which racism, sexism, and classism exist as entities that cannot be separated. This intermingling of oppressions has taken many names: *manifold and simultaneous oppressions, matrix of domination, intersectionality, inter-relatedness of oppression*, and *triple oppression*.[21] Ever since the Zapatista uprising in Chiapas in 1994, Zapatista women have denounced the violence they suffer as not only due to their gender. Comandanta Esther noted: "We have to fight more because as indigenous we are triply looked down upon: as indigenous women, as women, and as poor women."[22]

Indigenous women recognize a realm of existence beyond the material. They defend these other realms, too, which include the sacred and the guardians of the forest, the river, and the mountain, because they are fundamental to existence itself. These realms, considered by the logic of modernity to be irrational, are ones they recognize alongside their communities. They resort to that "irrationality" because it is from there that they forge other, non-colonial relations whose demands do not assume an anthropocentric vision according to which the human owns everything that exists. They therefore reinforce "irrational" practices and knowledges and from there promote resistances in favor and defense of life.

Their wagers seek to overcome the theory-practice binary: women discuss, theorize, and analyze the conditions in which they make decisions, and know that they face corporations with national and international capital as well as their government-represented interests. From this space they think, act, and generate "other" theoretical-political reflections. Women defenders of life have been able to walk, learn, discuss, contribute, theorize, and act as part of the struggle itself—the struggle for life. Thus, the dichotomous and hierarchical separation of individual/community and individual/nature is questioned in their concrete sites of resistance to reaffirm that the individual—be it man or woman—cannot be thought without community or the relationship with nature. Nature is not an object divorced from the individual; it is Pachamama, *madrecitatierra*, which provides sustenance, the sacred, life and that is why communities gather in it and ponder what is at stake, for it is not possible to live except in relation to everything that inhabits the territories, humans and non-humans alike.

These community women are aware of the power they have, but also of the risk of being seen as enemies of the capitalist system and the governments that promote it. They are repressed, threatened, dispossessed, displaced, murdered, not just because they are women but because they are poor Indigenous women who are tough and conscientious and who know to raise their voice and make themselves heard. Being women does not exempt them from the repression, criminalization, and death to which their male counterparts are subjected. They, too, are prosecuted, threatened, tortured, incarcerated, displaced, or raped.

In these struggles, decoloniality is not a project of returning to the past, but a project of sowing the seeds of the present and the future, always with an eye to the past. These struggles are formed with our feet on the ground and with the roots this ground grants and they are expressed in "other" epistemologies and ontologies—non-Western ways of seeing the world that have resisted colonization. These are worldviews that could not be annihilated, that persisted and continue to persist, and that people never stopped holding and renewing against the colonizer.

Colonial domination inaugurated a violent transformation of community relations that guaranteed the dispossession and exploitation of the colonized with the end goal of fracturing the ways of life of Indigenous peoples, thereby preventing their resistance. For this reason, coloniality sought to destroy their vital spaces and their modes of life. In spite of this, colonial history is marked by stories of resistance and anticolonial and decolonial wagers ranging from the quotidian to armed rebellions. Colonialism, as well as the coloniality it produces, is a reality and today it finds itself in a state of greater intensification as multiple mechanisms generate the conditions for its global reproduction. Today the colonial crusade requires bodies at its service, springs, mountains, minerals, winds, rains, ancestral wisdom, genetic information, etc., and the main obstacle to this predatory system are communities in resistance.

Therefore, Indigenous campesina women and Black racialized women do not speak only of the liberation of women and many of them do not call themselves feminists. When women participate in struggles alongside their communities, they fight for their rights as women, but they do not do so as a separate fight from the defense of their lands and territories, for they affirm that they cannot speak of their rights as women when their territories are being pillaged. This does not mean that their rights as women take a back seat, but rather that they cannot think as either individuals or collectives without the territories that guarantee them life.

The struggles of Indigenous and campesina women call into question the methods and demands of hegemonic feminist theory to the extent that it does not account for the realities of racialized women in our own contexts. And in that sense,

> White-bourgeois feminism that aspires to overcome "gender inequality" or the domination and oppression of women is no longer just unsustainable, but also an impediment to a real transformation that disrupts the modes of community social organization and of the historical-political-economic order as a whole and that reverses the notion of the human against the non-human and the episteme of hierarchical differentiation between what is considered the one and the other.[23]

Hegemonic feminism has seldom concerned itself with these women's struggles since these women's demands do not correspond to their own. Hegemonic feminists see Indigenous campesina women as "guardians of culture," not as ideologues, activists, radical thinkers within their communities, women who question the interlocking oppressions to which they are subjected alongside the men of their communities and fight against these oppressions to create an other world. Faced with this deadly system, the struggles of these women and their communities pose a radical decolonial wager for life.

When speaking of the commitment to life, I am not only referring to a wager for human life, but for life in its multiple expressions: water, wind, rain, animals, mountains, the sacred. The defense of territory and the sacred that exists within this wager for life is another element that radically questions the principles of enlightened modernity in its placing of man above other beings that inhabit the planet. The human/nature binary places the former as superior in a hierarchical relation that does not coincide with the cosmovision of Indigenous peoples. So the demands of Indigenous women are not limited to the recognition of their rights as people, as women, but instead concern themselves with the defense of life in all its forms. Therefore, the demands of Indigenous women who fight alongside their communities go beyond the demands of hegemonic feminism and pose radical challenges to their principles.

Conclusion

> My parents are the lake and the mountains.
> My siblings are the peoples who defend life.
> —San Salvador Atenco, Texcoco, Mexico.

Second Meeting on the Defense of the Lake

We will win this fight. . . . the river said so.
—Berta Cáceres (1969–2016)

Indigenous and campesina women fight from their kitchens, fields, and streets, protest inside and outside their homes, organize the sowing of the plot, select the seeds, know nature's cycles, and speak in their assemblies, making contributions and motivating the men and women of their communities to participate in the struggle for the defense of their land-territories, which is to say, in the struggle for the defense of their lives. The paths they pave contribute to the theoretical-practical and political construction of anticolonial and decolonial wagers that question multiple forms of oppression. Yet these women's struggles are not always recognized by hegemonic feminism, which believes that they are not sufficiently aware of gender oppression. Hegemonic feminism, then, sees these women as passive victims incapable of liberating themselves, but reality shows us otherwise.

The struggles of Indigenous and campesina women are not new: they have their origins in daily life, where our mothers, grandmothers, and sisters resist against the current predatory capitalist system. They defend themselves against the false idea of progress and modernity/coloniality imposed by neoliberal governments and multinational corporations that threaten their sacred lands and territories as well as their forms and ways of life. Indigenous and campesina women fight their battles with their feet on the ground and occupy a radical space aware of the multiple forms of oppression that are part of everyday life. From there, they recognize that not all women are equal and that only by recognizing not just our differences, but also the hierarchies that affect us, will we be able to build bridges and bring about change to really transform our conditions.

The struggle of women in defense of land-territory does not pretend to "save" others, but intends the defense of the communal, which allows for the continuation of life for the collectives that inhabit the territories. They do not build a "them," but an "us." The war against the peoples is a reality and women and men, as well as the waters, forests, winds, mountains, and everything that exists in the territories are targets of oppression. The community women in the struggle for the defense of land-territory know that their fight is for life in all its expressions and it is therefore fundamental to recognize that the battlefronts are multiple and inseparable. These struggles are the way forward if we want to build a world where all worlds belong.

NOTES

1. Mine is a willful choice not to translate *campesina/o*. Campesinxs are people who not only work the land, but also have an intimate relation with it. Their ways of life are inextricably tied to the land, as they do not only work in rural areas, but also live there and their labor is a form of sustenance and community. This community aspect is a cornerstone of the culture associated with the lifestyle of campesinos. Thus, the term "farm-worker" is not appropriate because it does not connote the culture of this life and work. I also reject "peasant," a popular translation, both for its derogatory connotations of ignorance and because it does properly signify that to be a campesinx is to hold an honorable profession. I also take this opportunity to note that translations of epigraphs are my own.—*Trans.*

2. "Más tierra para las mujeres, mejor seguridad alimentaria para todos," *Organización de las Naciones Unidas para la Alimentación y Agricultura* (FAO), published 2013, http://www.fao.org/americas/noticias/ver/es/c/320313/.

3. *Tequio* is an Indigenous concept referring to community work for collective benefit.—*Trans.*

4. Yuderkys Espinosa Miñoso, Diana Gómez, and Karina Ochoa Muñoz, eds, *Tejiendo de otro modo: Feminismo, epistemología y apuestas descoloniales en Abya Yala* (Popayán: Universidad de Cauca, 2014), 28.

5. Ramón Grosfoguel, "The Implications of Subaltern Epistemologies for Global Capitalism: Transmodernity, Border Thinking, and Global Coloniality," in *Critical Globalization Studies,* eds. Richard P. Appelbaum and William I. Robinson (New York/London: Routledge 2005), 284, 289.

6. Nelson Maldonado-Torres, "La descolonización y el giro des-colonial," *Revista Tabula Rasa,* no. 9 (July-December 2008): 64.

7. Aníbal Quijano, "Colonialidad del poder y clasificación social," in *Cuestiones y horizontes: De la dependencia histórico-estructural a la colonialidad/descolonialidad del poder,* ed. Danilo Assis Clímaco (Buenos Aires: *CLACSO,* 2014): 325.

8. Maldonado-Torres, "Descolonización," 64.

9. Frantz Fanon, *The Wretched of the Earth,* trans. Richard Philcox (New York: Palgrave, 2004): 3.

10. Rita Segato, "Género y colonialidad: del patriarcado de bajo impacto al patriarcado moderno," in *Des-posesión: Género, territorio y luchas por la autodeterminación,* eds. Marisa Beausteguigoitia Rius and María Josefina Saldaña-Portillo (Mexico: PUEG-UNAM, 2015), 332.

11. María Lugones, "Colonialidad y género: Hacia un feminismo descolonial," trans. Pedro DiPietro with María Lugones, in *Género y descolonialidad,* ed. Walter Mignolo, (Ediciones de Signo, 2008), 47.

12. Breny Mendoza, *Ensayos de crítica feminista en Nuestra América* (Mexico: Herder Editorial, 2014), 53 (emphasis by the author).

13. Ibid., 54.

14. Raúl Zibechi, *Latiendo resistencia: Mundos nuevos y guerras de despojo* (Oaxaca, Mex: El Rebozo, 2015), 16.

15. Sylvia Marcos, "Feminismos en camino descolonial," in *Más allá del feminismo: Caminos para andar,* ed. Márgara Millán (Mexico: UNAM, 2014), 21.

16. María Antonia Ramírez, member of Frente de Pueblos en Defensa de la Madre Tierra in the San Francisco Xochicuautla community, in the municipality of Lerma in the state of Mexico, in personal communication on November 15, 2015. Frente de Pueblos en Defensa de la Madre Tierra was created to defend the Otomí-Mexica sacred forest after the 2006 announcement of the construction of the Naucalpan-Toluca Airport Highway, a private highway whose layout affects 230 hectares of the forest and the lives of the communities in the region, among other things. Since then, the communities directly affected have founded the Frente and have been fighting against the imposition of this project by the Mexican government and Grupo Higa, the Mexican company that received the permit for the construction of the highway.

17. Francisco López Bárcenas, "Territorios indígenas y conflictos agrarios en México," *Estudios Agrarios* 12, no. 32 (2006): 91.

18. Francisco López Bárcenas, *¡La tierra no se vende! Las tierras y los territorios de los pueblos indígenas en México*, 2nd ed (Mexico: CLASCO, EDUCA A.C, ProDESC, COAPI, Centro Intradisciplinar para la Investigación de la Recreación, 2017), 82.

19. Ibid., 79–80.

20. Trinidad Ramírez, personal communication with author, March 15, 2016. Trinidad Ramírez is a member of Frente de Pueblos en Defensa de la Tierra (FPDT) in San Salvador Atenco, state of Mexico. In 2002, under the slogan "La tierra no se vende, se ama y se defiende" ("The Land is not for Trading, it is for Loving and Defending"), stopped the expropriation of 5,000 hectares on which the Mexican government wanted to build an airport. Since then, Trinidad is an acclaimed member in her community and in Mexico for her fight for the defense of the land, a fight that has not stopped and which resulted in the definitive cancellation of the airport project in November 2018. [The literal translation of the 2002 slogan is "The Land is Not for Sale, it is Loved and Defended," but I choose to translate it as "The Land is not for Trading, it is for Loving and Defending" to keep the rhyme of the original.—*Trans.*]

21. The Combahee River Collective, "A Black Feminist Statement," *Women's Studies Quarterly* 42, no. 3/4 (2014): 271; Patricia Hill Collins, *Black Feminist Thought: Knowledge, Consciousness, and the Politics of Empowerment,* 2nd edition (London: Routledge, 2014), 18; Kimberle Crenshaw, "Demarginalizing the Intersection of Race and Sex: A Black Feminist Critique of Antidiscrimination Doctrine, Feminist Theory and Antiracist Politics," *University of Chicago Legal Forum* 1989, no. 1 (1989): 140; bell hooks, *Feminist Theory: From Margin to Center* (Cambridge: South End Press, 1984), 14; Indigenous women of the Zapatista Uprising of 1994.

22. "International Day of the Rebel Woman," in *Dissident Women: Gender and Cultural Politics in Chiapas*, eds. Shannon Speed, R. Aída Hernández Castillo, and Lynn M. Stephen (Austin: University of Texas Press, 2006), 28.

23. Espinosa Miñoso, Gómez and Ochoa Muñoz, *Tejiendo,* 31.

Chapter 11

Resisting, Re-existing, and Co-existing (De)spite the State

Women's Insurgencies for Territory and Life in Ecuador

Catherine Walsh

We continue and we will continue

cultivating life, and flowering rebellion.

—Katy Machoa[1]

For María Lugones,

long-time friend and comrade of struggle,

who asked me to write this text.

In Ecuador, as in much of the territory long ago baptized "Latin America" by colonial invaders, the Church, and creole elite, *his*tory erases women—women′s subjectivities, agency, and voice—and, most especially, women-led struggles. It is a *his*tory of geopolitical, hetero-patriarchal, and racialized nature, project, and form. The violence of this *his*tory continues until today, replicated and reconstructed in what Breny Mendoza calls the male ethos of state, an ethos reified in the ten-year reign of Ecuador's "progressive" president Rafael Correa.[2]

Although my interest here is not with the state per se, the project of Correa's state and its authoritarian, patriarchal, racialized, gendered, hetero-normative, and extractivist politics are what give context and reason to this chapter. My interest instead is with the *her*stories of resistance, re-existence, and co-existence that spite this state.[3] Most especially, it is with the emergent and rising insurgencies of community-based women to defend territory and life against the spoliation, pillage, land grabbing, destruction, and death that in Ecuador is the state-led capitalist extractivist policy-project.

Of course, the very idea of women's insurgencies challenges not only the male ethos of state, but also the male ethos present in many—if not most—of Indigenous and Black communities. While women have always been a fun-damental—if not central—part of territory-based struggles, seldom are they recognized, even within communities themselves, as protagonists, insurgents, leaders, and carriers of the struggle, of knowledge, and of the word.

In the last couple of years of his life, Juan García Salazar, "worker of the process" and guardian of Afro-Pacific oral tradition and collective memory, recognized his own omissions in this regard:

For so many years I have assumed that the words and teachings of *Abuelo* (Grandfather) *Zenón* represent the voice of collective memory of the Afro-Pacific, that the words of Zenón are also present in the memory of women, including my *Abuela Débora.* The absence of the voice-seed of *Abuela Débora* and all the *Abuelas* in my texts reflect my "*de-formación*" (my bad training) that is part of the coloniality of gender that makes us (males) think that the man represents the woman. This is not my intention, nor is it my thought. Today I recognize the pending debt, a charge that is not only mine but of all Afro-Ecuadorian men and women, especially women in making visible their own thinking and planting (of seeds of memory and thought) as and for women, but also as teachings for all.[4]

The foundational texts of María Lugones have taught us that the coloniality of gender permeates virtually all territories, spaces, places, and aspects of life.[5] It is part of a patriarchal and racialized geopolitics that works globally, nationally, and in urban, rural, and ancestral communities not only to omit, negate, and exclude, but to also render extraordinary and strange women-led and women-conceived insurgencies. When recognition does appear, it is most often as individual, isolated, and exemplary cases sometimes long after the women have died. Such are the cases in Ecuador of Dolores Cacuango and Tránsito Amaguaña, historical Kichwa figures—Cacuango in the 1940s and Amaguaña in the 1960s—described by the Kichwa intellectual and lawyer Nina Pacari as "pioneers in the struggle, not only for land and education, but also for their philosophical profoundness."[6] Similarly, in the Black ancestral lands of the Afro-Andean Chota-Mira Valley, the eighteenth century freedom fighter Martina Carrillo has become in recent years "the" historical female figure, as if there were and have been no others.

The passing in 2017 of another Black woman leader and native of this Valley, Doña Zoila Espinoza, further exemplifies the problem. "Mama Zoilita," as she was known by many, carried in her body both the wisdom and struggle of her female ancestors. In announcing her passing, the public and private media was quick to laud her folkloric contributions in the realms of music and dance. Folklore, of course, is the acceptable domain of recognition in the racist and sexist society that is contemporary Ecuador. Rendered invisible was her leadership among women of all ages, and most especially with other women elders, in defense of territory, territory-based knowledges, and women-based collective memory, that which for centuries has sustained life despite the violences of enslavement, internal colonialism, and state.

Of course, the problem here is not with much due recognitions. Rather, it is with the ways "national" (that is, public nation-based) recognitions work to shroud—to make invisible and relegate as non-existent—the multiple, ongoing, and everyday knowledges, practices, and forms of Indigenous and Black women's subjectivity, agency, and insurgency of resistance, re-existence, and co-existence. But the problem is also of the persistence of a patriarchal and male-dominated framework and logic, including in rural communities, that portends to define leadership, insurgency, and struggle.

For example, and despite Indigenous cosmological-cultural claims of gender parity, complementarity, alliance, and relation, men remain the "usual" protagonists and leaders of both Andean and Amazonian community-based Indigenous governance and organization. While a man and woman may together assume leadership roles, or while men and women may occasionally alternate roles, men typically delineate and circumscribe the criteria, model, relational sphere, and voice of "leader." The lived experience of a Nasa *cabildo* leader in southern Colombia's Cauca region is illustrative:

> My leadership is constantly put in question just because I am a woman; some immediately look to highlight my weaknesses and faults, and many of the women who I thought would support and ally with me in a collaborative and communal sense lead the scrutiny and critique. I thought it would be possible to build a different practice of leadership: collective, communal, and relational in a much more female-sense, of women thinking and acting together. Instead I find myself mostly alone in this pursuit. The logic and frame remain that of men, generalized as cultural and cosmological by most in the community.[7]

The concerns of this leader as well as those of this chapter are not with the role of individual women in leadership, nor are they with increasing female representation. While such concerns——part of the Western principle and logic of equality—may be important for white, whitened, and urban feminisms and feminists, they are not typically so for grassroots and community-based Indigenous and African-descended women. "There is a code at work in the question about women's role and representation in communities and community leadership," Nina Pacari contends, "and this code is Western in logic and stance."[8] Undoing the centrality and supposed universality of this code can, as this chapter will suggest, open and push considerations of and toward feminism's pluriversals, including with respect to women-led insurgencies, struggles, praxis, and thought. Some may refer to this resurgence and insurgence of thought-action as feminist, locating it within the pluriversal of decolonial feminisms present beyond and despite the West. As we will see later, others, particularly women from rural communities, tend to shy away from this label.

The aim of this chapter is to make present the increasing force (most especially in Ecuador) of women-conceived and women-led struggles; that is, of insurgencies understood as collective actions, strategies, and methodologies/pedagogies of praxis that do not only resist but, more crucially, create and construct possibilities of re-existence, co-existence, and inter-existence (that is, of life). The focus, in specific, is with the Indigenous women-led insurgencies that sustain and re-vindicate life against the violences of global capital, its patriarchal and colonial culture, and its project of pillage, spoliation, land grabbing, destruction, and death. It is with the insurgencies and praxis of resistance, re-existence, and co-existence for life that in the specific case of Ecuador contest, dispute, and challenge the so-called progressive state and (now ex) President Rafael Correa's three-pronged amalgam, project, and rallying cry of extractivism, anti-poverty development, and modernization.[9]

The organization of the chapter is in three parts. The first is focused on the politics, policies, and problematic of Ecuador's "progressive" state under the reign of the now ex-President Rafael Correa. It moves from a brief description of the 2008 Constitution to a consideration of the foundational triad President-Government-State and its three-pronged project of extractivism–antipoverty development–modernization which defined and organized the "Citizens Revolution," also referred to, more broadly, in its earlier years, as Twenty-first Century Socialism and in the last years as Twenty-first Century Capitalism. The second part opens reflection on women-led insurgencies, giving specific attention to the insurgent praxis, most especially of Amazonian women, against the state project of extractivism–as development–as modernization. It explores the strategies, methodologies/pedagogies, and praxis of these insurgencies and considers how they create and construct ways to resist, persist, re-exist, and co-exist against and despite state, giving credence to the Constitution's plurinationalizing, interculturalizing, and decolonizing propositions and intentions. Finally, the third part affords broader reflections on feminism's pluriversal and the otherwise that is decolonial praxis.

Suffice it to say that this is not an ethnographic study, a research-based analysis, an academic treatise, or a theory-inspired paper. It is reflective, in great part, of ongoing conversations and participation over the course of the last three decades in Ecuador, in social movement and community-based processes and struggles (at the movements' and communities' request). In addition, it is reflective of my own active involvement in the conceptualizing and making of Ecuador's 2008 Constitution and in the collective hope-filled processes to build a radically distinct social and political project, processes which were undercut by Correa's government and state. I am not a disinterested observer. I am a militant intellectual, an engaged feminist, and a vocal critic that has refused to be silenced, as well as an immigrant from the North to the South who continues to unlearn in order to relearn, and to make this unlearning and relearning constitutive of my engagement, commitment, and praxis. To listen to, accompany, and walk, think, and learn with and from social movements, communities, and their members means to challenge the apparatus of research, the hierarchical binary of theory versus practice, and the authority and universalizing pretentions of academic knowledge. All of this is part of my decolonial pedagogical/methodological praxis and stance, a praxis and stance that is never stable but always becoming.

THE POLITICS, POLICIES AND PROBLEMATICS OF ECUADOR'S "PROGRESSIVE" STATE

In 2008, Ecuador approved in popular referendum a Constitution considered by many as the most radical in the world. By making Nature the subject of rights, establishing *buen vivir*[10]—living in harmony and plentitude—as the transversal principal and the horizon of a distinct social project, and giving recognition and base to an Intercultural and Plurinational State—among other aspects—, the Constitution took a historical step toward the decolonization of Ecuador.

As I have argued elsewhere, both the Constitutional Assembly (in which I had the privilege to participate as an "unofficial" advisor) and the Charter itself were the reflection and result, in large part, of the political and epistemic insurgency of social movements in the decades before. These movements, most especially the Indigenous movement, gave impetus to a proposition, project, and thought that proffered to transform the state, interculturalizing and pluriversalizing the here-to-fore monocultural and uninational social-political order. With the Constitution and the government-named "Citizen's Revolution" came the idea and belief of substantial and profound change. President Rafael Correa repeated on numerous occasions that the long neoliberal night had finally ended. His political project was to recuperate national sovereignty, redistribute wealth, and propel productive forces through alliances with certain progressive and leftist sectors.[11] Neoliberalism was to be replaced by a new moment in which the "Citizen's Revolution" and "Twenty-first Century Socialism" (the latter linking Ecuador and Bolivia with Hugo Chavez's Venezuela) promised transcendental shifts and transformative horizons.

Certainly one of the most transcendental shifts was with regard to Nature. As Ecuador's Constitution states:

> Article 71: Nature or Pacha Mama, where life is materialized and reproduced, has the right to an integral respect of its existence and the right to the maintenance and regeneration of its life cycles, structure, functions, and evolutionary processes.
> Article 72: Nature has the right to be restored.[12]

Here *Pachamama* (Mother Nature or Mother Earth) is a living being with intelligence, sentiments, and spirituality. Nature is neither an object nor a use-based exploitable good controlled and dominated by humans; it is an integral part of life itself.

In the language of the Charter, natural resources and the environment are also differentially positioned; "persons, communities, peoples, and [ancestral] nation[alities] shall have the right to benefit from the environment and natural wealth enabling them to enjoy the good way of living ['buen vivir']," but exploitation cannot put in permanent danger natural systems or permanently alter Nature's genetic makeup.[13] With such declaration, it was thought that the colonial matrix and extractive tradition would end and with it, the massive exploitation and contamination associated with capital and national, foreign, and transnational interests.

The Yasuni-ITT initiative launched in 2007 by President Correa and the then Minister of Energy Alberto Acosta (subsequent Constitutional Assembly president) seemed to solidify the path toward postextractivism. The Initiative asked the international community to compensate Ecuador with $3.6 billion (half of what Ecuador would have realized in revenue from exploiting the resources at 2007 prices), for keeping 850 million barrels of unexploited oil in the ground. The argument was that this would avoid the emission of 407 tons of CO_2 into the atmosphere, protect Indigenous peoples living in voluntary isolation, and preserve the Yasuni National Reserve, considered the most biologically diverse in the world.[14]

In its communication within the country and to the world, the Ecuadorian government described the Initiative as historic for its questioning of the model of life and consumption of contemporary society. "It symbolizes an example of the willingness of a country to change the playing rules of energy consumption," said the National Secretariat of Planning and Development, and it marks a "transition toward a model of sustainability. It is a wager for life and the planet."[15] However, in 2013, President Correa cancelled the Initiative, arguing monetary issues, and announced the forthcoming exploitation of oil—an unavoidable evil, the president said, for eradicating poverty, particularly in the Amazon.[16]

Postextractivism, it seems, was never part of the President's and "his progressive" state's agenda. In December 2008, less than three months after the approval of the Constitution, Correa pushed through a new Mining Law, enabling the exploitation of previously unexplored resources, and opening the door to megaprojects of open-sky mining. With declining oil reserves, Correa argued, mining is an economic necessity, a policy and public good that will contribute to development, the elimination of poverty, and modernization. Development-poverty/elimination-modernization became, from here on in, the foundational project and rallying cry not only of the President himself but, more crucially, of "his" government, state, and political-economic venture of "progressive extractivism." So took form another foundational triad and triumvirate: President-Government-State, here understood as a paternal-heteropatriarchal formation of inseparable unity in which Correa became—and was—both government and state. That is, the father who intended to control and wield power over virtually all aspects of governance, but also of life, including what he referred to in the later years of his reign,as the ideology of gender and sexuality. This ideology is "an offence against all natural laws," said Correa in one of his Saturday broadcasts; men need to act and look like men, and women need to act and look like women."[17]

Along with the Mining Law came the criminalization of protest under the legal-penal figure of "acts of terrorism" and "state sabotage." Acosta, who left the Constitutional Assembly in its last months because of his differences with Correa, became an outspoken critic of what he called "the hand of Twenty-first Century neoextractivism." The fighters for life are pursued and persecuted as terrorists so that the transnationals can loot natural resources and attack Nature and communities, Acosta said. "Repressive practices constitute an inheritance of old politics, oriented to disavow, disqualify, and even punish social movements."[18]

So too began the President's ongoing attacks in his weekly Saturday radio and television broadcasts—and in the media in general—on social movements and their leaders. In ways that reproduced and replicated coloniality's racialized and genderized violences, Correa repeatedly used the trope of infantilization to discredit Indigenous leaders, ecological feminists and environmental activists, and their organizations and movements. His ongoing references to "the infantile indigenous movement" and "the infantile ecologists" worked to wrest rationality and make child-like the leaders and activists struggling against extractive policies and for life, territory, and nature. "We've already lost too much time for development," said Correa. "Those that make us lose time are demagogues, 'no to mining, no to oil,' enough with these stupidities! We will not permit the infantile Left, with feathers and ponchos, to destabilize this process of change."[19]

The assault was not just discursive. Up until the end of his presidential term (May 2017), Correa endeavored not only to continue to discredit but also even to close the women-run NGO *Acción Ecológica* (Ecological Action), this because of its documentation of the criminalization of protest against extractive projects and its defense of the collective rights of Indigenous peoples against extractivism and territorial displacement and destruction.[20] Similarly, the National Confederation of Indigenous Peoples of Ecuador (CONAIE) was a principal and ongoing target of attack. The idea of a Plurinational state, the initiatives of extractivism, and the public policies regarding Indigenous peoples were points of tension from the beginning. However, as CONAIE's opposition to the government took more visible form—including in the 2009 mobilizations against the Mining Law, the March for Life and Water in 2012, and the actions against the Law of Lands, among others—the President-Government-State's attack also intensified. The criminalization of Indigenous men and women leaders swelled. At the same time, spaces won through CONAIE's historic struggle, such as the autonomy of Indigenous bilingual intercultural education, were eliminated; thousands of community-based schools (sites of social-cultural-political organization) were closed, replaced by large modern "millennial schools" (often far from the communities themselves) with a nationalized curriculum and instruction in Spanish only. In the Amazonian region most impacted by extractivism, "Millennial Cities" were built, forcing families and clans to relocate and "urbanize" so that extractive industries could do their work. Of course, the repression and disciplinization did not stop there. In 2015, the triumvirate attempted (unsuccessfully) to evict CONAIE from the building it has legally occupied since 1991 (part of the agreements reached between the Indigenous organization and the government after the 1990 historic uprising).

Certainly, the examples are excessively many to continue to elaborate here. Suffice it to say, as Cartuche clearly argues, "state modernization for capitalist development [i.e., Correa's project] needs the disciplining of critical social organizations."[21]

> The government argues the need for a re-centralization of the state and its institutions in order to liberate itself from "particularized interests" of organizations, unions and associations. This implies, according to the government, the need to construct a politics from the state that helps to counter the excess of autonomy of some public institutions; a politics that also closes paths of influence,

including that of indigenous organizations and peoples. This anti-corporative politics is aimed at neutralizing the influence not of all sectors, but only those who dispute and question the character of the state in the "citizen's revolution." The criminalization of protest focused on organizations like CONAIE and those with an anti-mining stance, is the result of a centralized politics of state in benefit of certain groups of economic power.[22]

Authoritarianism, in this sense, was deemed a necessary and component part of the centralized and consolidated state regime; a state–as president–as government that, under the banners of revolution, progressivism, and modernization-progress, promoted the individual inclusion of historically subalternized sectors (e.g., women, and Indigenous and Afro-descendant peoples) while at the same time negating and severely repressing their collective rights, stance, and struggle. With the extractive industries of mining and oil passed, during the Correa government, into the hands of Chinese public and private companies (the result and condition of a debt with China that in at the end of 2017 totaled more than 8 billion dollars, and that includes the obligatory hand over of most all of oil production to this nation until 2021), extractivism became the activity, project, and motor of the economy.[23] It is the state against territory and life.

FLOWERING REBELLION, RE-EXISTING, AND CULTIVATING LIFE

In Ecuador, as is true in much of Latin America/Abya Yala's south today, it is women who are leading the struggles against extractivism and global capitalism's predatory and pillage-oriented model of development. These are struggles of and for territory and life against and (des)spite state.

As Katy Machoa (director of women's issues in CONAIE's governing council from 2014–2017) sustains, these struggles are part of a historical continuum. They have root in colonization and its civilizatory project: in the diverse forms of violence—territorial, ideological, and knowledge and existence-based—that this process and project continue to manifest. "Here the relation of *runa*-nature [human being-nature] has been particularly impacted, leaving Indigenous women with an overload of disadvantages as compared to men. Numbered are the historical registers that recognize and take up the process of struggle of women. For us [women], they dug a deeper hole," says Machoa.[24]

> They erased us from history, from philosophy, from science and from society, but we never stopped being there. I remit to the present and I listen; as we take

the streets of the capital city, the most felt voices that chant "the land isn't for sale" are those of women. We know that we were present before because today we are fiercely defying the obstacles of the femicidal society. We continue giving birth to Quilago, Dolores Cacuango, Tránsito Amaguaña, Manuela León, to the indomitable Amazonas and so many others that, like us, forged the history of resistance told not from the official sources but from the mobilizations that push us and from the inherited dignity. We continue and we will continue cultivating life, flowering rebellion so that the new era —the pachakutik—does not come upon us by surprise.[25]

Indigenous women have always been component parts of resistance-based struggles, including in the numerous uprisings and mobilizations of the decade of the 1990s, when CONAIE and the Indigenous movement established themselves as political actors that the state could no longer negate, disregard, and dismiss. Yet there is a marked difference in women's protagonism, agency, and participation today. While the national and regional organizations continue to be predominantly male-led, women are at the lead of many of the territory-based struggles, most especially in the Amazon where the bulldozer of state propelled extractivism moves ahead with full force.

THE RESURGENCE OF AMAZONIAN
WOMEN WARRIORS

In recent years, Amazonian women have come together in Ecuador as a formidable, plurinational, insurgent force. These women-conceived and women-led resurgence and struggle have as their principal objective the protection and defense of territory, forest, rivers, families, Indigenous nations, and life itself: understood in an integral and relational sense as Mother Forest, Mother Nature, or Mother Earth. Such protection and defense have meant mobilizing against extractivism, massive deforestation, and the immense contamination of the ground, rivers, and streams. The images made viral in the now infamous Texaco-Chevron litigation (a case filed in 1992 by the Siona and Secoya nations against the multinational, and which—thanks to the power of capital—continues in 2021 without final resolution), afford just a small glimpse of the toxic legacy that Amazonian peoples struggle against.

This legacy and threat has not only been perpetuated, but also made much worse by the policies and project of Rafael Correa's so-called "progressive" state—policies and projects propelled by Chinese capital with little or no concern for the forest, the living beings, and life-as cosmos-as territory and land. Machoa explains:

The state's presence in the region is with police and armed guards in order to protect the Chinese; we do not exist for the state, and, as a result, the state does not exist for us. What is the state when it negates life, when it negates access to schooling and health as has occurred with the establishment of a state of exception in the Shuar community of Nankits, justifying state violence, subjugation, and aggression, massive displacements, and even threats by police of the rape of women and young girls, all to enable the go-ahead of copper mining?[26]

"We are the makers of our history. We are Amazonian women warriors fighting for dignity and territory-life, for an 'other' model, system, way and plan of living and life," Machoa goes on to say.[27] "Our territories continue to be threatened, and we continue to defend the inheritance of our children. We have the force, determination, and courage to do so. We women are together in the struggle, we will not be bought, and we will not be sold. We have dignity. So we are the women of the Amazon."[28]

The examples of Amazonian women's resurgence, insurgence, and defense against oil and mining and for territory-life are present both within communities and the various Indigenous nations, as well as in the collective alliances and actions that cross nation, region, and language. For the Sapara nation, for instance, these struggles are literally about survival. With only approximately 400 members left, this nation, whose language was declared by UNESCO as World Cultural and Immaterial Heritage, is struggling against the threat of extinction. "The oil project puts in question our survival as a peoples," argues Gloria Ushigua, leader of the Sapara Women's Association, defense of our territory is defense of life. "Those that want to take out the oil won't be affected, but we will all die."[29]

The first visible public manifestation of an Amazonian-wide women-led and conceived insurgency occurred on October 16, 2013. Approximately a hundred women from the Kichwa, Sapara, and Waorani nations organized under the banner of "Women mobilized in defense of life" arrived to Quito, many with their children and in what they termed a "March for Life," to demand that the crude in the Yasuni Park remain in the ground. The march was a response to Correa's announcement several months before of the end of the Yasuni-ITT initiative and the beginning of oil exploration and exploitation in the Yasuni Park, the most bio-diverse rainforest in the world.

Among the women's objectives and motivations: to evidence the ransacking of natural resources through extractivism and within a model of capitalist accumulation, and to socialize and make visible their community-based model of life *"Kawsak Sacha"* (the living forest), a concept integral to the defense of Nature and *Sumak Kawsay* or *Buen Vivir*. The communiqué circulated before their arrival to Quito, Ecuador's capital, described the reason for their march: "As women we feel from the deepness of our wombs, the threats of extractivism; we consider as urgent the need to open debate in this critical moment generated with regard to Yasuní-ITT and to come out in defense of our nourishing mother (Mother Forest or Mother Nature) that gives birth, raises and protects her children without distinction to ethnicity or social class."[30]

The Amazonian women's petitions to meet with then-President Correa were denied. Rather than return home, they decided to extend their time in Quito, calling for the national solidarity of all women to the cause, and convoking from the *Arbolito* Park—a central meeting place in the last several decades for Indigenous mobilizations—women, youth, and the masses to enter into dialogue with them and assume this women-led struggle for Life and Nature. By so doing, these women used the urban space as an educational forum, building understandings of their struggles, life-visions, and realities while, at the same time, positioning and linking these life-visions and struggles to the broader project of *Buen Vivir* as a shared project and new "interversal" that endeavors to move beyond capitalist exploitation and accumulation. The fact that they did this as women broke the mold of contemporary male-dominated Amazonian-Indigenous politics in which men, more often than not, assume both public and organizational leadership, decision-making, and voice. However, it also brought to attention what is increasingly evident throughout the region, and that is women's insurgent leadership in today's struggles for territory, Nature and Life. It is an insurgency that confronts the coloniality of power, of being, of existence, and of gender all intertwined, an insurgency of decolonial prospect, politic, and action that the so-called "progressive" state and much of the traditional Left (including white/whitened and western/westernized feminists) are still unable and unwilling to recognize or fathom.

"BE CAREFUL WITH YOUR LIFE, YOU COULD DIE"

The 2013 action ushered in a women-conceived and women-led insurgent practice that has continued to evolve and grow. Yet with it, persecution also expanded.

The words "be careful with your life, you could die" ("cuidado con tu vida puedes morir") were posted on Alicia Cahuiya's house shortly after the 2013 march, alongside her dead dog. Alicia, founder and president of the Waorani Women's Association, had, for months, fought off threats and pressure by male leaders to accept the government's plan for oil extraction in her birthplace of Yasuni. She had refused—and continues to refuse—to bend to the continued questioning, intimidation, persecution, and aggression of government officials. Alicia is not alone in this struggle against persecution. In fact, when police stopped the bus of women returning to the Amazon after the 2013 march and asked which one was Alicia, all the women present cried out "I am Alicia." The next day the death threat was found on Alicia's door.

Alicia is one of five women defenders of nature who presented their testimonies in a hearing in Washington, D.C. in October 2015, denouncing the actions of the Correa government against them. The testimonies were part of a petition by Earth Rights International and the previously mentioned Ecuadorian NGO Acción Ecológica.[31]

In her testimony, Alicia recounts how she returned to her territory at the age of 16, leaving a missionary boarding school to follow her grandmother's wise counsel: to defend the territory where she was born. "I returned to find a highway built on top of the cemetery where my grandparents are buried. I began to work to defend my grandparents' rights, to defend our territory."[32] She recalls the work with the National Huaorani Organization (ONHAE) at the beginning of her militancy, including the march of men, women, and children to Quito in the late 1990s to denounce oil exploitation.

[After the march,] the men leaders signed agreements with the oil companies and divided our peoples. They want development, while those who live inside the jungle already have all we need.

ONHAE was run by men; men made the decisions and women could not. . . . It is for this reason that I fought for our own women's organization to administer our territory. That's how the Waorani Women's Association (AMWAE) was made. I listened to the voices of my ancestors telling me "enough with oil companies, because they are contaminating and reducing our territories." The ancestors left their voices in me.[33]

In 2013, Alicia was elected vice president of the Waorani Amazon Nation.[34] "They asked me my position. I responded: to continue to defend our territory as a woman's struggle. . . . They said I had to continue to struggle so that new oil exploration would not occur." However, this is when the persecution by the Correa government began full force, she explained, when the threats of prison, when the vigilance, and when the death threats became everyday occurrences. It is also when the men in the organization began to insist that she accept the exploration and extraction of oil. This complicity makes the strategies of persecution and intimidation more complex. It is also one of the ways the government works to discredit leaders, particularly when those leaders are women.[35]

Gloria Ushigua, who also gave her testimony at the October 2015 Washington hearing, is another case in point. As with Alicia, the persecution of Gloria began in 2013. In December of that year, and after a November mobilization in front of the Ministry of Hydrocarbons in Quito, the government began its systematic attack. "Five days after the mobilization, the government launched a two-week television campaign to discredit me. The campaign showed my photo in my native dress with a caption saying that I dressed like a clown. They used the photo to discredit my work and to intimidate me."[36]

After the campaign, the persecution took on force. The government continued to threaten, harass, and intimidate Gloria and her family members, and to make her the target of various forms of aggression and violence. In 2013, she was judicially accused of terrorism, sabotage and obstruction of a public way (related to the hydrocarbon mobilization), charges still in force in mid-2018. In 2015, police broke into her home spraying tear gas in her face, affecting the other women and children present, and physically and verbally abusing her. Her office was broken into and her computer destroyed.[37]

In her 2015 testimony, Gloria explained the significance of her struggle, which is a struggle of women defenders of territory and life.

Our territory is our ancestral heritage that the ancestors left for Indigenous human life. Land is for the future of our children. I am a defender because I defend my territory and my culture; water is life for all beings that live on earth. One of the differences between women and men is that men sell the land more quickly, but we women are defenders and protectors of the land, of territory and life.

In order to reproduce and take care of nature, we Amazonian Indigenous peoples live very different from those who live in cites. We have our own architecture and the cosmovision of our ancestors to look beyond. Our men were territorial defenders and were treated badly. And now we women are in front of the defense asking that our rights, territory, and forest be respected.

Oil exploitation stays underground; neither the oil nor the air of Sapara territory are for sale.[38]

Gloria, Alicia, and other Amazonian women leaders once again made the news in another mobilization in March 2016, this one confronting the government's concession and sale to Andes Petroleum, a Chinese oil consortium, of two large blocks of the southern Amazon. This concession extends into the territories of the Sapara, Kichwa, and Waorani peoples, and the previously protected Yasuni Park, including the designated "intangible zone" where the Tagaeri and Taromenane peoples live in voluntary isolation. It includes 40% of Sapara territory. It also includes part of Sarayaku, the Kichwa community that in 2012 won litigation in the Inter-American Human Rights Court against the Ecuadorian state's attempt of oil exploration and extraction.[39] Sarayaku is widely known for its resistance against the state, not only the present state but also its predecessors. Women have been important protagonists in these struggles.

The 2016 march brought women from all these communities together. Photos circulated in the social media showed images of women with babies on their backs, navigating the rivers in the midst of the midday heat to come together in the provincial capital of Puyo to march in celebration of International Women's Day, but, most especially, to denounce Correa's agreement with the Chinese consortium. "Our territory is threatened by transnational Chinese companies. Our nation and our families see our rights violated in the loss and contamination of this territory. We are ready to protect, defend, and die for our rainforest, families and nation," said a representative of the Sapara Women's Association.[40]

Two months after this march, Gloria's sister-in-law was brutally assassinated while working in a garden that she shares with Gloria. The assumption is that Gloria was the target.

In response to these cumulative violences and aggressions, the initiative Women, Territories, and Environment of the Latin American and Caribbean Urgent Action Fund (made up of organizations and activists from Ecuador, Honduras, Guatemala, El Salvador, Mexico, Colombia, Peru, Chile, Bolivia, Uruguay, Paraguay, and Argentina), along with other environmental, Indigenous and Black women's organizations, released a public statement in June 2016 in defense of and in solidarity with Gloria, her family, and the Sapara Women's Organization. The statement called for investigation into the perpetuated aggressions and removal of the still-pending criminal charges against her. It demanded that the government desist in criminalizing Indigenous leaders for defending nature and human rights. It called for the establishment of mechanisms of protection and vigilance for Gloria and all others at risk for defending nature and life, and the nullification of illegal and illegitimate oil concessions that violate the Constitution, its principles of *buen vivir*, and nature's rights. Moreover, it linked the case of Gloria to other defenders of territory and nature:

> As Latin American women defenders of territory, nature and life, we reject the imposition of oil exploitation and extractive projects, which infringe upon the self-determination of peoples and which violate our bodies and our lives. We demand justice and an end to criminalization, assassinations, and all types of aggression against defenders, men and women, of water, land, and life in Latin America and the world.[41]

Of course, the cases of Alicia and Gloria are not isolated, nor are Amazonian women leaders the only targets. In Ecuador, mestiza women actively involved in both supporting these Amazonian women's struggles and in other related struggles against extractivisms, free trade, and women's and Indigenous rights have also been the targets of intimidation, aggression, and persecution. Margoth Escobar, Paulina Muñoz, and Esperanza Martinez are three of many. Their testimonies, similarly presented in Washington and documented by *Plan V*, detail the violences that they continue to confront as women insurgents resisting the extractivist, developmentalist, and anti-poverty policies of Correa´s ten-year regime.[42]

WALKING THE WORD: CHASKI-WARMI ABYA YALA

We, Indigenous women of the Amazonian forests, the rivers, the highlands, and the mountains of Abya Yala, have traveled our territories. In these lands, we recognize and encounter ourselves. We are part of *Pachamama* (Mother Earth); because of the way we relate with her, we feel climate change from the experience and everyday relation of living with our territories. . . . We feel the crisis caused by extractivist policies and models, of oil and mining, the contamination of water and the atmosphere, and the destruction of forests and of the plant cover of *Pachamama*, all of which has produced grave effects in our lives.[43]

The above words form part of the Declaration presented by the Indigenous women messengers of Abya Yala (*Chasqui Warmikuna* or *Chaski-Warmi*) to the COP22 meeting on Climate Change held in Morocco in November 2016. The Declaration was signed by Blanca Chancosa, then Vice-President of the Ecuadorian regional highland Indigenous organization ECUARUNARI; Nancy Santi of the Amazonian Kichwa Peoples; Marta Cecilia Ventura, Maya Quiche and part of the National Indigenous and Peasant Coordinator (Guatemala); Cecilia Flores of the Aymara peoples of Chile; Gladis Panchi of the Embera peoples of Colombia; Silvia Lupo of the Leco peoples of Bolivia; Alicia Cahuiya, vice president of the Waorani peoples' organization in Ecuador; Carmen Lozano, women's coordinator in ECUARUNARI; and Ivonne Ramos, coordinator of Saramanta Warmikiuna (Ecuador). It is the message of the many who struggle daily against national and global policies that cause the destruction of Nature.

Of course, it is no coincidence that women are at the forefront of this struggle. Indigenous women, as the Declaration sustains, lead the defense of territory. They live domestic violence, the social, environmental, and political violence of states, and the violence of the impoverishment of the conditions of life, all constitutive of extractivism and its results, and component parts of coloniality in all its dimensions, most especially gender. "The violence against Pachamama extends in a direct way to Indigenous women," the Declaration argues, "reflected in the criminalization, imprisonment, assassination, capture, persecution, of the women and men custodians of Pachamama." In this sense, "from our experience, we can make visible the fact that climate change is not an abstract concept but something palpable in health, in the change of agricultural cycles, in increased work for women, and in the violence against Pachamama or Mother Earth."[44]

Despite government rhetoric about the need to address climate change, states continue to implement and give incentives for the development of extractivist policies and programs in Indigenous territories and ancestral lands. States and governments of both the Right and the so-called Left are at the center of the problem, the Declaration contends.

> At the same time that national and global policies portend to address climate change, they promote extractive policies that increase the local and global climate crisis, and promote false solutions. They neither recognize nor consider the historical role that we Indigenous people have had with Nature, particularly Indigenous women, nor do they take into account our concrete contributions in the search for solutions that come from knowledge of the territory that we inhabit and our cosmovisions based in ancestral wisdoms.[45]

Through this Declaration, the Chaski-Warmi Indigenous women's collective makes clear that climate change is not just about environment; more crucially, it is about existence itself. Their words announce and articulate lived knowledges, actions, and activisms that exhort a decolonial feminism of sorts, a feminism—if we can use that word—that is not about specific women's issues having to do with sex and reproduction only or with the supposed domestic-public/economic separation.[46] It is a women-led insurgency of and for life. Such insurgency certainly prompts reflections about the significance, character, and composition of decolonial struggle in Abya Yala today, and, in particular, about the ways Indigenous women are challenging the traditional tenets of feminism and approaches toward the coloniality of gender. Brought to the fore here is the essence for these women of decolonial and decolonizing work understood as not only about the restitution and of what coloniality has taken but also, and possibly more crucially, about the co-creation in the present of conditions of re-existence defined communally, integrally, and in their terms.

While the Declaration presents a series of proposals to both the region's governments and the United Nations—all of which, not surprisingly, have gone unconsidered—it also offers proposals to the women of Abya Yala. These latter proposals include, among others, the need to organize, join forces, and come together in *Chaski-Warmi Abya Yala* to defend Mother Nature and walk the word in order "to be able to reach spaces of community-based, national and international decision making with a more profound knowledge of our realities and our cosmovision as Indigenous women." The Declaration, in this sense, is not just a statement of *Chaski-Warmi*, but also a call to and for its strengthening and growth.

Chaski-Warmi, "Women Messengers" or more broadly "Women Messengers in Defense of Mother Nature," began in 2015 as a kind of walking methodology/pedagogy among Indigenous women. Chaski-Warmi's project—in Ecuador but also in Colombia, Bolivia, Chile, and Guatemala—is to listen to what community-based Indigenous women have to say about their struggles in defense of Nature, about the effects of extractivism and climate change at the local level, and about the traditional practices of women and communities to confront these effects and to create alternatives to survive.

The first experience in Ecuador was *Yaku Chaski Warmikuna* (Women Messengers of the Water or River). During eight days in July 2015, a group of Amazonian Kichwa and Waorani women traveled the Bobonaza river basin in order "to help make aware and spread the word about extractivist conflicts that affect our communities, to work as women for territorial defense, and to promote the strategy to leave oil underground as the only real solution to climate change."[47] They carried messages against oil companies' strategies of aggression and land grabbing and alerted about the cooptation, buying off, and even assassination of community leaders. With these messages they helped construct, articulate, and support resistance and the demands for self-governance and self-determination, while at the same time making evident the contradictions between the Constitution (with its recognition of collective rights and nature's rights, and its call for *buen vivir*) and government sponsored extractivism. "The defense of territory by women against extractivism is a strategy that contributes to the Indigenous efforts being woven in the Province, most especially the efforts against the Ecuadorian government's 11th Oil Round (2015) that persecutes, harasses, and violates all community efforts to defend human rights, and the rights of nature and territory," the press statement published on their web said. "We categorically reject and denounce all extractivist proposals and actions in our territory, which for us constitutes a unique, indivisible and millennial heritage inherited from our ancestors."[48]

Yamila Gutierrez Callisaya, Aymaran Bolivian and part of the May 2017 *Chaski-Warmi* experience in Ecuador's southern Amazon region focused specifically on mining, describes how the project—most especially in the Ecuadorian context—works to recuperate "from below" the idea and role of the messenger (*chaski*) historically present throughout Abya Yala.[49] "Its objective," says Gutierrez, "is to build a process of dialogue among Indigenous women, convened by Indigenous women, about the problematic of extractivism, a problem that affects us as women." The experience of

Chaski-Warmi makes visible and gives presence to the thought and the political role of Indigenous women; "it is a dialogue among equals, in our own languages, and in and from our own territory, community, and place. Herein lies its value."[50]

As the *Chaski* or messenger who before the existence of cell phones and WhatsApp carried messages from community to community, here women messengers—tied to regional and national Indigenous organizations—listen to, carry, communicate, and walk women's territorially grounded words from river to river, from mountain to mountain, from community to community. Such experience serves to generate reflection, discussion, and debate between and among Indigenous women about the local and lived consequences of mining and oil, agroindustry, and other extractivisms, and about concrete practices and strategies of resistance, existence, and defense of Mother Nature or Mother Earth. In so doing, it helps plant seeds of awareness and concern, alerting populations about the death that is extractivism, then carrying this message from place to place. But, as Gutierrez argues, it also serves to inform the Indigenous organizations themselves, strengthening contact between the organization and their community base, and giving concretion, substance, and form to the organization's actions, struggles, and demands with respect to government policy.

Chaski-Warmi, in this sense, is a methodology/pedagogy constructed *desde lo propio*—an Indigenous women's methodology/pedagogy in which the political, territorial, spiritual, cosmogonic, cultural, affective, epistemic, existential, and organizational are all intertwined. While the methodology/pedagogy does not exclude men, it is women-centered and focused. In rural communities and in Indigenous organizations where men continue to be the most visible actors, protagonists, and spokespeople, *Chaski-Warmi* underscores and articulates women's force, thought, and voice, Gutierrez maintains. Furthermore, it builds women's own sense of capacity in contexts where women often devalue themselves and other women, thus helping to weave new communal and collective links and relations.[51]

Chaski-warmi, along with the other examples detailed here, make evident what Katy Machoa calls the flowering of women's rebellion, but also the women-led and women-conceived insurgencies that both challenge the policies, practice, and project of Ecuador's "progressive" state, and construct forms of resistance, re-existence and co-existence for territory and life.

ON FEMINISMS, PLURIVERSALS, AND
THE DECOLONIAL AS OTHERWISE

Can all of the above be considered as part and parcel of a kind of feminism––a feminism-otherwise? When I asked Yamila this question, she was adamant in her reply.

> For me, feminism remains a Western, anthropocentric, and individualist posture or position. It seems to suggest a disassociation or an unlinking from something, a setting off from the integral whole, from the activity of existence, of life, which is shared among all beings, including with the ancestors. The person is not just a person, the person is not a person alone, nor is her thought separate from the integral sphere of territory, beings, the cosmos, etc. As Indigenous women we have, feel, and create a connection and relation. We also know, recognize, and struggle against the machismo and male privilege present in our families, communities, and *ayllus*. *Chaski-Warmi* strengthens our connection and relation, and it helps build our collective power and force, a power and force that does not exclude others but that is women-focused, women-centered, and women-inspired. Feminism is not the word we use, nor does its concept and standpoint—born and constructed outside of our contexts—adequately reflect our project. While some Indigenous women, like Lorena Cabnal and Julieta Paredes, refer to communitarian feminisms, this reference is not widely shared. Our actions and thought, including the methodology here of *Chaski-Warmi*, have their own significance that do not necessarily need to be named as feminism or understood in feminist terms.[52]

From a related but somewhat different perspective, the Kichwa lawyer, intellectual, and historical leader Nina Pacari (also part of the 2017 *Chaski-Warmi* experience) underscores the importance of recuperating the visibility, presence, and participation of women "from our own parameters, vision, and community codes, but with much more horizontal perspectives, including with respect to the exercise of power":

> While machismo is a Western notion, Indigenous communities are not self-enclosed. Machismo exists. It is a factor present in and within the movement, and in and within communities, their contexts, processes, and practice. The increased presence and visibility of women today is a result of these debates that began [in Ecuador] in the 90s. Today our work is not just about the presence of women. More crucially, it is about the active role of women in decision-making. It is about recuperating the fundamentals and philosophical principles of the *ayllu*, not just as a stance against machismo but also as a way to build solidarity, complementarity, and a different logic, practice, and exercise of authority and power.[53]

Within this prospective frame of thought, Pacari opens a reflection on feminisms and the gender-based notion of woman.

> Woman is not 100% woman. She is part of an equilibrium man-woman; there are other codes at work with regards to personality and spirituality in both women and men and this has repercussions in a general sense in the ways that we conceive sex and sexuality, making our societies more open in ways that even traverse the gendered binary of men-women. For this reason, feminist movements cannot approach indigenous and non-indigenous women using the same codes; our codes are other and feminism needs to recognize this diversity not just of women, but also of culturally lived logics, philosophies, and codes.[54]

As I have argued elsewhere (Walsh, 2015; 2016), gender constructions in Andean and Amazonian societies (as well as in Mesoamerica) have been understood (particularly before the European invasion but also beyond) as dynamic, fluid, open, and non-hierarchical.[55] They have been based less on anatomical distinctions and more on performance, with what people do, and their ways of being in the world, ways in constant movement, shift, modification and fluid equilibrium.[56] Here, "gender" is probably not the best word; the relational duality of the feminine-masculine (which includes what I have described as the androgynous creative force and whole) opens up other cosmogonic, spiritual, and existence-based conceptions and practices that disturb polarity, its antagonistic dichotomy, and its totalizing rationality constructed in and through gender.

This, of course, is not to essentialize Indigenous difference, nor is it to negate machismo and patriarchy, and its violences, practices, and structures that have deepened with extractivism. Recalled is the analysis of the Peruvian peasant leader Lourdes Huanca from FEMUCARINAP, made in the context of the meeting of the Network of Women Defenders of Social and Environmental Rights held in Quito in October 2013: "For us, extractivism is rape and invasion," said Huanca, a violation that takes place on "the territory of our bodies." Women are the most affected by extractivism in terms of sexual violence and abuse, but also in health, in economic and social spheres, family instability, and territorial displacements. Nevertheless, there is also an additional problem, Huanca explained, and that is the way that the extractive industry affects community dynamics, relations, and structures, reinforcing male-dominated culture and behaviors. And it is the way that community men are using the Andean principles of duality and parity as conceptual tools that play into male superiority—"of the power of the testicles"—justifying men's exertion of force over female bodies as nature. For Huanca, this is the context and reason for women-led resistance, rebellion, and defense.[57]

Huanca's affirmation brings to the fore the problem today of male dominated conceptions and interpretations of Andean cosmology, and the use of
these conceptions and interpretations as tools of domination over women.
In so doing, she brings to mind the ongoing debate about historical and
present-day structures and practices of patriarchy within Indigenous cultures
and communities.[58] While much could be said about the distinct postures
and positions in this debate, that is not my interest here. My interest instead
is with present-day women-led struggles of resistance, re-existence, and
co-existence (de)spite state—struggles, that as the Amazonian and Andean
women in this text make clear, carry the collective memories of the rebellion of their female ancestors against coloniality and, with it, patriarchy, in
its different manifestations and forms (collective memories of rebellion for
territory and life). For some, these insurgent struggles—not just of Andean
and Amazonian women, but more broadly of Indigenous, Black, and peasant
women today—are in essence decolonial feminist struggles, with or without
the necessity of adjectives or labels.

Betty Ruth Lozano, for example, argues for the increasing association
today of decolonial feminisms with the struggle and political proposal of life.
Thinking from and with the cultural, social, spiritual, and existence-based
practices of struggle of blackwomen (her way of emphasizing the inseparability of being a woman and being Black) in the territory-region of the
Colombian Pacific, Lozano makes clear the relation for her of decolonial
feminisms and insurgency. Insurgency here refers to those processes and
possibilities of collective analysis, collective theorization, and collective
practice—all intertwined—that help engender an otherwise of relational
being, thinking, feeling, doing, and living in a place marked by the extremes
of violence, racism, and patriarchy in today's matrix of global capitalism/
modernity/coloniality. In this context, "blackwomen are not just impotent
victims, they also exercise power beyond resistance and survival; they are
insurgents," Lozano contends.[59] Of course, "feminism" is not always the
term that women use to describe, define, or orient their insurgent actions.
For Lozano (self-described as an Afro-Colombian decolonial feminist), the
non-naming of feminism is part of the decolonial feminisms—the "feminisms
otherwise"—that are "constructed in the struggles for the defense and reproduction of nature, territory, and collective rights . . . in the transformation of
conditions of life."[60]

The issue here is not with the politics of naming. Rather, it is with the ways
that Black and Indigenous women in Abya Yala are thinking, conceiving,
constructing, and leading resistances, rebellions, and resurgent and insurgent
actions that challenge state, move away from capitalism and its savage project, and move toward de-patriarchalizations, decolonizations, and the recreat-
ing of communal practices of leadership, governance, and autonomy (despite

state). In their insurgent thought-actions, territorial defense, and push for re-existence (this understood as the struggle and project of dignity and life) and co-existence (existence "with"), these women are enabling more complex analyses and articulations of gender, race, sexuality, patriarchy, capitalism, and the continual reconfigurations of the modern/colonial matrices of power. Moreover, they are revealing the lived significance of an "otherwise" that is decolonial praxis.

Whether or not "feminism" is the referent is not the point. With or without the label, these women's insurgent praxis engenders important considerations about the pluriversals and interversals of which decolonial feminisms are a necessary and fundamental part. In ways radically distinct from the postures and standpoints of feminisms in the West and in many of Latin America's westernized and whitened cities, here the project is one of relation; the relation rooted in territory-and-as-life. That is, the relation of knowledges, wisdoms, beings, and the cosmos, in and as Nature. It is a relation that works to dismantle and disarticulate the matrices of power, their hierarchical and dichotomous binaries (including of gender and sexuality), and their modern/colonial rationalities and foundations, thus engendering and enabling the "otherwise" as a radically distinct prospect of resistance, re-existence, and co-existence, a radically distinct prospect of life.

In closing, I once again recall the poignant words of Katy Machoa: "We continue and we will continue cultivating life, flowering rebellion so that the new era—the pachakutik—does not come upon us by surprise."[61] These words bring forth those of another Indigenous woman intellectual-activist (and writer, artist, and musician): Leanne Betasamosake Simpson, Mississaugua Nishnaabeg from Abya Yala's north or Turtle Island. As Simpson cries out: "Rebellion is on her way."[62]

NOTES

1. Katy Machoa was the director of women's issues in the National Governing Council of the National Confederation of Indigenous Peoples of Ecuador-CONAIE from 2014–2017. This epigraph was taken from the text "El florecimiento de la rebeldía" (The flowering of rebellion), presented in the photographic exhibit "Mujeres en la lucha social ecuatoriana" (Women in the Ecuadorian Social Struggle), organized by El Colectivo Desde el Margen, Universidad Andina Simón Bolívar, Quito, November 21–25, 2017.

2. Breny Mendoza, "La epistemología del sur, la colonialidad del género y el feminismo latinoamericano," in *Aproximaciones críticas a las prácticas teórico-políticas del feminisimo latinoamericano*, ed. Yuderkys Espinoa Miñoso (Buenos Aires: En la frontera, 2010).

3. I use the term re-existence here following the Afro-descendant decolonial thinker and artist Adolfo Albán Achinte. That is as: "The mechanisms that human groups implement as a strategy of questioning and making visible the practices of racialization, exclusion and marginalization, procuring the redefining and re-signifying of life in conditions of dignity and self-determination, while at the same time confronting the bio-politic that controls, dominates, and commodifies subjects and nature" (my translation). See: Adolfo Albán Achinte, "¿Interculturalidad sin decolonialidad? Colonialidades circulantes y prácticas de re-existencia," in *Diversidad, interculturalidad y construcción de ciudad*, ed. Wilmer Villa and Arturo Grueso (Bogotá: Universidad Pedagógica Nacional/Alcaldía Mayor, 2008), 85–86.

4. Juan García Salazar and Catherine Walsh, *Pensar sembrando/Sembrar pensando con el Abuelo Zenón* (Quito: Cátedra de Estudios Afro-Andinos, Universidad Andina Simón Bolívar and Ediciones Abya Yala, 2017), 30 (my translation).

5. María Lugones, "The Coloniality of Gender," *World & Knowledges Otherwise* 2, no. 2 (Spring 2008), https://globalstudies.trinity.duke.edu/sites/globalstudies.trinity .duke.edu/files/file-attachments/v2d2_Lugones.pdf.

6. Andrés Ortiz Lemos, "Lo que la sociedad mestiza puede aprender de las mujeres indígenas, según Nina Pacari," *Plan V,* published June 2017, https://www.planv.com .ec/historias/sociedad/lo-que-la-sociedad-mestiza-puede-aprender-mujeres-indigenas -segun-nina-pacari (my translation; henceforth, all quotes that appear in this chapter from this article are my translations).

7. Personal conversation, Popayan, Colombia, May 2017 (my translation).

8. Ortiz Lemos, "Lo que la sociedad mestiza puede aprender."

9. This is not to suggest that Indigenous women are the only ones fighting against the extractivist policy-project and for territory and life. However, both for reasons of space and because Indigenous women are affording the most organized and visible insurgency today against and despite the Ecuadorian state, this is the focus and attention here.

10. "In its most general sense, buen vivir denotes, organizes, and constructs a system of knowledge and living based on the communion of humans and nature and on the spatial-temporal-harmonious totality of existence—that is, on the necessary interrelation of beings, knowledges, logics, and rationalities of thought, action, existemce, and living. This notion is part and parcel of the cosnmovision, cosmology, or philosophy of the Indigenous peoples of Abya Yala but also, and in somewhat different ways, of the descendants of the African diaspora." Catherine Walsh, "Development as Buen Vivir. Institutional Arrangements and (De)Colonial Entanglements," in *Constructing the Pluriverse. The Geopolitics of Knowledge,* ed. Bernd Reiter (Durham: Duke University Press, 2018), 188.

11. Inti Cartuche Vacacela, "El conflicto entre la CONAIE y la Revolución Ciudadana," *Revista Digital La Linea de Fuego*, published March 2015, https://lalineadefuego.info/2015/03/31/el-conflicto-entre-la-conaie-y-la-revolucion -ciudadana-por-inti-cartuche-vacacela/.

12. "Constitution of the Republic of Ecuador," *Political Database of the Americas, Georgetown University,* published October 2008, https://pdba.georgetown.edu/ Constitutions/Ecuador/english08.html.

13. Ibid. Article 74.

14. Carlos Larrea, *Iniciativa Yasuní-ITT: La Gran Propuesta de un País Pequeño* (Ecuador: United Nations Development Programme, 2007).

15. Secretaria Nacional de Planificación y Desarrollo (SENPLADES), "Boletín de Prensa No. 395 Iniciativa Yasuni-ITT: Una apuesta ecuatoriana que marca un cambio de era" (Quito: SENPLADES, 2013), https://www.planificacion.gob.ec/wp-content/uploads/downloads/2013/02/BOLET%c3%8dN_395_YASUN%c3%8d_FANDER_08-02-13.pdf.

16. See Joan Martínez-Alier, Nnimmo Bassey and Patrick Bond, "Yasuni-ITT is dead. Blame President Correa," *Mapping Environmental Justice,* August 17, 2013 http://www.ejolt.org/2013/08/yasuni-itt-is-dead-blame-president-correa/.

17. See "Enlace Ciudadano Nro. 354 desde Guayaquil, Guayas," SECOM Ecuador, published December 2014, https://www.youtube.com/watch?v=ODXFdqtGsyo, with particular attention to 1:45:00 to 1:49:50. See also: Francisca Bozzo, "Feminazismo, hembrismo e ideología de género: Las respuestas del patriarcado a la revolución feminista," *Errancia 17* (April 2018), https://www.iztacala.unam.mx/errancia/v17/PDFS_1/LITORALES%203%20FEMINAZISMO.pdf. (my translation; henceforth, all quotes that appear from this article are my translation).

18. Alberto Acosta, "El uso de la justicia como mecanismo de terror," *El Universo,* published February 2011, https://www.eluniverso.com/2011/02/08/1/1363/uso-justicia-como-mecanismo-terror.html (my translation).

19. "Rafael Correa defiende contrato para la explotación minera," *El Universo,* published March 2012, https://www.eluniverso.com/2012/03/10/1/1355/rafael-correa-defiende-contrato-explotacion-minera.html.

20. In 2009 the government unsuccessfully attempted to close the NGO because of its frontal positions against extractivism and the destruction of territory/nature. In December 2016, the government began procedures of dissolution again, this time using the presidential Decree 739, which authorized mechanisms of control over the activities of civil society organizations, repeating the strategy used with another activist NGO, the Pachamama Foundation. In its notification to Acción Ecológica, the government gave as reasons the fact that "the organization, through its publications in social networks, has made manifest its support of the actions of the Shuar community [against the occupation of 41,760 hectares of ancestral land by Explorcobres, a subsidiary of the Chinese Tongling Nonferrous Metals Group], making affirmations about the grave impact to the environment and ecosystem caused by the extractive activities . . . , promoting social mobilization and the support of confrontations, and in consequence generating a grave affectation and social commotion in Ecuadorian society." While the government succeeded with Pachamama, it was unable to do the same with Acción Ecológica due to the outburst of national and international support and pressure. See: "Ecuador: Decisión arbitraria de disolución de la ONG Acción Ecológica," *Acción Ecológica*, published December 2016, https://www.accionecologica.org/ecuador-decision-arbitraria-de-disolucion-de-la-ong-accion-ecologica/.

21. Cartuche Vacacela, "El conflicto entre la CONAIE y la Revolución Ciudadana" (my translation).

22. Ibid. (my translation).

23. Alberto Acosto and John Cajas, "La deuda eterna contrataca," *La Línea de Fuego,* published July 2017, https://lalineadefuego.info/2017/07/27/la-deuda-eterna -contrataca-por-alberto-acosta-john-cajas-guijarro/.

24. Machoa, "El florecimiento de la rebeldía" (my translation).

25. Ibid. (my translation).

26. Comments by Machoa in my course "Contemporary Feminist Theory, State, and Interculturality," November 28, 2017 (my translation).

27. Ibid.

28. Machoa, quoted in Jaime Giménez, "Mujeres indígenas contra petroleras chinas en Ecuador: 'Estamos dispuestas a morir por nuestra selva,'" *El Diaro,* published March 2016, https://www.eldiario.es/desalambre/amazonicas-ecuador-defienden -territorio-supervivencia_1_5863501.html (my translation).

29. Gloria Ushigua, quoted in ibid. (my translation).

30. Orlan Cazorla and Miriam García Torres, "Mujeres por la vida marchan desde la Amazonía hasta Quito," *Rebelión,* published October 2013, http://www.rebelion .org/noticia.php?id=175630 (my translation).

31. "Cinco Mujeres Denuncian el Gobierno." *Plan V.* Published October 2015. https://www.planv.com.ec/historias/politica/cinco-mujeres-denuncian-al-gobierno.

32. Ibid. (my translation; henceforth, all translations from this document are my own).

33. Ibid.

34. "Waorani" is the preferred written form today, replacing the previously written form of "Huaorani."

35. "Cinco Mujeres Denuncian el Gobierno."

36. Ibid.

37. Ibid.

38. Ibid.

39. For a summary in English of this case, see Inter-American Court of Human Rights, *Case of The Kichwa Indigenous People of Sarayaku V. Ecuador*, accessed November 25, 2020, https://www.corteidh.or.cr/docs/casos/articulos/resumen_245 _ing.pdf.

40. Quoted in Jaime Giménez, "Mujeres indígenas contra petroleras chinas en Ecuador: 'Estamos dispuestas a morir por nuestra selva,'" *El Diaro,* published March 2016, https://www.eldiario.es/desalambre/amazonicas-ecuador-defienden-territorio -supervivencia_1_5863501.html (my translation). Also see M. Castillo, J. Félix, C. Mazabanda, M. Melo, M. Moreno de los Ríos, R. Narváez, B. Páez, and M. Ushigua, *La cultura sapara en Peligro ¿El sueño es posible? La lucha de un pueblo por su supervivencia frente a la explotación petrolera* (Quito: Terra Mater, la Nación Sapara del Ecuador y NAKU, 2016), https://www.pachamama.org.ec/wp-content/uploads /2019/06/La-Cultura-Sapara-en-Peligro.pdf.

41. Fondo de Acción Urgente por los Derechos de las Mujeres, "Public Communiqué Regarding the Increased Attacks Against Gloria Ushigua and The Sápara Women's Association of The Ecuadorean Amazon," published June 2016, https:// fondoaccionurgente.org.co/site/assets/files/1323/comunicado_a_la_opinion_publica

_ante_el_incremento_de_los_ataques_contra_gloria_ushigua_y_la_asociacion_de
_mujeres_sapar-2.pdf.

42. "Cinco Mujeres Denuncian el Gobierno."

43. B. Chancosa, N. Santi, M.C. Ventura, C. Flores, G. Panchi, S. Lupa, A. Cahuiya, C. Lozano, I. Ramos, "Mujeres indígenas de latinoamerica enfrentan el cambio climático desde sus procesos de adaptabilidad cultural. Chasaqui warmikuna del Abya Yala frente al cambio climático 'Haciendo caminar la palabra,'" document prepared for the COP22 meeting in Morroco (Quito: Ecuarunari, 2016); Also see "Chaski Warmi call for climate solutions," YouTube, published November 2016. https://www.youtube.com/watch?v=LMrEVJ3xw_s&feature=emb_logo; Herrera, Carolina. "Mujeres indígenas: defensoras del medio ambiente." Natural Resources Defense Council. Published August 2017. https://www.nrdc.org/es/experts/carolina -herrera/mujeres-indigenas-defensoras-medio-ambiente-america-latina#:~:text=Las %20Chaski%20Warmi%20del%20Abyayala,que%20trascienden%20comunidades %20y%20nacionalidades.&text=El%20di%C3%A1logo%20hizo%20hincapi%C3 %A9%20espec%C3%ADficamente,el%20campo%20del%20cambio%20clim%C3 %A1tico.

44. Chancosa et. al, 2016.

45. Chancosa et. al, 2016.

46. I thank Maria Lugones for highlighting this point and for her comments which have helped me clarify some of the arguments here.

47. Braulio HyC, "Yaku Chaski Warmi Kuna: mujeres mensajeras por el petróleo baja la tierra." *Tegantai. Agencia de Noticias Ecologistas*, July 27, 2015 (my translation). Also see Braulio HyC, (Video) Yakuchaski Warmikuna: Mensajeras del Río Curaray," May 23, 2016. http://www.saramanta.org/video-yakuchaski-warmikuna -mensajeras-del-rio-curaray/.

48. "Yaku Chaski Warmi kuna finaliza primera etapa," Press release, Puyo, Pastaza Province, Ecuador, July 27, 2015 (my translation).

49. For Gutierrez, the Ecuadorian experience stands out precisely because it is grassroots, "from below," and intimately connected to the historical and ongoing political struggle of Indigenous organizations and Indigenous men and women. In this, the active involvement of the country's two most important historical Indigenous women leaders, Blanca Chancosa and Nina Pacari, has been key. In Bolivia, she argues, *Chaski-Warmi* has functioned more as a research project in search of "results" rather than political incidence and transformation.

50. Personal conversation, Quito, June 2, 2017 (my translation).

51. Ibid.

52. Ibid.

53. Ortiz Lemos, "Lo que la sociedad mestiza puede aprender" (my translation).

54. Ibid.

55. Catherine Walsh, "Life, Nature, and Gender Otherwise: Feminist Reflections and Provocations from the Andes," in *Practising Feminist Political Ecologies. Moving Beyond the "Green Economy,"* ed. Wendy Harcourt and Ingrid Nelson (London: Zed, 2015);

Catherine Walsh, "On Gender and Its 'Otherwise,'" in *The Palgrave Handbook of Gender and Development*, ed. Wendy Harcourt (London: Palgrave Macmillan, 2016).

56. See: Michael Horswell, *Decolonizing the Sodomite: Queer Tropes of Sexuality in the Andean Culture* (Austin: University of Texas Press, 2005); Sylvia Marcos, *Taken from the Lips. Gender and Eros in Mesoamerican Religions* (Boston: Brill, 2006); Irene Silverblatt, *Moon, Sun, and Witches. Gender Ideologies and Class in Inca and Colonial Peru* (Princeton: Princeton University Press, 1987).

57. Walsh, "Life, Nature, and Gender Otherwise," 120.

58. See, for example, Lorena Cabnal, "Acercamiento a la construcción de la propuesta de pensamiento epistémico de las mujeres indígenas feministas comunitarias de Abya Yala," *Feminismos diversos: El feminismo comunitario,* ed. Feminista Siempre (Madrid: Acsur-Las Segovias, 2010); Aura Estela Cumes, "Mujeres indígenas, patriarcado y colonialismo: un desafía a la segregación comprensiva de las formas de dominio," *Anuario Hojas de Warmi* No.17 (2012); and Julieta Paredes, *Hilando fino desde el feminismo comunitario* (Querétaro, Mexico: Colectivo Grietas, 2012). For perspectives from Turtle Island, see, for example, Leanne Simpson, "Queering Resurgence: Taking on Heteropatriarchy in Indigenous Nation-Building," *Mamawipawin: Indigenous Governance and Community Based Research Space,* June 2012, https://blogs.cc.umanitoba.ca/mamawipawin/2012/06/01/queering-resurgence-taking-on-heteropatriarchy-in-indigenous-nation-building/.

59. Betty Ruth Lozano,"Pedagogías para la vida, la alegría y la re-existencia: Pedagogías de mujeres negras que curan y vinculan," in *Pedagogías decoloniales: Prácticas insurgentes de resistir, (re)existir y (re)vivir)*, Vol. 2, ed. Catherine Walsh (Quito: Ediciones Abya-Yala, 2017), 288–89.

60. Betty Ruth Lozano, "El feminismo no puede ser uno porque las mujeres somos diversas. Aportes a un feminismo negro decolonial desde la experiencia de las mujeres negras del Pacífico colombiano," in *Tejiendo de otro modo: Feminismo, epistemología y apuestas descoloniales en Abya Yala,* eds. Yuderkys Espinosa Miñoso, Diana Gómez and Karina Ochoa (Popayán: Universidad de Cauca, 2014), 348–49 (my translation).

61. Machoa, "El florecimiento de la rebeldía."

62. Leanne Betasamosake Simpson, *This Accident of Being Lost: Songs and Stories* (Toronto: House of Anansi, 2017).

References

Abu-Lughod, Lila. *Writing Women's Worlds*. Berkeley: University of California Press, 1993.

Acosta, Alberto. "El uso de la justicia como mecanismo de terror." *El Universo*. Published February 2011. https://www.eluniverso.com/2011/02/08/1/1363/uso -justicia-como-mecanismo-terror.html.

Acosta, Alberto and John Cajas. "La deuda eterna contrataca." *La Línea de Fuego*. Published July 2017. https://lalineadefuego.info/2017/07/27/la-deuda-eterna -contrataca-por-alberto-acosta-john-cajas-guijarro/.

Albán Achinte, Adolfo. "¿Interculturalidad sin decolonialidad? Colonialidades circulantes y prácticas de re-existencia." In *Diversidad, interculturalidad y construcción de ciudad*, edited by Wilmer Villa and Arturo Grueso, 64–96. Bogotá: Universidad Pedagógica Nacional/Alcaldía Mayor, 2008.

American Psychiatric Association. *Diagnostic and Statistical Manual of Mental Disorders,* 4th ed. (DSM-IV). Ann Arbor: University of Michigan Press, 2000.

Amos, Valerie, and Pratibha Parmar. "Challenging Imperial Feminism." In *Feminism and "Race,"* edited by Kum-Kum Bhavnani, 17–32. Oxford: Oxford University Press, 1984.

Antillón, Camilo, Arnin Córtez, Juan Pablo Gómez, Jessica Martínez-Cruz, and Ligia Peña. "Lecturas subalternas a los procesos de modernización en Nicaragua, 1893–1933." Managua: Mimeo, 2017.

Arboleda, Javier, "HH contó cómo fue la entrada al Valle y el Cauca," *VerdadAbierta.com*, January 22, 2009, accessed June 8, 2021, https://verdadabierta .com/hh-o-carepollo/

Arévalo, Andrés. "La configuración temporal del orden mundial: una mirada moderno/colonial." *Trabajos y ensayos*, no. 9 (2009): 1–20.

"The Autonomy Statue (Law No. 28)." *Centro de Asistencia Legal a Pueblos Indígenas*. Published 2010. https://www.calpi-nicaragua.com/the-autonomy-statute -law-28/.

Avance y ajustes de la política de participación y equidad para las mujeres (CONPES 2941). Bogotá: Departamento Nacional de Planeación, 1997.

Bell, Charles Napier. "Remarks on the Mosquito Territory, its Climate, People, Productions." *Journal of the Royal Geographical Society* 32 (1862): 242–68.

Bell, Charles Napier. *Tangweera: Life and Adventures Among Gentle Savages.* London: Edward Arnold, 1899.

Bhabha, Hommi. *The Location of Culture.* 1st ed. New York/London: Routledge, 1994.

Birn, Anne-Emanuelle, Sarah Zimmerman, and Richard Garfield. "To Decentralize or Not to Decentralize, It That the Question? Nicaraguan Health Policy under Structural Adjustment in the 1990s." *International Journal of Health Services* 30, no. 1 (2000): 111–28

Blaser, Mario. *Storytelling Globalization from the Chaco and Beyond.* Durham: Duke University Press, 2010.

Bozzo, Francisca. "Feminazismo, hembrismo e ideología de género: Las respuestas del patriarcado a la revolución feminista." *Errancia 17* (April 2018). https://www.iztacala.unam.mx/errancia/v17/PDFS_1/LITORALES%203%20FEMINAZISMO.pdf.

Branche, Raphaëlle. "Sexual Violence in the Algerian War." In *Brutality and Desire: Genders and Sexualities in History,* edited by Dagmar Herzog, 247–260. London: Palgrave Macmillan, 2009.

Butler, Judith. *Bodies That Matter.* 1st ed. New York/London: Routledge, 1993.

Butler, Judith. *Undoing Gender.* New York/London: Routledge, 2004.

Cabnal, Lorena. "Acercamiento a la construcción de la propuesta de pensamiento epistémico de las mujeres indígenas feministas comunitarias de Abya Yala." *Feminismos diversos: El feminismo comunitario,* edited by Feminista Siempre (Madrid: Acsur-Las Segovias, 2010).

Cabnal, Lorena. "De las Opresiones a las Emancipaciones: Mujeres Indígenas en Defensa del Territorio Cuerpo-Tierra." Pueblos–Revista de Información y Debate. Published February 2015. http://www.revistapueblos.org/blog/2015/02/06/de-las-opresiones-a-las-emancipaciones-mujeres-indigenas-en-defensa-del-territorio-cuerpo-tierra/.

Cannadine, David. "Civilization." *The Yale Review* 101, no. 1 (2013): 1–37.

Cánovas, Carlos J. Echarri. *La violencia feminicida en México: aproximaciones y tendencias 1985–2016.* Mexico: SEGOB, Secretaría de Gobernación INMUJERES, Instituto Nacional de las Mujeres ONU Mujeres, Entidad de las Naciones Unidas para la Igualdad de Género y el Empoderamiento de las Mujeres, 2017.

Caputi, Jane and Diana E. H. Russell, "Femicide: Sexist Terrorism against Women." In *Femicide: The Politics of Woman Killing,* edited by Jill Radford and Diana E. H. Russell, 13–21. New York: Twayne, 1992.

Cariño, Carmen, Aura Cumes, Ochy Curiel, Maria Teresa Garzón, Bienvenida Mendoza, Karina Ochoa, and Alejandra Londoño. "Pensar, sentir y hacer pedagogías feministas descoloniales: Diálogos y puntadas." In *Pedagogías decoloniales: Prácticas insurgentes de resistir, (re)existir y (re)vivir.* Vol. 2, edited by Catherine Walsh, 509–536. Quito: Ediciones Abya-Yala, 2017.

Carneiro, Sueli. "Ennegrecer al Feminismo." Presented at the seminar "La situación de la Mujer negra en América Latina, desde una perspectiva de genero," São Paulo, 2001.

Carrie, Heather, Tim K. Mackey, and Sloane Laird. "Integrating Traditional Indigenous Medicine and Western Biomedicine into Health Systems: a Review of Nicaraguan Health Policies and Miskitu Health Services." *International Journal for Equity in Health* 14, no. 1 (2015).

Cartuche Vacacela, Inti. "El conflicto entre la CONAIE y la Revolución Ciudadana." *Revista Digital La Linea de Fuego*. Published March 2015. https://lalineadefuego .info/2015/03/31/el-conflicto-entre-la-conaie-y-la-revolucion-ciudadana-por-inti -cartuche-vacacela/.

Casimir, Jean. *Haití de mis amores*. Isla Negra, Chile: Ambos Editores, 2012.

Castillo, Diana, Glenda Godfrey, Nelly Miranda, and Jessica Martínez-Cruz. *Mujeres Jóvenes Multiétnicas Costa Caribe Sur, Participación Ciudadana y Violencia de Género*. Maryland: Global Communities, 2017. http://www.globalcommunities.org .ni/media/documentos/12-inf-violencia-global-julio-2017.pdf.

Castillo, M., J. Félix, C. Mazabanda, M. Melo, M. Moreno de los Ríos, R. Narváez, B. Páez, and M. Ushigua. *La cultura sapara en peligro ¿El sueño es posible? La lucha de un pueblo por su supervivencia frente a la explotación petrolera* (Quito: Terra Mater, la Nación Sapara del Ecuador y NAKU, 2016). https://www.pachamama.org .ec/wp-content/uploads/2019/06/La-Cultura-Sapara-en-Peligro.pdf

Castro-Gómez, Santiago. "Decolonizar la universidad. La hybris del punto cero y el diálogo de saberes." In *El giro decolonial. Reflexiones para una diversidad epistémica más allá del capitalismo global*, edited by Santiago Castro-Gómez and Ramón Grosfoguel, 79–92. Bogotá: Siglo del Hombre, 2007.

Castro-Gómez, Santiago. *Crítica de la razón latinoamericana*. 2nd ed. Bogotá: Editorial Pontificia Universidad Javeriana, 2011.

Castro-Gómez, Santiago. "La filosofía latinoamericana como ontología crítica del presente. Temas y motivos para una 'Crítica de la razón latinoamericana.'" Accessed April 22, 2014. https://www.insumisos.com/lecturasinsumisas/LA%20 FILOSOFIA%20LATINOAMERICANA%20COMO%20ONTOLOGiA%20 CRiTICA%20DEL%20PRES.pdf.

Castro-Gómez, Santiago. *Historia de la gubernamentabilidad I: Razón de Estado, liberalismo y Neo-liberalismo en Michel Foucault*. Bogotá: Siglo del Hombre Editores, 2010.

Castro-Gómez, Santiago. *La hybris del punto cero ciencia, raza e ilustración en la Nueva Granada (1750–1816)*. Bogotá: Editorial Pontificia Universidad Javeriana, 2005.

Castro-Gómez, Santiago. *Tejidos oníricos: movilidad, capitalismo y biopolítica en Bogotá (1910–1930)*. Bogotá: Editorial Pontificia Universidad Javeriana, 2009.

Castro-Gómez, Santiago and Ramón Grosfoguel, "Giro decolonial, teoría crítica pensamiento heterárquico." In *El giro decolonial. Reflexiones para una diversidad epistémica más allá del capitalismo global,* edited by Santiago Castro-Gómez and Ramón Grosfoguel, 9–24. Bogotá: Siglo del Hombre, 2007.

Cazorla, Orlan and Miriam García Torres. "Mujeres por la vida marchan desde la Amazonía hasta Quito." *Rebelión*. Published October 2013. http://www.rebelion .org/noticia.php?id=175630.

Censo general de población. Colombia: Departamento Administrativo de Estadísticas, 2005. Accessed November 22, 2020. https://www.dane.gov.co/index.php/estadisticas-por-tema/demografia-y-poblacion/censo-general-2005-1.

Chancosa, B., N. Santi, M.C. Ventura, C. Flores, G. Panchi, S. Lupa, A. Cahuiya, C. Lozano, I. Ramos. "Mujeres indígenas de latinoamerica enfrentan el cambio climático desde sus procesos de adaptabilidad cultural. Chasaqui warmikuna del Abya Yala frente al cambio climático 'Haciendo caminar la palabra.'" Document prepared for the COP22 meeting in Morroco. Quito: Ecuarunari, 2016.

"Chaski Warmi call for climate solutions." YouTube. Published November 2016. https://www.youtube.com/watch?v=LMrEVJ3xw_s&feature=emb_logo.

Collins, Patricia Hill. *Black Feminist Thought: Knowledge, Consciousness, and the Politics of Empowerment.* London: Routledge, 2014.

Collins, Patricia Hill. *Black Feminist Thought: Knowledge, Consciousness, and the Politics of Empowerment.* New York/London: Routledge, 1990.

The Combahee River Collective. "A Black Feminist Statement." *Women's Studies Quarterly* 42, no. 3/4 (2014): 271–80.

"Constitution of the Republic of Ecuador." *Political Database of the Americas, Georgetown University.* Published October 2008. https://pdba.georgetown.edu/Constitutions/Ecuador/english08.html.

Conzemius, Eduard. "Ethnographical Survey of the Miskito and Sumu Indians of Honduras and Nicaragua." *Bureau of American Ethnology Bulletin* 106 (1932): 1–191.

Cox, Avelino. *Cosmovisión de los Pueblos de Tulu Walpa: Según los Relatos de los Sabios Ancianos Miskitos.* Managua: URACCAN, 1998.

Cox, Avelino. *Sukias y Curanderos: Isigni en la Espiritualidad.* Managua, Nicaragua: URACCAN and BID, 2003.

Crenshaw, Kimberlé. "Demarginalizing the Intersection of Race and Sex: A Black Feminist Critique of Antidiscrimination Doctrine, Feminist Theory, and Antiracist Politics." In *Feminist Legal Theory: Foundations,* edited by D. Kelley Weisberg, 383–398. Philadelphia: Temple University Press, 1993.

Crenshaw, Kimberle. "Demarginalizing the Intersection of Race and Sex: A Black Feminist Critique of Antidiscrimination Doctrine, Feminist Theory and Antiracist Politics," *University of Chicago Legal Forum* 1989, no. 1 (1989): 139–67.

Crenshaw, Kimberlé. "Gender-Related Aspects of Race Discrimination." Background paper for Expert Meeting on Gender and Racial Discrimination, Zagreb, Croatia (EM/GRD/2000/WP.1, November 21–24, 2000).

Crewe, Emma. "The Silent Traditions of Developing Cooks." In *Discourses of Development: Anthropological Perspectives,* edited by R.D Grillo and R.L Stirrat, 59–80. Oxford: Berg, 1997.

Cumes, Aura. "Cosmovisión maya y patriarcado: una aproximación en clave crítica." Paper presented at the Centro Interdiciplinario de Estudios de Género de la Universidad de Chile. Santiago, Chile, 2014.

Cumes, Aura. "El feminismo debe luchar contra las múltiples opresiones que enfrentamos las mujeres indígenas y afrodescendientes." Presented at II Encuentro de Estudios de Género y Feminismos, Guatemala, 2011.

Cumes, Aura. "Multiculturalismo, género y feminismos: Mujeres diversas, luchas complejas." In *Participación y políticas de mujeres indígenas en América Latina,* edited by Andrea Pequeño, 29–52. Quito: FLACSO Ecuador/ Ministerio de Cultura, 2009.

Cumes, Aura Estela. "Mujeres indígenas, patriarcado y colonialismo: un desafía a la segregación comprensiva de las formas de dominio." *Anuario Hojas de Warmi,* No.17 (2012): 1–16.

Curiel, Ochy. "Los Aportes de las Afrodescendientes a la Teoría y la Práctica Feminista. Desuniversalizando el Sujeto 'Mujeres.'" In *Perfiles del Feminismo Iberoamericano.* Vol. 3, edited by María Luisa Femenías, 163–190. Buenos Aires: Catálogos, 2007.

Curiel, Ochy. *La nación heterosexual. Análisis del discurso jurídico y el régimen heterosexual desde la antropología de la dominación.* Bogotá: Brecha Lésbica-*en la frontera,* 2013.

Dagnino, Evelina. "Sociedad Civil, Participación y Ciudadanía en Brasil." Presented at UNICAMP, São Paulo, Brazil, 2005.

Davis Rodríguez, Sandra, Sasha Marley, and Gerhild Trübswasser. *Algo anda mal. El Bla o Wakni en el río Coco.* RACCN: URACCAN, 2006.

de Lauretis, Teresa. *Technologies of Gender: Essays on Theory, Film, and Fiction.* 1st ed. Bloomington: Indiana University Press, 1987.

"Una declaración feminista autónoma. El desafío de hacer comunidad en la casa de las diferencias." *Rumbo al Encuentro Feminista Autónomo.* Published May 2009. http://feministasautonomasenlucha.blogspot.com/.

Du Bois, W.E.B. *The Souls of Black Folk.* New York: Penguin, 1989.

Deare, Craig A. "La Militarización en América Latina y el Papel de los Estados Unidos." *Foreign Affairs Latinoamérica* 3, no. 3 (2008): 22–34.

Dennis, Philip A. "Grisi siknis una enfermedad entre los Miskito." *Revista Wani,* no. 24 (December 1999).

Dennis, Philip A. "Part three: Grisi Siknis Among the Miskito." *Medical Anthropology* 5, no. 4 (1981): 445–505.

Diaz, Daniel. "Raza, pueblo y pobres: las tres estrategias biopolíticas del siglo XX en Colombia (1873–1962)." In *Genealogías de la Colombianidad: Formaciones discursivas y las tecnologías de gobierno en los siglos XIX y XX,* edited by Santiago Castro-Gómez and Eduardo Restrepo, 42–69. Bogotá: Editorial Pontificia Universidad Javeriana, 2008.

DiPietro, Pedro, Jennifer McWeeny, and Shireen Roshanravan, eds. *Speaking Face to Face: The Visionary Philosophy of María Lugones* (Albany: SUNY Press, 2019).

Dirlik, Arif. *Postmodernity's Histories: The Past as Legacy and Project.* Lanham: Rowman & Littlefield, 2000.

Dixon, Bernardine and Torres, María Olimpia. *Diagnóstico de género en las Regiones Autónomas de la Costa Caribe. Cuaderno 3, Serie Cuadernos de Género para Nicaragua, Banco Mundial,* 2008. http://siteresources.worldbank.org /INTLACREGTOPGENDERINSPA/Resources/Cuaderno3costa_caribe.pdf.

Dorlin, Elsa. *Sexo, género y sexualidades.* 1st ed. Buenos Aires: Ediciones Nueva Visión, 2009.

Dunbar-Ortiz, Roxanne. *An Indigenous Peoples' History of the United States (Revisioning American History)*. Boston: Beacon Press, 2014.

Dussel, Enrique. "Beyond Eurocentrism: The World-System and the Limits of Modernity." In *The Cultures of Globalization*, edited by Fredric Jameson and Masao Miyoshi, 3–31. Durham: Duke University Press, 1998.

Dussel, Enrique. "Europe, Modernity, and Eurocentrism." *Nepantla: Views from South* 1, no. 3 (2000): 465–78.

Dyer, Richard. *Gays and Film*. London: British Film Institute, 1977.

"Ecuador: Decisión arbitraria de disolución de la ONG Acción Ecológica." *Acción Ecológica*. Published December 2016. https://www.accionecologica.org/ecuador -decision-arbitraria-de-disolucion-de-la-ong-accion-ecologica/.

EFE. "Detectan nuevos casos de 'locura colectiva' en el norte de Nicaragua." *El Nuevo Diario*. Published December 2017. https://www.elnuevodiario.com.ni/ nacionales/450267-detectan-nuevos-casos-locura-colectiva-norte-nicar/.

Ejecuciones extrajudiciales en el contexto de la militarización de la seguridad pública. Mexico: Comisión Mexicana de Defensa y Promoción de los Derechos Humanos, A.C, 2013. http://cmdpdh.org/publicaciones-pdf/cmdpdh-ejecuciones -extrajudiciales-en-el-contexto-de-la-militarizacion-de-la-seguridad-publica.pdf.

"Encuentro Feminista de América Latina y el Caribe." *Viva Historia*. Accessed November 21, 2020. https://en.vivahistoria.org/eflac.

"Encuentro Lésbico Feminista de Abya Yala." *Memoria X*. Published August 2016. https://glefas.org/download/biblioteca/lesbianismo-feminista/memoria-x-elfay -colombia-2014-v.pdf.

"Enlace Ciudadano Nro. 354 desde Guayaquil, Guayas." SECOM Ecuador. Published December 2014. https://www.youtube.com/watch?v=ODXFdqtGsyo.

Escobar, Arturo. "Worlds and knowledges otherwise: The Latin American Modernity/Coloniality Research Program." *Cultural Studies* 21, no. 2–3 (2007): 179–210.

Escobar, Arturo. *Encountering Development: The Making and Unmaking of the Third World*. 1st ed. Princeton: Princeton University Press, 1995.

Escobar, Arturo. *Encountering Development: The Making and Unmaking of the Third World*. 2nd ed. Princeton: Princeton University Press, 2012.

Escobar, Arturo and Álvaro Pedrosa, eds. *Pacífico ¿Desarrollo o diversidad?* Bogotá: CEREC, ECOFONDO, 1996.

Espinosa, Yuderkys, Diana Gómez, Karina Ochoa, and María Lugones. "Reflexiones pedagógicas en torno al feminismo descolonial. Una conversa en cuatro voces." In *Pedagogías decoloniales. Prácticas insurgentes de resistir, (re) vivir y (re)vivir*, edited by Catherine Walsh, 403–42. Quito: Ediciones Abya Yala, 2013.

Espinosa-Miñoso, Yuderkys. "Una crítica descolonial a la epistemología feminista crítica." *Revista El Cotidiano* 29, no. 184 (Spring 2014): 7–12.

Espinosa-Miñoso, Yuderkys, "De por qué es necesario un feminismo descolonial: diferenciación, dominación co-constitutiva de la modernidad occidental y el fin de la política de identidad," *Solar* 12, no.1 (2016): 141–71.

Espinosa-Miñoso, Yuderkys. "Ethnocentrism and Coloniality in Latin American Feminisms: The Complicity and Consolidation of Hegemonic Feminists in

Transnational Spaces." Translated by Ana-Maurine Lara. *Venezuelan Journal of Women Studies* 14, no. 33 (2009): 37–54.

Espinosa-Miñoso, Yuderkys. "Etnocentrismo y colonialidad en los feminismos latinoamericanos: Complicidades y consolidación de las hegemonías feministas en el espacio transnacional." *Revista Venezolana de Estudios de la Mujer* 14, no. 33 (2010): 37–54.

Espinosa-Miñoso, Yuderkys. "Feminismos descoloniales de Abya Yala." In *Le Dictionnaire universel des Créatrices. A paraître à l'automne.* Paris: Des Femmes-Antoinette Fouque Publishing, 2013.

Espinosa-Miñoso, Yuderkys. "Las feministas antirracistas teorizando la trama compleja de la opresión," Paper presented at "Género y Etnicidad: Reflexiones desde el Sur del Mundo," Centro Interdisciplinario de Estudios de Género, Universidad de Chile, Santiago, 2014.

Espinosa-Miñoso, Yuderkys. "La política sexual radical autónoma, sus debates internos y su crítica a la ideología de la diversidad sexual." In *Pensando los feminismos en Bolivia,* edited by Patricia Montes, 113–126. La Paz: Conexión Fondo de Emancipación, 2012.

Espinosa-Miñoso, Yuderkys, Diana Gómez y Karina Ochoa. "Introducción." In *Tejiendo de otro modo: Feminismo, epistemología y apuestas descoloniales en Abya Yala,* edited by Yuderkys Espinosa Miñoso, Diana Gómez y Karina Ochoa, 13–40. Popayán: Universidad de Cauca, 2014.

Espinosa-Miñoso, Yuderkys, Diana Gómez y Karina Ochoa, eds. *Tejiendo de otro modo: Feminismo, epistemología y apuestas descoloniales en Abya Yala.* Popayán: Universidad de Cauca, 2014.

Fagoth, Ana R., Fulvio Gioanetto, and Adan Silva. *Wan Kaina Kulkaia: Armonizando con Nuestro Entorno.* Managua, Nicaragua: Imprimátur Artes Graficas, 1998.

Fanon, Frantz. *Black Skin, White Masks.* Translated by Richard Philcox. New York: Grove Press, 2008.

Fanon, Frantz. *The Wretched of the Earth.* Translated by Richard Philcox. New York: Grove Press, 2004.

Fassin, Éric. "La democracia sexual y el choque de civilizaciones." *Mora (B. Aires)* 18, no. 1 (July 2012). Accessed September 17, 2015. http://www.scielo.org.ar /scielo.php?script=sci_arttext&pid=S1853-001X2012000100001&lng=es&nrm =iso.

"El feminicidio en México y Guatemala." *Federación Internacional de los Derechos Humanos,* no. 446/3 (2016).

"El feminicidio más allá de Ciudad Juárez." *Observatoria Ciudadano Nacional del Feminicidio.* Published 2008. http://observatoriofeminicidio.blogspot.mx/.

Fondo de Acción Urgente por los Derechos de las Mujeres. "Public Communiqué Regarding the Increased Attacks Against Gloria Ushigua and The Sápara Women's Association of The Ecuadorean Amazon." Published June 2016. https: //fondoaccionurgente.org.co/site/assets/files/1323/comunicado_a_la_opinion _publica_ante_el_incremento_de_los_ataques_contra_gloria_ushigua_y_la _asociacion_de_mujeres_sapar-2.pdf.

"Foto de soldados gays israelíes causa controversia." *BBC News* June 13, 2012. https://www.bbc.com/mundo/noticias/2012/06/120612_soldados_gay_israel_facebook_jgc.

Foucault, Michel. *History of Sexuality*. New York: Random House, 1978.

Foucault, Michel. *The History of Sexuality. Vol 2: The Use of Pleasure*. Translated by Robert Hurley. New York: Vintage Books, 1985.

Foucault, Michel. "Nietzsche, Genealogy, History." In *The Foucault Reader*, edited by Paul Rabinow, 76–100. New York: Pantheon Books, 1984.

Foucault, Michel. "Politics and the Study of Discourse." In *The Foucault Effect Studies in Governmentality*, edited by Graham Burchell, Colin Gordon, and Peter Miller, 53–72. Chicago: University of Chicago Press, 1991.

Freyre, Gilberto. *The Masters and the Slaves: A Study in the Development of Brazilian Civilization*. Translated by Samuel Putnam. Berkeley: University of California Press, 1986.

Freyre, Gilberto. *O mundo que o português criou* (São Paulo: É Realizações, 2010).

Gallardo, Jose Francisco. *Always Near, Always Far: The Armed Forces in Mexico*. San Francisco: Global Exchange, 2001.

García Salazar, Juan and Catherine Walsh. *Pensar sembrando/Sembrar pensando con el Abuelo Zenón*. Quito: Cátedra de Estudios Afro-Andinos, Universidad Andina Simón Bolívar, Ediciones Abya Yala, 2017.

García, Salvador and Jessica Martínez-Cruz. *Significados y trayectorias sobre el bienestar y la felicidad: Una aproximación relacional y participativa Comunidades del Alto Wangki y Bocay*. Managua: Mimeo, 2014.

Gallargo, Francesca. "Cartas van, cartas vienen. Para una crítica de las exclusiones en el feminismo y los usos de la decolonialidad." *Francesca Gargallo*. Published November 2014. https://francescagargallo.wordpress.com/2014/11/06/cartas-van-cartas-vienen-para-una-critica-de-las-exclusiones-en-el-feminismo-y-los-usos-de-la-decolonialidad/.

Gargallo, Francesca. *Feminismos desde Abya Yala. Ideas y proposiciones de las mujeres de 607 pueblos en nuestra América*. Bolivia, La Paz: Editorial Autodeterminación, 2013.

Gargallo, Francesca. *Ideas feministas latinoamericanas*. México, DF: Universidad Autónoma de la Ciudad de México, 2004.

Giménez, Jaime. "Mujeres indígenas contra petroleras chinas en Ecuador: 'Estamos dispuestas a morir por nuestra selva.'" *El Diario*. Published March 2016. https://www.eldiario.es/desalambre/amazonicas-ecuador-defienden-territorio-supervivencia_1_5863501.html.

Gonçalvez, Luis. "La metodología genealógica y arqueológica de Michel Foucault en la investigación en psicología social." Accessed April 22, 2019. http://www.fadu.edu.uy/estetica-diseno-ii/files/2015/06/transitos-de-una-psicologia-social-genealogi%CC%81a-y-arqueologi%CC%81a.pdf.

Gonzales, Lélia. "A categoria político-cultural de amefricanidade." *Tempo Brasileiro*, no. 92/93 (1988).

González Casanova, Pablo. "Colonialismo interno (una redefinición)." In *Conceptos y fenómenos fundamentales de nuestro tiempo*. Mexico City: Instituto de

Investigaciones Sociales, Universidad Nacional Autónoma de México, 2003. http://conceptos.sociales.unam.mx/conceptos_final/412trabajo.pdf.

Gónzalez, Miguel. "La Costa del comandante Campbell." *Confidencial.* Published August 2015. https://confidencial.com.ni/archivos/articulo/22630/la-costa-del-comandante-campbell.

Granada, Henry. "Intervention of Community Social Psychology: The Case of Colombia," *Applied Psychology* 40.2 (1991): 165–79.

Grosfoguel, Ramón. "The Implications of Subaltern Epistemologies for Global Capitalism: Transmodernity, Border Thinking, and Global Coloniality." In *Critical Globalization Studies,* edited by Richard P. Appelbaum and William I. Robinson, 283–292. New York/London: Routledge 2005.

Grosfoguel, Ramón. "The Structure of Knowledge in Westernized Universities." *Human Architecture: Journal of the Sociology of Self-Knowledge* 11, no. 1 (2013): 73–90.

Guía Latinoamericana de Diagnóstico Psiquiátrica. Asociación Psiquiátrica de América Latina, Sección de Diagnóstico y Clasificación, 2003. http://www.sld.cu/galerias/pdf/sitios/desastres/guia_latinoamerticana_diagn_psiq_gladp.pdf.

Guido, Rigoberto, Catalina Yunkiath, and Serafina Espinoza Blanco. "Percepción sobre *Isigni* de la comunidad de Sawa, Waspam, Río Coco." *Revista Caribe URACCAN* 16, no. 1 (2016): 21–25.

Hall, Stuart. "The Spectacle of the 'Other.'" In *Representation: Cultural Representations and Signifying Practices,* edited by Stuart Hall, 223–290. London: London Sage Publications and Open University, 1997.

Hall, Stuart. "When was 'The Post-colonial'? Thinking at the Limit." In *The Postcolonial Question: Common Skies, Divided Horizons,* edited by Ian Chambers and Lidia Curti, 242–260. New York/London: Routledge 1995.

Haraway, Donna. *Primate Visions: Gender, Race and Nature in the World of Modern Science.* New York: Routledge, 1998.

Haraway, Donna. *Simians, Cyborgs and Women: The Reinvention of Nature.* New York/London: Routledge, 1991.

Harding, Sandra. "A Socially Relevant Philosophy of Science? Resources from Standpoint Theory's Controversiality." *Hypatia* 19, no. 1 (2004): 25–47.

Harding, Sandra. "Feminism, Science, and the Anti-Enlightenment Critiques." In *Women, Knowledge, and Reality: Explorations in Feminist Philosophy,* edited by Ann Garry and Marilyn Pearsall, 298–320. New York/London: Routledge, 1996.

Harding, Sandra. "Introduction: Is There a Feminist Method?" In *Feminism and Methodology,* edited by Sandra Harding, 1–14. Bloomington: Indiana University Press, 1987.

Harding, Sandra. *The Science Question on Feminism.* Ithaca: Cornell University Press, 1986.

Harding, Sandra. *Whose Science? Whose Knowledge?: Thinking from Women's Lives.* New York: Cornell University Press, 1991.

Hartsock, Nancy. "The Feminist Standpoint: Developing the Ground for a Specifically Feminist Historical Materialism." In *Discovering Reality: Feminist Perspectives on Epistemology, Metaphysics, Methodology and Philosophy of Science,* edited by Sandra Harding and Merrill Hintikka, 283–310. Dordrecht: Reider Publishers, 1983.

Henríquez Levas, Cipriano, Norberto Chacón Mendoza, and Serafina Espinoza Blanco. "Percepción y prácticas de atención del *Grisi siknis* de la comunidad de krin krin, Waspam, Río Coco." *Revista Caribe URACCAN* 16, no. 1 (2016): 14–20.

Hernández Morales, Iris. "Aportes, problemáticas y desafíos que la noción de ciudadanía movilizada por el Movimiento de Diversidad Sexual y sus fragmentos LTGBI y lesbofeminista antirracista decolonial significan a la radicalización del pluralismo." PhD Diss., Universidad de Chile, 2016.

Hernández Morales, Iris "Arroz con leche ¿Me quiero casar?" *Revista Sociedad & Equidad*, no. 3 (2012).

Hernández Morales, Iris. "Colonialidad, diversidad sexual y puntos de fuga a la opresión: Apuntes generales." *Nuevas Voces Descoloniales de Abya Yala*. Madrid: Editorial Akal-GLEFAS, 2017.

Hernández Morales, Iris. Unpublished manuscript. Presented at Encuentro Feminista Nacional de Arica, 2016.

Herrera, Carolina. "Mujeres indígenas: defensoras del medio ambiente." *Natural Resources Defense Council*. Published August 2017. https://www.nrdc.org/es /experts/carolina-herrera/mujeres-indigenas-defensoras-medio-ambiente-america -latina#:~:text=Las%20Chaski%20Warmi%20del%20Abyayala,que%20 trascienden%20comunidades%20y%20nacionalidades.&text=El%20di%C3 %A1logo%20hizo%20hincapi%C3%A9%20espec%C3%ADficamente,el%20 campo%20del%20cambio%20clim%C3%A1tico.

Hincapié, Laura Marcela. "Violencia sexual, delito invisible detrás del conflicto armado." *El País*. Published August 2011. http://www.elpais.com.co/judicial/ violencia-sexual-delito-invisible-detras-del-conflicto-armado.html.

Hinkelammert, Franz. *Yo soy, si tú eres. El sujeto de los derechos humanos*. Mexico City: Centro de Estudios Ecuménicos, 2010.

Hobbes, Thomas. *Leviathan*. Indianapolis: Hackett Classics, 1994.

Hobson, John M. *The Eastern Origins of the West*. Cambridge: Cambridge University Press, 2004.

Hobson, John M. *The Eurocentric Conception of World Politics*. Cambridge: Cambridge University Press, 2012.

Hoffman, Odile. *Comunidades negras en el Pacífico colombiano*. Quito: Ediciones Abya-Yala, 2007.

hooks, bell. "Black Women: Shaping Feminist Theory." In *Feminist Theory: from Margin to Center*, 1–15. Boston: South End Press, 1984.

hooks, bell. *Feminist Theory: From Margin to Center*. Cambridge: South End Press, 1984.

Horswell, Michael. *Decolonizing the Sodomite: Queer Tropes of Sexuality in the Andean Culture*. Austin: University of Texas Press, 2005.

Huntington, Samuel. *The Clash of Civilizations and the Remaking of World Order*. New York: Simon & Schuster, 1996.

HyC, Braulio. "Yaku Chaski Warmi Kuna: mujeres mensajeras por el petróleo baja la tierra." *Tegantai. Agencia de Noticias Ecologistas*. July 27, 2015.

HyC, Braulio. "Yakuchaski Warmikuna: Mensajeras del Río Curaray," May 23, 2016. http://www.saramanta.org/video-yakuchaski-warmikuna-mensajeras-del-rio -curaray/.

The ICD-10 Classification of Mental and Behavioral Disorders: Diagnostic Criteria for Research. World Health Organization. Published 1993. https://www.who.int/ classifications/icd/en/GRNBOOK.pdf.

"La impunidad reina en el caso de los feminicidios en Buenaventura." *Asociación de Cabildos Indígenas del Cauca.* Published October 2013. http://anterior.nasaacin .org/index.php/2013/10/12/buenaventurala-impunidad-reina-en-el-caso-de-los -feminicidios-en-buenaventura/.

Inter-American Court of Human Rights. *Case of The Kichwa Indigenous People of Sarayaku V. Ecuador.* Accessed November 25, 2020. https://www.corteidh.or.cr/ docs/casos/articulos/resumen_245_ing.pdf.

"International Day of the Rebel Woman" in *Dissident Women: Gender and Cultural Politics in Chiapas,* eds. Shannon Speed, R. Aída Hernández Castillo, and Lynn M. Stephen, 28–32. Austin: University of Texas Press, 2006.

Jamieson, Mark. "Masks and Madness. Ritual Expressions of the Transition to Adulthood Among Miskitu Adolescents." *Social Anthropology* 9, no. 3 (2001): 257–72.

Joyce, Rosemary A. *Gender and Power in Prehispanic Mesoamerica.* Austin: University of Texas Press, 2000.

Kabengele, Munanga. *Rediscutindo a mestiçagem no Brasil: Identidade nacional versus identidade negra.* Petrópolis: Vozes, 1999.

Kant, Immanuel. "An Answer to the Question: 'What is Enlightenment?'" In *Kant: Political Writings,* edited by Hans Siegbert Reiss, 54–60. Cambridge: Cambridge University Press, 1991.

Kant, Immanuel. *Critique of Pure Reason.* New York: Penguin Classics, 2008.

Keating, Christine. *Decolonizing Democracy.* University Park: Pennsylvania University Press, 2011.

Kuagro Ri Ma Changaina Ri PCN (Women's Collective of the Black Communities Process). "Shadow Report to the Committee for the Elimination of Discrimination Against Women." United Nations CEDAW Convention to Eliminate All Forms of Discrimination Against Women (2013). http://www.afrocolombians.com/pdfs/ AfroColombianWomen-AbstractCEDAWReport2013.pdf.

Kusch, Rodolfo. *Indigenous and Popular Thinking in America.* Durham: Duke University Press, 2010.

Kymlicka, Will. "Las políticas del Multiculturalismo." *Ciudadanía Multicultural: Una teoría liberal de los derechos de las minorías.* Barcelona: Paídos, 1996.

Lagarde y de los Ríos, Marcela. "Introducción." In *Feminicidio: Una perspectiva global,* edited by Diana E.H. Russel and Roberta A. Harmes, 15–42. Mexico, D.F: Universidad Nacional Autónoma de México, Centro de Investigaciones Interdisciplinarias en Ciencias y Humanidades, 2006.

Lander, Edgardo. "Ciencias sociales: saberes coloniales y eurocéntricos." In *La colonialidad del saber. Eurocentrismo y Ciencias Sociales. Perspectivas latinoamericanas*, edited by Edgardo Lander, 11–40. Buenos Aires/Caracas: CLACSO/UNESCO, 2000.

Larrea, Carlos. *Iniciativa Yasuní-ITT: La Gran Propuesta de un País Pequeño.* Ecuador: United Nations Development Programme, 2007.

"Las epidemias de *grisi siknis* en la Costa Atlántica." IMTRADEC/URACCAN (n.d).

Lazano Jackson, Norman and Peter Jackson, trans. *Law 70 of Colombia (1993): In Recognition of the Right of Black Colombians to Collectively Own and Occupy their Ancestral Lands.* Accessed November 22, 2020. https://www.wola.org/sites/default/files/downloadable/Andes/Colombia/past/law%2070.pdf.

Leal, Claudia. "Recordando a Saturio. Memorias del racismo en el Chocó (Colombia)." *Revista de Estudios Sociales*, no. 27 (Summer 2007): 76–93.

Londoño López, Marta Cecilia. "Políticas públicas para las mujeres en Colombia. Interlocución movimiento social de mujeres-estado-movimiento social de mujeres. El caso de Cali." Master's Thesis, Universidad Nacional de Colombia Bogotá, 1999.

Lopez Astrain, Martha Patricia. *La Guerra de Baja Intensidad en Mexico.* Mexico, D.F.: Universidad Iberoamericana and Plaza y Valdes Editores, 1996.

López Bárcenas, Francisco. "Territorios indígenas y conflictos agrarios en México." *Estudios Agrarios* 12, no. 32 (2006): 85–108.

López Bárcenas, Francisco. *¡La tierra no se vende! Las tierras y los territorios de los pueblos indígenas en México.* 2nd ed. Mexico: CLASCO, EDUCA A.C, ProDESC, COAPI, Centro Intradisciplinar para la Investigación de la Recreación, 2017.

Lorde, Audre. 1984. "The Master's Tools Will Never Dismantle the Master's House." *Sister Outsider: Essays and Speeches.* Berkeley, CA: Crossing Press. 110–14.

Lorde, Audre. "Poetry Is Not a Luxury." Accessed November 19, 2020. https://makinglearning.files.wordpress.com/2014/01/poetry-is-not-a-luxury-audre-lorde.pdf.

Lozano, Betty Ruth. "El feminismo no puede ser uno porque las mujeres somos diversas. Aportes a un feminismo negro decolonial desde la experiencia de las mujeres negras del Pacífico colombiano." In *Tejiendo de otro modo: Feminismo, epistemología y apuestas descoloniales en Abya Yala,* edited by Yuderkys Espinosa, Diana Gómez and Karina Ochoa, 335–52. Popayán: Universidad de Cauca, 2014.

Lozano, Betty Ruth. "El feminismo no puede ser uno porque las mujeres somos diversas. Aportes a un feminismo negro decolonial desde la experiencia de las mujeres negras del Pacífico." *La manzana de la discordia* 5, no. 2 (2010): 7–24.

Lozano, Betty Ruth. "Estar del propio lado." *Boletín Territorio Pacífico,* no. 1 (2007): 9–13.

Lozano, Betty Ruth. "Pedagogías para la vida, la alegría y la re-existencia: Pedagogías de mujeres negras que curan y vinculan." In *Pedagogías decoloniales: Prácticas insurgentes de resistir, (re)existir y (re)vivir).* Vol. 2, edited by Catherine Walsh, 273–90. Quito: Ediciones Abya-Yala, 2017.

Lugones, María. "A Decolonial Revisiting of Gender." Unpublished manuscript.

Lugones, María. "Colonialidad y género: hacia un feminismo descolonial." Translated by Pedro DiPietro with María Lugones. *Género y descolonialidad.* Edited by Walter Mignolo, 13–54. Buenos Aires: Ediciones del Signo, 2008.

Lugones, María. "The Coloniality of Gender." In *The Palgrave Handbook of Gender and Development,* edited by Wendy Hartcourt, 13–33. London: Palgrave MacMillan, 2016.

Lugones, María. "The Coloniality of Gender." *World & Knowledges Otherwise* 2, no. 2 (Spring 2008): 1–17. https://globalstudies.trinity.duke.edu/sites/globalstudies .trinity.duke.edu/files/file-attachments/v2d2_Lugones.pdf.

Lugones, María. "Gender and Universality in Colonial Methodology." *Critical Philosophy of Race* 8, nos. 1–2 (2020): 25–47.

Lugones, María. "Heterosexualism and the Colonial Modern Gender System." *Hypatia* 2, no. 1 (Winter 2007): 186–209.

Lugones, María. "Introduction." *Worlds and Knowledges Otherwise* 2, no. 2 (2008): n.p. https://globalstudies.trinity.duke.edu/projects/wko-gender.

Lugones, María. "Methodological Notes Towards a Decolonial Feminism." In *Decolonizing Epistemologies: Latina/o Theology and Philosophy*, edited by Ada Maria Isasi Diaz and Eduardo Mendieta, 68–86. New York: Fordham University Press.

Lugones, María. *Pilgrimages/Peregrinajes: Theorizing Coalition Against Multiple Oppressions.* Lanham: Rowman & Littlefield, 2003.

Lugones, María. "Radical Multiculturalism and Women of Color Feminisms." *Journal for Cultural and Religious Theory* 13, no. 1 (2014): 68–80.

Lugones, María. "Toward a Decolonial Feminism." *Hypatia* 25, no. 4 (Fall 2010): 742–59.

Machoa, Katy. "El florecimiento de la rebeldía." Text presented in the photographic exhibit "Mujeres en la lucha social ecuatoriana" organized by El Colectivo Desde el Margen. Universidad Andina Simón Bolívar, Quito, November 21–25, 2017.

Maese-Cohen, Marcelle. "Introduction: Toward Planetary Decolonial Feminisms." *Qui Parle: Critical Humanities and Social Sciences*, 18, no. 2 (2010): 3–27.

Maldonado-Torres, Nelson. "El caribe, la colonialidad, y el giro decolonial." *Latin American Research Review* 55, no. 3 (2020): 560–573. https://larrlasa.org/articles /10.25222/larr.1005/.

Maldonado-Torres, Nelson. "The Decolonial Turn." *New Approaches to Latin American Studies: Culture and Power*. Edited by Juan Poblete, 111–27. London: Routledge, 2018.

Maldonado-Torres, Nelson. "Decoloniality at Large: Towards a Trans-Americas and Global Transmodern Paradigm (Introduction to Second Special Issue of 'Thinking Through the Decolonial Turn')." *Transmodernity* 1, no. 3 (2012): 1–10. https:// escholarship.org/uc/item/58c9c4wh.

Maldonado-Torres, Nelson. "La descolonización y el giro des-colonial." *Revista Tabula Rasa,* no. 9 (July-December 2008): 61–72.

Maldonado-Torres, Nelson. "On the Coloniality of Being: Contributions to the Development of a Concept." *Cultural Studies* 21 no. 2–3 (2007): 240–70.

Maldonado-Torres, Nelson. "Thinking Through the Decolonial Turn: Post-Continental Interventions in Theory, Philosophy, and Critique—An Introduction." *Transmodernity*, 1, no. 2 (2011): 1–15. https://escholarship.org/uc/item/59w8j02x.

McClintock, Ann. "The Angel of Progress: Pitfalls of the Term 'Post-Colonialism.'" *Social Text,* no. 31/32 (1992): 84–98.

Mann, Charles C. *1493: Uncovering the New World Columbus Created.* New York: Vintage Books, 2011.

Marcos, Sylvia. "Feminismos en camino descolonial." In *Más allá del feminismo: Caminos para andar,* edited by Márgara Millán, 15–34. Mexico: UNAM, 2014.

Marcos, Sylvia. *Taken from the Lips: Gender and Eros in Mesoamerican Religions.* Leiden: Brill, 2006.

Martínez-Alier, Joan, Nnimmo Bassey and Patrick Bond. "Yasuni-ITT is dead. Blame President Correa." *Mapping Environmental Justice.* August 17, 2013. http://www.ejolt.org/2013/08/yasuni-itt-is-dead-blame-president-correa/.

Martínez-Cruz, Jessica. "Whose Knowledge Counts? Harmony and Spirituality in Miskitu Counter-Narratives." In *Latin American Perspectives on Global Development,* edited by Mahmoud Masaeli, Germán Bula, and Samuel Ernest Harrington, 309–29. Newcastle Upon Tyne: Cambridge Scholars Press, 2018.

"Más tierra para las mujeres, mejor seguridad alimentaria para todos." *Organización de las Naciones Unidas para la Alimentación y Agricultura* (FAO). Published 2013, http://www.fao.org/americas/noticias/ver/es/c/320313/.

"Master Plan Buenaventura 2050." *Grupo Gonval.* Published July 2014. https://www.grupogonval.com/2014/10/master-plan-buenaventura-2050.html.

Méndez, Georgina, Juan López, Sylvia Marcos and Carmen Osorio, eds. *Senti-pensar el género. Perspectivas desde los pueblos originarios.* Guadalajara: Taller Editorial la Casa del Mago, 2013.

Méndez Gutiérrez, Luz and Amanda Carrera Guerra. *Mujeres Indígenas: Clamor por la Justicia. Violencia Sexual, Conflicto Armado y Despojo Violento de Tierras.* Guatemala: Equipo de Estudios Comunitarios y Acción Psicosocial, 2014.

Mendoza, Breny. *Ensayos de crítica feminista en Nuestra América.* Mexico: Herder Editorial, 2014.

Mendoza, Breny. "La epistemología del sur, la colonialidad del género y el feminismo latinoamericano." In *Aproximaciones críticas a las prácticas teórico-políticas del feminisimo latinoamericano*, edited by Yuderkys Espinosa Miñoso, 19–36. Buenos Aires: En la frontera, 2010.

Mendoza, Breny. "La epistemología del sur, la colonialidad del género y el feminismo latinoamericano." In *Tejiendo de otro modo: Feminismo, epistemología y apuestas decoloniales en Abya Yala*, edited by Yuderkys Espinosa Miñoso, Diana Gómez Correal, and Karina Ochoa, 91–104. Colombia: Editorial Universidad del Cauca, 2014.

Mendoza, Breny. "La cuestión del imperio español y la Leyenda Negra," *eHumanista: Journal of Iberian Studies* 50 (2022): 87–105.

Menéndez, Amparo. "El lugar de la ciudadanía en los entornos de hoy. Una mirada desde América Latina." *Revista Ecuador Debate,* no. 58 (2003): 181–222.

Mezzadra, Sandro and Federico Rahola. "The Postcolonial Condition: A Few Notes on the Quality of Historical Time in the Global Present." *Postcolonial Text* 2, no. 1 (2006). http://postcolonial.org/index.php/pct/article/view/393/819.

Mignolo, Walter. *The Darker Side of the Renaissance.* 2nd ed. Ann Arbor: Michigan University Press, 2003.

Mignolo, Walter. *The Darker Side of Western Modernity.* Durham: Duke University Press, 2011.

Mignolo, Walter. *Local Histories/Global Designs.* Princeton: Princeton University Press, 2012.

"Militarización y Violencia Patriarcal en Haití o Cómo se Asocian Dos Viejos Amigos Ante el Desastre." Grupo Antimilitarista Tortuga. Published January 2011. http://www.grupotortuga.com/Militarizacion-y-violencia.

"Una Mirada al Feminicidio en México 2009–2010." *Observatoria Ciudadano Nacional del Feminicidio.* Accessed November 23, 2020. https://observatoriofeminicidio.files.wordpress.com/2011/09/informe-ocnf-2009-2010.pdf.

Misión Permanente por la Vida en Buenaventura. "S.O.S. from Colombia's Largest Port." *Solidarity Collective.* Published January 2014, accessed June 8, 2021. https://www.solidaritycollective.org/post/s-o-s-from-colombia-s-largest-port---s-o-s-del-puerto-principal-de-colombia.

Mohanty, Chandra. "'Under Western Eyes' Revisited: Feminist Solidarity through Anticapitalist Struggle." *Signs* 28, no. 2 (2003): 499–535.

Mohanty, Chandra. "Under Western Eyes: Feminist Scholarship and Colonial Discourses." *boundary 2* 12, no. 3 (1984): 333–58.

Moreno, Hortensia. "La noción de 'tecnologías de género' como herramienta conceptual en el estudio del deporte." *Revista Punto Género*, no. 1 (2011): 41–62.

Mueller, Adele. "Power and Naming in the Development Institution: the 'Discovery' of Women in Peru." Presented in the 14th Annual Third World Conference, Chicago, 1987.

Mujeres constructoras de paz y desarrollo. Bogotá: Consejería Presidencial para la Equidad de la Mujer, 2003.

Muller, Pierre. *Las políticas públicas.* 2nd ed. Bogotá: Universidad Externado de Colombia, 2006.

Nascimento, Abdias do. *O genocídio do negro brasileiro: Processo de um racismo mascarado.* Rio de Janeiro: Paz e Terra, 1978.

Nichols, Robert. "Contract and Usurpation: Enfranchisement and Racial Governance in Settler-Colonial Contexts." In *Theorizing Native Studies*, edited by Audra Simpson and Andrea Smith, 99–121. Durham: Duke University Press, 2014.

Nichols, Robert. "Realizing the Social Contract: The Case of Colonialism and Indigenous Peoples." *Contemporary Political Theory* 4, no. 1 (2005): 42–62.

Olivera, Mercedes. *Violencia feminicida en Chiapas: razones visibles y ocultas de nuestras luchas, resistencias y rebeldías.* Chiapas: Colección Selva Negra and Universidad de Ciencias y Artes de Chiapas, 2008.

Ortiz, Fernando. *Cuban Counterpoint: Tobacco and Sugar.* Durham: Duke University Press, 1995.

Ortiz Lemos, Andrés. "Lo que la sociedad mestiza puede aprender de las mujeres indígenas, según Nina Pacari." *Plan V.* Published June 2017. https://www.planv.com.ec/historias/sociedad/lo-que-la-sociedad-mestiza-puede-aprender-mujeres-indigenas-segun-nina-pacari.

Oyěwùmí, Oyèrónkě. *The Invention of Women: Making an African Sense of Western Gender Discourses*. Minneapolis: University of Minnesota Press, 1997.

Pacheco, Avila and Wilson L. Peña Meléndez. *Ramón Grosfoguel. La Descolonización de la Economía Política*. Bogotá: Universidad Libre, 2010.

Palermo, Zulma. "Conocimiento 'otro' y conocimiento del otro en América Latina." *Estudio*, no. 21 (Fall 2009): 79–90.

Palermo, Zulma. "La opción decolonial." *CECIES: Pensamiento Latinoamericano y Alternativo*. Accessed October 3, 2013. http://www.cecies.org/articulo.asp?id=227.

Pan-American Health Organization. *Health Systems Profile in Nicaragua: Monitoring and Analyzing Health Systems Change/Reform*. 3rd ed. Washington, D. C.: PAHO, 2009. https://www.paho.org/hq/dmdocuments/2010/Health_System_Profile -Nicaragua_2008.pdf.

Pappé, Ilán. *The Ethnic Cleansing of Palestine*. Oxford: Oneworld Publications, 2006.

Paredes, Julieta. *Hilando fino desde el feminismo comunitario*. La Paz, Bolivia: El Rebozo, Zapateándole, Lente Flotante en Cortito que's p'a largo y Alifen AC, 2010.

Paredes, Julieta. *Hilando fino desde el feminismo comunitario*. Querétaro: Colectivo Grietas, 2012.

Paredes, Julieta. *Una sociedad en estado y con estado despatriarcalizador*. Bolivia, La Paz: Ministerio de Justicia, 2008.

Pateman, Carole. *The Sexual Contract*. Palo Alto: Stanford University Press, 1988.

Pateman, Carole and Charles Mills. *Contract and Domination*. Cambridge: Polity Press, 2007.

Patiño, Germán. "Prologue." In *Ensayos escogidos: Rogerio Velásquez*, edited by Germán Patiño, 9–36. Bogotá: Ministerio de Cultura de Colombia, 2010.

Peña Torres, Ligia. "Entre curanderos y médicos: disputas por las prácticas médicas curativas en el contexto de la modernización de la salud pública (1915–1928)." Presented at VI Congreso Centroamericano de Estudios Culturales, Managua, Nicaragua, July 11–13, 2017.

"Piden a grandes tiendas que ofertas y formularios para novios incluyan al Acuerdo de Unión Civil." *Movilh*. Published July 27, 2015. http://www.movilh.cl/piden -a-grandes-tiendas-que-ofertas-para-matrimonios-se-apliquen-expresamente-a -convivientes-civiles/.

Política de participación y equidad para las mujeres (CONPES 2726). Bogotá: Departamento Nacional de Planeación, 1994.

Política de salud para las mujeres "Salud para las Mujeres, Mujeres para la Salud" (Resolución 1531). Bogotá: Ministerio de Protección Social, 1992.

La política genocida en el conflicto armado en Chiapas: reconstrucción de hechos, pruebas, delitos y testimonios. San Cristóbal de Las Casas, Chiapas: Centro de Derechos Humanos Fray Bartolomé de Las Casas, 2005. https://frayba.org.mx/ historico/archivo/informes/050201_la_politica_genocida_en_el_conflicto_armado _en_chiapas.pdf.

Política integral para la mujer (CONPES 2626). Bogotá: Departamento Nacional de Planeación, 1992.

Política nacional para la mujer campesina (CONPES 2109). Bogotá: Departamento Nacional de Planeación, 1984.

Política para el desarrollo de la mujer rural. Bogotá: Ministerio de Agricultura y Desarrollo Rural, 1994.

Política pública nacional de equidad de género para las mujeres (CONPES 161). Bogotá: Departamento Nacional de Planeación, 2013.

Pratt, Mary Louise. *Imperial Eyes: Travel Writing and Transculturation.* New York/London: Routledge, 2008.

Puar, Jasbir. "Homonationalism As Assemblage: Viral Travels, Affective Sexualities." *Jindal Global Law Review* 4, no. 2 (2013): 23–43.

Quijano, Aníbal. "¿Bien vivir?: Entre el 'desarrollo' y la des/colonialidad del poder." In *Cuestiones y horizontes: de la dependencia histórico-estructural a la colonialidad/descolonialidad del poder,* edited by Danilo Assis Clímaco, 847–859. Buenos Aires: CLACSO, 2014.

Quijano, Aníbal. "Colonialidad del poder, eurocentrismo y América Latina." In *Colonialidad del Saber, Eurocentrismo y Ciencias Sociales*, edited by Edgardo Lander, 201–246. Buenos Aires: Consejo Latinoamericano de Ciencias Sociales, 2000.

Quijano, Aníbal. "Colonialidad del poder, globalización y democracia." *Revista de Ciencias Sociales de la Universidad Autónoma de Nuevo León*, 4, nos. 7–8 (2002): 58–89.

Quijano, Aníbal. "Colonialidad, modernidad/racionalidad." *Perú Indígena*, 13, no. 29 (1992): 11–29.

Quijano, Aníbal. "Colonialidad del poder y clasificación social." In *Cuestiones y horizontes: De la dependencia histórico-estructural a la colonialidad/descolonialidad del poder,* ed. Danilo Assis Clímaco, 285–330. Buenos Aires: *CLACSO, 2014.*

Quijano, Aníbal. "Colonialidad del poder y clasificación social." *Journal of World-Systems Research* XI, no. 2 (Summer/Fall 2020): 342–86.

Quijano, Aníbal. "Coloniality and Modernity/Rationality." *Cultural Studies* 21, nos. 2–3 (2007): 168–178.

Quijano, Aníbal. "Coloniality and Modernity/Rationality." In *Globalization and the Decolonial Option*, edited by Walter D. Mignolo and Arturo Escobar, 22–32. New York/London: Routledge, 2010.

Quijano, Aníbal. "Coloniality of Power, Eurocentrism, and Latin America." *Nepantla: Views from South* 1, no. 3 (2000): 533–80.

Quijano, Aníbal. "Que tal raza!" *Revista Venezolana de Economía y Ciencias Sociales* 5, no. 1 (2000): 37–45.

Radford, Jill. "Introduction." In *Femicide: The Politics of Woman Killing,* edited by Jill Radford and Diana E. H. Russell, 3–12. New York: Twayne, 1992.

"Rafael Correa defiende contrato para la explotación minera." *El Universo.* Published March 2012. https://www.eluniverso.com/2012/03/10/1/1355/rafael -correa-defiende-contrato-explotacion-minera.html.

Redacción Noticiero 90 Minutos, "Desempleo en Buenaventura: un panorama crítico, especialmente para los jóvenes," February 11, 2021, accessed June 8, 2021, https: //90minutos.co/desempleo-buenaventura-panorama-critico-jovenes-11-02-2021/.

Regulatory situation of herbal medicines: a worldwide review. World Health Organization. Published 1998. https://apps.who.int/iris/bitstream/handle/10665 /63801/WHO_TRM_98.1.pdf?sequence=1&isAllowed=y.

Revista La Cicuta. "Lanzamiento *La Cicuta Revista*: Santiago Castro-Gómez-'Michel Foucault: El oficio del genealogista." YouTube. Published October 4, 2013. https: //www.youtube.com/watch?v=033YTK-t0zo.

Rigouste, Mathieu. *L'ennemi Intérieur: La Généalogie Coloniale et Militaire de l'Ordre Sécuritaire dans la France Contemporaine.* Paris: Découverte, 2009.

Rivera Cusicanqui, Silvia. *Ch'ixinakax utxiwa. Una reflexión sobre prácticas y discursos descoloniales.* Buenos Aires: Tinta y Limón/Retazos, 2010.

Rivera Cusicanqui, Silvia. "El potencial epistemológico y teórico de la historia oral: de la lógica instrumental a la descolonización de la historia." *Voces Recobradas, Revista de Historia Oral* 21 (2006): 12–22.

Rivera Cusicanqui, Silvia. *Violencia (re)encubiertas en Bolivia.* Bolivia, La Paz: La Mirada Salvaje, 2010.

Riveros Rueda, Alexandra. "¿Por qué nos duele Buenaventura? Feminicidio, racismo, etnocidio e impunidad." *Feminismo Afrodiaspórico.* Published November 2013, accessed June 8, 2021. https://feministasafrodiasporicas.blogspot.com/2013/11/ deja-de-normalizar-el-asesinato-las.html.

Robin, Marie-Monique. *Death Squadrons: The French School.* New York: First Run/ Icarus Films, 2003.

Rodríguez, C. and J. Hamersma. *Las contrapartes en salud de América Central y el Caribe. 25 años después de Alma Ata: Experiencia en cuatro países.* Guatemala: CORDAID, 2006.

Rodríguez, Stella. "Fronteras fijas, valor de cambio y cultivos ilícitos en el Pacífico caucano de Colombia." *Revista Colombiana de Antropología* 44, no.1 (January-June, 2008).

Rojas, Jeannette, Danelly Estupiñán and Teresa Casiani. *Derrotar la Invisibilidad. Un Reto para Las Mujeres Afrodescendientes en Colombia: El Panorama de la Violencia y la Violación de los Derechos Humanos Contra las Mujeres Afrodescendientes en Colombia, en el Marco de los Derechos Colectivos.* Colombia: Proyecto Mujeres Afrodescendientes Defensoras de Derechos Humanos, 2012.

Rousseau, Jean Jacques. *Émile.* Create Space Independent Publisher Platform, 2017.

Ruiz, Edgardo. *Cultural Politics and Health: The Development of Intercultural Health Policies in The Atlantic Coast of Nicaragua.* PhD Diss., University of Pittsburg, 2006.

Sachs, Wolfgang. "The Archaeology of the Development Idea." *Interculture* 23, no. 4 (1990): 1–37.

Said, Edward. *Orientalism.* New York: Pantheon, 1978.

Sánchez, Gonzalo and Martha Nubia Bello. *¡Basta Ya! Colombia: Memories of War and Dignity.* Translated by Jimmy Weiskopf and Joaquín Franco. Bogotá: National Center for Historical Memory, 2016. http://www.centrodememoriahistorica.gov.co /descargas/informes2016/basta-ya-ingles/BASTA-YA-ingles.pdf.

Santos, Boaventura de Sousa. "Beyond Abyssal Thinking: From Global Lines to Ecologies of Knowledges." *Review*, 30, no. 1 (2007): 45–89.

Santos, Boaventura de Sousa. *Descolonizar el saber, reinventar el poder.* Santiago de Chile: LOM Ediciones, 2013.

Santos, Boaventura de Sousa. "Toward a Multicultural Conception of Human Rights." In *Moral Imperialism: A Critical Anthology*, edited by Berta Hernández-Truyol, 39–60. New York: New York University Press, 2002.

Scott, Joan Wallach. "The Evidence of Experience." *Critical Inquiry* 17, no. 4 (1991): 773–97.

Scott, Joan Wallach. *Gender and the Politics of History.* New York: Columbia University Press, 1999.

Secretaria Nacional de Planificación y Desarrollo (SENPLADES). "Boletín de Prensa No. 395 Iniciativa Yasuni-ITT: Una apuesta ecuatoriana que marca un cambio de era." Quito: SENPLADES, 2013. https://www.planificacion.gob.ec/wp-content/uploads/downloads/2013/02/BOLET%c3%8dN_395_YASUN%c3%8d_FANDER_08-02-13.pdf.

Segato, Rita Laura. "Colonialidad y patriarcado moderno: expansión del frente estatal, modernización y la vida de las mujeres." In *Tejiendo de otro modo: Feminismo, epistemología y apuestas decoloniales en Abya Yala*, edited by Yuderkys Espinosa Miñoso, Diana Gómez, and Karina Ochoa, 75–90. Colombia: Editorial Universidad del Cauca, 2014.

Segato, Rita. "Género y colonialidad: del patriarcado de bajo impacto al patriarcado moderno." In *Des-posesión: Género, territorio y luchas por la autodeterminación*, edited by Marisa Beausteguigoitia Rius and María Josefina Saldaña-Portillo, 125–162. Mexico: PUEG-UNAM, 2015.

Segato, Rita. *Género y colonialidad en ocho ensayos.* Buenos Aires: Prometeo, 2015.

Segato, Rita Laura. "El sexo y la norma: frente estatal, patriarcado, desposesión, colonidad." *Revista Estudos Feministas* 22, no. 2 (May/August 2014): 593–616.

Serrano Amaya, José Fernando. "La doble salida del clóset de Simon Knkoli: heterosexismo y luchas anti-apartheid." *Ciudad Paz-Ando*, 7, no. 1 (2014): 86–105.

Sequeira Magda, Henry Espinoza, Juan José Amador, Gonzalo Domingo, Margarita Quintanilla, and Tala de los Santos. *The Nicaraguan Health System: An Overview of Critical Challenges and Opportunities.* Seattle: PATH, 2011. http://www.path.org/files/TS-nicaragua-health-system-rpt.pdf.

Shohat, Ella. "Notes on the 'Post-colonial.'" *Social Text* no. 31/32 (1992): 99–113.

Sillitoe, Paul. "Local Science vs. Global Science." In *Local Science vs. Global Science: Approaches to Indigenous Knowledge in International Development*, edited by Paul Sillitoe, 1–22. New York: Bergahn Books, 2007.

Silverblatt, Irene. *Moon, Sun, and Witches. Gender Ideologies and Class in Inca and Colonial Peru.* Princeton: Princeton University Press, 1987.

Simpson, Leanne. "Queering Resurgence: Taking on Heteropatriarchy in Indigenous Nation-Building." *Mamawipawin: Indigenous Governance and Community Based Research Space.* June 2012. https://blogs.cc.umanitoba.ca/mamawipawin/2012/06/01/queering-resurgence-taking-on-heteropatriarchy-in-indigenous-nation-building/.

Simpson, Leanne Betasamosake. *This Accident of Being Lost: Songs and Stories.* Toronto: House of Anansi, 2017.

Slater, David "The Geopolitical Imagination and the Enframing of Development Theory." *Transactions of the Institute of British Geographers* 18, no. 4 (1993): 419–37.

Smith, Dorothy E. "Women's Perspective as a Radical Critique of Sociology." *Sociological Inquiry* 44, no. 1 (1974): 7–13.

Smith, Dorothy E. "Women's Standpoint: Embodied Knowledge versus Ruling Relations." In *Gender Inequality: Feminist Theory and Politics*, edited by Judith Lorber, 185–191. New York: Oxford University Press, 2010.

Smith, Dorothy E. *The Everyday World as Problematic: A Sociology for Women.* Boston: Northeastern University Press, 1987.

Sommer, Doris. "A Vindication of Double Consciousness." In *A Companion to Postcolonial Studies*, edited Henry Schwarz and Sangeeta Ray, 165–179. Malden: Blackwell, 2000.

Spillers, Hortense. "Mama's Baby, Papa's Maybe: An American Grammar Book." *Diacritics* 17, no. 2 (Summer 1987): 65–81.

Spivak, Gayatri. "Can the Subaltern Speak?" In *Marxism and the Interpretation of Culture*, edited by Cary Nelson and Lawrence Grossberg. Urbana: University of Illinois Press, 1988.

Stamp, Loyda. *Prácticas de Atención y Tratamiento del Grisi siknis utilizadas por los médicos tradicionales en los municipios Puerto Cabezas y Waspam.* Managua: IMTRADEC-URACCAN, 2006.

Thomson, Sinclair. "Claroscuro andino: Nubarrones y destellos en la obra de Silvia Rivera Cusicanqui." In *Violencias (re) encubiertas en Bolivia,* edited by Silvia Rivera Cusicanqui, 7–24. Bolivia, La Paz: La Mirada Salvaje, 2010.

Torres, Marisol. "Sobre la sospecha, la crítica y la feminidad. Reflexiones tras el ELFAY." *Menjunje Lesbiano.* Published December 2014. https://marisoultorresjimenez.wordpress.com/2014/12/10/sobre-la-sospecha-la-critica-y-la-feminidad-reflexiones-tras-elflay-bogota-2014/.

Towns, Ann. "Civilization." In *The Oxford Handbook of Feminist Theory*, edited by Lisa Disch and Mary Hawkesworth, 79–99. New York: Oxford University Press, 2015.

Traver, Albert. "El Gobierno colombiano militariza a Buenaventura, la ciudad más violenta de ese país." *La información.* Published March 22, 2014, accessed June 8, 2021, https://www.lainformacion.com/espana/el-gobierno-colombiano-militariza-la-ciudad-mas-violenta-del-pais_4e33aBQli2PFJLsiGQLjA1/.

Truth, Sojourner. "Ain't I a Woman?" Women's Convention, Akron, Ohio, 1851.

Tzul Tzul, Gladys. *Sistemas de gobierno comunal indígena. Mujeres y tramas de parentesco en Chuimeq'ena.'* Guatemala: SOCEE/Maya'Wuj Editorial, 2016.

"Ventajas Competitivas." Cámara de Comercio de Buenaventura. Accessed November 22, 2020. https://www.ccbun.org/articulos/ventajas-competitivas.

Violencia contra las mujeres en el Distrito de Buenaventura: Informe Temático. Defensoría delegada para la evaluación del riesgo de la población civil como consecuencia del conflicto armado Sistema de Alertas Tempranas (SAT). Bogotá: Defensoría del Pueblo, 2011. https://www.sdgfund.org/sites/default/files/Colombia_VBG%20Buenaventura.pdf.

"Violência sexual, violência de gênero e violência contra crianças e adolescentes." *Relatório da Comissão Nacional da Verdade*. Vol I. Brasilia: Comissão Nacional da Verdade, 2014. http://cnv.memoriasreveladas.gov.br/images/pdf/relatorio/volume _1_digital.pdf.

Waiselfisz, Julio Jacobo. *Mapa da Violência 2015: Homicídio de Mulheres no Brasil.* Brasilia: Faculdade Latino-Americana de Ciências Sociais, 2015. http://www .onumulheres.org.br/wp-content/uploads/2016/04/MapaViolencia_2015_mulheres .pdf.

Walsh, Catherine. "Development as Buen Vivir. Institutional Arrangements and (De)Colonial Entanglements." In *Constructing the Pluriverse. The Geopolitics of Knowledge,* edited by Bernd Reiter, 184–196 (Durham: Duke University Press, 2018).

Walsh, Catherine. "Life, Nature, and Gender Otherwise: Feminist Reflections and Provocations from the Andes." In *Practising Feminist Political Ecologies. Moving Beyond the "Green Economy,"* edited by Wendy Harcourt and Ingrid Nelson, 101–128. London: Zed, 2015.

Walsh, Catherine. "On Gender and Its 'Otherwise.'" In *The Palgrave Handbook of Gender and Development*, edited by Wendy Harcourt, 34–47. London: Palgrave Macmillan, 2016.

Walsh, Catherine. "Shifting the Geopolitics of Critical Knowledge: Decolonial Thought and Cultural Studies 'Others' in the Andes." *Cultural Studies* 21, no. 2–3 (2007): 224–39.

Wedel, Johan. "Involuntary mass spirit possession among the Miskitu." *Anthropology & Medicine* 19, no. 3 (2012): 303–14.

Weheliye, Alexander. *Habeas Viscus: Racializing Assemblages, Biopolitics, and Black Feminist Theories of the Human.* Durham: Duke University Press, 2014.

Wekker, Gloria. *The Politics of Passion: Women's Sexual Culture in the Afro-Surinamese Diaspora.* New York: Columbia University Press, 2006.

Werneck, Jurema. "Of Ialodes and Feminists: Reflections on Black Women's Political Action in Latin America and the Caribbean." *Cultural Dynamics* 19, no. 1 (2007): 99–113.

Widdicombe, Rupert. "Nicaragua Village in Grip of Madness: Doctors and Traditional Healers Reach Remote Jungle Community where 60 people are Suffering from Mysterious Collective Mania." *The Guardian.* Published December 2003. http:// www.guardian.co.uk/world/2003/dec/17/1.

Wynter, Sylvia. "1492: A New World View." In *Race, Discourse, and the Origin of the Americas.* Edited by Vera Lawrence Hyatt and Rex Nettleford, 5–57. Washington, D.C.: Smithsonian Institution Press, 1995.

Zarco, Fernando. *Masculinidad y homoerotismo desde el pensamiento decolonial.* Barcelona: Universidad Autónoma de Barcelona, 2009.

Zibechi, Raúl. *Latiendo resistencia: Mundos nuevos y guerras de despojo.* Oaxaca, Mex: El Rebozo, 2015.

Index

interculturality/*interculturalidad*, 8, 175, 177, 179, 187, 191, 192, 193, 195, 221
internal colonialism, 26, 34, 117, 219
intersectionality, ix, xv, xvii, xix, xxv, 53, 70, 97–99, 210; and fusion, 98, 100–102

Jackson, Andrew, 4
Jamieson, Mark, 180, 182

Kant, Immanuel, 10, 36–37, 74
Keating, Christine, 78–79
Knkoli, Simon, 93, 95–96
knowledge production, xii, xvi–xvii, xix, 32, 34, 36–38, 46, 50, 191–94, 207–8; experience as source for, xiv, 27, 32–33, 34, 47, 52, 54, 97, 221; "from below," xxvi, 16, 234; situated, 27, 51–52, 155, 176–77, 221; and subject-object relation, 53–56; Western scientific, xxii, 17, 19, 27, 32–33, 116, 177, 189–92, 194, 199n63. *See also* community: and knowledge production; epistemic violence; Indigenous knowledge
Kusch, Rodolfo, 13–14

la otra de la otra, 26
Lagarde, Marcela, 133–34, 151n5
Laird, Sloane, 178
land-territory, 203, 205, 206–7, 211, 213, 214n1. *See also* movements: women in defense of land-territory; nature/Nature; women: defending land, territory, nature, life
Latin America, x, xi, xii, xix, 26, 28, 30, 32, 46, 146, 149, 175, 179, 194, 217, 225, 239; discourses of, 28–31, 36, 94; feminism in. *See* feminism: in Latin America; history of coloniality, xxi, 28, 30, 44, 79, 85, 94, 140, 149, 225; identity of, xix, 28, 149; philosophy in, xvi, xvii, 27–28, 47, 175; and Reason, xxi, 27, 35;

state of, 55, 92, 94, 146, 149. *See also* Abya Yala
Latin Americanness, 28, 30. *See also* Latin America: philosophy in
Latour, Bruno, 190
León, Manuela, 226
LGBTI movements, xx, 84, 85, 90–93, 94–96, 102, 103n18, 104n33; and gender, 93; and homonationalism, 96, 104n28; racism of, 93, 95–96; and state discourse, 90, 92, 94. *See also* rights: LGBTI
liberation, 8, 20, 180, 213; and citizenship, 89, 90; global program for, xvii, 37, 49, 83, 96; interconnected struggles for, 20, 88, 91, 93, 211; philosophies of, 13, 54; as pretext, 78, 89, 114, 224. *See also* subject: of liberated gender and sexuality
life and care, reproduction of, xvi, 6, 17, 33, 55, 181, 202, 205, 230, 238
Locke, John, 63, 74, 76
López de Gómara, Francisco, 3
Lorde, Audre, 15, 86
Lozano, Carmen, 232
Lugones, María, ix–x, xi, xxiv–xxv, xxvin1, xxviin2, 20n1, 47, 53, 56, 84, 88, 93, 98, 100, 132, 217; on category of "woman," xviii, 109, 112, 114, 120, 136–37; on colonial/modern system, 120, 123n23, 136–37, 153n44, 205; on coloniality of gender, xv, 48, 70–71, 87, 109, 137, 205, 218
Lupo, Silvia, 232

Machoa, Katy, 217, 225, 226–27, 235, 239, 239n1
Mackey, Tim, 178
Maese-Cohen, Marcelle, xxviin2
Maldonado-Torres, Nelson, x, xxiv–xxv, xxviin4, 14, 20n1, 49, 67, 70
male ethos of state, 217, 218
Mapuche, the, 3, 99